Cultural Studies of LEGO

Rebecca C. Hains · Sharon R. Mazzarella
Editors

Cultural Studies of LEGO

More Than Just Bricks

Editors
Rebecca C. Hains
Department of Media and Communication
Salem State University
Salem, MA, USA

Sharon R. Mazzarella
School of Communication Studies
James Madison University
Harrisonburg, VA, USA

ISBN 978-3-030-32663-0   ISBN 978-3-030-32664-7   (eBook)
https://doi.org/10.1007/978-3-030-32664-7

This Palgrave Macmillan imprint is published by the registered company Springer Nature Switzerland AG
The registered company address is: Gewerbestrasse 11, 6330 Cham, Switzerland

For Theo, Alex and Xavier, who make everything awesome
—Rebecca C. Hains

For Jeff, who has taught me one is never too old to "play well"
—Sharon R. Mazzarella

Preface

As a children's media culture scholar, I observed with professional interest LEGO's transformation from a children's toy into a transnational, transmedia brand with immense cultural power. My research has always considered the cultural implications of major media phenomena, such as girl power's rise in the 1990s, and the Disney Princess brand's ascendency after the turn of the millennium. The latter subject built upon a wealth of previous scholarship, as scholars and other critics have been interrogating Disney for decades. But not so with LEGO: It only recently emerged as a transmedia brand that boasts, among other properties, blockbuster animated films. So, one day, not too long after the release of *The LEGO Batman Movie* in 2017, I asked Sharon: What if we were to give LEGO the Disney treatment? That question guided us as we developed this volume.

We created this book for scholars, students and readers from the general public alike. It will appeal to those with an interest in the LEGO brand, as well as in children's media culture more broadly. In this volume, essays examine LEGO from an array of critical/cultural studies approaches, with attention to its ideological power, influence and status as a major transnational media brand. While our contributors' work focuses on LEGO, their findings reflect broader trends in the children's media landscape. As such, these chapters have implications for those who are interested in cultural studies, media studies and the array of additional disciplines that our contributors represent, including literature, psychology, religious studies and sociology. We also value that our contributors bring to bear perspectives from a variety of nations, as they hail from Canada, Germany, England, Australia, The Netherlands, Norway and locations across the United States.

Sharon and I owe these amazing scholars a huge shout-out for being part of our team. This collection's high quality derives from their passion for the topic, their intellectual expertise and their understanding of the importance of subjecting popular cultural artifacts to in-depth critical/cultural analyses. Over the past year or so, it has been a genuine pleasure to work with them: We admire their good humor, willingness to stick with us as this collection evolved and overall commitment to our project. Finally, we appreciate the contributions of everyone involved in the editorial and production processes at Palgrave Macmillan: their commitment to providing a space for academic exploration and intellectual interrogation of popular culture artifacts made this project possible.

Salem, USA   Rebecca C. Hains

Contents

Notes on Contributors

Shannon Brownlee is appointed to the Cinema and Media Studies program and the Gender and Women's Studies program of Dalhousie University in Halifax (Canada). Her research focuses on animated film and film adaptation from a range of media. Her previous work on LEGO animation includes a 2016 article for *Film Criticism*.

Lincoln Geraghty is professor of media cultures in the School of Film, Media and Communication at the University of Portsmouth (England). He serves as editorial advisor for *The Journal of Popular Culture, Transformative Works and Culture, Journal of Fandom Studies* and *Journal of Popular Television* with interests in science fiction film and television, fandom and collecting in popular culture. Major publications include *Living with Star Trek: American Culture and the Star Trek Universe* (IB Tauris, 2007), *American Science Fiction Film and Television* (Berg, 2009) and *Cult Collectors: Nostalgia, Fandom and Collecting Popular Culture* (Routledge, 2014).

Joyce Goggin is a senior lecturer in literature, film and media studies at the University of Amsterdam (The Netherlands). She publishes widely on gambling and finance in literature, painting, film, TV and computer games. Her recent publications include "Everything is Awesome": The LEGO Movie and the Affective Politics of Security, *Finance and Society*; "Crise et comédie: Le système de John Law au théâtre néerlandais," *La réception du Système de Law* (Rennes, 2017); "Trading and Trick Taking in the Dutch Republic," *Playthings in Early Modernity* (Western Michigan University, 2017); and a co-edited volume entitled *The Aesthetics and Affects of Cuteness* (Routledge, 2017).

Rebecca C. Hains is professor of media and communication at Salem State University (United States). The author of *Growing Up with Girl Power: Girlhood on Screen and in Everyday Life* (Peter Lang, 2012) and *The Princess Problem: Guiding Our Girls Through the Princess-Obsessed Years* (Sourcebooks, 2014), and the co-editor of *Princess Cultures: Mediating Girls' Imaginations and Identities* (Peter Lang, 2015), her research appears in many scholarly anthologies and journals including *Feminist Media Studies, Popular Communication* and *Girlhood Studies*.

Kyra Hunting is an assistant professor of media arts and studies at the University of Kentucky (United States). Her research focuses on gender and sexuality in media for children and teens, fandom and children's media apps. Her work has appeared in *Feminist Media Studies*; *Critical Studies in Media Communication*; *Mass Communication and Society*; *Spectator*; *The Quarterly Review of Film and Video*; and *Cinema Journal*, as well as several anthologies.

Nancy A. Jennings is professor and director of the Children's Education and Entertainment Research Lab (CHEER) in the Department of Communication at the University of Cincinnati (United States). Dr. Jennings studies the impact of media on the lives of children and their families, and public policies and practices involved with children's media. She has authored one book, *Tween Girls and Their Mediated Friends* (Peter Lang, 2014), and co-edited another book, *20 Questions about Youth and the Media* (Peter Lang, 2018) with Sharon Mazzarella. She has published in peer-reviewed journals, many chapters in various books and handbooks, as well.

Derek Johnson is professor of media and cultural studies in the department of communication arts at the University of Wisconsin–Madison (United States). He is the author of *Transgenerational Media Industries: Adults, Children, and the Reproduction of Culture* (Michigan, 2019) and *Media Franchising: Creative License and Collaboration in the Culture Industries* (NYU, 2013). He has edited or co-edited the books *From Networks to Netflix: A Guide to Changing Channels* (Routledge, 2018), *Point of Sale: Analyzing Media Retail* (Rutgers, 2019), *A Companion to Media Authorship* (Wiley-Blackwell, 2013) and *Making Media Work: Cultures of Management in the Entertainment Industries* (NYU, 2014).

Jared LaGroue is a Ph.D. candidate in the Donald P. Bellisario College of Communications at Penn State and an instructor of communication at Juniata College (United States). His research focuses on critical-cultural media studies and the philosophy of communication. He has published research in *Computers in Human Behavior* and has presented at several conferences including the International Communication Association, National Communication Association, Popular Culture Association and the Association for Education in Journalism and Mass Communication.

Jonathan Rey Lee teaches interdisciplinary humanities and writing at the University of Washington and Cascadia College in Seattle (United States). He received his Ph.D. in comparative literature from the University of California, Riverside. He currently studies play media and has published several articles on tabletop games and LEGO. In addition, he is currently completing a book on deconstructing the LEGO medium (forthcoming from Palgrave).

Ari Mattes is lecturer in communications and media, and English literature, at the University of Notre Dame Australia. He has written widely on contemporary screen culture, publishing in Australian and international journals. His current book project involves the representation of accidents in disaster films.

Sharon R. Mazzarella is professor of communication studies at James Madison University (United States). She is the author of *Girls, Moral Panic and News Media: Troublesome Bodies* (Routledge, 2020) and the editor or co-editor of seven academic collections. She also edits "Mediated Youth" (Peter Lang), a series of cutting-edge books on cultural studies of youth.

Matthew P. McAllister is professor of communications, communication arts and sciences, and women's, gender, and sexuality studies at Penn State (United States). His research focuses on political economy of media and critiques of commercial culture. He is the author of *The Commercialization of American Culture* (Sage, 1996), and the co-editor of *Comics and Ideology* (Peter Lang, 2001), *Film and Comic Books* (Mississippi, 2007), *The Advertising and Consumer Culture Reader* (Routledge, 2009) and *The Routledge Companion to Advertising and Promotional Culture* (2013).

Debra Merskin is professor of media studies in the School of Journalism & Communication at the University of Oregon (United States). Her research focuses on intersectionality and media re-presentation as it applies to race, gender, species and identity. In particular, her work considers how media portrayals impact the lived experiences of all beings. She is the author of *Media, Minorities, & Meaning: A Critical Introduction* (Peter Lang, 2011), *Sexing the Media: How and Why We Do It* (Peter Lang, 2014) and *Seeing Species: Re-presentations of Animals in Media & Popular Culture* (Peter Lang, 2018).

Jennifer W. Shewmaker serves as the dean of the College of Education and Human Services and professor of psychology at Abilene Christian University (United States). She has taught courses in child psychology, intelligence theory and assessment, exceptionalities and the liberal arts core. Her research focuses on child development and the influence of popular culture on identity development, and she has written and spoken at state, national and international levels on these topics. She is a nationally certified school psychologist who has worked with hundreds of families, children, teachers and community organizations.

Sissel Undheim is professor in the study of religion at the University of Bergen (Norway). In addition to her interest in LEGO and religion, her publications include books and articles on didactics of religion and religion and youth culture. She has also specialized in religions of antiquity and late antiquity. Here, her most recent publication is the monograph *Borderline Virginities: Sacred and Secular Virgins in Late Antiquity* (Routledge, 2017).

Matthias Zick Varul is an independent cultural sociologist (Germany) who focuses on the moral and religious implications and dimensions of capitalist practices of production, exchange and consumption. He is particularly interested in gauging the potential of such cultural practices for dialectical transcendences of capitalism, both utopian and dystopian.

List of Figures

1

"Let There Be LEGO!": An Introduction to *Cultural Studies of LEGO*

Sharon R. Mazzarella and Rebecca C. Hains

Upon entering the historic National Cathedral in Washington D.C. in May 2019, the second editor of this book was intrigued to see a large sign announcing "Let There Be LEGO!" The sign, featuring the image of a LEGO minifigure gargoyle, further read, "Help Washington National Cathedral become the world's largest LEGO cathedral." As part of a fundraising effort to repair significant damage from a 2011 earthquake, the cathedral had just launched a $19 million (US) campaign to sell $2.00 (US) LEGO bricks to build a LEGO replica of the cathedral, stationed in the cathedral's gift shop. In-person visitors could add their purchased bricks to the model—guided, of course, by designated

S. R. Mazzarella (✉)
School of Communication Studies, James Madison University,
Harrisonburg, VA, USA
e-mail: mazzarsr@jmu.edu

R. C. Hains
Department of Media and Communication, Salem State University,
Salem, MA, USA
e-mail: rhains@salemstate.edu

R. C. Hains and S. R. Mazzarella (eds.), *Cultural Studies of LEGO*,
https://doi.org/10.1007/978-3-030-32664-7_1

volunteers using official blueprints. When the replica is completed in two to three years, it is expected to stand 8 feet high, 13 feet long, contain half a million LEGO bricks and weigh 1350 pounds (Washington National Cathedral 2019). In fact, a volunteer explained that once completed, the replica would be too large to move from that room, as it would no longer fit through the doorway. It would become an enduring part of the public's experience touring the cathedral.

We begin our introduction to this volume, *Cultural Studies of LEGO: More Than Just Bricks*, with this story to show the near-ubiquity of LEGO as a cultural artifact. The little plastic bricks and representations of them seem to be nearly everywhere.[1] Let there be LEGO, indeed!

LEGO is the world's largest toy manufacturer[2] and an international, multimedia conglomerate. Due to its popularity among consumers, its marketing budget and its profitability, *Brand Finance* (Kauflin 2017) declared LEGO the world's most powerful brand in 2017, with *Business Insider* (Rath 2017) noting that LEGO's popular film properties contributed significantly to its rise to the top. While LEGO did not maintain this position the following year, it is still notable that they so recently ranked ahead of global behemoths including Google and Amazon.

While many still think of LEGO as the colorful building block toys they grew up with, toy production company The LEGO Group has grown its brand into a multimedia/multi-experiential phenomenon that includes seven Legoland theme parks spanning the globe from Denmark to Dubai. Moreover, LEGO boasts over 100 Lego Store retail shops worldwide, as well as videogames, board games, movies, television shows, books, a magazine, and even LEGO Wear children's clothes. LEGO's bricks and robotics kits have given the brand significant credibility as a STEM-oriented educational toy that is inherently wholesome and good for children. Still, however, the company considers the brick to be their "most important product" (Mortensen 2017). According to The LEGO Group, "the foundation remains the traditional LEGO brick" (Mortensen 2017).

Given the brand's reach, popularity and ubiquity, LEGO is ripe for serious critical/cultural interrogation of the kind offered by the chapters in this book. In this chapter, we begin by introducing the reader to the history, evolution and expansion of the LEGO brand over the past 80+ years. We then briefly situate our project within the broader field of Cultural Studies before introducing each chapter.

History, Evolution and Expansion of the LEGO Brand

Named "'Toy of the Century' in 2000 by both *Fortune* magazine and the British Association of Toy Retailers" (LEGO, n.d.), LEGO has a long and storied history within the international cultural landscape. Attesting to its longevity and diversity as a cultural artifact, in 2018, The LEGO Group experienced three notable milestones: The plastic LEGO bricks as we know them today turned 60; the first LEGOLAND theme park (in Billund, Denmark, where The LEGO Group is head-quartered) turned 50; and the LEGO minifigure turned 40. But LEGO's history has not been an entirely upward trajectory, and in this section, we cover some notable events and time periods in the LEGO brand's evolution. Individual chapters feature additional key dates and events, such as movie and product line release dates, when relevant to their topics.

Founded in Billund, Denmark in 1932 by Ole Kirk Kristensen, the same family still privately holds The LEGO Group, which boasts a long history of family leadership (Jensen 2015). The word LEGO is a con-traction of the Danish "leg godt," meaning "play well," which, accord-ing to the LEGO Group Web site, is "our name and it's our ideal" (Mortensen 2017). Coincidentally, the company later realized that in Latin, the word *lego* appropriately means "I put together" (Lauwaert 2008).

As a toy company, LEGO began first by producing wooden toys (Konzack 2014; Lauwaert 2008), moving to "the now famous auto-matic Binding Bricks" in the late 1940s (Schultz and Hatch 2003, p. 7). The company launched "the revolutionary 'LEGO System of Play'" in 1955 (Mortensen 2017) which, according to the company, essentially means that [bricks] can easily be combined in innumerable ways—and just as easily be dismantled. The more LEGO bricks you have, the more fertile your creativity can become. The combination of a structured system, logic and unlimited creativity encourages the child to learn through play in a wholly unique LEGO fashion. (Jensen 2015)[3]

In addition, in that same year, the company began what it describes as "The first real export of LEGO" (in this case to Sweden) (Mortensen 2017). As of this year, LEGO products are available in over 140 countries (Mortensen 2017).

It wasn't until 1958 that "the brick in its present form was launched" (Mortensen 2017) and "the familiar stud-and-tube interlocking system was patented" (Schultz and Hatch 2003, p. 7). Indeed, in her technological history of LEGO, Maaike Lauwaert (2008) itemizes "three major instances in the history of the LEGO company" (p. 221)—the first being this transition from wood to plastics. Contrary to popular lore, however, some historians assert that LEGO did not invent the plastic brick toy (Lauwaert 2008). Rather, they "were inspired" by self-locking bricks called Kiddicraft that a man named Hillary Page had designed earlier in England, and in 1981, LEGO paid an out-of-court settlement for "residual rights" to the new owners of Mr. Page's company (Lauwaert 2008, p. 223). Interestingly, as Lauwaert notes, this latter part of the evolution of LEGO bricks typically is omitted from the many published histories of the product.

While the company thrived for decades, Schultz and Hatch (2003) identify four broader social, cultural and technological changes that affected the LEGO brick's viability and popularity by the end of the twentieth century:

1. the pace of child development sped up such that kids aged out of playing with such toys at younger ages;
2. competition from new digital technology including video games and digital toys took kids' attention from simpler toys;
3. overall trends in the toy industry resulted in toys going out of fashion more quickly;
4. and toy companies began partnering with "global mega-brands" such as film franchises.

Moreover, the last of LEGO's patents expired in 1998, resulting in the market being flooded with a range of copycat products (Einwächter and Simon 2017). As a result, according to Lauwaert (2008), the second notable phase in LEGO's historical evolution, what she calls "a rather unfortunate episode" (p. 221), occurred in the period from the late 1990s through the early 2000s. In an attempt to compete and stay viable in this new environment, LEGO shifted emphasis from its bread-and-butter construction toys to a more varied yet less creative product line focused on role playing (often tied in with other media products, which required LEGO to pay hefty licensing fees) (Lauwaert 2008).

These dramatic shifts resulted in a "huge deficit" (Mortensen 2017) in the early 2000s that "made clear that brand extension through product differentiation had not been successfully executed" (Lauwaert 2008, p. 227). In 2004, LEGO announced a 7-year strategy to revitalize the company, including the reintroduction of the classic construction toys as a core product line. The plan was so successful that, according to the company's Web site in 2013, "In less than 10 years, the company has quadrupled its revenue" (Mortensen 2017).

By 2017, LEGO had surpassed Mattel as the "world's largest toy manufacturer" (Van Looveren 2017), with the company attributing a large part of that success to its licensing deals with such transmedial juggernauts as Star Wars and Harry Potter. According to Sophie Einwächter and Felix Simon (2017), LEGO's deal with Lucasfilm for the licensing rights to Star Wars "equipped Lego (sic) with a powerful weapon in the competition for market share" (n.p.). Indeed, in his cultural history of LEGO, Lars Konzack (2014) identifies several epochs in the development of the brand, with the latest one being what he calls "transmedial," or spanning multiple media platforms using an array of technologies. Mark J. P. Wolf (2014, p. xxiii) sees LEGO as both transmedial and transfranchisal, or bridging multiple franchises (ranging from Disney films to Star Wars to DC Comics to Harry Potter to the Simpsons), while Sondra Bacharach and Roy T. Cook (2017) describe LEGO bricks as "the building blocks of a transgenerational multimedia empire" (p. 1), appealing a wide range of ages and abilities, including children of all ages and adults alike.

In the process of becoming a transmedia and transfranchisal phenomenon, LEGO came to reflect both "toyetics" and "toyesis" as phenomena. When considering greenlighting media texts, producers and other gatekeepers have long evaluated them for whether they are "toyetic": "suitable to be merchandised across a range of licensed tie-ins: including toys, games and novelties" (Bainbridge 2017, p. 24), as well as other cultural artifacts with playful qualities, such as foods and apparel (p. 24). Building upon the concept of "toyetics," Jason Bainbridge (2017) has suggested that "toyesis" is a kind of "reverse toyetics": a free-flow of ideas between licensed toys and media texts (like films and television shows) that enriches toys and media texts alike. As such, the original media text may be considered "erased," enabling more free flow across media platforms (p. 26). As Bainbridge has explained: "Whereas toyetic implies a one-way adaptation from screen/literary text to a physical paratext (through merchandising), toyesis implies movement both ways across platforms to point the that the distinction between different texts becomes obscured and therefore less important" (p. 26)— which in many ways characterizes the LEGO brand.

Einwächter and Simon (2017) discuss how LEGO's realization of the importance of "transmedial stories" (n.p.) for its toy sales informed the highly successful (and highly toyetic) *The LEGO Movie*, the main concept of which is "transmedia world-building" (n.p.). As the highest-grossing animated film of 2014, *The LEGO Movie* (Einwächter and Simon 2017) paved the way for a range of additional LEGO-related movies, many of which are discussed later in this volume.

LEGO's fan outreach has been another component, its resurrection (Einwächter and Simon 2017; Lauwaert 2008). Whether soliciting fan involvement in product development such as the programmable robotic kits Mindstorms 2.0 and Mindstorms NXT (Lauwaert 2008), building community through such programs as the LEGO Ambassador Program (Lauwaert 2008), or supporting adult fans of LEGO (AFOLs) in other ways (Einwächter and Simon 2017), one of LEGO's most important changes in recent years has been "the strategy of bringing fans into the company, for tapping into the user-driven innovative fan culture" (Lauwaert 2008, p. 232). (See Nancy Jennings' chapter in this volume for an in-depth discussion of AFOLs.)

Jason Mittell (2014) has pronounced LEGO to be "an unusual company" in that it was "globalized prior to the era of globalization, connected to a web of other cultural industries but structurally independent from them, and innovating trends like transmedia convergence long before such terms were coined" (p. 270). Indeed, for these reasons, LEGO is worthy of critical/cultural academic inquiry. While in this book we do not seek to establish or contribute to a sustained, formalized field of LEGO Studies—something Mittell argues against—we do acknowledge the LEGO brand's global reach, influence, and importance. As such, through this book, we seek to interrogate critically many of LEGO's interrelated cultural artifacts.

This Collection

Cultural Studies

Over the past several decades, LEGO has emerged as one of the most studied cultural artifacts in history. The lions' share of this scholarship, however, is experimental in nature, as scholars have sought to measure and document the effects of a range of LEGO artifacts on young people. Evidencing the wealth of scientific examination of LEGO's effects, recent studies range from how LEGO products affect the gendering of children's play (Fulcher and Hayes 2018), to the effectiveness of LEGO Therapy for youth with autism (e.g., Lindsay et al. 2017), to the role of LEGO building toys in improving children's problem-solving skills and overall STEM learning (e.g., Li et al. 2016; Moreau and Engeset 2016), to the integration of LEGO robotics (Mindstorms) in the classroom (e.g., Afari and Khine 2017).

As LEGO has grown to enjoy unprecedented commercial success, however, a growing body of critical scholarship—grounded in more humanistic inquiry—has begun interrogating LEGO as a seemingly ubiquitous cultural artifact. Much of this scholarship, including the chapters in this book, is situated in the interdisciplinary field known as Cultural Studies.

Before discussing Cultural Studies as a field, it is imperative first to address what we mean when we talk about "culture," and specifically about LEGO as a cultural artifact. As eloquently described by Meenakshi Gigi Durham and Douglas H. Kellner (2012), culture "constitutes a set of discourses, stories, images, spectacles, and varying cultural forms and practices that generate meanings, identities, and political effects" (p. 4). One cannot separate culture from the broader system of ideologies at play—specifically its link to a dominant ideology or hegemony (Durham and Kellner 2012; Kellner 2015). Large, powerful, multinational corporations like LEGO and Disney, for example, can perpetuate their worldview across the range of cultural artifact they produce by telling the stories they want audiences to hear. They are likely to prioritize stories whose worldviews promote the corporations' self-interests (such as financial success), with the cultural needs of their audience members (such as inclusivity and the breaking-down of harmful stereotypes) playing a secondary role. The chapters in this collection therefore offer diverse critical/cultural studies perspectives on what we see as the "storytelling" of the LEGO franchise.

It is imperative, then, that scholars have the necessary tools to interrogate the relationship between culture and (dominant) ideology, and Cultural Studies, as an umbrella, provides us with those tools (Kellner 2015). While it is beyond this introduction's scope to provide a historical and epistemological overview of Cultural Studies, interested readers could follow up with Simon During's *The Cultural Studies Reader (3rd ed.)* (2007) for a comprehensive historical evolution of the field and/or Durham and Kellner's *Media and Cultural Studies: Keyworks (2nd ed.)* (2012) for an equally detailed introduction to key theoretical perspectives and approaches within the field. For our purposes, Cultural Studies, according to Douglas Kellner (2015), is characterized by a focus on the connections between ideology and representation, specifically the examination of the relationships between popular culture artifacts and the dominant ideologies of a particular time and place. Moreover, Kellner (2015) asserts:

Cultural studies insists that culture must be studied within the social relations and systems through which culture is produced and consumed and that the study of culture is thus intimately bound up with the study of society, politics and economics. (p. 8)

In a nutshell, Cultural Studies' concern is with how meaning is made and transmitted, even through something as seemingly innocuous as a LEGO brick. Scholars working within this tradition therefore engage in "more differentiated political, rather than aesthetic valuations of cultural artifacts" (p. 8).

While, as During (2007) notes, Cultural Studies "possesses neither a well-defined methodology nor clearly demarcated fields for investigation" (p. 1), Kellner (2015) identifies three components that link Cultural Studies: (1) political economy (going behind the scenes, so to speak, to examine cultural artifacts within their broader systems of production); (2) textual analysis (deconstructing the "ideological positions," "narrative strategies" and "image construction" within cultural texts, broadly defined) (p. 12); and (3) audience reception (how audiences, including fans, negotiate their relationship with cultural artifacts). The various chapters in this collection represent these three traditions, although the chapter authors' use of theories and lenses to engage with these traditions varies.

In recent years, critical/cultural studies scholars have made the discourses and representations within children's culture a significant area of study. We situate this volume within this broader critical/cultural interrogation of children's culture including American Girl dolls (Zaslow 2017); Disney (Cheu 2013); Nickelodeon (Banet-Weiser 2007; Hendershot 2004); princess culture (Forman-Brunell and Hains 2013); video games (Cassell and Jenkins 2000); and more.

Chapters

This book is divided into three parts. The first, "LEGO as Media Text" focuses on LEGO films and various other mediated representations of the LEGO brand. Part II examines "Creativity in the LEGO Universe" by covering the phenomenon of creativity with and within LEGO cultural artifacts, as well as how LEGO fans and writers create with LEGO. Finally, Part III, "The Politics of Representation in the LEGO

Franchise," addresses the representation of diversity (or lack thereof) in LEGO artifacts.

LEGO as Media Text. In this book's first part, our authors engage with various LEGO "texts," such as assorted LEGO playsets, books and videogames; films like *The LEGO Movie, The LEGO Movie 2, The LEGO Batman Movie,* and *The LEGO Ninjago Movie;* and LEGO's DC Super Heroes media properties. In their chapters, the authors draw upon an array of critical/cultural studies perspectives to unpack various ideologies embedded into these texts, shedding light on the worldviews conveyed by the LEGO brand and their possible cultural significance.

The first two chapters focus on LEGO Batman—significant for its focus on a transfranchise title character that has been a toyetic and transmedia success for decades—within a political economy context. In their chapters, Lincoln Geraghty (Chapter 2) and Matthew McAllister and Jared LaGroue (Chapter 3) argue that LEGO Batman serves as a crossover, cross-promotional character that, in the marketplace, greatly benefits both the LEGO and the DC Comics brand.

In Chapter 2, called "In a 'Justice' League of their Own: Transmedia Storytelling and Paratextual Reinvention in LEGO's DC Super Heroes," Geraghty explores LEGO's collaborative working relationship with licensing partner DC Comics, which owns the Batman franchise. Examining a range of LEGO artifacts and paratexts (including playsets, minifigures, films, videogames and books) primarily related to the LEGO Batman character, he documents how the connections between corporate initiatives and content creation result in the construction of "transmedia worlds." These transmedia worlds catalyze new stories and franchise marketing opportunities for LEGO and also function to direct LEGO fans to engage further with DC's Batman, which has a lengthy and extensive transmedia history. Geraghty concludes that the collaboration between DC and LEGO strategically diversifies the brands' potential markets and "transforms Batman into a transmedia franchise character"—an insight that is helpful in understanding wider shifts in the toy and entertainment industries.

In Chapter 3, called "'Hey, Kids. Who Wants a Shot from the Merch Gun?!': LEGO Batman as a Gateway Commodity Intertext," McAllister and LaGroue build upon the idea that from a strategic corporate standpoint, LEGO Batman's various appearances in LEGO films and other LEGO media functioned to extend both the LEGO and Batman brands. McAllister and LaGroue consider the marketing of LEGO Batman products, such as toys and books, and note that these cross-media products targeted children as young as three years of age. Taking a holistic view of LEGO Batman in the marketplace, and the array of strategic cross-promotion opportunities LEGO has created, McAllister and LaGroue conclude that a primary goal of LEGO Batman's marketing is the socialization of young viewers into consumer culture, to the benefit of its own brand and those of its franchise partners.

Then, in Chapters 4, 5 and 6, our authors offer textual analyses that read LEGO media for other ideological positions: neoliberalism, religion, and gender and race, respectively. In Chapter 4, titled "Everything is Awesome When You're Part of a List: The Flattening of Distinction in Post-Ironic LEGO Media," Ari Mattes examines LEGO films and videogames for their use of lists and irony. Through his analysis, Mattes reveals that an apolitical, uncritical perspective is embedded throughout LEGO media at the narrative level. This, Mattes argues, reflects a neoliberal dream of an apolitical world in which individual choice and self-celebration are paramount, rather than structural matters. By reducing social and political conflict to matters of individual choices and morality, LEGO media suggest that it is entirely possible for every member of society to win: "that everything *is* awesome, if you've got the right attitude." Mattes sees LEGO's characteristic list-based, ironic humor as "attempting to evacuate and negate the political through the annihilation of a critical position."

In Chapter 5, "Made Up Prophecies: Metamodern Play with Religion, Spirituality and Monomyth in the LEGO Universe," Sissel Undheim considers *The LEGO Movie* and *The LEGO Movie 2: The Second Part* from a religious studies perspective. Although she notes that some may find the idea of LEGO mixing religion and popular culture blasphemous, she is interested in interrogating how LEGO's diverse media and platforms approach religion. As LEGO primarily targets child audiences, Undheim notes that LEGO has received less attention from scholars in her field than have other, similarly influential transnational media phenomenon that target adult audiences. In her analysis, she finds that while most of the themes sold on the LEGO Shop Web site seem secular, LEGO products and media are filled with new-age spiritualities that are vague and nearly unnoticeable. Undheim concludes that LEGO celebrates rule-breaking opposing dogmatism, with a "kind of 'spiritual secularity' [that] emerges through tongue-in-cheek puns, play, and chaotic pop-cultural mash-ups."

The final chapter in the "LEGO as Media Text" part of this volume, written by Matthias Zick Varul (Chapter 6), is called "The Accursed Second Part: Small-Scale Discourses of Gender and Race in *The LEGO Movie 2*." Varul argues that while at first glance, *The LEGO Movie 2: The Accursed Second Part* seems to offer a scathing critique of toxic masculinity, it does not subvert the cultural dominance of the patriarchy or present a meaningful challenge to White, male privilege. Instead, Varul explains, the film positions the character Emmet as a "White savior" when Duplo aliens—led by a queen that the film presents as both gendered and racialized—invade Bricksburg. Problematizing these representations, Varul argues that the film supports a patriarchal, middle-class ideology by perpetuating the stereotypical idea that masculinity, Whiteness and order are dichotomously opposed to femininity, Blackness and disorder—making the former a necessary corrective for the threat presented by the latter.

"Creativity in the LEGO Universe." Part II of this volume considers the phenomenon of creativity with and within LEGO artifacts. While the first chapter (Chapter 7) examines the LEGO brand's own representation of LEGO as a creative medium, the other chapters consider the creative works of individuals—some of whom (as in Chapters 8 and 10) receive forms of compensation or reward from LEGO, but some of whom (as seen in Chapter 9) would receive no patronage from the company, as they create works that are entirely contrary to LEGO's brand image.

The part begins with "Master Building and Creative Vision in *The LEGO Movie*" (Chapter 7), which bridges the focus on LEGO as a media text and LEGO creativity. In this chapter, author Jonathan Rey Lee examines LEGO's representation of Master Builders in *The LEGO Movie*, specifically as this intersects with LEGO toy play. Organized using Csikszentmihalyi's five stages of creativity as adopted by

The LEGO Foundation—preparation, incubation, insight, evaluation and elaboration—Lee deconstructs how LEGO works to construct a particularly LEGO version of creative vision. His chapter begins by analyzing two reports commissioned by The LEGO Foundation which, taken together, articulate a theory of creativity that links to the need for development by activity such as building with LEGO. Moreover, he examines how this vision of creativity is played out in *The LEGO Movie* and its playsets, demonstrating that the film's messages about play, creativity and work are in discourse with central, crucial aspects of the LEGO brand's identity and philosophy. Lee concludes that LEGO has constructed a vision of creativity that fits into a commercial imperative, problematically advancing a consumerist ethic.

In Chapter 8, "Toyetics and Novelizations: Bringing *The LEGO Movie* to the Page," Joyce Goggin examines one of the least-studied and least-respected forms of popular culture: novelizations, or novels based on previously released films. She critically interrogates novelizations of *The LEGO Movie* and *The LEGO Batman Movie* by examining their content; interviewing women who write LEGO media novelizations; and bringing a political economy perspective to a range of intersecting issues related to the novelizations' production. These include the gendering of novelizations (as they are mostly written by women); cultural capital; pedagogy; and appeal to readers. While novelizations often receive criticism for their perceived role as unimaginative marketing vehicles for the films upon which they are based, Goggin argues that novelizations are linked historically to other cultural artifacts typically written by women, such as Harlequin Romances, and likewise devalued in part due to their reputation as a feminized form of labor. In her analysis, Goggin demonstrates that LEGO novelizations have links to "affective labor," women's perceived roles as caretakers, a focus on the "cuteness" of LEGO characters, and a pedagogy that is at times grounded in neoliberalism.

Chapter 9 turns to a type of creative work not conducted under the aegis of LEGO: "brickfilming" (Brownlee 2016; Einwächter and Simon 2017), or amateur stop motion films made primarily by LEGO fans. Noting that there is a long history of this LEGO fan creative practice, Shannon Brownlee's chapter narrows the study of such productions specifically to LEGO pornography. In "LEGO Porn: Phallic Pleasure and Knowledge," Brownlee offers a textual analysis of numerous videos posted primarily on YouTube. She reveals LEGO pornography to be both "phallic and phallocentric," in part as informed by the design of LEGO minifigures and the bricks themselves. This design, she argues, along with the use of metaphors and insinuations by LEGO porn creators, results in a genre grounded in the exploration of an overriding theme of penetration.

In Chapter 10, informed primarily by ethnographic research and situated within the seemingly unrelated academic fields of fan studies, labor relations and public relations, author Nancy Jennings takes the reader into the multifaceted relationship between Adult Fans of LEGO (AFOLs) and the company itself. Her chapter, called "'It's All About the Brick': Mobilizing Adult Fans of LEGO," is more than just an investigation into AFOLs: She also explores of how LEGO "mobilizes" those fans—specifically, the roles that LEGO invites AFOLs to play in the company's marketing and public brand management initiatives. Jennings demonstrates how, through their engagement with LEGO as artists, collectors, designers, and user community members, these fans also serve as free labor for the LEGO brand. For the AFOL, however, "it's all about the brick."

The Politics of Representation in the LEGO Franchise. The chapters in our third part focus upon the LEGO franchise's inclusivity and diversity (or lack thereof), examining matters of race and gender. In Chapter 11, titled "'I Just Don't Really, Like, Connect To It': How Girls Negotiate LEGO's Gender-Marketed Toys," Rebecca Hains and Jennifer Shewmaker begin by reviewing how LEGO began creating and marketing products in differing, gender-stereotypical ways to boys and girls in the 1980s, and have continued doing so ever since. Hains and Shewmaker then turn to their qualitative research with twenty girls, ages six to eleven, whom the authors individually interviewed and invited to engage in free play with the materials from several LEGO playsets. The authors found that their participants could readily tell them which products LEGO meant "for girls" or "for boys," and that some—but not all—participants expressed personal preferences for LEGO sets along such gender stereotypes (finding girl-oriented sets more appealing, and boy-oriented sets less relatable). When the participants played with the mixed-together pieces from the LEGO sets, however, away from the contexts of their often gender-stereotypical packaging, many girls were active, creative and generative—demonstrating significantly different behaviors and interests than those that are assumed by marketing and cultural stereotypes about girls' interests and pastimes.

Then, in Chapter 12, "Mia Had a Little Lamb: Gender and Species Stereotypes in LEGO Sets," Debra Merskin conducts an examination of a range of LEGO sets available for purchase on the LEGO Shop Web site that include animal figures. She closely reads these sets for their "re-presentation" of human–animal relationships, particularly in relation to gender. Using intersectionality as a critical lens, she finds that while the LEGO sets in her study include boy and girl characters, there are gendered differences that impact the representation of both human and animal figures in the sets: Sets meant for boys tended to present male characters in dominant positions over unnamed animals (such as farm animals), while sets meant for girls tended to present female characters as caretakers who nurtured named animals (such as pets). Merskin concludes that the storytelling in these building sets perpetuates hegemonic ideas, promoting an ideological perspective in which boys, girls, women, men and animals alike are assumed to be suited for predetermined, stereotypical roles. She argues that the brand's current offerings miss the opportunity for gender-inclusivity in their offerings and for fostering children's empathy for animals.

Drawing from a range of theoretical literatures including queer theory, LEGO Studies, feminist media studies, and children's media studies, Kyra Hunting (Chapter 13) examines the representation of masculinity within *The LEGO Batman Movie*. In "The Man Behind the Mask: Camp and Queer Masculinity in *LEGO Batman*," Hunting offers a nuanced analysis of how the film draws from and remixes several other previous cinematic incarnations of Batman. Her analysis articulates how the film's use of parody and privileging of the 1960s queer, camp *Batman* TV series undermines the heteronormative, hypermasculinity of some earlier Batman representations. She concludes by arguing that *The LEGO Batman Movie*, like LEGO bricks, enables its filmmakers to construct something new out of seeming disparate pieces that fit together to create something entirely different than what is expected.

Finally, positioned at the intersection of representational politics and corporate social responsibility, Derek Johnson in Chapter 14 ("A License to Diversify: Media Franchising and the Transformation of the 'Universal' LEGO Minifigure") situates LEGO products as what he calls "building blocks of embodied difference." According to Johnson, since 2015, LEGO products have evidenced more racial and gender diversity than ever before. While LEGO minifigures have long been characterized by the "universal" yellow brick, Johnson argues that LEGO's licensing agreements with such transmedia phenomena as Star Wars have led to more diversity within LEGO products themselves. As Star Wars diversified their character lineups, LEGO has followed suit in their toyetic representations of these diverse characters. Johnson goes on to also examine how this new embrace of diversity has played out in other new, non-licensed LEGO products. He argues that while LEGO and their licensees have embraced representational diversity in their offerings, these corporations' embrace of diversity is inherently tied into broader corporate branding initiatives.

"Let There Be LEGO!": The Concluding Part

Given the ubiquity, diversity and reach of LEGO cultural artifacts, The LEGO Group has emerged as a significant and powerful producer of culture in today's world. No single volume can address all things LEGO: As is the case when playing with LEGO toys, imagination is the only limit on the possible inquiries into the brand.

Our anthology offers nuanced, critical-cultural explorations into a wealth of LEGO artifacts, stories and actors, but many more critical/cultural studies of LEGO could be undertaken. In his musings on the wisdom of institutionalizing a field of "LEGO Studies," Jason Mittell argues instead that "what we need from LEGO Studies is fluidity and flexibility, the ability to put unlikely pieces together while also being able to dismantle and reconfigure what has already been done" (2014, p. 272). Following from that, we hope this volume inspires further research on the political economy, ideological storytelling and audience reception of the LEGO brand, toys, media and products. When engaging with our contributors' chapters, it is worth attending to the stories our authors tell *and* those that they do not. For example, consider *LEGO Magazine*, which targets children ages five to ten with commercial content about the brand; LEGO webisodes, available on the LEGO Web site, that tell animated stories based on themes like Friends and Elves; LEGO robotics clubs, some of which engage in tournaments and other competitions, but in which girls and children of color are often not well represented; and LEGO's theme parks, found in locations around the world, offering visitors of all ages immersive brand experiences. All these subjects are ripe for analyses from fresh perspectives, with the potential to offer insights about LEGO as a cultural storyteller and producer of ideology, politics and meaning-making.

At first glance, some might dismiss the LEGO brand as mere child's play, unworthy of deep critical thought. In fact, dismissal is a relatively common reaction to pop culture topics, and children's culture topics especially. For example, in response to a Washington Post article about Barbie's cultural significance that this volume's lead editor authored, one commenter sniped: "Barbie and Legos – you can be a Professor of just about anything in our great country" (Hains 2019). Amusing though those business cards would be, our universities don't need to make us Professors of Barbie and LEGO for us to know that trivializing of children's popular culture is problematic. Doing so ignores meaningful complexities and affords wealthy transnational corporations *carte blanche* in consumer socialization and hegemonic, ideological messaging. For this reason, we are pleased to present in this volume an alternative perspective about the significance of children's products and entertainment. Because of its power and influence in the global marketplace, LEGO truly is more than just bricks.

Notes

1. We do not claim that LEGO products are found in every country, but as of 2015, LEGO products were sold in more than 140 countries (Mortensen 2017).
2. Interestingly Bacharach and Cook (2017) remind us that LEGO "doesn't actually make toys" (p. 2). Rather, they make building materials.
3. In a 2018 study, Christoph Bartneck and Elena Moltchanova found that LEGO products' complexity and specialization has increased over the years, "resulting in sets sharing fewer bricks" (p. 1). They argue that this favors "skilled builders" while disadvantaging young builders, for the latter are overwhelmed by the complexity.

References

Afari, E., & Khine, M. S. (2017). Robotics as an educational tool: Impact of LEGO mindstorms. *International Journal of Information and Education Technology, 7*(6), 437–442. https://doi.org/10.18178/ijiet.2017.7.6.908.

Bacharach, S., & Cook, R. T. (2017). Introduction: Play well, philosophize well! In R. T. Cook & S. Bacharach (Eds.), *Lego philosophy: Constructing reality brick by brick* (pp. 1–3). Hoboken, NJ: Wiley-Blackwell.

Banet-Weiser, S. (2007). *Kids rule! Nickelodeon and consumer citizenship.* Durham, NC: Duke University Press.

Bartneck, C., & Moltchanova, E. (2018). LEGO products have become more complex. *PloS one, 13*(1), e0190651. https://journals.plos.org/plosone/article?id=10.1371/journal.pone.0190651.

Bainbridge, J. (2017). From toyetic to toyesis: The cultural value of merchandising. In S. Harrington (Ed.), *Entertainment values* (pp. 23–39). London: Palgrave Macmillan.

Brownlee, S. (2016). Amateurism and the aesthetics of Lego stop-motion on YouTube. *Film Criticism, 40*(2). http://dx.doi.org/10.3998/fc.13761232.0040.204. Accessed on July 1, 2019.

Cassell, J., & Jenkins, H. (Eds.). (2000). *From Barbie to Mortal Kombat: Gender and computer games.* Cambridge, MA: MIT Press.

Cheu, J. (Ed.). (2013). *Diversity in Disney films: Critical essays on race, ethnicity, gender, sexuality and disability.* Jefferson, NC: McFarland.

Durham, M. G., & Kellner, D. M. (2012). Adventures in media and cultural studies: Introducing the keyworks. In M. G. Durham & D. M. Kellner (Eds.), *Media and cultural studies: Keyworks* (2nd ed., pp. 1–23). Malden, MA: Wiley-Blackwell.

During, S. (Ed.). (2007). Introduction. In S. During (Ed.), *The cultural studies reader* (3rd ed., pp. 1–31). New York, NY: Routledge.

Einwächter, S. G., & Simon, F. M. (2017). How digital remix and fan culture helped the Lego comeback. *Transformative Works and Cultures, 25*. https://journal.transformativeworks.org/index.php/twc/article/download/1047/892?inline=1.

Forman-Brunell, M., & Hains, R. C. (Eds.). (2013). *Princess cultures: Mediating girls imaginations and identities*. New York: Peter Lang.

Fulcher, M., & Hayes, A. R. (2018). Building a pink dinosaur: The effects of gendered construction toys on girls' and boys' play. *Sex Roles, 79*(5–6), 273–284. https://doi.org/10.1007/s11199-017-0806-3-3.

Hains, R. C. (2019). Barbie is 60. And she's reinventing herself: Mattel's changes to an iconic doll reflect evolving demographics. *The Washington Post*. https://www.washingtonpost.com/outlook/2019/03/07/barbie-is-shes-reinventing-herself/?utm_term=.347406632659. Accessed on July 30, 2019.

Hendershot, H. (Ed.). (2004). *Nickelodeon nation: The history, politics, and economics of America's only TV channel for kids*. New York: New York University Press.

Jensen, M. V. S. (2015, February 12). *The LEGO group*. https://www.lego.com/en-us/aboutus/lego-group. Accessed on June 20, 2019.

Kauflin, J. (2017, February 14). The most powerful brands in 2017. *Forbes*. https://www.forbes.com/sites/jeffkauflin/2017/02/14/the-most-powerful-brands-in-2017/#862c07df1f84. Accessed on June 28, 2019.

Kellner, D. (2015). Cultural studies, multiculturalism, and media culture. In G. Dines & J. M. Humez (Eds.), *Gender, race and class in media: A critical reader* (4th ed., pp. 7–19). Los Angeles: Sage.

Konzack, L. (2014). The cultural history of LEGO. In M. J. Wolf (Ed.), *LEGO studies: Examining the building blocks of a transmedial phenomenon* (pp. 1–14). New York: Routledge.

Lauwaert, M. (2008). Playing outside the box—On LEGO toys and the changing world of construction play. *History and Technology, 24*(3), 221–237. https://doi.org/10.1080/07341510801900300.

LEGO. (n.d.). *National Toy Hall of Fame*. https://www.toyhalloffame.org/toys/lego. Accessed on June 20, 2019.

Li, Y., Huang, Z., Jiang, M., & Chang, T. W. (2016). The effect on pupils' science performance and problem-solving ability through Lego: An engineering design-based modeling approach. *Journal of Educational Technology & Society, 19*(3), 143–156. https://www.jstor.org/stable/jeductechsoci.19.3.143.

Lindsay, S., Hounsell, K. G., & Cassiani, C. (2017). A scoping review of the role of LEGO® therapy for improving inclusion and social skills among children and youth with autism. *Disability and Health Journal, 10*(2), 173–182. https://doi.org/10.1016/j.dhjo.2016.10.010.

Mittell, J. (2014). Afterword: DIY disciplinarity–(dis) assembling LEGO studies for the academy. In M. J. Wolf (Ed.), *LEGO studies: Examining the building blocks of a transmedial phenomenon* (pp. 268–275). New York: Routledge.

Moreau, C. P., & Engeset, M. G. (2016). The downstream consequences of problem-solving mindsets: How playing with LEGO influences creativity. *Journal of Marketing Research, 53*(1), 18–30. https://doi.org/10.1509/jmr.13.0499.

Mortensen, T. F. (2017, October 17). *The LEGO group history*. https://www.lego.com/en-us/aboutus/lego-group/the_lego_history. Accessed on June 20, 2019.

Rath, J. (2017, February 25). The 10 most powerful brands in the world. *Business Insider.* http://www.businessinsider.com/the-worlds-10-most-powerful-brands-2017-2. Accessed on June 28, 2019.

Schultz, M., & Hatch, M. J. (2003). The cycles of corporate branding: The case of the LEGO company. *California Management Review, 46*(1), 6–26. https://doi.org/10.2307/41166229.

Van Looveren, Y. (2017, October 3). LEGO is world's largest toy manufacturer for first time. *Retail Detail.* https://www.retaildetail.eu/en/news/general/lego-worlds-largest-toy-manufacturer-first-time. Accessed on June 27, 2019.

Washington National Cathedral. (2019). *Help build a LEGO replica of the National Cathedral.* https://cathedral.org/lego/. Accessed on June 26, 2019.

Wolf, M. J. (Ed.). (2014). *LEGO studies: Examining the building blocks of a transmedial phenomenon* (pp. xxi–xxv). New York: Routledge.

Zaslow, E. (2017). *Playing with America's doll: A cultural analysis of the American girl collection.* New York: Springer.

Part I

LEGO as Media Text

2

In a "Justice" League of Their Own: Transmedia Storytelling and Paratextual Reinvention in LEGO's DC Super Heroes

Lincoln Geraghty

For Derek Johnson (2013), "transmedia storytelling suggests cultural artistry and participatory culture," while "'franchising' calls equal if not more attention to corporate structure and the economic organization of that productive labor" (p. 33). For the LEGO Corporation, that "cultural artistry" and "productive labor" is epitomized by the multiple collaborative partnerships the company shares with the likes of Disney and Warner Bros., who own iconic and popular entertainment franchises including *Star Wars*, Marvel, *Harry Potter* and DC. With its partners, LEGO has designed and released hundreds of playsets and minifigures based on characters that populate the ever-expanding worlds of TV, film and comics. From humble beginnings as an educational toy manufacturer, LEGO is now the world's largest toy company, and their strategic financial plan centers on its licensed products for global media franchises. For example, in 2018, LEGO released 37 sets for its most prolific licensed theme, *Star Wars*—the most of any theme that year ("Crunching the Numbers" 2019, p. 10). Moreover, following a 17%

L. Geraghty (✉)
University of Portsmouth, Portsmouth, UK
e-mail: lincoln.geraghty@port.ac.uk

© The Author(s) 2019
R. C. Hains and S. R. Mazzarella (eds.), *Cultural Studies of LEGO*,
https://doi.org/10.1007/978-3-030-32664-7_2

drop in profits in 2017, the company saw a 4% rise in 2018, thanks largely to products associated with blockbuster *Jurassic World* and franchises like *Star Wars* and *Harry Potter* (Wharfe 2018, p. 8).

Product diversification drives part of this success: It's not just about the toys, but also the media content and video games that LEGO now commission. TV series and short films based on *Star Wars*, Marvel and DC characters such as *LEGO Star Wars: The Freemaker Adventures* (2016-present), *LEGO Marvel Superheroes: Maximum Overload* (2013) and *LEGO Batman: The Movie—DC Heroes Unite* (2013) exemplify LEGO's drive to create new, original content that extends the parent universe's traditional format, adding their own brand of humor and character interpretations. Popular LEGO games by British video game developer Traveller's Tales (now TT Games, owned by Warner Bros.) expand the fictional worlds of *Star Wars*, *The Avengers* and *Batman* even further. Catering to a knowing fan audience, they allow people to "play" the superhero, as well as literally rebuild and reenact iconic movie scenes. Titles based on established media franchises have proliferated, reflecting the financial importance of intellectual property and cinematic world-building in contemporary Hollywood.[1]

Therefore, I argue in this chapter that LEGO's original content is an example of brand synergy across transmedia platforms. The toys, animated series and associated merchandise like books, guides and video games contribute to a complex narrative network of texts, working in tandem to underscore the new storytelling strategy's preeminence: television and films "reimagine" classic movie and comics scenes; reference books fill in backstories to characters from the expanded universes; toys and video games allow players/gamers/fans to adapt and control characters in self-created narratives and spaces. Where Robert Buerkle (2014) suggested that "LEGO acts as a signifier for childhood and toy play," creating nostalgia for past texts within a "toydom" framework (p. 148), I further argue that LEGO's animated series are part of their strategy for creating brand synergy. These series reinvent established canon through paratextual production to create new audiences and offer franchise partners space to retell and resell older characters and storylines. Thus, this chapter seeks to highlight the interconnected nature of corporate production, media content creation and transmedia world-building in the contexts of character development. For those interested in studying the ever-closer relationships between the media and entertainment industries, my focus on how LEGO works with its licensing partners to create new products from older brands will elucidate some recent debates within media studies concerning technology and content production, global reception and the flow of texts across media platforms.

In this chapter, I analyze the LEGO DC Super Heroes brand and how Batman, in particular, represents LEGO's attempts to create a self-contained narrative world that reimagines, recycles and remediates familiar stories, villains and heroes from the DC comics universe. While this might suggest a breakaway from comic canon and previous versions of the Caped Crusader, it in fact underscores the adaptability of the core character and his story, the importance of multiplicity in sustaining a franchise and, ultimately, how LEGO has become a medium for both play and transmedia storytelling. Exploring how LEGO adds to and transforms DC's transmedia Batman franchise helps us understand wider entertainment and toy industry shifts. At the forefront of toy design for decades, LEGO's ability to take pre-established, globally recognized entertainment franchises like Batman, *Star Wars* and Harry Potter and turn them into distinct, successful brands suggests audiences seek new ways of engaging with those fictional texts. Likewise, those franchises are keen to access new markets.

Marc Steinberg's discussion of what he termed anime's "media mix" provides a helpful framework for understanding the multiple versions of transmedia Batman. Media mix, a "term for the cross-media serialization and circulation of entertainment franchises" (Steinberg 2012, p. viii), shares much with Henry Jenkins' (2006) examination of contemporary convergence culture. However, Steinberg traced a longer history of the term, suggesting it starts with anime's emergence on the 1960s Japanese television. More than a style, anime is a mode of cultural production and consumption where animated characters and franchises mix and merge across multimedia platforms. Audience consumption of these franchises and animated characters is about both possession (purchasing and collecting merchandise and images) and participation (entering the fictional world through the various incarnations of the characters in question). Thus, according to Steinberg (2012), the anime media mix simultaneously creates (1) the character merchandise as material object, (2) the world to which the character merchandise belongs, and (3) the character as immaterial connective agent guaranteeing the consistency of this ever-expanding world. (p. 200)

Throughout this chapter, I discuss how DC's partnership with LEGO has created a "media mix" that spreads Batman's established world into parallel incarnations characterized by parody and humor, immersion and play. Analyzing the reference books, animated movies and video games that expand the LEGO DC universe, I argue that LEGO Batman is a consistent part of DC's world that also offers opportunities for the toy company to take the character into interesting new directions.

Rebuilding the Brand: From Construction Toy to Licensed Product

Danish toy company LEGO has been a perennial favorite with children and adults since its mass marketing rebirth in the 1950s and 1960s. The attraction of being able to build almost anything a child can imagine from a pile of colorful interlocking bricks proved a valuable selling point for parents concerned that their children should learn something as they played (Cross 1997). During the 1970s and 1980s, however, fantasy and action toys became central components of movie merchandise and licensing agreements in the American toy industry. Following this, LEGO added to its offerings its own ranges of themed building sets and minifigure characters. As a consequence, since the 1980s, many LEGO consumers and fans have followed architectural blueprints and built within prescribed "systems": city, space, medieval, pirates, etc. (Kline 1993). Beyond this, Adult Fans of LEGO (AFOLs) use bricks and minifigures to produce and/or modify their own creations, displaying and building at conventions around the world (as detailed in Nancy Jennings' chapter in this volume). Often working without sanction, adult enthusiasts can turn the children's toy into a playful, subversive medium characterizing their subcultural fan identity.

In 1999, LEGO bought into the merchandising market, starting with *Star Wars*-themed sets tied into the release of prequel film *The Phantom Menace* (Lipkowitz 2009, p. 29). For Maaike Lauwaert (2008), LEGO's attempts at product diversification—partnering with other companies to produce themed sets—symbolized its shift in emphasizing narrative over construction:

> Toys that centered on stories and themes allowed both for the development of more diverse products that did not necessarily have the brick and construction play at its basis (product differentiation) and the integration of the product with other media and other areas of the child's world (brand integration). (p. 227)

By the mid-1990s, LEGO produced more sets that allowed children to play with characters from established media franchises. Despite lucrative deals with Disney, LEGO's high production costs and brand overextension resulted in corporate restructuring in the early 2000s. Lauwaert has argued that having to rethink what lines and other media relationships LEGO wanted to continue meant it could refocus on the "system" as brand and concentrate on developing toys that emphasized narrative as well as construction (p. 228). We see this most vividly in the products, publications and media content released for Disney's *Star Wars* (Geraghty 2018a) and, as I will analyze in this chapter, DC's *Batman*.

LEGO's shift to producing licensed movie tie-ins is supported by the brand's popular range of video games and the creation of online fan clubs. This convergence of popular fandom, narrative, nostalgia and contemporary toy culture suggests that the lines between past and present; technology and culture; and childhood and adulthood are increasingly porous. Memory is an important component of being a fan, and the retelling of popular franchise stories through LEGO bricks and the remediation of toys through video games help to reconstruct memories of youth used to negotiate digital collaborative spaces shared by other fans. LEGO, a children's toy originally based on the physicality of construction, has taken on new significance in contemporary media culture as it allows adult fans to reconnect with their past and define a fan identity through more ephemeral and digital interaction.

David Buckingham (2011) argued that in a risky and flooded toy marketplace, "Integrated marketing, strong branding and the incessant recycling of past successes (particularly those that capitalize on parents' nostalgia for the toys of their own childhood) have become crucial in the attempt to manage the market" (p. 95). Now that the LEGO "system" incorporates global franchises like *Star Wars*, Marvel and DC Superheroes, Minecraft and historical titles such as *Indiana Jones, Pirates of the Caribbean, Harry Potter* and Pixar's *The Incredibles*, fans of one brand crossover to become fans of the other. Therefore, LEGO's shift from educational children's toy to media content provider is the characteristic of contemporary convergence culture, "where the property is proliferated by authorized licensees as well as consumers who make bottom-up contributions to the content network" (Johnson 2014, p. 33). It highlights nostalgia's importance in influencing which childhood media texts get remembered, and also how nostalgia acts to expand the original potentials of those remediated texts across different transmedia platforms (Geraghty 2018b).

It is worth noting, as I have argued elsewhere, that LEGO minifigures in particular have become popular articles of collecting, trade and fan work because they are easily manipulated and represent LEGO's universal playability and versatility. Either as part of a set or stand-alone, the minifigure literally embodies the player's actions in the LEGO world (Geraghty 2014, 170). Small enough to fit into the built environment the builder has created, they thus become the physical avatar of the master who controls their domain. Licensed franchise universes continually unfold, yet the LEGO minifigure becomes a transformative extension of the self and character inserted into the physical recreation of the fictional narrative: the playset. They allow fans to become part of, and own, the very text they adore. Minifigures combine the physical elements of toydom, play and adaptability with the familiar visual characteristics of the iconic on-screen characters. Their use in retelling the familiar story or elaborating on specific in-between moments from movies, television and comics highlights important transmedia qualities as they take the story from screen to page, text to paratext.

World-Building, Brick by Brick: LEGO DC Super Heroes

Batman was not the first superhero to receive his own line of sets and minifigures. LEGO released a series of Spider-Man themed sets in 2002 on the back of Sam Raimi's *Spider-Man* (2002), the first of three films starring Tobey Maguire. Working with DC, LEGO launched the Batman toy line in 2006, which included minifigures of a number of his most infamous foes: Joker, Riddler and Poison Ivy, to name a few. Two years later, *Batman: The Video Game* confirmed LEGO Batman as a fully transmedia character, bringing his adventures in Gotham City to life through an original animated storyline and interactive game-play. While the game was the first LEGO Traveller's Tales production to feature a brand-new story through which players could navigate (i.e., not based on a previous movie or comic book storyline), and new vocal effects that gave voice to iconic characters, it featured music from Danny Elfman's score for Tim Burton's *Batman* (1989). Such aural connection to what many critics and fans consider an authentic adaptation of the Batman story, and one that brought both the character and superhero genre into the Hollywood mainstream market, gives the LEGO Batman brand a sense of legitimacy within the wider universe of DC comic adaptations. This is important, as I will elucidate later, in terms of how convincing the LEGO Batman world is in brick form compared to its original comic book and blockbuster progenitors.

In 2012, LEGO expanded the Batman comic universe by releasing new sets under the DC Super Heroes brand. LEGO introduced Superman, Wonder Woman and Lex Luthor, among others, in minifigure form. That same year, LEGO also worked with DC's rival Marvel, releasing sets based on well-known characters such as Spider-Man (not Raimi's films, but the comics), the X-Men (again from the comics rather than films), and The Avengers (centered on the Cinematic Universe created by Marvel Studios). Alongside the expansion in characters and related storyworlds in toy form, LEGO supported DC Super Heroes with new games and an animated television movie. *Batman 2: DC Super Heroes* as a game broke free from Batman's traditional Gotham City confines and included Metropolis as playable setting, with other Justice League members joining him in stopping Joker and Lex Luthor from stealing the presidential election. The first animated Batman movie based on the LEGO toys, *LEGO Batman: The Movie—DC Heroes Unite*, followed in 2013. In contrast, *The LEGO Batman Movie* (2017; hereafter referred to as LBM) is based not on previous toys, but rather on the Batman character created for *The LEGO Movie* (2014; hereafter *TLM*). Utilizing cut scenes from the game interwoven with new scenes, the 2013 movie told a traditional Batman story and established the character as a Justice League leader. Again, as I will discuss further in the next section, LEGO's transmedia storytelling strategy (supporting the toy line through games and animation) helps promote the brick Batman alongside other versions of the character brought to life on the page and big screen.

In the same way, popular books and guides commissioned by LEGO offer further promotional and narrative opportunities to expand the brand. Dorling Kindersley Publishing (DK), part of the Penguin Random House group, published *LEGO DC Super Heroes: The Awesome Guide*, which serves as a compendium to the sets and minifigures released since 2006; but it also serves as an encyclopedic collection of facts, stats and information that add depth and narrative detail to the characters and back story of the LEGO DC universe. Author Cavan Scott (2017) outlined the important heroes and villains that have made an appearance in LEGO form and summarized the many times Batman and the Justice League have faced off against their familiar foes. DK's *Character Encyclopedia* (Hugo and Scott 2016) and two editions of the *Visual Dictionary* (Lipkowitz 2012; Dowsett and Kaplan 2018) likewise present the LEGO DC brand as a complete narrative universe with connections between different LEGO versions of Batman, his suits and vehicles, as well as alternative examples of characters based on either the comics or more recent Warner Bros./DC live-action movies: *Man of Steel* (2013), *Batman vs. Superman: Dawn of Justice* (2016), *Justice League* (2017), *Wonder Woman* (2017) and *Aquaman* (2018). All books add to the textual depth of the universe and come with an exclusive minifigure to collect. They help maintain and explain the Batman "media mix," allowing for both the repetition of and divergence from the central story and character arc. Clear examples of transmedia paratexts, they extend the LEGO DC Super Heroes story beyond toys, movies and games—filling in narrative gaps to help create immersive experiences for players, viewers and fans.

Audiences make sense of complex narrative forms through practices of orientation and mapping. They create and seek out what Jason Mittell (2015) termed "orienting paratexts" (p. 261) to help decipher the original and primary text. Such paratexts could include lists, maps, guides, reference works and encyclopedias. These are not always transmedia but help to make sense of the storyworld from a distance:

> Orientation is not necessary to discover the canonical truth of a storyworld but rather is used to create a layer atop the program to help figure out how the pieces fit together or to propose alternative ways of seeing the story that might not be suggested by or contained within the original narrative design. (Mittell 2015, p. 262)

In this fashion, the LEGO books and guides published by DK for the DC Super Heroes brand act as "orienting paratexts." They help to establish and contain the comic book world LEGO has built around Batman and associated DC characters. LEGO and DK are important partners in telling a connected story and establishing brand synergy across transmedia platforms. The toys, associated merchandise, books, guides and video games all contribute to a complex narrative network of DC Super Heroes texts, working in tandem to underscore the preeminence of LEGO's transmedia strategy: animated movies "reimagine" classic heroes and villains from the comic books; reference books fill in backstories and details of ancillary characters and exclusive minifigure releases; and the toys and video games allow players/gamers/fans to adapt and control characters in self-created narratives and spaces.

As the chapters in this book highlight, LEGO is a multifaceted company with interests across different industry sectors. From toys to theme parks, LEGO has diversified its portfolio considerably since foundation. Mark J. P. Wolf (2014) described LEGO as a "medium, a mediating substance through which ideas can be expressed, and with which art can be created" (p. xxii). As a medium, LEGO lends itself to adaptation, as can be seen in the multiple DC sets and characters released since 2006; but it is also a transmedia company that produces texts, objects and content that "can produce meanings and structure play, creativity, and even identity" (p. xxiii). Their franchise links with Disney, Marvel, DC and Warner Bros. offer endless potential for storytelling and extending familiar characters and worlds into new territories and new scenarios. Such production could threaten established canon and offer contradictory information to what is seen on screen, yet LEGO's transmedia content complements rather than challenges what has come before. Wolf has argued that canonicity is not an issue for LEGO, as the stories mean to promote the minifigures and building sets rather than offer faithful versions of Batman, Superman or others seen in comics and films. They are "adaptations distinct and different from their source material, which all find common ground in the minifigure format … the minifigures nonetheless evoke the characters they are modeled on, and are more than simply minifigures putting on costumes" (p. xxiii). I will expand this discussion of the nature of the LEGO minifigure and the Batman character in the next section, but it is important to underscore here the flexible quality of LEGO as medium. For comics, a medium renowned for its reliance on often labyrinthine canon, LEGO's flexibility offers narrative potentials that open out, rather than limit, the franchise. It adds to and affirms the Batman "media mix" rather than subtracting from or diluting it.

Canon is important in maintaining and sustaining a franchise as it adapts to changes within the entertainment industries. Yet, canon can also be reformed and refashioned to offer new directions for storytelling and character development at the precise moment when franchises seek new audiences and large sales. Superhero comics commonly feature revisions to canon, offering alternate versions of characters and their backstories and providing writers and artists new opportunities to improve upon or correct mistakes in the original text. While LEGO DC Super Heroes does not necessarily improve upon or correct original characters and stories drawn from the comics, the brand does add to the original's potential for new forms of narrative. The retcon (or retroactive continuity) is a comic book staple, offering writers the chance to revisit "past installments in order to revise and rewrite them to create new narrative potential in the present (and thus in the future)" (Friedenthal 2017, p. 6). As such, we might consider LEGO DC stories as retcons of a sort: designed to offer new storytelling to new audiences who play with and enjoy LEGO, rather than necessarily knowing all there is to know about the DC comic book universe. They add to the world of DC, offer brick versions of established characters, but do not reboot the franchise in any meaningful way. In an age of "retroactive continuity" in all forms of popular culture, Andrew Friedenthal (2017) has argued that retconning is most explicit in the world of comic book superheroes published by DC and Marvel. The unfolding and ever-growing stories on page and screen actively require retcons in order to overcome challenges to the canon, to make sense of stories regularly published over the past 80 years. Comic book retconning is defined by "plasticity," as events and characters offer endless possibilities for storytelling despite what might have been written before (p. 9). Therefore, LEGO DC Super Heroes is literally and metaphorically a plastic world created to tell and retell well-known stories without changing or detracting from the original's nature as defined by canon.

If comic book superheroes emblematize a fascination for retroactive continuity, with LEGO creating parallels texts and paratexts that fill out the DC universe, then their continued popularity and prevalence may arguably represent convergence culture's effect. In the age of media convergence, Jenkins argues, "old and new media collide" (2006, p. 2). Newly reborn, these once-forgotten icons, symbols, images, sounds and series from music, comics, film and television attract new fans. Jenkins further asserts that convergence allows for the archiving of and searching for new forms of entertainment where "the flow of content across multiple media platforms" (p. 2), linking the web with older media forms such as comics, film and television. In this context, multiple versions and iterations of the same text can coexist due to constant content creation, mediation and consumption. For the superhero genre, with a history of stories, characters, authors and artists behind it, the need for continuity is replaced by a desire for "multiplicity." Jenkins (2009), in his essay on the history of silver age comics, described "multiplicity" as a system where "readers may consume multiple versions of the same franchise, each with different conceptions of the character, different understandings of their relationships with the secondary figures, different moral perspectives, exploring different moments in their lives, and so forth" (pp. 20–21). As such, LEGO DC Super Heroes continues in the multiplicity of the Batman and Justice League universe.

However, LEGO's foray into the DC universe, which already has multiple variations and versions of the same characters and stories, is not entirely at odds with what has come before. Johnson (2017) argued that multiplicity requires careful management, with creators and owners collaborating to produce franchise texts that can share the same world, but not necessarily refer to or impact each other. He described "media franchising as a site of struggle and negotiation within the cultural industries … [and] that the worlds brought into being by franchising engage, resolve, and ultimately manage those conflicts and tensions" (p. 131). The following comment from LEGO DC Super Heroes designer Justin Ramsden highlights the management of multiplicity between both creative partners:

> We work very closely with DC Comics to create the best toys possible. For instance, when designing sets for an upcoming film, we usually get to read the script way in advance of the movie being launched and decide on the moments (and characters) in the film that would translate best into LEGO sets. We also get sent a vast amount of reference images that we can base our models on. (quoted in Dowsett and Kaplan 2018, p. 121)

Further, in his interview published in Dowsett and Kaplan's (2018) *Visual Dictionary*, Ramsden noted, "design at the LEGO Group is a collaborative process," both in terms of within the design team at LEGO HQ in the small Danish town of Billund and in partnership with DC (p. 121). Design Master Adam Corbally echoed this sentiment in response to design process questions. He said that after referring to comics and images provided by DC, representatives from LEGO and DC discuss plans for new minifigures before LEGO sends final drafts to production (p. 121). The established worlds of DC Comics on page and screen inform the LEGO DC Super Heroes world, contributing to the toy or animated character's final design. However, while it seems DC has a huge say in what LEGO produces for the brand, designers point out that at the end of the day, they are making characters and sets that fit into LEGO's world—not just new toys for DC Comics. The *Visual Dictionary* quoted design manager and LEGO DC Super Heroes team member Jesper C. Nielsen as saying, "we make toys that inspire kids to construct, dream, and play in a fantastic universe" (p. 123)—core values at the heart of the LEGO Group from the very beginning. In effect, Nielsen describes how LEGO aids in players' creation of imaginary worlds, young and old alike. While LEGO seems to be working for DC in creating new versions of established characters for a new market, the toy's inherent, limitless creativity suggests LEGO can also work around DC's franchise guidelines.

The term "fantastic universe" used by Nielsen chimes with Wolf's (2019) description of "transmedial worlds": "world materials, stories, and characters appearing across a range of different media" (p. 141). As is the case for LEGO DC Super Heroes, this world stems from an original first created for comic books that then spread to radio, TV, film and video games. The original inspired each version, yet different authors created them, depending on medium and owner. The expansion of both the transmedial world and the franchise necessitates partnerships. For Wolf (2019), they "almost always require multiple authors or a hierarchy of authors overseen by the originator of the world, without whom the world could not be constructed" (p. 144). In the animated movies discussed in the next section, I argue that while LEGO developed and built this transmedial world using the origins and characteristics of Batman presented in comics and films, LEGO's toyetic nature itself was influential. One informs the other to present a fully realized world that is both recognizably DC and unmistakably LEGO. This is again the characteristic of Batman's "media mix" which sees various forms and iterations of the character merge to build a multifaceted yet consistent universe.

LEGO *Batman*: Same but Different

Several academic works have examined Batman as cultural icon and transmedia hook to a global comic book franchise. He has been adapted for radio, film, television, video game and more, suggesting he is a malleable figure and recurring cultural trope that acts a signifier for broader themes of heroism, crime fighting and the gothic. Batman expert and enthusiast Will Brooker (2000) argued that the character has many lives—both literally and figuratively. Rebranded and remade over eight decades, Bruce Wayne/Batman has undergone multiple changes to suit audience taste and market forces, literally changing costume and mood to fit different production eras. The Wayne/Batman character has also changed figuratively in terms of meaning, how he has been interpreted, and what he represents for different audiences at different times. Brooker (2000) explained, "the Batman image is open not just to two but to a multiplicity of readings; and … no reading, however absurd it seems … can be ruled out" (p. 23). In this sense, then, LEGO Batman is one of many literal and figurative interpretations of the character which has multiple meanings.

Over time, Batman's iterations have shifted between opposite levels of importance; Christopher Nolan's trilogy, heralded as more realistic and gritty, replaced Burton's movie version, hailed as most authentic. Brooker (2012) argued, "the sense that Batman is ungraspable, elusive, everywhere (and therefore potentially nowhere) has intensified," and as such, "he is everything he has ever been—a combination of a thousand variations, an overlapping of alternates" (p. xi). Authorial voices form and control public and private hierarchies at different production moments: from those who draw him for the comics to those who adapt the character for the big screen. Overall, there is not one author, but many. Issues of authorship are important, as I have already discussed; LEGO works with DC to create a version of Batman that fits with both companies' overarching visions. Matthew Freeman (2017), in his history of transmedia storytelling, pointed out that Batman has had so many different "authors" that maintaining the core character is a difficult balancing act, and identifying one transmedia narrative across history is impossible:

> Batman has moved across the hands of countless creative personnel work-
> ing in comics publishing, film and television production, merchandising
> outlet subsidiaries and marketing divisions … with so many authorial
> hands and influences over so many years across industries, it is hard to
> claim that the entire back catalogue of Batman constitutes transmedia
> storytelling. (pp. 35–36)

With LEGO Batman, however, both companies have collaborated to create a distinct narrative universe spread across film, television, games and toys that makes sense within its own internal logic. Batman is still comic Batman (dark, brooding and a crime fighter), but he is also LEGO Batman (humorous and contingent upon his toyetic features). Roberta Pearson (2017) has argued that differences between versions of the Dark Knight can be ascribed to world-building logics and copyright control: In the first half of the twentieth century, "corporate control ensured that the characters' multiple incarnations were consecutive and consensual … In the 1980s, corporate strategy changed from consecutive and consensual transformation to concurrent exploitation of multiple and divergent Batmen across multiple platforms" (p. 120). Thus, the superhero's "multiplicity" allows LEGO to offer a different, more comical, Batman compared to the darker adaptations produced by Warner Bros. and DC. The Batman "media mix" is therefore made up of comics and films, serious character development and a lighter sense of humor.

Such humor features notably in *LBM*, a Warner Bros., DC, RatPac-Dune Entertainment co-production. First introduced in *TLM* as a Master Builder who helps Emmet save the world from President Business, this LEGO Batman (voiced by Will Arnett) is a pastiche of the Wayne/Batman character: an egotistical loner played for laughs. *LBM* offers an origin story of sorts (showing how Robin becomes the Boy Wonder, for example) and simultaneously plays with familiar Batman traits. Reliant on gadgets, Batman's overconfidence detracts from his intelligence: luck and happenstance, rather than skill, often aid his victories over Joker and the usual suspects. Yet, the familiar backstory (Wayne's parents died when he was young, leaving Alfred to raise him) and character relationships (Commissioner Gordon sees Batman as Gotham's protector) continue to inform our understanding of why he fights crime. This LEGO retelling's lampooning of both story and characters resembles fans' creation of parodic paratexts celebrating the main text. Specifically, I would apply the term "pragmatic parody" to this film and to the multiple LEGO Batman films. In *Playing Fans*, Paul Booth (2015) argued, "pragmatic parody invocates both subculture and culture by commodifying and appropriating simultaneously" (p. 102). As an appropriation strategy employed by LEGO, this form of parody follows in the "reproduction of specific fan practices" (p. 21); like many fan videos and fiction, *LBM* is both mocking and subversive while also reveling in Wayne/Batman's characterization as brooding, self-obsessed vigilante.

Batman's leadership of the Justice League is also played for comedic effect in both the *LEGO Batman: The Movie—DC Heroes Unite* and *LEGO DC Comics Super Heroes: Justice League: Gotham City Breakout* (2016), two feature-length animations produced by Warner Bros. Animation and TT Animation. In the former, Batman remains staunchly serious and is rarely the butt of any jokes, unlike in Arnett's version; but his relationship with Superman and the Justice League offers narrative scope to play with Batman's personality. He likes working alone, putting up with Robin's exuberance thanks to a sense of duty, and resists asking Superman for help. By the end of the film, when Batman grudgingly accepts help from Superman, Cyborg and Wonder Woman to defeat Joker and Lex, he remains suspicious of the League's intentions. In fact, he believes they don't take crime fighting seriously enough and resolves to lead and teach them how to be better, more serious, superheroes. *Gotham City Breakout* again parodies his sense of duty, to the extent that any humor is seen as weakness, when the League forces Batman to take a holiday. Unbeknown to Superman and the others, however, Batman arranges a working vacation that ends up in a mission to defeat Deathstroke and Bane. The tension between Batman's attitude to relaxation and Superman's attempts to get him to relax reinforces the Dark Knight character while breaking down prescribed features: Like the other superheroes, Batman could work on his sense of humor.

Paralleling the company's shift in the 1970s, when it created systems to frame its various building sets, LEGO introduced games based on certain themes or worlds: City, Knights' Kingdom, Racer, Bionicle and Pirates. In 2008, LEGO released the first DC tie-in game, *LEGO Batman: The Video Game*, closely followed by *LEGO Batman 2: DC Super Heroes* in 2012. As the titles suggest, the first game linked to Batman's Gotham crime fighting exploits, and players could interact with all manner of characters and gadgets associated with him and his notable cast of super villains. The second game further expanded gameplay by giving players the opportunity to play through an expanded saga as famous characters from the wider DC universe, from Superman to The Flash. *LEGO Batman 3: Beyond Gotham* (2014) shifts the story and locations even further from Gotham to the outer reaches of space, pitting Batman and The Justice League against intergalactic foes and drawing less well-known DC characters into the action. The games' success—the first sold over 12 million copies three years after release (Graser 2011)—showed LEGO the limitless potential and profit in promoting tie-in games alongside licensed toys.

Clearly, part of the games' attraction is that they tie gameplay directly to the original Batman source text's overarching narratives. So, for example, in the first game, players can experience familiar scenarios from the comics and movies, where Batman and Robin tackle Joker (who is holding Gotham to ransom) and play through various levels, encountering major villains such as the Penguin and Poison Ivy. The second and third games link Batman with Justice League heroes, pitching them against other DC universe villains such as Lex Luthor and Brainiac. Their stories force you to play not just Batman, but also other League members, such as Superman and Green Lantern, to complete levels and defeat bosses (computer-controlled enemies that appear at crucial stages in a game). Gamers can also enjoy extra missions and tasks linked to the game's overall theme, driven more by exploration than the original story's limits. Across all LEGO games, this adventurous play, called "free play," allows for greater experimentation and immersion. In his discussion of video game adaptations of television series, Jonathan Gray (2014) argued that a game's "ability to capture minutiae of their respective worlds and allow exploration and interaction" appeals to both players and reviewers (p. 63). This is in part due to video games' inherent interactive nature, which not only tells an adapted story but also allows for the development of "tone, timbre, pace, and experience" through the expanded virtual world created in game (p. 59). In the *LEGO Batman* games, the tone follows that of the animated movies discussed above: self-referencing, reflective, mocking and subversive.

While playing the story, players may collect money to buy access to extra levels, new characters and abilities, greatly enhancing the freedom to explore. Once they have opened all levels and abilities, gamers can create their own characters, My Own Creations (MOCs), and play as them within the story and "free play." Narrative and digital play thus become more personalized, with a player's own LEGO character (individually designed and named) engaging with LEGO Batman, Joker and so on. Analyzing the *Star Wars* LEGO video games, Buerkle (2014) argued that they become "a manner of retelling this familiar story" (p. 143): "Playing the game and recognizing its many narrative references validates one's membership in the *Star Wars* fan community – ratifying group membership [through the production of shared memories, feelings and values]—and by extension, validates one's claim to the franchise" (Buerkle 2014, p. 144). I would stress further that the games' MOC element allows for fan identity and fictional narrative to converge, making the experience more individual, real and affective.

Each game version of the Batman character adds another level of meaning and depth to the comic book original, adding to the Batman "media mix." With MOCs also part of this transmedia process, gamers can move the story from the real world (physical toy) to the fictional (virtual avatar), and back, playing through the narrative in ways not achievable by rewatching the films, reading the comics and building the toys. As gamers play through the levels as their MOC, they can interact with original characters from the DC universe and place themselves in Gotham or Metropolis to explore the related fictional world. Dan Fleming (1996) recognized this shift in toy culture, stating they "are not the only mediatory objects in our lives; not the only objects to function transitionally for us," and arguing that technological objects like video consoles are not so much "toys for big boys and girls" but "they generate a safe feeling when we give ourselves over to them" (p. 195). Building on this, I argue that the LEGO game versions of established franchise storyworlds are now as much part of the transmedia narrative as are the toys, merchandise, spin-off books or other digital paratexts. Playing as

MOCs (making and collecting, playing with and as story characters) brings that narrative to life for all fans, regardless of age or gender.

The LEGO medium's representations of Batman achieve balance through economy of design and recognizability of salient features. By showing Batman as an animated minifigure in movies, and making his gadgets buildable and playable toys that fans can have at home, Wolf's (2014) reflections upon LEGO *Star Wars* playsets are relevant: "Instead of merely adapting a narrative, a playset … provide[s] its user all the elements needed to reenact a particular narrative, without requiring that the narrative be reenacted" (p. 20). The LEGO DC Super Heroes minifigures' popularity—in toy, movie and video game form—is in large part due to "character abstraction," where the conflict inherent in the figure of the "doubled avatar" (the character in an animation compared to its source material original, for example) is alleviated through the "winsome, if somewhat mocking, representations of their cinematic selves" (Aldred 2014, p. 106). Minifigures represent important characters in the DC Batman transmedia narrative "built" from LEGO, but they are also "figurative" characters in their own right. Thus, the animated films' and video games' humor is more appropriate and believable in LEGO form, yet it does not distract from the fact that the character is still Batman. He is the same and different.

Conclusion

In the recent run-up to the release of *The LEGO Movie 2: The Second Part* (2019), LEGO's vice president of licensing Jill Wilfert outlined the company's approach to signing new brand partners and developing famous properties such as *Star Wars*: "We're able to convince partners about the way kids play with Lego [sic]. Kids don't follow whether characters are from DC or Lucasfilm, they play with them all as Lego [sic] characters and mix them together" (cited in McCarthy 2019). Following what I have argued throughout this chapter, Wilfert's remarks make clear that LEGO sees itself as a unique media content provider. Its toys, movies and games give established characters new life, blending elements from canon to tell new stories across transmedia platforms.

DC gains from such a relationship: According to Wilfert, brands look to LEGO to access their global footprint. LEGO also benefits, as "beloved properties help 'lift' the Lego [sic] brand and drive engagement" (McCarthy 2019). Such franchise partnerships will inevitably continue as global media franchises seek to extend their reach for new audiences, and LEGO remains committed to producing new media content.

The character of Batman discussed in this chapter demonstrates LEGO's DC Super Heroes media mix—texts and paratexts, animation and films, toys and games, history and narrative merging together across multiple continuities. Crossover characters act as catalysts for new stories and new franchise marketing opportunities but also function as familiar narrative signposts directing fans to important moments and events within the transmedia story of DC's Batman. This chapter has outlined how license owners Warner Bros. and DC work with social partners such as LEGO and DK Publishing to retell and reimagine the Batman story over multiple platforms, reworking the DC Super Heroes brand for different audiences. Investigating such a relationship highlights canon's importance in maintaining and sustaining a media franchise as it adapts to changes within the wider entertainment industries. From this, we can see how DC's strategy of working with LEGO on reimagining Batman as toy, in animation and as video game character, diversifies their potential market and transforms Batman into a transmedia franchise character.

Note

1. To date, the LEGO games based on successful media franchises are: *Indiana Jones: The Original Adventures* (2008) and *Indiana Jones 2: The Adventure Continues* (2009), *Batman: The Video Game* (2008), *Batman 2: DC Super Heroes* (2012), *Batman 3: Beyond Gotham* (2014) and *DC Super-Villains* (2018), *Harry Potter: Years 1–4* (2010) and *Harry Potter: Years 5–7* (2011), *Pirates of the Caribbean: The Video Game* (2011), *Jurassic World* (2015), *Lord of the Rings* (2001) and *The Hobbit* (2014), *Marvel Super Heroes* (2013), *Marvel's Avengers* (2016),

and *Marvel Super Heroes 2* (2017), *Star Wars: The Video Game* (2005), *Star Wars II: The Original Trilogy* (2006), *Star Wars: The Complete Saga* (2007), *Star Wars III: The Clone Wars* (2011) and *Star Wars: The Forces Awakens* (2016) and *The Incredibles* (2018). *Star Wars: The Skywalker Saga* is planned for release in 2020. *LEGO Dimensions* (2015), an original title, can also be included in this list as it combines multiple characters and scenarios owned by the likes of Warner Bros., BBC, Universal Studios and Fox—as well as some of LEGO's own original properties including *The LEGO Movie Videogame* (2014), *The LEGO Movie 2 Videogame* (2019) and *LEGO Worlds* (2017).

References

Aldred, J. (2014). (Un)Blocking the transmedial character: Digital abstraction as franchise strategy in Traveller's Tales' LEGO games. In M. J. P. Wolf (Ed.), *LEGO studies: Examining the building blocks of a transmedial phenomenon* (pp. 105–117). New York: Routledge.

Booth, P. (2015). *Playing fans: Negotiating fandom and media in the digital age.* Iowa City: University of Iowa Press.

Brooker, W. (2000). *Batman unmasked: Analyzing a cultural icon.* New York: Continuum.

Brooker, W. (2012). *Hunting the Dark Knight: Twenty-first century Batman.* London: I.B. Tauris.

Buckingham, D. (2011). *The material child: Growing up in consumer culture.* Cambridge: Polity Press.

Buerkle, R. (2014). Playset nostalgia: LEGO *Star Wars: The Video Game* and the transgenerational appeal of the LEGO video game franchise. In M. J. P. Wolf (Ed.), *LEGO studies: Examining the building blocks of a transmedial phenomenon* (pp. 118–152). New York: Routledge.

Crunching the Numbers. (2019, February). *Blocks: building, collecting and customising your LEGO*, pp. 10–11.

Cross, G. (1997). *Kid's stuff: Toys and the changing world of American childhood.* Cambridge: Harvard University Press.

Dowsett, E., & Kaplan, A. (2018). *LEGO DC super heroes: Visual dictionary.* London: Dorling Kindersley.

Fleming, D. (1996). *Powerplay: Toys as popular culture.* Manchester: Manchester University Press.

Freeman, M. (2017). *Historicising transmedia storytelling: Early twentieth-century transmedia story worlds.* New York: Routledge.

Friedenthal, A. J. (2017). *Retcon game: Retroactive continuity and the hyperlinking of America.* Jackson: University Press of Mississippi.

Geraghty, L. (2014). *Cult collectors: Nostalgia, fandom and collecting popular culture.* London: Routledge.

Geraghty, L. (2018a). Nostalgia, fandom and the remediation of children's culture. In P. Booth (Ed.), *A companion to media fandom and fan studies* (pp. 161–174). Oxford: Wiley Blackwell.

Geraghty, L. (2018b). (Re-)Constructing childhood memories: Nostalgia, creativity, and the expanded world of the LEGO fan community. In E. Wesseling (Ed.), *Reinventing childhood Nostalgia: Books, toys, and contemporary media culture* (pp. 66–83). London: Routledge.

Graser, M. (2011, July 19). WB builds on LEGO partnership: Toymaker gets full access to DC's characters, stories. *Variety.* Retrieved from https://variety.com.

Gray, J. (2014). In the game: The creative and textual constraints of licensed video game. In D. Mann (Ed.), *Wired TV: Laboring over an interactive future* (pp. 53–71). New Brunswick: Rutgers University Press.

Hugo, S., & Scott, C. (2016). *LEGO DC comics super heroes: Character encyclopedia.* London: Dorling Kindersley.

Jenkins, H. (2006). *Convergence culture: Where old and new media collide.* New York: New York University Press.

Jenkins, H. (2009). "Just men in tights": Rewriting silver age comics in an era of multiplicity. In A. Ndalianis (Ed.), *The contemporary comic book superhero* (pp. 16–43). New York: Routledge.

Johnson, D. (2013). *Media franchising: Creative license and collaboration in the culture industries.* New York: New York University Press.

Johnson, D. (2014). Authorship up for grabs: Decentralized labor, licensing, and the management of collaborative creativity. In D. Mann (Ed.), *Wired TV: Laboring over an interactive future* (pp. 32–52). New Brunswick: Rutgers University Press.

Johnson, D. (2017). Battleworlds: The management of multiplicity in the media industries. In B. Marta (Ed.), *World building: Transmedia, fans, industries* (pp. 129–142). Amsterdam: Amsterdam University Press.

Kline, S. (1993). *Out of the garden: Toys and children's culture in the age of TV marketing.* London: Verso.

Lauwaert, M. (2008). Playing outside the box: On LEGO toys and the changing world of construction play. *History and Technology: An International Journal, 24*(3), 221–237.

Lipkowitz, D. (2009). *The LEGO book*. London: Dorling Kindersley.

Lipkowitz, D. (2012). *LEGO DC universe super heroes: Batman visual dictionary*. London: Dorling Kindersley.

McCarthy, J. (2019, February 6). How Lego gets the world's largest entertainment brands to play nice together. *The Drum*. Retrieved from https://www.thedrum.com.

Mittell, J. (2015). *Complex TV: The poetics of contemporary storytelling*. New York: New York University Press.

Pearson, R. (2017). World-building logics and copyright: The Dark Knight and the Great Detective. In B. Marta (Ed.), *World building: Transmedia, fans, industries* (pp. 109–128). Amsterdam: Amsterdam University Press.

Scott, C. (2017). *LEGO DC super heroes: The awesome guide*. London: Dorling Kindersley.

Steinberg, M. (2012). *Anime's media mix: Franchising toys and characters in Japan*. Minneapolis: University of Minnesota Press.

Wharfe, C. (2018, November). Rebuilding revenues: The LEGO group's finances have stabilised after a disappointing 2017. *Blocks: building, collecting and customising your LEGO*, pp. 8–9.

Wolf, M. J. P. (2014). Prolegomena. In M. J. P. Wolf (Ed.), *LEGO studies: Examining the building blocks of a transmedial phenomenon* (pp. xxi–xxv). New York: Routledge.

Wolf, M. J. P. (2019). Transmedia world-building: History, conception, and construction. In M. Freeman & R. Rampazzo Gambarato (Eds.), *The Routledge companion to transmedia studies* (pp. 141–147). New York: Routledge.

Filmography: Films Featuring LEGO Batman

LEGO Batman: The Video Game (2008).
LEGO Batman 2: DC Super Heroes (2012).
LEGO Batman: The Movie—DC Heroes Unite (2013).
LEGO DC Comics: Batman Be-Leaguered (2014).
LEGO Batman 3: Beyond Gotham (2014).
The LEGO Movie (2014).
LEGO DC Comics Super Heroes: Justice League vs Bizarro League (2015).

LEGO DC Comics Super Heroes: Justice League: Attack of the Legion of Doom! (2015).
LEGO DC Comics Super Heroes: Justice League: Cosmic Clash (2016).
LEGO DC Comics Super Heroes: Justice League: Gotham City Breakout (2016).
The LEGO Batman Movie (2017).
LEGO DC Comics Super Heroes: The Flash (2018).
LEGO DC Comics Super Heroes: Aquaman: Rage of Atlantis (2018).
LEGO DC Super-Villains (2018).
The LEGO Movie 2: The Second Part (2019).

3

"Hey, Kids. Who Wants a Shot from the Merch Gun?!": LEGO Batman as a Gateway Commodity Intertext

Matthew P. McAllister and Jared LaGroue

The LEGO Batman Movie (McKay 2017; referred to from this point as *LBM*) realized both popular and critical success. With a reported $80 million production budget, the film generated more than $311 million at the worldwide theatrical box office and another $50 million in DVD and Blu-ray sales (BoxOfficeMojo 2017; The Numbers 2017). Reviewers also widely praised *LBM*, with 90% of critics rating it positively (Rotten Tomatoes 2017). Some critics placed it at or near the top of all Batman films: a Tribune News Service reporter called it "Quite possibly the best Batman movie ever made" (Walsh 2017).

Other critics, however, commented on *LBM*'s obvious roots in commercial and promotional culture. *The New York Times*' Manohla Dargis (2017) especially foregrounded the tension between *LBM*'s aesthetic/entertainment achievement and its commodified core. Her review began, "As gateway drugs go, 'The Lego Batman Movie is pretty

M. P. McAllister (✉) · J. LaGroue
Penn State University, State College, PA, USA
e-mail: mpm15@psu.edu

J. LaGroue
e-mail: jal570@psu.edu

R. C. Hains and S. R. Mazzarella (eds.), *Cultural Studies of LEGO*,
https://doi.org/10.1007/978-3-030-32664-7_3

irresistible," and it ended, "as far as commercials go, 'The Lego Batman Movie' is just swell." While appreciative of the film's entertainment value, Dargis characterized *LBM* as "corporate-brand storytelling" and noted that the "primary function" of the film is to "[extend] the two brands—LEGO and Batman."

Created from a partnership between The LEGO Group and Warner Media, two powerful brand-oriented entities, *LBM* is many things: a spin-off from *The LEGO Movie* (hereafter referred to as *TLM*); a cross-promotion between two brands (LEGO and Batman); a film-length promotion for a series of tie-in toys and licensing; and an extension of the existing LEGO Batman brand. The idea of LEGO Batman as a "gateway" commodity invokes a marketing logic that appears designed to socialize viewers, especially younger ones, as participants in multiple modes of consumption. These modes include commodity culture (by teaching that aspects of media culture, such as LEGO sets, can be for sale), media franchises (including LEGO, Batman and related licenses released over long periods of time) and brand extensions (e.g., different versions of licensing associated with LEGO Batman). *LBM* also was the cumulation of a decade-long "commodity intertext" involving LEGO Batman that included several LEGO Batman toy sets (2006), video games (2008), direct-to-home films (2013) and a major role in *TLM* (2014). Such firm integration of children's culture in commodification and merchandising, as in LEGO Batman, raises issues of how such commodification affects storytelling targeting children, the linking of entertainment pleasure to purchasing and the disappointments/tensions associated with class differences where not all may afford the cost of associated merchandise.

In this chapter, we argue that LEGO Batman's expansive commercialism positions it as a "gateway commodity intertext" that socializes young consumers within a branded and commodified society. We begin by reviewing a critical theoretical orientation that applies a political-economic framework to children's media and consumerism, with a focus on extending Meehan's (1991) concept of a commodity intertext as a form of consumer socialization. Next, we examine Batman's history as a branded, media-licensed character that offers a unique and contradictory relationship to other licenses, making it especially attractive to a cross-promotional partner like LEGO. This is followed by a brief section detailing LEGO Batman's development. In the main analyses sections, we explore three characteristics of LEGO Batman: the commodity-friendly elements of the character, especially the narrative of his conversion from being a loner to a team player; the influence of LEGO's commodity iconography; and the role of third-party cross-promotional partners such as Apple's iPhone in the franchise. Finally, we conclude with a summary and discussion of the implications of LEGO Batman as a gateway commodity intertext.

Intertextual Commodities, Consumer Socialization and Children's Media Culture

Our examination of LEGO Batman combines a critical political-economic framework with textual analysis. Critical political economy focuses on how media economics may influence the content, access and use of media, especially as affected by power inequalities in society (Hardy 2014). A key aspect of the media's political economy is commodification: How media define what can be bought and sold. Modern for-profit media institutions are heavily embedded in commodity logic. This includes the commodification of audiences in advertising-based media, as well as media content's commodification, whether through direct payment from audiences for original or recirculated media content, through promotions with other marketers to generate publicity and production revenue, and/or through branded commodities' licensing to industrial partners such as other media outlets, clothing, food and toy companies. Media companies like Disney and DC Entertainment can therefore be viewed as licensing companies that substantially monetize themselves by leveraging their own branded media licenses.

Meehan (1991) argues that multimedia corporations such as Warner Media (formerly Time Warner) and Disney strive to create "commodity intertexts" where the same branded characters and worlds are placed in media outlets that the corporations own or are in partnership with. A particular character or story can be commodified in different outlets simultaneously with different textual versions (i.e., in movies, comics and video games). Industry executives seek to create long-term multimedia franchises (Johnson 2013) that produce predictable and enduring revenue levels, leading to endless brand extension variations that generate "perpetual commodification" (Lizardi 2012, p. 33).

Children's branded licenses that are tied to media outlets have special commodifying qualities. As potential long-time consumers, the young can be socialized into consumer culture in a variety of ways (Ekström 2015), including through exposure to media's commodity orientation and promotion. Much of our media culture is tied to toys and games. Bainbridge (2017) suggested that, given the significant, intertextual and cross-mediated influence of toy-based properties, we should consider what he terms "toyesis": the influence of toys as a driving cultural force. Our culture includes both media content based on toy licenses and media content that spawns its own toys. In both cases, media content itself often remains continually reflexive and adaptable to the toys' popularity and commercial success.

Toyesis and the prominent role of toys in children's culture—along with the commodity logic it brings—have a history. In 1984, the Federal Communications Commission (FCC) dismissed the possibility of limitations on advertising during children's television programming or requirements that broadcasters provide educational programs for children (Kunkel 1988). This deregulatory environment gave rise to children's television programs that Engelhardt (1986) described as "program-length commercials" (p. 74)—television programs based on toys that have incentives to create multiple brand extensions *and* narratives portraying how these extensions work together. Weak US policy over children's media continues to facilitate this strategy. Engelhardt dubbed this marketing trend "The Shortcake Strategy," named for *Strawberry Shortcake*, a toy-based program with a large number of characters and stories celebrating the value of friendship and connection that exemplified the "program-length commercials" trend. In such programs, team-based narratives encouraged multiple licensed-toy purchases to allow children to duplicate episode plotlines in their own play. Similarly, Cross (1997) argued that *Star Wars* action figure and playset expansions—in which even minor characters became toys—encouraged a change in how consumers thought of, collected, and played with these action figures.

However, consumers' ultimate uses of and meaning-making from licensed-based properties are not inherently determined. Hains (2012) posited that even the most ideologically problematic toys and dolls (such as Bratz) may be semiotically flexible in actual children's play; Jenkins (2012) noted that even prior to YouTube, the many action figures of franchises like *Star Wars* facilitated fans' creation of video-texts that played with the meanings of "official" media productions. However, regardless of how children play with licensed merchandise, their promotion, availability and influence on children's culture remains vibrant, including the licensed merchandise associated with one particular long-standing character: Batman.

Batman as a Master (License) Builder

Batman is an enduring license that has been popular in many different media outlets and can be used to promote other licenses to multiple markets. Jenkins (2009) proposed that Batman's multiple instantiations across this ever-widening intertext ultimately encourage new consumers to join in Batmania by attempting to "reboot the continuity." Rather than isolating the Dark Knight's appeal to comic book fans familiar with his extensive history, new versions of Batman often serve to recruit new fans and promote existing assets by encouraging all fans to "consume multiple versions of the same franchise, each with different conceptions of the character, different understandings of their relationships with the secondary figures, different moral perspectives, exploring different moments in their lives, and so forth" (Jenkins 2009). As one media licensing Web site noted, "The Batman brand today is one of the most exciting superhero properties with extremely high visibility" (Brandora Licensing 2019).

Given its longevity and complexity, Batman as a character and license is contradictory. Batman is at once a traumatized and scary character that appears to belie a child-friendly appeal, while at the same time, a long history exists wherein these aspects have been blunted by revisions to the character and through various licensing connections. LEGO Batman navigates this binary in a particular way that actually accentuates the character's commodity value.

In terms of the character's fearsome and solitary tendencies, Batman became a superhero because of trauma: He witnessed his parents' murder—a tragic backstory that could potentially frighten children. Batman uses fear as a weapon, choosing the bat as his symbol since "criminals are a superstitious and cowardly lot," a decision he makes while alone in his mansion (Finger and Kane 1939). In modern versions of the character, Batman intimidates and is judgmental of other superheroes, often expressing his preferences for working alone (McAllister and Cruz, 2020). Graphic novels such as *The Dark Knight Returns* and more adult-oriented movie versions directed by Tim Burton and Christopher Nolan reinforce the loner and violent nature of the character (for discussions of Batman's cultural meanings, see Brooker 2001; Pearson et al. 2015).

Contrastingly, for nearly all of his existence Batman has been a popular multimedia character who often has been paired with other characters, especially other superheroes (much of the below history is from Daniels 1999). Less than a year after Batman's 1938 comic book debut, his crime-fighting partner and young ward Robin was introduced. In the 1940s, Batman (with Robin) appeared on the radio program *The Adventures of Superman*; in the 1950s, the comic book series *World's Finest Comics* began to feature regular team-ups of Superman and Batman.

In the 1960s, the popular but short-lived ABC network television program *Batman* presented a campy, friendlier version of the character and introduced television versions of Batgirl and Green Hornet (Yockey 2014). Batman became the featured character in the comic book *The Brave and the Bold* in the 1960s, which teamed him up in each issue with other DC Comics characters. The character is or has been a member of several superhero groups, like the Justice League of America, Justice League International, The Outsiders, Batman Incorporated and the child-friendly *Super Friends* on ABC television in the 1970s and 1980s.

Premiering in 1992, the TV program *Batman: The Animated Series* featured a noir-like look and more intense tone than other cartoon versions; nevertheless, the program aired on the Fox Kids programming block and included both Robin and Batgirl. In the 2000s, a team-up-based animated series *Batman: The Brave and the Bold* (2008–2011) debuted on Time Warner-owned Cartoon Network; here, Batman was paired with b- and c-list DC characters, using Batman's popularity to elevate them; the program also featured a long list of tie-in merchandise including a comic book, video game and toy line (Roman and McAllister 2012).

Both versions of Batman—the frightening loner and the supportive team member—arguably reinforce each other. The more intense, scarier versions (in graphic novels and film) attract adult audiences with the money to purchase expensive publications and the autonomy to attend PG-13 films, while Batman is made more accessible and "toyetic" (Bainbridge 2017) in youth-targeted appearances that emphasize fun gadgets and relationships with other licensed characters. Batman's licensing potential is also enhanced by different versions of his costume and his various gadgets, vehicles and locations: his utility belt, the Batmobile and the Batcave, respectively.

This point-counterpoint is seen throughout Batman's history. Batman and Superman's good-natured team-ups in *World's Finest* contrasted with the moral panic over horror comics in the early 1950s. ABC's *Batman* and its wave of "Batmania" marketing alleviated the more complex themes introduced in comic books by 1960s Marvel heroes like Spider-Man. The major theatrical film *Batman* (1989), which involved a plot of the Joker poisoning consumer goods, was met with a wave of age-diverse merchandise (Meehan 1991). Corresponding with the character's 50th anniversary, then-Warner Communications (WCI) coordinated its owned media outlets and partnerships to create an expansive cultural and commercial presence for Batman across the film, commercials, product tie-ins, comic book stories, music video and books. This included widening Batman's audience appeal by leveraging other Warner assets, such as Prince's recording of "Batdance," which "crossed over" between White female and African American male demographics (Meehan 1991). *Batman: The Animated Series* (1992–1995) is a friendlier version of Tim Burton's *Batman Returns* (1992); the latter featured BDSM-style costumes and a plot to murder children. Cartoon Network's *Batman: The Brave and the Bold* (2008–2011) sanitizes Batman's brute vigilantism and the Joker's sadism presented in

The Dark Knight (2008). Most relevant for this chapter, the premiere of *LBM* in February 2017 contrasted with the grim Batman portrayed in the live-action DC Extended Universe movies, especially in *Batman v Superman: Dawn of Justice*, released less than a year earlier.

As we explore in the following sections, the LEGO version of Batman significantly informed and referenced this yin-yang of scary vs. approachable Batmen and their appeal to different demographic age groups, alongside the character's license-friendly nature.

A Genealogy of LEGO Batman

Although *LBM* constitutes the most culturally visible version of the LEGO and Batman mega-brands' partnership, it wasn't the first. Their cross-promotion began approximately 11 years prior to 2017 film's release (see Table 3.1) with an initial run of six LEGO toy sets sold beginning in 2006 (Szadkowski 2006). A teaser-trailer released earlier that year introduced these sets (*Batman Lego Teaser Trailer* 2006); eventually, 13 sets were actively manufactured until 2009 (Hamill 2012). Commercials, a hybrid comic book/catalog, and a novelty life-size LEGO Batman display in New York's FAO Schwarz promoted the 2006 sets (Dorfman 2006). The comic book intermixed photos of the toys with a drawn comic-panel story about LEGO-styled Batman, Robin and Nightwing (the adult Dick Grayson) foiling the Joker, Two-Face and other "Rogue" villains (*LEGO Batman Secret Files and Origins* 2006).

The next LEGO Batman licensing wave began in 2008 with the first LEGO Batman video game's release, boasting more than 11 million copies sold worldwide. The video game provided the ability to play as both a hero (e.g., Batman or Robin) or villain (e.g., the Joker) (Warner Bros. Interactive 2012). The 2012 video game sequel *LEGO Batman 2: DC Super Heroes* was accompanied by the release of LEGO toy sets and an on-demand animated film in 2013 containing the same basic plot. Promotional in-store events at the now-defunct retail chain Toys "R" Us also supported the second video game's release by offering Batman and Superman LEGO playsets and serving "as a reminder to the children's

Table 3.1 LEGO Batman timeline

Time period	Event
Spring-Summer 2006	LEGO Batman toy sets released
November 2006	Novelty lifesize LEGO Batman figure released
September 2008	*LEGO Batman: The Video Game* released
2008	*LEGO Batman: The Video Game* McDonald's Happy Meal Toys released
2012	DC Superheroes toy sets released, including a LEGO Batman
May 2012	*LEGO Batman 2: DC Super Heroes* video game trailer debuts
June 2012	*LEGO Batman 2: DC Super Heroes* video game released
October 2012	*LEGO Batman: The Movie—DC Super Heroes Unite* movie trailer released
May 2013	*LEGO Batman: The Movie—DC Super Heroes Unite* on-demand video released
February 2014	*The LEGO Movie* premieres
October 2014	*LEGO DC Comics: Batman: Be-Leaguered* airs on The Cartoon Network
November 2014	*LEGO Batman 3: Beyond Gotham* video game released
March 2016	Two teaser trailers for *LBM* theatrical film released
July 2016	*LBM* full trailer shown at ComiCon
July 2016	*LEGO DC Comics Superheroes: Justice League—Gotham City Breakout*, on-demand video released
November 2016	*LBM* trailer 4 released
February 2017	*LBM* theatrical film premiere
June 2017	DVD and on-demand release of *LBM*
February 2019	*The LEGO Movie 2: The Second Part* theatrical film premiere

parents that it's only a few more weeks until 'The Dark Knight Rises'… hits theaters" (Shirey 2012).

All this occurred before Batman's scene-stealing appearance (voiced by Will Arnett, who mimicked the deep-voiced Christian Bale version) in *TLM* (Lord and Miller 2014). A box-office success, *TLM* featured LEGO versions of many franchised and original characters and emphasized themes of teamwork and the pleasure of building from a large number of components. (It also triggered mixed feelings from reviewers regarding art vs. commerce.) However, the Batman character "proved a hit with audiences," and as a result, Warner Brothers may have "prioritise[d]" the stand-alone *LBM* spin-off over the sequel to *TLM* (Pulver 2014). Multiple trailers supported *LBM* (including two released in the same week), as well as several tie-in books, toy sets, a comic book and cross-promotional efforts.

LEGO Batman, as we argue below, embraced a particular version of commodification that exploited Batman's contradictory appeal, especially in ways that appear designed to appeal to the young. In 2007, Paul Levitz, then-President of DC Comics, observed, "There's a special magic to the LEGO incarnation of Batman that makes him accessible to a younger generation of his fans" (Warner Bros. Interactive 2007). When examining LEGO Batman's various versions since 2006, and focusing on the character's status as a licensed commodity intertext, three themes stand out that highlight this "special magic" of commodity appeal: (1) the multi-commodifiable elements embedded in various merchandise and licensing outlets, including the constructed narrative of these elements; (2) the influence of LEGO in the look and narrative of LEGO Batman's different versions; and (3) the partnership with cross-promotional brands that span different age groups. Each of these will be discussed in the sections that follow.

LEGO Batman as Commodity Team Player

Batman is an especially valuable LEGO commodity partner for several reasons: (1) the character's various specialized costumes, gadgets and settings, all of which are easily "toyified"; (2) the many supporting characters (e.g., Alfred, Robin, Nightwing) and antagonists (e.g., the Joker, Poison Ivy) in the Batman narrative universe; (3) the thousands of characters in the larger DC universe (e.g., Superman, Wonder Woman, Cyborg); and (4) the use of the character's solitary tendencies as a narrative device for stressing the value of friendship and teamwork. These attributes lend themselves to the creation of LEGO Batman figures and playsets with multiple parts and manifestations and are the likely reasons why Batman (instead of Superman) was chosen as the first LEGO/DC partnership. LEGO itself also stresses cooperation and teamwork in its non-Batman variants—values that further maximize its commodity value since sets can involve hundreds (or more) interlocking parts and can be combined with other sets for massive play extravaganzas, as shown in *TLM*. The fun of expansive commodification is reflected in the theme song of that 2014 film, which posits that being a member of a team makes everything cool.

The "gadget-ish" nature of Batman/Bruce Wayne—a technological, billionaire genius with unlimited resources and control over a massive organization, Wayne Enterprises—therefore lends itself to a company like LEGO that is premised on offering complex toy sets that sometimes contain thousands of parts. The toy sets released in 2006 and 2012 illustrate this symbiosis between Batman's superhero tendencies and LEGO's marketing strategies. The first sets included the LEGO Batman Batcave, Batmobile and Batwing, among others. LEGO Batman—The Batcave: The Penguin and Mr. Freeze's Invasion (#7783) consisted of 1075 pieces and included characters in the Batman narrative world such as Alfred, Robin and the two title villains (in 2019, a collector set of this model could be purchased for $581). Among those early toys, LEGO Batman's Tumbler (#7888) had a specific movie tie-in, with the vehicle originating in the Christopher Nolan movies (Lipkowitz 2018, p. 215). In what now may be called "content marketing," the comic/catalog *LEGO Batman Secret Files and Origins* (2006) visualizes many of these sets, with a photo of the set box (and its LEGO number) inserted somewhere on the page that also features a large photo of the toy. The inside cover, for instance, is "Secret Files and Origins: Batman" offering a profile of the Caped Crusader. Only a small photo of LEGO Batman is shown, however, whereas the page features two much larger images of the LEGO Batwing, including one of the original boxes the toy comes in; the front cover also features that same Batwing. The 2012 playsets—ones that tied in with the *LEGO Batman 2* video game and the *LEGO Batman: The Movie—DC Superheroes Unite* (Burton 2013) on-demand video—added other DC superheroes, including Superman and Wonder Woman, and non-Batman villains such as Lex Luthor. These playsets were still Batman-centric, featuring settings like Arkham Asylum, Jokerland and an updated Batcave (Lipkowitz 2018).

LBM makes full use of merchandise tie-ins that mirror particular sets and even scenes from the film. As *The LEGO Book* proudly notes:

The Joker Manor is the largest The LEGO BATMAN MOVIE set and includes 3,444 pieces and 10 minifigures. The Joker's renovated version of Batman's home, Wayne Manor, features a wraparound roller coaster, buildable bombs, and a giant Joker head with a tube slide (Lipkowitz 2018).

TV commercials encouraged consumers to purchase multiple sets in tandem. One commercial uses on-screen narration ("You can transform Bruce Wayne into Batman, and help him build the powerful Scuttler"), hands-assisted playing and autonomous animated movement of the toys to construct a narrative of Batman building his Scuttler in the Batcave and chasing down the Joker and Harley Quinn in the Jokermobile (Mr Toys Toyworld YouTube 2017). The three sets (Batcave, Scuttler and Jokermobile) combined, as the commercial suggests they should be, would total 2255 pieces. As of January 2019, they cost $235 on Amazon.

The Scuttler, a battle vehicle with legs and introduced in *LBM*, is especially pervasive in *LBM* tie-in media. It is featured prominently in the *LEGO Batman Junior Novel* (Lane 2017), a novelization of the film for young readers (for more on novelizations of LEGO films, see Chapter 8 in this volume, "Toyetics and Novelizations: Bringing *The LEGO Movie* to the Page" by Joyce Goggin). Lane's (2017) *LEGO Batman Junior Novel's* abbreviated movie narrative foregrounds the Scuttler:

'Computer, initialize MasterBuild music!' he called. 'I need to take out multiple targets with minimal damage. Hopefully.'
   'May I suggest the Scuttler, sir?' Computer replied.
   'Perfect,' said Batman. He began Master-Building one of his favorite vehicles. (pp. 60–61)

The novel later describes it as "an awesome machine with legs instead of wheels—good for climbing stairs, walls, and ceilings—and all kinds of other features" (p. 62). An even younger readership learns about the Scuttler (with pictures) in *LEGO Team Batman* (DK Level 1, for "Learning to Read" children aged 3–8) with simplified descriptions: "Batman loves cool vehicles. Alfred helps him build them. This is the

Scuttler. It is shaped like a bat. It has lots of gadgets" (Dewin 2017, p. 14). A photo of the Scuttler also appears on the "Quiz" pages, asking, "What animal is the Scuttler shaped like?" (The answer is a bat.) The vehicle/toy even has its own entries in the book's index and table of contents, where it is again prominently pictured. In such ways, these cross-media versions promote to young fans the merchandise featured in the movie and available for purchase as LEGO sets.

LBM self-reflexively winks at its own consumer-culture status, raising the issue of when a promotional text perpetuates, or satirizes, commodification. One reviewer noted, "There's a cute 'merchandising' sequence at an orphanage that pokes fun at the relentless commercial imperative of the movie (for LEGO and Warner Bros, the movie-rights holder)" (Maher 2017). In this scene, Batman visits the orphanage with a "merch gun" that fires bat-logoed lunchboxes and other items at the orphans. The scene is funny. But how much can a scene "poke fun" when a franchise's own merchandizing duplicates this logic, and this exact example? *The LEGO Batman Junior Novel* (Lane 2017) repeats this bat merch gun scene; however, it reads as less ironic without the clever visuals, edits and sounds of the movie:

> "Hey, kids," Batman called out. "Who wants a shot from the merch gun?"
>
> "I do, I do!" the kids replied, jumping up and down.
>
> "Great!" Batman shot the gun, and it launched an impressive variety of Batman gear over the orphanage fence. The kids scrambled to snatch up the prizes. (p. 31)

In other manifestations, bat merch and the merch gun teach young fans life lessons about how bat merch (or "prizes" in the quote above) can lead to being "cool" or even "cooler." The "cool" lesson in the companion book *LEGO Batman's Guide to Being Cool* (Dewin 2017) is to make sure you have your personal branded "symbol" (a bat logo, in Batman's case) and share it with others—rather than practicing moderation in your licensed product purchasing or use. On one page, depicted with the merch gun, LEGO Batman explains, "So you've perfected your symbol and put it on a bunch of stuff. Great! But what good is all that stuff if you don't have friends to share it with?" (Dewin 2017,

p. 95). The companion book, *LEGO Robin's Guide to Being Cool(er)* (Rusu 2017), reinforces this lesson when Robin advises:

> When I was at the orphanage, my dream was to be like Batman. That was the dream of all the other kids, too. (It was a popular dream.) We always wore our Batman merch to show our Caped Crusader pride! (p. 44)

Images from the movie of LEGO kids with a Batman mug, Batman t-shirt and Batman Lunch Box accompany this text (Rusu 2017, pp. 44–45). Finally, the bat merch gun is itself "merch." *LBM*'s tie-in Batmobile Building Kit (#70905) comes with Batman, Robin, and several bat-gadgets, including the same bat merch gun used in the movie (the box shows Robin holding it). This also flows with another lesson in Batman's Guide: "No Gadgets → Less Cool." "Gadgets → More Cool" (Dewin 2017, pp. 88–89).

Aside from the expensive, cross-promoted and intertwined toy sets, Batman encourages large-scale licensing consumption in another way: It plays on the "Dark Knight" version of Batman as a loner, but one who, paradoxically, has relationships with many other licensed characters. Early versions of the LEGO Batman franchise included only characters associated with the Batman narrative universe. The 2006 toy sets and the first 2008 video game mostly featured Batman allies and villains battling in Batman settings. However, beginning with the 2012 playsets, video game and on-demand movie, Batman interacted with other DC characters like Superman. This, of course, expands the amount of LEGO licenses that may be purchased and integrated into play. *LBM* embraces this even more; in the movie, Batman battles well over 30 Batman-universe villains and visits an engorged Justice League that includes characters from the Super Friends. Batman also meets Über-villains in *LBM*, including many Warner-related characters such as *Harry Potter*'s Voldemort and *Lord of the Ring*'s Sauron. Notably, ancillary media such as the *Junior Novel* omit these trademarked characters, perhaps due to copyright permission expenses, although The Ultimate Batmobile set (#70917) includes the Wicked Witch of the West and her flying monkeys as action figures.

LBM leverages Batman's solitary nature to drive the narrative of teamwork's importance, a clear theme of the film. The second trailer released in March 2016 ("When you're as super as me, you don't just get one trailer, you get two trailers, in one week") emphasizes Batman's loneliness, as does the film itself. Batman declares to Joker early in the movie, "There is no 'us.' Batman and Joker are not a thing. I don't need you. I don't need anyone. You mean nothing to me. No one does." The narrative arc follows Batman's attitude change as he realizes he needs others to help him, and to be part of a family, in this case, Robin, Barbara Gordon/Batgirl, and Alfred (see also Chapter 13, "The Man Behind the Mask: Camp and Queer Masculinity in *LEGO Batman*" by Kyra Hunting in this volume). Perhaps the ultimate "pairing" of LEGO Batman with other characters occurs in *The LEGO Movie 2: The Second Part* (Mitchell 2019). A key plot point is Batman uniting two LEGO universes by marrying Queen Watevra Wa'Nabi, a character unique to the LEGO movie narrative world. Batman, therefore, "settles down," both in terms of marriage but also in terms of domesticating his loner status in service of a LEGO multi-toy ethos.

Earlier LEGO Batman media emphasized the "it's cool to be part of a team" moral before *TLM* and *LBM*. These media teach about the dangers of isolation through stories of Batman's relationship to other (branded) superheroes. The plots of both the second video game and on-demand video (2012–2013) involve Batman's hesitation to team up with Superman: "We don't need him…The only people we can rely on are ourselves," he tells Robin (Burton 2013). Superman along with other DC superheroes end up helping Batman despite his protests. Batman concludes, "I have to admit, I couldn't have done it without a little help from my friends." This theme is even stronger in Cartoon Network's special *LEGO DC Comics: Batman: Be-Leaguered* (Morales 2014). The Justice League tries to recruit Batman, who declines: "I am perfectly capable of handling this all by myself"; "As for your club, I Batman will never join your Justice League." Again, in the end he does join, and he admits he finally saw "how childish I was being about insisting on working alone." This also plays out in the tie-in comic book for *Be-Leaguered*: "I see now…my own weakness is I always want to work alone" (Lee and Lareau 2014). The DK Reading Level 1 LEGO *Team Batman* cover observes, "Sometimes even Batman™ needs friends" (Dewin 2017).

Teamwork is a fine value to teach young readers/viewers, but like the Shortcake Strategy, it is a commercial narrative theme that strategically fits LEGO and DC's larger promotional goals. Teamwork among many licensed characters encourages play involving multiple action figures and sets. Batman learns, over and over, that working alone is not good; he needs other characters/figures/toys to be a better person and hero. Fans, then, must purchase other figures—Batman characters, DC characters, classic villains and all of the figures in both versions of *TLM*—if they wish to model the climatic scenes in these stories and Batman's self-actualization.

LEGO-fied Batman

Writing before LEGO Batman existed, Phillips (2002) argued that Batman is a "textual object" with roots in media texts, compared to the toy-based Barbie, a "plastic object" with meaning constructed primarily through the various toys (p. 123). However, LEGO Batman extends beyond the Batman license alone; it combines two major brands. The one listed first in the character's title—the toy company with meaning constructed in plastic—fundamentally shapes his world, appearance and adventures. Obviously, the characters' particular shape and appearance are as LEGO minifigures, with branded heads (drawn faces; pop-on hair/helmets), bodies (square) and feet (blocky, holey). They are accompanied by many settings and vehicles made of LEGO bricks. In the LEGO Batman videos, when buildings collapse and vehicles crash, LEGO bricks scatter and plastic clinks. In this section, we explore these formal cinematic elements and highlight how the various LEGO Batman plots feature LEGO attributes that flow with the concept of "toyesis" (Bainbridge 2017) and meaning constructed in plastic. As argued in the previous section, LEGO Batman likes merch so much he shoots it out of a gun. We argue here that LEGO Batman is, himself, ontologically "merch."

In some ways, the LEGO-ization of *LBM* could be more explicit and doesn't mirror the degree to which the LEGO-brand influences the plot of both *TLM* 1 and 2. The actual Batman stories virtually never use the word "LEGO," except in the title. This is a big "except for," of course, given the title's use in promotional materials, which primes viewers to think of the property as LEGO. The same is true of LEGO TV programs like Ninjago: The program doesn't mention LEGO, but the brand is made visible through supplemental texts including LEGO commercials aired before and after (but not during) Ninjago; concurrently, the digital program guides describing Ninjago emphasize the LEGO name and connection (McAllister and Buckley 2014).

However, LEGO emphasizes its presence in the *LBM* plot through other means, such as the function and symbolism of "bricks." The early LEGO Batman video games presented gold bricks as valuable icons. In *LBM*, a giant talking brick is a character: Phyllis (voiced by Ellie Kemper), the Phantom Zone's manager. A key plot device in some LEGO Batman stories involves villains threatening the world by uncoupling bricks. In 2013s *LEGO Batman—DC Super Heroes Unite*, Lex Luthor uses a weapon called "The Deconstructor" to pull apart black bricks; he uses it to entice the Joker to join him, so that the Joker can pull apart Batman's vehicles and gadgets. One of Batman's gadgets in *Justice League: Gotham City Breakout* (Peters and Zwyer 2016) is the "Bat Brick Separator," which mimics an actual device LEGO sells (the Brick Separator 630) that makes it easier to separate small pieces. In Batman's case, he uses it to escape from a dungeon.

TLM established that Batman is a Master Builder, allowing him to create complex gadgets and vehicles from the various LEGO bricks in his environment. This attribute continues in *LBM*. In preparing to save Jim Gordon's retirement party from a Rogues villain invasion, Batman says, "Computer, initialize Master Build music." At his computer's suggestion, Batman builds The Scuttler from other surrounding structures' bricks. He also teaches Robin how to Master Build, and in the climactic sequence wherein Gotham City is being physically pulled apart because of a Joker bomb, Batman saves the day by connecting the heads and feet of the (LEGO-bodied) characters (accompanied with a satisfying "CLICK," the sound effect when the pieces are joined). This is highlighted in the *Junior Novel* as well: "Batman used his lightning-quick reflexes to place brick after brick with precision. The others watched in awe of his brilliant brick instincts and started to help, trying to keep up" (Lane 2017, p. 126).

In these ways, Batman is LEGO-ized, where the logic of the plastic toy permeates, and perhaps overwhelms, an icon with a textual history going back to the 1930s. This is not a typical superhero team-up that emphasizes the thrill of the encounter: Batman meets LEGO. This is more of an assimilation: Batman becomes LEGO.

Cross-Promoted LEGO Batman

The combination of LEGO and Warner Media licenses is not the only promotional partnerships surrounding LEGO Batman. Although third-partner marketers go back to at least 2008, when McDonald's released a series of LEGO Batman Happy Meal toys to tie into the video game (Happy Toy 2017), such partnerships amped up with *LBM*. As one marketing executive argued, "There was no such thing as too many tie-ins for the 'LEGO Batman' campaign" (Pasquarelli 2017). McDonald's released eight sets in 2017 to cross-promote with *LBM*, and they touted more than just *LBM* and McDonald's. As seen in a YouTube review (FastFoodToyReviews 2017), several sets included a Six Flags theme park coupon picturing the Batman ride and a promotional disk with a plug for the McPlay app—McDonalds' version of a half-promotion/half-video game, sometimes called an "advergame" (Grimes 2015).

Corporate-synergy tie-ins involved animations of LEGO Batman interacting with Warner characters on television. He appeared in DC superhero promotions in The CW Network's "Arrowverse," including Arrow and The Flash, all voiced by the live-action actors and Arnett (Warner Bros. Television Group 2017). Arnett also voiced LEGO-ized promotions for the then-prime time CBS series *The Big Bang Theory* (Pasquarelli 2017). Produced by Warner Television, *The Big Bang Theory* shares a corporate owner with both DC Entertainment and Warner Bros. Animation. The connection between the sitcom and *LBM* is thus more than Sheldon and Leonard being comics fans: Virtually all of Sheldon's superhero t-shirts, the superhero background props and the comics sold in the fictional "The Comic Center of Pasadena" are DC-licensed.

Two other cross-promotions involved adult-oriented brands: Apple and Chevrolet. Apple's personal voice assistant "Siri" served as the voice of Batman's computer—often called 'Puter by Batman—and is one of the few non-fictional character product placements in *LBM*. Furthermore, when the Flash asks Batman to take a photo of the Justice League party, he hands Batman an iPhone. Robin has an iPhone as well, using it in a key moment when he takes a selfie of the Bat family. The cross-promotion also extended to real-life consumer interactions with Apple products such as the iPhone. If an individual activates Siri using phrases like "Hey 'Puter," it responds to the request as if the user were LEGO Batman, with quips such as "You have a message from the Condiment King. It says 'Pbbbffftttt!'" (Pasquarelli 2017). This expands the tie-in to everyday life, both in terms of promotional activity and data collection of such activity—wherever and whenever one uses an iPhone. As of October 2019, this feature was still functional.

Chevrolet cross-promoted with *LBM* by creating an animated LEGO version of their campaign featuring a focus-group facilitator quizzing (and often tricking) participants about Chevy's wonderful attributes. In this case, the focus-group members ("Real LEGO® minifigures. Not actors")—which include LEGO Batman (again voiced by Arnett)—humorously examine "The new LEGO Batmobile, from Chevy," a 344,000-piece construction on display that year at the Detroit Auto Show (Pasquarelli 2017). The jokes mostly played on themes from the movie, including Batman's presumed loneliness ("Look, there's no back seat. Probably not many friends," observes one LEGO-bodied focus-group member).

The cross-promotion of adult-marketed Chevrolet and Apple alongside child-friendly LEGO Batman may seem to make strange bedfellows, but several marketing strategies may be at play: The cross-market appeal to children and adults of *LBM*, the goal of inculcating a life-long brand loyalty in young consumers (perhaps especially true with Apple's iPhone) and the hope that child may serve as an "influence market" in expensive family purchases like smartphones and automobiles (Schor 2005). That the iPhone was integrated into *LBM*'s storyline, and that the Chevy commercial was created in *LBM*'s animated style, seems to indicate that children were key targets for these marketing activities.

Conclusion

This story of the young socialized consumer-viewer of *LBM* doesn't end in complete triumph for the forces of capitalism, showing that even the most coordinated efforts are not totalizing. Sales for *LBM* toys were labeled as "weak" and may have contributed to layoffs at LEGO, although the popularity of video games and other digital forms of entertainment also present the company with long-term marketing challenges (Bloomberg News 2017). Reviewers of the next LEGO movie, *The LEGO Ninjago Movie*, released in September 2017, were more uniform in foregrounding the concept's commercialistic nature than in typical reviews of *LBM* (see, e.g., Andersen 2017). With such indicators of commercial imperfection, it may be tempting to assume that LEGO Batman was all sound and fury, signifying little in terms of ideological impact.

LEGO toy sales are but one measure of the impact of a commodified media text, however, and the long-term efforts were impressively coordinated, enduring and culturally visible. LEGO Batman paired expensive and complex toy sets with a character known for gadgets, whose backstory included both a scary and isolated nature that could be reformed with the help of other characters *and* a track record of partnering with, and promoting, other branded characters. Cross-media intertexts (including video games, comic books, books, on-demand video, TV specials and appearances in TV series) plugged the toys and the celebration of the commodity form for different age groups. This appeal started with those as young as three years old, if the suggested age range for DK Level 1 books like *LEGO Team Batman* are taken at face value. "Gadgets" are cool, as young fans are told overtly, and as is constantly illustrated in the stories. Children who wish to copy LEGO Batman's media narratives know that for Batman to be happy and defeat his many foes, he needs his Bat family and other superheroes' help. Without these, he continues to be lonely. In fact, in *The LEGO Movie 2*, Batman is crucial in creating group unity, completely subverting his loner image. Meanwhile, cross-promotional partnerships targeted both younger (through fast-food Happy Meals) and older markets (through Chevy), while Siri spread the *LBM* brand well after *LBM* left theaters.

Finally, while LEGO may not have achieved its short-term sales hopes during the *LBM* release window, Batman and the continued prominence of superhero narratives remained triumphant. For DC Entertainment, which functions more as a licensing company than a comic book company, LEGO Batman once again showed the durability and malleability of the branded character. Their strategy is the long game, and the LEGO partnership marked the first points scored. In LEGO Batman toys in McDonald's Happy Meals, in first-level early-reader books, in giveaway promotional comic books, in TV specials on the Cartoon Network, and in the PG-rated big screen movie, Warner and LEGO marketing executives worked to ensure that young fans will learn to love Batman and, as they grow older, to continue loving the Batmen created for older demographics, as well as whatever cross-promotional partners are part of the team.

References

Andersen, S. (2017, September 20). 'The Lego Ninjago Movie' review. *Seattle Times*. From the database NewsBank. Accessed on January 3, 2019.

Bainbridge, J. (2017). From toyetic to toyesis: The cultural value of merchandising. In S. Harrington (Ed.), *Entertainment values: How do we assess entertainment and why does it matter* (pp. 23–39). New York: Springer.

Batman Lego Teaser Trailer. (2006). YouTube video. https://www.youtube.com/watch?v=WywgtUdWtx8. Accessed on January 3, 2019.

Bloomberg News. (2017, September 5). Lego cuts 1,400 jobs as sales slump on weak 'Batman Movie' toy demand. *Advertising Age*. https://adage.com/article/cmo-strategy/lego-cuts-1-400-jobs-sales-slump-weak-batman-demand/310340/. Accessed on January 3, 2019.

BoxOfficeMojo. (2017). *The LEGO Batman Movie*. https://www.boxofficemojo.com/movies/?id=lego2.htm. Accessed on January 3, 2019.

Brandora Licensing. (2019). http://www.brandlicensing.com/License.aspx?Lic=245&IzmLang=9. Accessed on January 3, 2019.

Brooker, W. (2001). *Batman unmasked: Analyzing a cultural icon*. London: Continuum.

Burton, J. (Director). (2013). *LEGO Batman: The Movie—DC Super Heroes Unite*. United States: DC Comics.

Cross, G. (1997). *Kids' stuff: Toys and the changing world of American childhood.* Cambridge, MA: Harvard University Press.

Daniels, L. (1999). *Batman: The complete history.* San Francisco: Chronicle Books.

Dargis, M. (2017, February 8). Review: In 'The Lego Batman Movie,' toys and heroes, what's not to like? *The New York Times.* https://www.nytimes.com/2017/02/08/movies/the-lego-batman-movie-review.html. Accessed on January 3, 2019.

Dewin, H. (2017). *LEGO The Batman Movie Batman's guide to being cool.* New York: Scholastic.

Dorfman, D. (2006, November 29). When money is no object. *New York Sun,* p. 19. From the database NewsBank. Accessed on January 3, 2019.

Ekström, K. M. (2015). Consumer socialization. In D. T. Cook & J. M. Ryan (Eds.), *The Wiley Blackwell encyclopedia of consumption and consumer studies* (n.p.). https://doi.org/10.1002/9781118989463.wbeccs060.

Engelhardt, T. (1986). The shortcake strategy. In T. Gitlin (Ed.), *Watching television* (pp. 68–110). New York: Pantheon.

FastFoodToyReviews. (2017, February 11). *The LEGO Batman Movie 2017 set of 8 McDonalds Happy Meal kids toys video review.* YouTube video. https://www.youtube.com/watch?v=fz7getbYocE. Accessed on January 3, 2019.

Finger, B., & Kane, B. (1939, November). The Batman wars against the dirigible of doom. *Detective Comics,* 33. New York: DC Comics.

Grimes, S. M. (2015). Playing by the market rules: Promotional priorities and commercialization in children's virtual worlds. *Journal of Consumer Culture, 15*(1), 110–134. https://doi.org/10.1177/1469540513493209.

Hains, R. C. (2012). An afternoon of productive play with problematic dolls: The importance of foregrounding children's voices in research. *Girlhood Studies, 5*(1), 121–140. https://doi.org/10.3167/ghs.2012.050108.

Hamill, S. D. (2012, July 15). Holy lodestone, Batman, those Legos are outta sight! *McClatchy—Tribune Business News.* From the database Proquest. Accessed on January 3, 2019.

Happy Toy. (2017, January 24). *McDonald's The LEGO Batman Movie Happy Meal toys 2017 sneak peek LEGO Batman The Video Game 2008 Kid.* YouTube video. https://www.youtube.com/watch?v=P0TM4xfW6aM. Accessed on January 3, 2019.

Hardy, J. (2014). *Critical political economy of the media: An introduction.* New York: Routledge.

Jenkins, H. (2009, February 2). The many lives of Batman (Revisited): Multiplicity, Anime, and Manga [Blog Post]. *Confessions of an Aca-Fan.*

http://henryjenkins.org/blog/2009/02/the_many_lives_of_the_batman_r.html. Accessed on January 3, 2019.

Jenkins, H. (2012). Quentin Tarantino's Star Wars? Digital cinema, media convergence, and participatory culture. In M. G. Durham & D. Kellner (Eds.), *Media and cultural studies: Keyworks* (2nd ed., pp. 452–470). Malden, MA: Wiley-Blackwell.

Johnson, D. (2013). *Media franchising: Creative license and collaboration in culture industries*. New York: New York University Press.

Kunkel, D. (1988). From a raised eyebrow to a turned back: The FCC and children's product related programming. *Journal of Communication, 38*(4), 197–209. https://doi.org/10.1111/j.1460-2466.1988.tb02072.x.

Lane, J. (2017). *LEGO The Batman Movie Junior Novel*. New York: Scholastic.

Lee, P., & Lareau, R. (2014). *LEGO DC Comics super heroes*. New York: DC Comics.

LEGO Batman secret files and origins. (2006). New York: DC Comics.

Lipkowitz, D. (2018). *The LEGO book* (new ed.). New York: DK.

Lizardi, R. (2012). DLC: Perpetual commodification of the video game. *Democratic Communiqué, 25*(1), 33–45. http://journals.fcla.edu/demcom/article/view/78739. Accessed on January 3, 2019.

Lord, P., & Miller, C. (Directors). (2014). *The LEGO Movie*. United States: Warner Bros.

Maher, K. (2017, February 10). Holy superhero satire, Batman! *The Times* (London). From the database NewsBank. Accessed on January 3, 2019.

McAllister, M. P., & Buckley, C. (2014, June 27). LEGO-based paratextual commodity flow in children's television. In N. Ahmed (Ed.), LEGO Week, *In Media Res*. http://mediacommons.futureofthebook.org/imr/2014/06/27/lego-based-paratextual-commodity-flow-children-s-television. Accessed on January 3, 2019.

McAllister, M. P., & Cruz, J. (2020). Critical theory: Celebrating the rich, individualistic superhero. In M. J. Smith, M. Brown, & R. Duncan (Eds.), *More critical approaches to comics: Theories and methods* (pp. 7–19). New York: Routledge.

McKay, C. (Director). (2017). *The LEGO Batman Movie*. United States: Warner Bros.

Meehan, E. R. (1991). 'Holy commodity fetish, Batman!': The political economy of a commercial intertext. In R. E. Pearson & W. Uricchio (Eds.), *The many lives of the Batman: Critical approaches to a superhero and his media* (pp. 47–65). New York: Routledge.

Mitchell, M. (Director). (2019). *The LEGO Movie 2: The Second Part.* United States: Warner Bros.

Morales, R. (Director). (2014). *LEGO DC Comics: Batman be-leaguered.* Warner Brothers Animation.

Mr Toys Toyworld YouTube. (2017, March 18). *The LEGO Batman Movie sets commercial.* YouTube video. https://www.youtube.com/watch?v=Zd-QFsZYUISE. Accessed on January 3, 2019.

Pasquarelli, A. (2017, February 20). Superfriends of marketing. *Advertising Age*, 8–10. https://adage.com/article/news/superfriends-marketing/308007?fbclid=IwAR39yn9kRzbbdQkQFuU_. Accessed on January 3, 2019.

Pearson, R., Uricchio, W., & Brooker, W. (2015). *Many more lives of the Batman* (2nd ed.). London: British Film Institute.

Peters, M., & Zwyer, M. (Directors). (2016). *Justice league: Gotham City Breakout.* United States: Warner Bros. Animation.

Phillips, K. R. (2002). Textual strategies, plastic tactics: Reading Batman and Barbie. *Journal of Material Culture, 7*(2), 12–136. https://doi.org/10.1177/1359183502007002510.

Pulver, A. (2014, October 14). Holy construction toys! Lego Batman to star in own spinoff movie. *The Guardian.* From the database Newsbank. Accessed on January 3, 2019.

Roman, Z., & McAllister, M. P. (2012). The brand and the bold: Synergy and sidekicks in licensed-based children's television. *Global Media Journal, 12*(20), 1–15. http://www.globalmediajournal.com/open-access/the-brand-and-the-bold-synergy-and-sidekicks-in-licensedbased-childrens-television.php?aid=35330. Accessed on January 3, 2019.

Rotten Tomatoes. (2017). *The LEGO Batman Movie.* https://www.rottentomatoes.com/m/the_lego_batman_movie. Accessed on January 3, 2019.

Rusu, M. (2017). *LEGO Robin's guide to being cool(er).* New York: Scholastic.

Schor, J. B. (2005). *Born to buy.* New York: Scribner.

Shirey, E. (2012, June 20). LEGO DC Universe super heroes event promotes new 'Batman 2 game.' *Dallas Examiner.* From the database Newsbank. Accessed on January 3, 2019.

Szadkowski, J. (2006, February 25). Lego builds its inventory of Batman-related figures. *The Washington Times.* From the database Newsbank. Accessed on January 3, 2019.

The Numbers. (2017). *The LEGO Batman Movie.* https://www.the-numbers.com/movie/Lego-Batman-Movie-The#tab=summary. Accessed on January 3, 2019.

Walsh, K. (2017, February 9). Review: Everything is awesome about 'LEGO Batman Movie.' *The Detroit Free Press*. https://www.freep.com/story/entertainment/movies/2017/02/09/lego-batman-movie-review/97665590/. Accessed on January 3, 2019.

Warner Bros. Interactive Entertainment and TT Games Announce LEGO(R) BATMAN(TM): THE VIDEOGAME. (2007, March 27). *Business Wire*. From the database Newsbank. Accessed on January 3, 2019.

Warner Bros. Interactive Entertainment, TT Games and The LEGO Group announce LEGO® Batman™ 2: DC Super Heroes. (2012, January 5). *Business Wire*. From the database Newsbank. Accessed on January 3, 2019.

Warner Bros. Television Group celebrates "The LEGO Batman Movie" with super-sized studio billboards, and LEGO Batman crashes The CW's super hero lineup. (2017, February 6). *PRWeb*. From the database Newsbank. Accessed on January 3, 2019.

Yockey, M. (2014). *Batman*. Detroit: Wayne State University Press.

4

Everything Is Awesome When You're Part of a List: The Flattening of Distinction in Post-Ironic LEGO Media

Ari Mattes

Imagine the following scenario. It is Christmas morning. Daylight breaks, and children wake each other up, gathering in bedrooms and peeping through gaps in doors. They speculate in whispers about the seen and unseen, anticipating potential treasures waiting for them beneath the tree. Stealthily, they make their way toward the living room; they raise wrapped parcels and shake them, ears carefully pressed to their sides. After what seems like an age, parents emerge with cups of tea and coffee, looking like they've been up half the night, and smile as their children shake with excitement. Go: Paper is ripped open, and boxes containing collections of plastic bricks called LEGO become the objects of squeals of delight.

Later that morning, the children sit down with their presents—perhaps the Duplo Steam Train or the Modular Skate House, or the Mindstorms Robot Kit with Remote Control for the older kids—and open the colorful boxes. The bricks look like fun, but, their parents tell them, the most important thing in the box is the booklet. Essentially a

A. Mattes (✉)
University of Notre Dame, Fremantle, WA, Australia
e-mail: ari.mattes@nd.edu.au

© The Author(s) 2019
R. C. Hains and S. R. Mazzarella (eds.), *Cultural Studies of LEGO*,
https://doi.org/10.1007/978-3-030-32664-7_4

list, the booklet pre-empts—like Hegel's acorn pre-empting the tree—the final construction. It is a list of parts, and a list of "building instructions"; like the lists that come with furniture from another successful Scandinavian company, IKEA, sometimes these instructions are easy to follow, sometimes more difficult. Thus begins a day of prescribed labor, with the children (and parents) interpreting the list, attempting to realize its proscriptive capacity.

Constructing LEGO is, after all, first and foremost a matter of checking items on and interpreting instructions from lists—documents that collect different elements and submit them to identical framing logics. The list—arguably, the formal paradigm of twenty-first-century online culture—indeed negates distinction and flattens difference. The list is defined through equation, congruence and presence or, to paraphrase Paul Virilio, presentation rather than representation (2009, p. 6). Assembly from component parts, clicking together interchangeable bricks, implies a logic of mass exchangeability that aptly reflects LEGO's commodity form, as mass-produced toy, containing a universe of necessary (and almost limitlessly accumulatable) parts, each with its own number; as an assembly-with-instructions toy, LEGO is ontologically indebted to lists and listing.

Given how critical the list is to LEGO as a toy, there is a certain poetic consonance to the fact that in recent LEGO films—*The LEGO Movie* (2014) (*TLM*), *The LEGO Batman Movie* (2017) (*LBM*) and *The LEGO Ninjago Movie* (2017) (*LNM*)—the form and logic of the list and practices of listing are critical to their comedic effects. This is realized in *TLM* at both the narrative level—the plot revolves around the notion of "building without instructions"—and as part of the logic of the film as a whole, in its assembly-style. Furthermore, numerous times throughout the three films, the process of assembling incongruous elements together under the aegis of a single list generates comedy. Toward the beginning of *TLM*, for example, protagonist Emmet reads "Instructions to fit in, have everybody like you, and always be happy." An image of LEGO people accompanies each section: three LEGO men in a line ("instructions to fit in"); five smiling LEGO people standing in a semicircle, the middle one being lifted by the two beside him ("have everybody like you"); and a solitary, smiling and waving LEGO man in the middle of being swallowed by a shark, the upper half of his torso poking out from the shark's jaws ("and always be happy").

Despite some recent scholarly interest in the list, primarily from Young (2013, 2017), not much has been written on the aesthetics of the list, and on the list as a form structuring aesthetic practices in the digital age, including listing as potentially generating comedic effects—my focus in this essay. In this essay, I address this elision, looking to interrogate the function of listing as a comedic device in the recent LEGO movies. I begin by analyzing the comedic function of listing in the three films, situating this discussion in the broader context of comedic theories of doubling, before suggesting that this formal regime is in consonance with the broader neoliberal messages of the three films, which emphasize the necessity for individual self-belief to resolve structural conflicts. I finish by suggesting that the LEGO movies' frenetic and banal humor both performs and reflects the negation of irony as bearer of critical meaning in twenty-first-century culture more broadly, reflective of the Internet age of unlimited exchange of and access to information (for some, if not others). But before we look at the LEGO movies in more detail, let's think a little more carefully about lists. What is a list? And, perhaps more importantly, what does a list do?

I Think, Therefore I List

Lists are everywhere. They "proliferate at every turn" (Young 2013, p. 497). Door lists, death lists, bucket lists, shopping lists, playlists, symptom lists, side effect lists, Christmas wish lists, top ten lists, lists of student results from high school, lists of student results from university, lists of the best universities, lists of the worst universities, lists of the wealthiest men, lists of the sexiest women, lists of the wealthiest companies, Oscar-nominee lists, electoral lists, countdown lists, lists of ingredients, lists of attendees, lists for national service, and, of course, lists of lists.

Lists are everywhere, and everywhere that is, terrestrially, can now be captured by Google Maps, a computational program—a list of processes, and sequences of numbers called algorithms—that recreates geographical space in the virtual, thereby realizing the cadastral dream that has sustained empires for thousands of years: whatever can be mapped can be bordered; whatever can be bordered—or "listed," as suggested by the etymology of the word "list," which comes from middle English for "border"—can be possessed, turned into private property.

If we accept the basic premise that the computational age features a shift in thinking about energy and matter from the ontological ("is") toward the functional ("does")[1]—most prominently pronounced, perhaps, in the reigning of technoscience over science, evident in the disproportionate funding of research into technology over philosophy—then the post-Enlightenment axiom of the twenty-first century must be "I think, therefore I list."[2] In the Internet age, the list of commands called protocol comes to pattern our rhythms of daily life, the algorithm the engine for our social existence—we check our emails on our phones, swipe our travel cards on buses, fill in tables on computers at work, and update our social media profiles while watching Netflix at night. The list becomes, much like the Library of Babel in Borges' (1998) fable, endlessly proliferating and self-generating. One list always seems to lead to more lists; be it top-ten lists of the biggest hunks or the best potatoes, the medium, in this case, is definitely the message. As Liam Cole Young (2017) points out in his brilliant analysis of lists and listing, *List Cultures: Knowledge and Poetics from Mesopotamia to Buzzfeed*, the most significant question is not what is on a list, or even what a list *is*, but, rather, what a list *does*.

The list does several things. Perhaps most clearly, it enacts control, by ordering information according to a specific functional principle. By being positioned as part of a list, the logic of the list applies. As James R. Beniger (1986) demonstrates in *The Control Revolution*, the list was a critical bureaucratic technology of the nineteenth and twentieth centuries, enabling the future to be shaped through its documentation of the past. At the same time, by both manifesting and fostering the desire for control, lists reveal a fundamental lack of control. Every list also points toward everything that is not on the list. The arbitrary application of a listing principle—these are the Hollywood hunks *I* like, or these are the best potatoes—reveals the sheer entropy against which the list must perpetually work in order to sustain itself. Lists also offer an avenue for the performance of a certain kind of cultural guardianship. The Australian radio station ABC Classic FM, for example, recently released a list of the top 100 classical music composers.[3] By publicizing that one is following this list—through social media updates, or through discussions with friends—one can appear as a "cultured" kind of person. In such cases, the list's release becomes a cultural event, distributing knowledge and mediating power.

There is, however, nothing modern about the list. As Young points out, the earliest writing, cuneiform, served a listing function, through its tabulation of stocks: "… with the onset of writing came the list" (2013, p. 500). The list has occupied a critical position in social and political life since administration began (and began with recording), existing as "a technique […] that can be found in practically all human communities" (Baetens 2019, p. 99). As Foucault (1970) demonstrates in the now classic *The Order of Things*, knowledge itself develops through a kind of schemata involving a tautology of listing: what is in the world can appear on the list called knowledge that records what is in the world; more lists means more knowledge, and the accumulation of lists becomes the central task of the French *encyclopaedists* of the eighteenth century.

And yet, perhaps the "ubiquity of lists in the contemporary cultural moment" (Young 2013, p. 499) represents "a broader shift toward […] the list as a dominant mediator of cultural information" (p. 507). If we think of the Internet as, essentially, a series of connecting lists of information—that is, Web sites channeling information stored in databases—then the exponentially increasing number of Web site searches[4] suggests a kind of frenetic desire for documentation, a graphomania, at rates unimaginable in earlier epochs. If the purview of modernity, as Adorno and Horkheimer (2016) famously argue, was total administration—and, thus, the keeping of lists on large scales, including the infamous Nazi death lists—what does today's listmania suggest regarding the administration of people and things in the twenty-first century? If modernity, as John Guillory (2004) suggests, is perfectly encapsulated in the often-overlooked material form of recording called the memo, then in this essay, I claim that the procedural form of the list best encapsulates what follows modernity. The metalogic of assembly that characterizes the list—the logic of protocol—underpins twenty-first-century network culture.[5] The "machinic functionality of the list," Young (2013) argues, "secures for it a privileged position in the digital logic of the database" (p. 512).

Despite the list's long history, and its association with the shaping of modern administered man, this pleasure of making, sharing and reading lists seems to be a more recent anthropological development. It may be that the performance of control facilitated by listing practices is in itself a source of pleasure for people and institutions, as suggested by David Graeber (2015) in *The Utopia of Rules*. As every procrastinator knows, making the "to-do list" often feels like more of an achievement than actually doing the tasks featured on it. In any case, what were once primarily arbiters of administrative control have become objects valued in their own right. And perhaps—and this marks the broader context of this essay—this is simply another example of the increasing management of the self concomitant with the unchecked acceleration of capitalism known by the moniker "neoliberalism."[6]

While some scholars have studied the pleasures of listing, there has been little scholarly discussion of the list as a comedic source. So: how can lists be funny?

Comedy in the LEGO Movies

Comedy is notoriously difficult to pin down. As Lauren Berlant and Sianne Ngai (2017) note, it thrives in ambiguity and the transgression of boundaries, aesthetic, social, linguistic, physical and moral; it may "dispel anxiety," but as "both an aesthetic mode and a form of life, its action just as likely produces anxiety: risking transgression, flirting with displeasure, or just confusing things in a way that both intensifies and impedes the pleasure" (p. 233). At the risk of overgeneralization, perhaps we could say that comedy always involves some kind of violence done upon the expectations of the ordinary. Verbal comedy may involve the literalization of a word—as in Harpo's presentation of a swordfish when asked the password to enter the exclusive club in *Horse Feathers* (1932)—or the ironic split between a word and its other; it may involve the deliberate misapplication of a commonly used word. Physical comedy may revolve around a mere accident—a man slips on a banana peel—or on a bizarre and unusual arrangement of the physical order, as in Charlie Chaplin's frenetic movements. As Berlant and Ngai (2017) note, "classic comedy theory points to a rapid frame breaking, including scalar shifts, as central to comedic pleasure. Scenes, bodies, and words dissolve into surprising component parts; objects violate physics or, worse, insist on its laws against all obstacles" (pp. 233–234).

Comedy thereby calls into question the boundaries between concepts, things and people, challenging borders that have structured western culture for thousands of years: good and evil, inside and outside, up and down. If a list draws attention to borders by reifying categories, through its "bordering" function, then comedy draws attention to these same edges through their deliberate subversion and dissolution. Comedians do this for multiple reasons, and comedy can encode opposing political ideologies. As Angela Nagle (2017) writes, nothing is inherently progressive about transgression.

Comedy always involves an existential doubling, a split between object or self and object or self with difference. A mimetic doubling is ever at play in the moment of comedy, which subverts the ordinary and the expected into something other in the space of representation, and it is this doubling with a difference that generates the humor (Dolar 2017). We expect the man to easily cross the road, but instead he slips on a banana peel, leaving us with the gap between man who crosses road, and man who slips on banana peel. In a verbal context, this is irony's domain—the exploitation of the gap between what *we know* a thing is and what it appears to be, between the scene of its representation and its normative, socially constructed meaning.

Things become more complicated when this split concerns our expectations regarding our participation in and observation of the art-event itself. For example, when watching a film or reading a book, we expect something notable will happen—that something interesting will transpire to maintain our interest, however minimally invested. The man slipping on the banana peel is funny because *something happens*; the man crossing the road is not, because it merely realizes what we thought would happen all along. But what if the fact that *nothing* happens becomes the source of the humor? We are watching a comedy, so we expect the man to slip on the banana peel, but he doesn't… A great deal of contemporary comedy seems to involve thus laying waste to our expectations of the extraordinary by presenting and reifying the ordinary and the repetitive. This is the comedy of the banal, of mere doubling *without* difference. Or, rather, the difference is in our expectation that something different will happen; the comedic moment is thereby transferred to the meta-textual level, rather than occurring within the world of the text. The mere presence of something banal, and its acknowledgment, becomes a source of comedic pleasure.

The LEGO movies' humor oscillates between these two poles. On the one hand, the films revel in the banality and formulaic nature of their narratives, explicitly staging, celebrating, and lampooning their dependence upon myriad clichés (while nonetheless still depending upon them). At a visual level, much of the films' comedy comes from the gap between the technically superb use of computer generated imagery and the ordinary "blockiness" of the source objects, the LEGO bricks themselves. This is simultaneously manifested in the films' intermittent fetishization of the amateurish nature of children's play, through their realization of this within the domain of a multi-million dollar Hollywood studio project. In *LBM*, for example, when characters are shooting at each other, the accompanying sound track features the "pew-pew-pew" noises of children staging a toy battle. Likewise, in *TLM*, when a spaceship takes off at a key moment, the image suddenly resembles an amateurish drawing lacking the virtual depth that defines the film's general visual language.

On the other hand, the films often generate comedy through outlandish (and completely unpredictable) events and characters, frequently realized through practices of listing, through the trope of creating a list that contains some radically incongruous elements. In this case, they set up the comedy by juxtaposing the bizarre element in relation to the previous cumulative effect of several logically related items appearing on the list. Violence is thereby done to our expectations regarding what befits the logic of a particular list, through the inclusion of the disparate and often asymmetrical element. Batman's playlists, for example, glimpsed early in *LBM* before he first battles the Joker, contains these titles: "Gym Workout; Super Cool Mega Mix; LET'S GET NUTS MIX; Batman Solos."

Aside from several "first order" gags populating the movies—in *TLM*, for example, Emmett, while taking a shower, says "Always be sure to keep the soap out of your—ahhhh!" as the soap goes in his eyes, and moments later laughs so hard while watching television he falls from the couch—the above poles capture the major branches of humor across the three films, which we can fit into three categories. The first involves the self-aware citation and parody of generic tropes and narrative structures; the second involves the parody of the source medium itself—the LEGO block—and milieu—children playing; and the third involves the shock effects concomitant with the practice of incorporating peculiar and unexpected elements into otherwise logically coherent lists. While the films' citations of generic tropes and the parody of the medium's blockiness do not exactly follow the logic of the comedic list, their prevalence is equally symptomatic and indicative of twenty-first-century network aesthetics.

The List as Comedic Trope: Random Lists, Lists of the Random

Before we examine listing practices across the LEGO films, brief synopses may be in order. *TLM* follows protagonist Emmet from nondescript construction worker to savior of the universe, as he teams up with a crew of master-builders—those who can "build without instructions"—and becomes a master-builder in his own right. The tyrant Lord Business (aka President Business) tries to generate the perfect world according to his vision, fixing people and things into position using his super weapon, The Kragle; Emmet and his team fight to liberate the people from the clutches of Business, teaching them to unlock the "special" potential within each of them. This struggle within the LEGO world, it is revealed toward the end of the film, is the product of a young boy's real-world play, and the struggles between Emmet and Business mirror the boy's clash with his father (Will Ferrell), who collects LEGO sets with which he doesn't allow his son to play; the father plans to glue all the LEGO sets he has built in the family basement in place using Krazy Glue ("KRA—GL-E"). The two worlds overlap in the film's final section, when Emmet/the boy save the LEGO world from being glued into place by showing Business/the dad that play and creativity are better than order and stasis.

The LNM and *The LBM* have the structures of more straightforward superhero action narratives. *TLM* is a martial arts film parody, set on the island of Ninjago that follows the attempts of evil warlord, Lord Garmadon, to conquer and rule Ninjago, and the efforts of a team of superhero ninjas—including Garmadon's son, Lloyd Garmadon— under the tutelage of Master Wu (who happens to be Garmadon's brother), to repel his efforts. Similar to its predecessor, it is resolved through the reconciliation of a father and son, proving that love, rather than violence, resolves the tensions upon which the narrative is built. Garmadon and his son eventually team up and defeat the ultimate monster, a live action cat, by placating it through tender pats and kind words.

The LBM has the largest archive of popular cultural resources from which to draw (see, in this volume, Chapters 3 and 13: "'Hey, kids. Who wants a shot from the merch gun?!': LEGO Batman as a gateway commodity intertext" by McAllister and LaGroue, and "The man behind the mask: Camp and queer masculinity in *LEGO* Batman" by Hunting) and its comparatively staid approach to its subject reflects this. It seems less frenetic than the other films; it derives much of its action from the viewer's assumed knowledge of Batman and his exploits saving Gotham City from the Joker. The plot involves new police commissioner Barbara Gordon taking over from Jim Gordon; Barbara is less inclined to allow Batman free rein as a vigilante and seeks to implement more socially conscious approaches to policing. Batman falls in love with her, adopts an orphan who becomes sidekick Robin, and acknowledges he has a symbiotic relationship with the Joker, who spends the film trying to get Batman to admit that he's his number one antagonist and that he couldn't live without his constant attacks on Gotham.

Gags litter the three films, offering persistent assaults on the comedic sensitivities of the viewer, but none more so than the first movie,

TLM. One suspects that the film's manic attempts to win over the viewer reflects its ontological status as an extended advertisement for the toy LEGO—evident even at the level of its title, which merely signifies that it is a movie based upon a toy. This is not the case with *LNM* and *LBM*, both of which are oriented by a pre-existing narrative-cultural space. From playing in the LEGO universe, viewers know that Ninjago is a kind of imaginary martial arts movie world and, of course, there is already a rich cultural archive concerning Batman, across comic books, television, film, cartoons, and costuming and merchandise. In contrast, *TLM* seems impelled to manically justify its existence—there are no a priori fictional universes upon which it can draw—and it seems to do this through its relentless assembly of comedic moments and its ceaseless demonstration of its own self-awareness, its hip media literacy.

Unsurprisingly, then, this first film features the largest number of gags about its genre and gags involving listing. During its ninety-two minutes of action (excluding end credits), *TLM* contains thirty-seven gags parodying its generic constitution and dependence upon formulae, and thirty-one involving lists and listing. Examples of the former include love interest Wyldstyle first meeting Emmet and saying, "Come with me if you want *not* to die," parodying the clichéd heroic line from numerous action narratives ("come with me if you want to live") and the "good cop, bad cop" cliché realized by having both exist in the same LEGO man who spins his head around to change faces. Examples of the latter include the list of products and services that President Business' Octan Corporation supply ("music, dairy products, coffee, TV shows, surveillance systems, all history books, voting machines") and the list of master-builders to whom Vitruvius introduces Emmet in Cloud Cuckoo Land, including: Robin Hood, Mermaid Lady, Gandalf, Swamp Creature, 1980-something Space Guy, 2002 NBA All Stars, Wonder Woman, Green Ninja, Millhouse, Nice Vampire, Michelangelo (painter) and Michelangelo (Teenage Mutant Ninja Turtle), Cleopatra, Abraham Lincoln, Superman and Green Lantern. Often this listing process involves a character assembling several items in a list together, interspersing random elements, or the list's logic proceeds from serious to ridiculous, with an increasing number of bizarre or inane elements introduced to it.

In contrast, during its ninety-six minutes (excluding end credits), *LBM* contains nineteen gags involving listing (such as the list of different Bat vehicles orphan Dick discovers in the Bat Cave: the Bat sub, the Bat spaceship, the Bat zeppelin, the Bat train, the Bat kayak, the Bat dune buggy, and Bat shark repellent) and thirty-seven parodying itself in terms of genre. It deliberately draws attention to the conventions of Hollywood superhero films from its opening sound, which plays on the serious affect of the Christopher Nolan Batman films, with Batman's voiceover stating: "Black. All important movies start with a black screen. And music. Edgy, scary music. That would make a parent or studio executive nervous. And logos. Really long and dramatic logos." Some gags blend the two categories. Alfred lists at one point, for example, every previous screen incarnation by year of the caped crusader, accompanied by a suitable LEGO tableau representing each version: "I've seen you go through similar phases in 2016 [*Batman v Superman: Dawn of Justice*] and 2012 [*The Dark Knight Rises*] and 2008 [*The Dark Knight*] and 2005 [*Batman Begins*] and 1997 [*Batman & Robin*] and 1995 [*Batman Forever*] and 1992 [*Batman Returns*] and 1989 [*Batman*] and that weird one in 1966 [*Batman* TV series]." It makes sense that a higher proportion of this film's gags involve genre, given Batman is one of the quintessential DC Comics' superheroes involving a rich pop-culture archive on which the film can parodically draw.

LNM has fewer gags involving genre and lists than the other two films. Post-*TLM*, it needed not struggle to establish itself as a franchise—it can peacefully exist as an entry in an already-established franchise—and therefore lacks the same parodic fuel as *LBM*. *LNM* features nineteen gags built around lists (a list of important birthdays, for example, features in the newscast *Good Morning Ninjago*; it includes "this hotdog guy, this panda, and Lloyd Garmadon") and twenty parodying genre (for example, the transformation of the opening Warner Bros. logo in line with the martial arts films it is parodying). In *LNM*, the evil Lord Garmadon, during a raid on the island Ninjago, orders his generals (listed by number) to perform several destructive acts. After some apparently serious commands—"General Number Five—take the TV station! General Number One—crash the stock market!"—he orders, "General Number Four—make that school bus dangle precariously over an overpass or something—I've never seen that before." Garmadon offers his own metacommentary on the narrative action—in the LEGO world, people seem to live according to a kind of set of hyper-generic expectations that transcend the diegetic edges of the world (literally realized in the real-life cat penetrating into the story world later in the film). The film knowingly asserts its self-awareness through its conscious invocation and activation of formulae associated with Hollywood—crime film clichés, and so on—while simultaneously relying on these formulae for narrative development.

Analyzing some examples in more detail can illustrate how the films employ the list as a source of comedy. As aforementioned, each film generates much comedic energy through creating bizarre lists (or sets) involving dissimilar and asymmetrical elements. In *LBM*'s opening sequence, the Joker hijacks a plane transporting an outlandish assortment of dangerous goods (listed by the pilot to the control tower when requesting permission to fly over the city), establishing the trajectory of the film's action to come: The Joker attacks Gotham City, and Batman stops him—so obvious, in the context of a Batman movie, that the parody of this obviousness becomes a structuring narrative element of the film, with the Joker constantly asking Batman to admit that he's his nemesis, and that he will continue to stop him when he tries to take over Gotham City.

As the Joker hijacks the plane, he explains to the pilot (and viewer) that the city is under attack from "Gotham's greatest criminal minds, including: The Riddler; Scarecrow; Bane; Two-Face; Catwoman." He introduces each character in a measured fashion, with a second or two of screen time dedicated to them. The Joker's voice is even: these are the expected villains, the baddies known and loved from the Batman world. Then the Joker continues: "And let's not forget: Clayface; Poison Ivy; Mr. Freeze; Penguin; Crazy Quilt; Eraser; Polka-Dot Man; Minae; Tarantula; King Tut; Orca; Killer Moth; March Harriet; Zodiac Master; Gentleman Ghost; Clock King; Calendar Man; Kite Man; Catman; Zebra Man; and the Condiment King." As the list becomes increasingly bizarre (with lesser-known villains like Kite Man appearing on it), Joker's delivery speeds up; the characters appear for only a microsecond. The humor of the presence in the film of these lesser known villains is emphasized by their sheer quantity, and the cumulative effect of listing exacerbates this humor. "Okay, are you making some of those up?" asks the Pilot. "Nope, they're all real. Probably worth a Google," replies the Joker, thereby assenting to the authority of a service that, essentially, lists Web sites, while simultaneously suggesting that the character recognizes the absurdity of the very frame in which he finds himself.

The films' redeployment of listing and lists—which usually, as Young (2013, 2017) shows, function as serious control tools—as sources of humor is most clearly demonstrated in the early news sequence in *LNM*, involving the parody of breakfast news programs, *Good Morning Ninjago*. The listing function of news—the distracting, pseudo-randomness with which different items are tacked together for entertainment, as discussed by Peter Sloterdijk (1988) in *Critique of Cynical Reason*—becomes the source of the comedy, as three different lists (a list of Garmadon's crimes, a list of ninjas and a list of important birthdays) are compounded upon one another in one large kind of news-list.

A cheesy announcer's voice-over introduces *Good Morning Ninjago* with a list: "When Garmadon attacks; when Garmadon crashes the stock exchange; when Garmadon defaces *Whistler's Mother*—we are there!" The juxtaposition of the high-seriousness of the first two entries (attacking and crashing the stock exchange seem like things any serious villain might do) and the third entry's absurdity (childishly defacing a painting seems less appropriate for a supervillain) generates the comedic effect. We expect the list's third element to be equivalent, according to the logic of continuity suggested by listing processes, yet it is massively incongruous and asymmetrical. This intrusion into the frame disrupts the frame, the trespass subverting our expectations and generating the comedy.

Yet in introducing Lord Garmadon's malevolence, the program *is* providing the film's viewer with key information for understanding the rest of the narrative. The news program then provides, in the form of another list, the other piece of key information for following a super-hero-style narrative: the heroes' identities. The program introduces the six ninjas who defend Ninjago against Garmadon in list form by name, accompanied by "Burning Questions" about each one. The sequence's call-and-response nature—with each Ninja given a split second of screen time following the anchorman's voice over—as well as the absurdity of the questions draws attention to the basic stupidity of news media in the celebrity age. This emphasizes the informational vacuity of the form itself—news programs list things deemed of significance to the viewer—while at the same time introducing the viewer to the heroes of the movie:

> *Anchor*: "Fire Ninja: Where is he on a scale of one to awesome?"
> *Fire Ninja*: "I'm not gonna lie… I'm awesome!"
> *Anchor*: "Earth Ninja: When will he upgrade to digital?"
>   [We see Earth Ninja spinning a record]
> *Earth Ninja*: "No I would never do that."
> *Anchor*: "Ice Ninja: Is he a real boy or a robot?"
> *Ice Ninja*: "How dare you. I'm a wild teen" [in a distinctly android voice].
> *Anchor*: "Lightning Ninja: Is he the bravest ninja of them all?"
>   [We see Lightning Ninja screaming as he flees some attackers].
> *Anchor*: "I'll take that as a yes!"
> *Anchor*: "Water Ninja: She's a girl, *and* a ninja. Can she really have it all?"
> *Water Ninja*: "You fellers need to inform yourselves of where we're at culturally."
> *Anchor*: "And finally the Green Ninja. He fights in the air, on the ground, and in the kitchen with the refrigerator [we see him hitting some shark men with the fridge door] but what is he hiding? And who is he really?"

The report suddenly cuts out, followed by yet another list: this time, of local notables' birthdays. "Celebrating birthdays today," says the anchor woman, "are this hot dog guy, this panda and, oh-oh, Lloyd Garmadon." "The son of evil Lord Garmadon," adds the anchor man. Our attention is again pulled in quaquaversal directions through the assembly of the list—a kind of news document linking the disparate in the present discursive moment.

The three films feature many similar jokes, and while none of the above-mentioned comedic tropes—listing, generic and medial citation—is original to the LEGO movies, each with its own (often related) legacy in literature (Swift, Sterne, etc.) and film (e.g., The Marx Brothers, Mel Brooks), the repetitive use of these tropes within the films and across the series perhaps indicates a fundamental insistence on the list, which reveals something more provocative about our current moment than more-considered and ironically charged versions of these tropes. The LEGO movies' humor often depends upon a dynamic fluctuating between these tropes, involving the statement of the banally, brutally obvious, involving self-referentiality *vis-à-vis* genre, and the outlandishly improbable (the contrast between wildly disparate and asymmetrical, disproportionally arranged, elements on the single list).

This logic of listing categorizes much of the humor of the three films at large, through their repetitive assembly of comically random lists, seeming to posit a world in which meaning can only be generated through citation of other citations. If everything becomes an index to something else, with references becoming ontologically determined only in relationship to other references, following the logic of the database, then signification becomes simply a matter of citation. Presence on a list—which, on the list of the World, includes, in Borgesian fashion, everything then, now and forever—seems to constitute value, and everything becomes endlessly exchangeable and interchangeable: any reference can be switched for any other reference. In the LEGO movies, the privilege narrative grants particular characters and figures seems to be revealed as accidental, with everything occupying equal relevance as a reference, the more arbitrary the more comical. *LNM* seems to suggest to the viewer that while it is about these characters, it could also be about the hotdog man or the panda. At the same time, the humor is generated through our paradoxical awareness of an existing hierarchy of objects, in terms of significance—the humor of the random is the humor of the unexpected, the element breaking open and revealing the a priori arbitrary and banal nature of the listing hierarchy.

The Politics of the List: Presentation and Representation

Peter Sloterdijk (1988) analyses the distracting and alienating effects of the list form in 1980s German news media in a way that both reflects the LEGO movies' ostensible critiques of mass media, entertainment and news, and shoots barbs directly at the movies' distracting, hyperactive, frenetic styles: "… for the consciousness that informs itself in all directions, everything becomes problematic and inconsequential" (p. 307). One of the two key cynicisms of professional journalism, Sloterdijk continues, is "the disinhibition of the currents of information in relation to the consciousnesses that absorb them" (p. 307). The news industry "floods the capacities of our consciousness in a downright anthropologically threatening way" (p. 308). The result is distraction and "deconcentration":

> We now regard it as normal that in magazines we find… all regions close to one another: reports on mass starvation in the Third World next to advertisements for champagne, articles on environmental catastrophes beside a discussion of the most recent automobile production. Our minds are trained to scan and comprehend an encyclopedically broad scale of irrelevancies—in which the irrelevance of the single item comes not so much from itself but from its being arranged in the flood of information from the media. … without intensive practice, people, if they do not want to risk some form of mental disintegration, cannot bear this continual flickering of important and unimportant items, the waxing and waning of reports that in one moment demand the highest attentiveness and in the next are totally passé. (p. 308)

Indeed, "an enormous simultaneity stretches itself out in our informed consciousness: Here, some are eating; there, some are dying" (Sloterdijk 1988, p. 309). This is, Sloterdijk suggests with his usual dose of irony, an "addiction and […] compulsion to live daily in the whirr of information and to tolerate the constant bombardment of our minds with unbelievable masses of indifferent-important, sensational-unimportant news" (p. 308).

In a networked age, in which all information is available online all the time, this database logic—the logic of the list—makes sense. To make an argument, or to generate affect, seems to be increasingly the domain of the assembly of bits of information. The modernist dream of shocking presence out of itself through representation—the domain of art—seems to have less consonance in the age of information online and accessible. In the networked, cybernetic present, everything has been documented, so art becomes the art of LEGO bricks: of the assembly of neatly cut, pre-made pieces, a space supporting the skillful archivist rather than the poet. Irony, the verbal equivalent of shocking sense into a concept through the presentation of it as its opposite—the exquisite polishing of the gap between object and concept—collapses in a context in which logics of presentation and assembly rather than semiosis and poetics dominate.

At the same time, in a hip, media literate world, the most generative dynamic seems to emerge from a system, concept, or work's perpetual demonstration of the understanding of its own borders. The LEGO movies' frequent parodic engagement of generic tropes serves as a kind of publication of knowingness, a performance of self-awareness. When knowledge of information no longer functions in the evaluation of intelligence, due to comprehensive database-lists of information like Wikipedia that devalue the cultural capital of information possession, systems awareness—and self-critique—seem to become the markers of knowledge; "wokeness" is contingent upon an explicit awareness of the mechanisms and processes structuring one's media ecology. The LEGO movies' performance of a generic trope accompanied by its simultaneous vocalization marks a kind of humor resounding in the statement of presence, of the reproduction of presence, and a "logic of affirmative accumulation" defines the list; what is to be added adds value in expanding the list and in generating more lists (Young 2013, p. 503). What does this do to irony, the base level trope at the core of both of these comedic effects in LEGO?

Doubling, here—of the act, and the recognition of the act, within the single system—serves as a kind of brute statement of presence, rather than an act of signification and ironic passage, suggesting its fundamental difference from the critical social function of the double in comedy, as discussed by Dolar (2017), and underpinning human culture more generally, as demonstrated in the work of René Girard (1988).[7] As Linda Hutcheon (1995) argues in her magisterial study of the politics of irony, *Irony's Edge*, irony is politically polysemous. It is, as evident in the recent popularity of the alt-right as iconoclastic provocateurs, never only radical or reactionary. At the same time, irony, as a trope signifying a fluctuation of meaning between radically different (or oppositional) terms, is clearly all pervasive at the level of both narrative and image in the media produced by the LEGO franchise. However, rather than generative of a rich multiplicity of critical meaning (historically irony's function), irony's sheer ubiquity in LEGO media leads to its flattening, negating irony's potential as bearer of critical meaning. The collapsing of the significance of the space between object and concept blunts what was "irony's edge." This, in turn, blunts the political (as the struggle for the distribution of resources), replacing it with what could be called "the administration of commodities," the manifestation of the dream of the neutral market of endless interchange and exchange replacing the politics of conflict between people.

Indeed, rather than seeing this kind of humor—equally fetishizing the bizarre and the obvious—as critically engaging with the world (along the lines of absurdist theater or existential philosophy, calling into question not only being, but the frame of being itself, the ontic and the ontological), it seems to signify a disappearance of the onus of representation (and the ethics associated with this),[8] attempting to evacuate and negate the political through the annihilation of a critical position. If comedy is characterized through the ultimate gap between act and context, then a kind of comedic trope emerges here that delights in its *annihilation of this gap*. This new(ly popular) comedic trope short-circuits the significance of signification. There is no longer a comic split between action and language, no slippage of meaning, but, simply, a banal doubling, an affirmation of a position on a list—a reification of sameness/identity underpinning the comic act. Its brutal banality, its almost post-artistic status, becomes the source of its comic energy. This doubling negates the signifier's value as politically charged referent, its transmutation of scene into obscene reminding us of Jean Baudrillard's (1990) definition of the obscene in *Fatal Strategies*:

Obscenity is the absolute proximity of the thing seen, the gaze stuck in the screen of vision—hypervision in close-up, a dimension without any distance, the total promiscuity of the look with what it sees. Prostitution. (p. 84)

This collapsing of critical distance reflects the neoliberal dream evident at the LEGO films' narrative level: that the world can be "apolitical," that everyone can be a winner (Dean 2009, p. 55), that everything *is* awesome, if you've got the right attitude. Each film resolves what are essentially struggles between structurally irreconcilable forces through individual good cheer. This kind of "Burbanking"—reducing social and political conflict to a matter of individual choice and morality—is nothing new, having characterized Hollywood cinema since its early days. *LNM* offers the message: Look at things from a different point of view /in a different way, and everything will be okay! *LBM* suggests that if you are willing to have friendships with people, then everything will be okay! And *TLM* offers a message of reappropriating and recycling what others have built, and building new things: assembly, reassembly, bricolage. This fits with its neoliberal celebration of the master-self, the creative-self, the ruling-self, the re-creating-self: all that's solid melts into air. "All of you have the ability inside you to be a groundbreaker," Lucy says in *TLM*. Later, Emmet says: "You are the Special. And so is everyone." "Believe," Vitruvius says to Emmet, for believing makes anyone "the Special."

The list privileges a logic of presence, of accumulation, over the dialogical force of irony. Steven Shaviro's (2010) discussion of the digital in *Post-Cinematic Affect* can perhaps begin to illuminate this style of non-critical irony success in the contemporary, which he argues is

> a world of hypermediacy and ubiquitous digital technologies, organized as a "timeless time" and a "space of flows" through which "divergent series are endlessly tracing bifurcating paths." Such a world cannot be *represented*, in any ordinary sense. There is no stable point of view from which we could apprehend it. Each perspective only leads us to another perspective, in an infinite regress of networked transformations—which is to say, in an infinite series of metamorphoses of capital. (p. 131)

"In the realm of digital media," Shaviro (2010) continues,

> binary code [...] is a universal equivalent for all data, all inputs, and all sensory modalities. Everything can be sampled, captured, and transcribed

into a string of ones and zeroes. This string can then be manipulated and transformed, in various measured and controllable ways. Under such conditions, multiple differences ramify endlessly; but none of these differences actually *makes a difference*, since they are all completely interchangeable. (pp. 132–133)

Perhaps the effectiveness of the LEGO movies' database humor signifies the omnipotence of a digital—or computational—*Geist*, recalling Virilio's (2009) (moralistic) denunciation of the present:

The whole world stage is turned upside down [...] to the point where *representations* gradually lose their pertinence—whether aesthetic, political or ethical… What is promoted instead is *presentation*, an untimely, out-of-place presentation that suppresses the depth of time for shared reflexion every bit as much as the depth of field of action and its displacements. (p. 6)

The dependence of the LEGO movies on list-effects certainly demonstrates the transformation of aesthetics by contemporary online digital culture. Whether this is awesome or not is a different matter.

Notes

1. This is the central thesis of David Golumbia's *The Cultural Logic of Computation.* See Golumbia (2009).
2. Equally present is its correlative, equally visible online and indicative of the dominance of identity politics—"I feel, therefore I am."
3. See the Australian Broadcasting Corporation's Classic Composer: The Composers You Can't Live Without (https://www.abc.net.au/classic/classic-100/composer/) countdown from the Australian radio station ABC Classic FM.
4. According to Bernard Marr (2018), in 2018 there are 2.5 quintillion bytes of data created each day, with 90 per cent of the data in the world created from 2016 to 2017. There are 5 billion Internet searches each day.

5. Regarding Wikipedia: "emergent forms of collaborative information/ knowledge projects, most notably *Wikipedia*, increasingly enable and encourage the unquestioned use of lists to prop up aesthetic claims" (Young 2013, p. 507).
6. For a discussion of neoliberalism, see Mattes (2017, pp. 626–628).
7. See Girard (1988).
8. See Hagi Kenaan's discussion and development of Levinas in *The Ethics of Visuality* (2013).

References

Adorno, T., & Horkheimer, M. (2016). *Dialectic of enlightenment* (J. Cumming, Trans.). London: Verso.

Australian Broadcasting Corporation. (2019). *Classic composer: The composers you can't live without.* https://www.abc.net.au/classic/classic-100/composer/. Accessed on June 6, 2019.

Baetens, J. (2019). *List cultures: Knowledge and poetics from Mesopotamia to Buzzfeed* by Liam Cole Young (review). *Leonardo, 52*(1), 98–99. https://doi. org/10.1162/LEON_r_01712.

Baudrillard, J. (1990). *Fatal strategies* (P. Beitchman & W. G. J. Niesluchowski, Trans.). Cambridge, MA and London: The MIT Press.

Beniger, J. R. (1986). *The control revolution: Technological and economic origins of the information society.* Cambridge, MA and London: Harvard University Press.

Berlant, L., & Ngai, S. (2017). Comedy has issues. *Critical Inquiry, 43*(2), 233–249. https://doi.org/10.1086/689666.

Borges, J. L. (1998). *Collected fictions* (A. Hurley, Trans.). London: Penguin.

Dean, J. (2009). *Democracy and other neoliberal fantasies: Communicative capitalism and left politics.* Durham and London: Duke University Press.

Dolar, M. (2017). The comic mimesis. *Critical Inquiry, 43*(2), 570–589. https://doi.org/10.1086/689659.

Foucault, M. (1970). *The order of things: An archaeology of the human sciences.* New York: Pantheon.

Girard, R. (1988). *To double business bound: Essays on literature, mimesis and anthropology.* Baltimore: Johns Hopkins University Press.

Golumbia, D. (2009). *The cultural logic of computation.* Cambridge, MA: Harvard University Press.

Graeber, D. (2015). *The utopia of rules: On technology, stupidity, and the secret joys of bureaucracy*. Brooklyn: Melville House.

Guillory, J. (2004). The memo and modernity. *Critical Inquiry, 31*(1), 108–132. https://doi.org/10.1086/427304.

Hutcheon, L. (1995). *Irony's edge: The theory and politics of irony*. London and New York: Routledge.

Kenaan, H. (2013). *The ethics of visuality: Levinas and the contemporary gaze*. London: I.B. Taurus.

Marr, B. (2018, May 21). How much data do we create every day? The mind-blowing stats everyone should read. *Forbes*. https://www.forbes.com/sites/bernardmarr/2018/05/21/how-much-data-do-we-create-every-day-the-mind-blowing-stats-everyone-should-read/. Accessed on May 1, 2019.

Mattes, A. (2017). Imagining excess: Ideology in contemporary Hollywood's Florida. *The Journal of Popular Culture, 50*(3), 622–645. https://doi.org/10.1111/jpcu.12562.

Nagle, A. (2017). *Kill all normies: Online culture wars from 4chan and Tumblr to Trump and the Alt-Right*. Winchester and Washington: Zero Books.

Shaviro, S. (2010). *Post cinematic affect*. Winchester and Washington: Zero Books.

Sloterdijk, P. (1988). *Critique of cynical reason* (M. Eldred, Trans.). Minneapolis: University of Minnesota Press.

Virilio, P. (2009). *The university of disaster* (J. Rose, Trans.). Oxford, UK and Boston: Polity Books.

Young, L. C. (2013). Un-black boxing the list: Knowledge, materiality and form. *Canadian Journal of Communication, 38*, 497–516. https://doi.org/10.22230/cjc.2013v38n4a2651.

Young, L. C. (2017). *List cultures: Knowledge and poetics from Mesopotamia to Buzzfeed*. Amsterdam: Amsterdam University Press.

5

Made Up Prophecies: Metamodern Play with Religion, Spirituality and Monomyth in the LEGO Universe

Sissel Undheim

From Bricksburg to Apocalypseburg[1]

The opening scenes of the first *LEGO Movie* (2014) (*TLM*) presents a condensed mash-up of myth, fiction and fantasy. A gigantic, monster-like Lord Business enters the cave of master builder Vitruvius, who most of all resembles a mix between the cartoon druid Panoramix (the chief druid in the Asterix series, also known as Getafix and Miraculix) and Gandalf in a tie-dyed t-shirt.[2] Pressured to surrender the missing Piece of Resistance, Vitruvius, wonderfully voiced by Morgan Freeman, utters a prophecy with the expected amount of drama and affect:

Vitruvius: Wait, there is a prophecy.
Lord Business: Aha, now there's a prophecy!
Vitruvius: About the Piece of Resistance.
Lord Business: Yes, the supposed missing Piece of Resistance, that can somehow magically disarm the Kragle. Give me a break!

S. Undheim (✉)
University of Bergen, Bergen, Norway
e-mail: Sissel.Undheim@uib.no

© The Author(s) 2019
R. C. Hains and S. R. Mazzarella (eds.), *Cultural Studies of LEGO*,
https://doi.org/10.1007/978-3-030-32664-7_5

> *Vitruvius*: One day, a talented lass or fellow,
>   a Special one with face of yellow,
>   will make the Piece of Resistance found
>   from its hiding refuge underground,
>   and with a noble army at the helm,
>   this Master Builder will thwart the Kragle and save the realm,
>   and be the greatest, most interesting, most important person of all times.
>   All this is true because it rhymes.
> *Lord Business*: That was a great legend. That you just made up! What a bunch of hippie, dippie baloney!

From then on, *TLM* establishes a stark contrast between the ordered and regulated city, Bricksburg, an apparently thoroughly secular place, reminiscent of the traditional LEGO City sets, and the ever-expanding LEGO Universe, of which Bricksburg is only one of countless "realms" or "dimensions." In Bricksburg, everyone follows instructions, unaware that Lord Business controls them all and also unaware of the other realms in their Universe. While Bricksburg may seem to have no room for religion, the LEGO Universe certainly has, although perhaps of a different kind than one might expect. The movie's play on the American monomyth's well-established clichés makes an action-filled roller-coaster ride through layers of pop- and self-referential fun. Some realms, such as the Old West and Middle Zealand, correspond to well-known Wild West and Castle theme LEGO sets, while Cloud Cuckoo Land is a burst-of-creativity-place where anything can happen. There, inhabitants from all the other realms, including Harry Potter's Hogwarts, Tolkien's Middle Earth and the world of DC-comics superheroes, meet and re-mix. When the fourth wall breaks down in the movie's last act, yet another meta-layer joins the narrative, and it easily lends itself to biblical interpretation. Although the narrative is vague on this point, the contrast between the stern father/creator figure and his liberator son, and their relationship to the creation, gives way to a number of exegetical readings. *TLM*'s abundant religious references were noticeable: While a number of online blogs cheered the savior motif and read it as a Biblical allegory (e.g.,

Caleb n.d.; O'Neil 2014; Perchlik 2014; cf. Weiss 2014), others claimed the film was an anti-Christian affront to Christian doctrines and values (Little Light Studios 2015; Newsome 2014).

How can we understand these diametrically opposed religious receptions of the same film? Is there actually anything religious in *TLM*? What kind of "religion" would that be?

Instead of looking for Judeo-Christian motifs, as others already have done (see, in this volume, Chapter 6: "The Accursed Second Part: Small-Scale Discourses of Gender and Race in *The LEGO Movie 2*" by Matthias Zick Varul), I will approach *TLM* with three different, yet somewhat merging and overlapping recent perspectives from religious studies. I will start with a discussion of religion and new age spiritualities and then move on to popular culture and religion. Secondly, I will discuss *The LEGO Movie* (*TLM*) (2014) and *The LEGO Movie 2: The Second Part* (*TLM2*) (2019) in light of recent approaches to narrative and fiction from scholars of religion, before I turn to media and theories of mediatization. Thirdly, I will reflect upon how the films' use of humor and play may shed some light on religion in the LEGO Movies. In conclusion, I suggest that in seeking to understand the combination of seriousness and playfulness we find in the LEGO Movies' light puns on and hints to religion, perhaps the best approach is to combine Jolyon Baraka Thomas's concept of "tongue in cheek religion" (2015) with Stig Hjarvard's concept of "banal religion" (2011) and the cultural discourse referred to as "metamodernism." I suggest that this neo-romantic turn, as described by Vermeulen and van den Akker (2010), may further help us grasp some of the "unnoticeable," multilayered and multimorphic "religion" we encounter in the LEGO Universe.

Religion, Secularity and New Age Spiritualities

An overarching paradigm for my approach is the rethinking of the concept of religion itself. As Ingvild Gilhus and Steven Sutcliffe have argued, a concept of religion that includes "new age beliefs and practices has the potential to construct a more complete and dynamic model of 'religion'" (2013, p. 262). As noted above, most of the online responses to *TLM*'s religious symbolism and motifs have been framed by Judeo-Christian theology. From such a perspective, the LEGO Movies can be seen as endorsing a "Christian message," as well as a message for heretical, anti-Christian forces. My approach to religion in *TLM* and *TLM2* as a reflection of contemporary religiosity is not meant to side with either position. Rather, I argue that the very success of LEGO's inclusive "spirituality" is the playfulness and vagueness that open for a range of interpretations. In the transnational, even global, pop-cultural toy and entertainment market LEGO aims for, this is a demanding balancing act that the producers appear to have brought to a charmingly self-conscious perfection.

What, then, do I mean by "new age spiritualities"? I take the term from Gilhus and Sutcliffe (2013), who argue:

The modern concept of "religion" is dependent on the coexistence end even cocreation with the category "secular", which means that religion tends to be an oppositional and pure category (Douglas 1966), and further, to be regarded as more "authentic" precisely to the extent that it is not mixed with other things. In strong contrast, even in opposition, to this ideal and purified category of religion, *new age spiritualities* are inherently composite and amalgamated: they are all mixed up with ideas and practices relating to health, well-being, leisure, relaxation, self-help, training, reading and entertainment. (p. 12, added emphasis).

While religious scholars and sociologists tend to look at institutional religion as the normal way of conceptualizing religion, Gilhus and Sutcliffe (2013) proposed McGuire's "lived religion" as the normal state of religion, which they argue is a category of "religion" that also encompasses new age spiritualities. The importance of this definitional change is evident in how such a new model also renders "insights into the production and distribution of religious representations in modern societies, especially in non-religious sectors" (Gilhus and Sutcliffe 2013, pp. 13–14). They also argued that it is necessary to recognize how Christianity historically has played a role as the "prototype" for conceptualizations of "religion." This has led to a devaluation or more-or-less implicit hierarchization of religion(s) that do not fit the monotheistic, protestant mold.[3] According to Gilhus and Sutcliffe, redefining religion by dismantling the polarization between religion and secularity, on the one hand, and, more importantly, by including new age spiritualities in the category "religion," can help us learn more about not only how religion is *lived*, but also *produced*. From this perspective, in particular, LEGO's products provide interesting material for religious studies.

In scholarship, the relation between the "religious" and the "secular" has often been conceived as a binary pair, as stark oppositions. With new empirical material and new theoretical approaches, such distinctions between the two prove more difficult to uphold. Linda Woodhead (2016) argued that a new and intensified kind of pluralism currently emerges. According to Woodhead, "religious ideas and symbols float free on a scale never seen before, becoming available to any 'seeker.'" She further argued that "religion has leaked into areas of life from which it was temporarily exiled by modern projects" (2016, p. 46). She called this process "a pluralism of religious de-differentiation and deregulation," which eventually makes the distinction between religious and secular meaningless (p. 44). This "leaking" seems to have much in common with Gilhus and Mikaelsson's description of contemporary new age spiritualities as "religion everywhere," and "spread thinly" in culture (2000, cf. Lied 2012; Undheim 2018b, p. 53).

Although culture can be more than religion, religion is always culture (Rothstein 2014). For the humanistic study of religion, there will not be an underlying or transcendent essence of "religion" that is expressed through or in "culture." Rather, religion is embedded in culture, and it ought to be studied from this perspective and in this context. Gilhus (2009) has compared religion and culture's relationship to that of magnesium and nature. Magnesium will never exist in a "pure form," but only in chemical mixtures. In the same way, no "pure religion" can be found in culture. According to Gilhus and Sutcliffe, historical and ideological processes have managed to separate "religious" from "secular" at significant sites in the modern world, but this artificial separation remains unstable (2013, p. 12, cf. Gilhus 2009). The notion of religion as an inextricably bound-up part of culture, where spirituality, religion and secularity blend and remix, leads us to the topic of religion and popular culture.

LEGO, Religion and Popular Culture

The rapidly expanding field that studies religion and popular culture has provided an abundance of new approaches and insights in the productive discourses and inter-relation of religion and culture. For many, the idea of mixing religion and popular culture will appear irreverent, bordering on blasphemous. This is based on an understanding of religion as essentially different and separated from politics and culture, where religion encompasses eternal truths belonging to a superhuman realm beyond what we can perceive in the material world.

While Bruce David Forbes in 2005 wrote about "religion in unexpected places," the fruitful cross-pollination between religion and pop culture has by now become a well-known, well-researched phenomenon. The relation between pop culture and religion works in a large variety of ways, however, all depending on the mix in question, as well as the innumerable kinds of stakes invested.

In LEGO's case, the large diversity of media and platforms also contribute to a dynamic, productive field. Because LEGO primarily aims its products at children, LEGO has perhaps also received less attention from religious scholars than other comparable phenomena with similar transnational reach. With the exception of Bado-Fralick and Norris (2010) and Bado and Norris (2015), the intriguing field of religion and toys has been largely ignored. As interest in religion and gaming enriches the larger field of religion and pop culture, and also religious studies as such (cf. Skjoldli 2017), the LEGO transmedia supersystems—combining actual bricks and toys with digital and mass media entertainment—provide interesting data relevant for the study of religion.

Most of the "themes" promoted on LEGO's Web site appear strictly secular, with no reference to religion. This is unsurprising, considering that LEGO's global market is similar to Disney's, for instance. LEGO's references to religion are strikingly non-specific, with no elements that may be identified as exclusive to any of the so-called World religions.[4] For instance, *TLM2* takes its audience to a post-apocalyptic landscape, fittingly called Apocalypseburg. Picking up a few years after the *TLM* ended, after the Duplo aliens' Taco Tuesday attack on Bricksburg, the inhabitants have rebuilt a rough society in a desert landscape. There, they constantly are under attack by plundering aliens from the Systar System and also face the imminent threat of "Armamageddon" [sic] that may eventually wipe out their existence.

This Universe features "temples" but no churches. Its subtle plays on Armageddons and apocalypses appear to refer not to biblical literature, but to the popular culture canon.[5] Religious vocabulary and references are detached from specific traditions, and are instead part of a free-floating pop-cultural repertoire.

LEGO's contribution to the ongoing and ubiquitous sprinkling of new age spiritualities can be seen in numerous LEGO products, reflecting LEGO's prominent part in a global, pop culture entertainment industry. The animated TV series *LEGO, Legends of Chima*, which still airs on Netflix and various children's television channels, is a good example of this.[6] Other strong examples of LEGO themes that flirt with new age spiritualities are Ninjago, Elves, Harry Potter, Star Wars and Marvel's Superheroes (https://www.LEGO.com/en-us/products/themes, cf. Undheim 2016, 2018a). These sets and their corresponding multimedia presence are firmly placed within fictional worlds, but they play with notions of superhuman entities and forces that to some can be interpreted as spiritual truths (cf. e.g., Davidsen 2016)—as I will discuss in more detail below. The two LEGO Movies, as well as the interactive LEGO Dimensions videogame, break down the boundaries between these LEGO themes or worlds, creating a Universe where characters and references can move freely between "dimensions." The first hint of this multi-universe with different Realms comes in the episode of Ninjago called "Curseworld II," the final episode of season 5. In this episode, Lloyd got the *Realm Crystal* and travelled through some of the Sixteen Realms, or parallel worlds—to the surprise of the Chima inhabitants who saw him fly by.[7] These known as well as unknown "realms" come together in *TLM*'s Cloud Cuckoo Land.

The notion of multiple, yet intersecting realms or worlds has since almost become a trademark of the boundary-breaking playfulness of LEGO's rebranding in the wake of *TLM*'s success. In an endless self-referential, pop-cultural play with everything, not least the well-known monomyth of American cinema, the movie manages to sway even those critical of their business. LEGO thus models and reconfigures itself as the resistance against the very rules and instructions that come with the brick sets. The movie turns into a celebration of creativity, adventure and play and of breaking the rules and opposing dogmatism. This exuberance of fun, thrill, puns and excitement is indeed what seems to have become LEGO's success recipe, which spilled over into the feature-length *The LEGO Batman Movie* and *The LEGO Ninjago Movie*, both of which were released in 2017.

Narrative

In his 2004 article on the mediatization of LEGO, Hjarvard identified narrativization as one of three intertwined processes that sparked LEGO's Phoenix-like rise in the early 2000s, after having verged on economic disaster. According to Hjarvard, narrativization describes the process where the focus in playing with LEGO shifted. From primarily having the focus on brick as tools to build with, the resulting constructions were now meant to be part of fictional narratives. Narrativization is intricately tied to the simultaneous process of imaginarization. According to Hjarvard, during the 1970s and 1980s, the thematic universes LEGO promoted moved away from "the real word." Although not completely replaced, these "real world" LEGO sets were gradually supplied with an increasing number of fantasy universes, inspired by fictional worlds circulated by popular media. Space travelers, pirates, Indians and knights provided new LEGO worlds. Combined with narrativization, the LEGO play no longer just indicated building with blocks, or construction work, but also the enactment of various narratives in these fictional worlds. The third process Hjarvard tied to mediatization of LEGO was virtualization, which entailed LEGO's increasingly availability in digital form, as video games or in digital communities. This mediatization thus explains LEGO's development from a construction toy to a global, multimedia brand.

Hjarvard's theories on LEGO's mediatization shed even more light on this topic when they are combined with his later theories about mediatization of religion. For the sake of this discussion, the term "banal religion" (Hjarvard 2011) is most relevant to understanding the processes in which popular culture represents, reproduces and disseminates religion.[8] Hjarvard underlined that by "banal religion," he did not mean one that is inferior or unimportant compared to other kinds of religion. Of particularly interest is the media's role as an agent in the actual (re-)production and spread of religion:

> The iconography and liturgical practices of both institutionalised religions and folk religions become stockpiles for the media's own production of factual and fictional stories about the world. In this way, the media distribute banal religious elements that may or may not be integrated into more coherent narratives with more explicit religious meanings. (Hjarvard 2011, p. 128)

One of the strengths of this kind of religion lies, according to Hjarvard, "in the ability to create representations that arrest attention, evoke emotions and support memory" (2011, p. 130). The affective power of narrative, particularly when narrated by multimodal media, is thus an important aspect—one I will return to in the conclusion.

Narrative has always been an important aspect of religious studies. Whereas "sacred texts" and mythology have held a special role, the field now shows an increasing interest in exploring the relationship between narrative, fiction and religion. A special issue of *Religion* was, for instance, dedicated to the topic in 2016, illustrating some of the compelling questions this field now addresses. To assist in the further discussion of *TLM* and *TLM2*, I will highlight two articles from this special issue.

Firstly, in her article about Harry Potter and religion, Laura Feldt (2016) pointed out how both J.K. Rowling and Philip Pullman's books have appealed to progressive Christians as well as spiritual seekers. Feldt argued,

> The popularity of supernatural narratives today suggests the wider importance of including communication about supernatural beings and powers, actions and domains, religiously tinged titillating entertainment, and emotions in our discussions of religion to a greater extent. (p. 551)

For our purposes, one of Feldt's most significant finds is how the fictional narratives

> reflect attitudes to religion as something to be explored freely, and as focused on pragmatic, material concerns, on entertainment, experimenting and playing with the religious and religion, in an atmosphere that recognises the validity and co-presence of multiple interpretations of other planes of reality. (p. 567)

In other words, fantasy fiction opens the potential for individual creativity and experimental play, by bringing in the element of other "realms" and something beyond the conceived reality of everyday life.

Dirk Johannsen's (2016) article in the same special issue highlighted how "the fantastic is defined by structural ambiguity: it is a literary genre which offers two conflicting interpretations of the described events, two options for the story's 'true genre'" (p. 591). He demonstrated how the introduction of the modern project in Scandinavian literature at the end of the nineteenth century sparked controversies over the relationship between religion and literature that lasted several decades. According to Johannsen (2016), this led to a reconfiguration of religion, where folk traditions and the fantastic could seemingly paradoxically provide freethinkers with means to oppose to the rigid rules of the modern project, and at the same time maintain the modern project's reaction against institutionalized Christian hegemony (pp. 592–593). Most relevant to our discussion of LEGO, Johannsen pointed out how novelists in this period came to see religion as a matter of choice, rather than truth. He identified an "ontological tension" (p. 593) as having emerged in this period. By including an element of doubt in the narrative structure, it is possible to introduce the supernatural, in these cases closer to folklore and fantasy than traditional "religion," "as *one* interpretation" (Johannsen 2016, p. 603). The element of individual choice is thus important for how the reader understands the supernatural elements in the narrative:

> The modernist freethinker stories put flesh on the classical criticism of religion and the subsequent reductive theorizing. Where ontological

naturalism had exposed the freethinker to an existence without meaning, and, later on, to an uncontrollable mind, he was left to believe in his own poetic imagination. In literature, the criticism of religion became religiously productive. (Johannsen 2016, p. 606)

Emmet as "The American Superhero"

Joseph Campbell is probably the American religious studies scholar who has had the most impact outside the Academy. Through his Jungian-inspired comparative mythology and phenomenological approach, Campbell struck a chord in Hollywood, particularly through George Lucas's interpretation of the hero's journey plotline in the first *Star Wars* trilogy.[9] In their book *The Myth of the American Superhero*, Robert Jewett and John Shelton Lawrence (1977) noted the importance of Joseph Campbell's presentation of the monomyth of the hero's journey. Although they identified a slightly different plot that they argue provided an easily-recognized framework for narrative structure in American popular culture, particularly in movies, it nevertheless shares many similarities with Campbell's putative universal hero.

> A community in a harmonious paradise is threatened by evil: normal institutions fail to contend with this threat, a selfless superhero emerges to renounce temptation and carry out the redemptive task: aided by fate, his decisive victory restores the community to its paradisal condition: the superhero then recedes into obscurity. (Jewett and Lawrence 1977, p. xx)

The constant reiterations of the monomyth, which can be (and often is) read as a version of the Christian salvation story, also reinforces the paradigm of how the story has to be told. *TLM's* remixing of the monomyth is perhaps most evident in its opening scene and in the prophecy theme that follows Emmet as "The Special." All the rules of storytelling are cynically broken, however, when Vitruvius dies as he's about to explain the prophecy. But because this is an alternative realm—because this is fiction, or LEGO, or even because it is true—what can happen is unlimited. When the situation is at its bleakest, and all hope seems lost, Vitruvius returns as a ghost to deliver his message:

Vitruvius: Emmet!

Emmet: Who said that?

Vitruvius: I did. I am ghost Vitruvius. [Vitruvius makes a ghostly "woo" sound.] Emmet, — you didn't let me finish earlier… because I died. The reason I made up the prophecy was because I knew that whoever found the piece could become the Special, because the only thing anyone needs to be special is to believe that you can be. I know that sounds like a cat poster, but it's true. Look at what you did when you believed you were special. You just need to believe it some more.

Emmet: How can I just decide to believe that I'm special, when I'm not?

Vitruvius: Because the world depends on it. [Vitruvius exits, making cartoonish "woo-woo" ghost sounds]

The scene plays on almost all the monomyth clichés we recognize from popular culture, from *Harry Potter* and *Star Wars* to *The Prince of Egypt* (think of Mariah Carey and Whitney Houston's hit, "When You Believe"). The well-known message is: Belief is all that is needed, alongside a heroic willingness to self-sacrifice for the community and a greater good. Only when the hero is willing to die will there be salvation.

The extra layer in *TLM* is, of course, that all this happens in a world imagined by an 8-year-old boy. The self-consciously left-unanswered question is thus: Does that make the story more, or less, true—like a motivational "Believe" cat poster hanging on the wall?

Religion and Play

In recent years, scholars have become increasingly interested in the role of play in the human and cultural production of religion. As Brent S. Plate (2010) underlined, "Games, and religions, are as much about creating ever-new worlds as they are conquering others" (p. 225). Like Plate, Carole Cusack also has applied the theories of John Huizinga from *Homo Ludens* to explain why fiction-based and so-called invented religions should be studied as religions. According to Cusack, "Invented religions also view fictions, the ludic and play as legitimate sources of ultimate meaning [...]" (2013, p. 371). She concluded that invented religions—a category that includes Wicca,[10] Disconcordianism, Church of All Worlds, Jediism and Matrixism, among others—should be seen as the authentic religious manifestations of our age. Significant sites of meaning-making, they combine play and seriousness. Nothing except their evidently fictional basis makes them different from other kinds of religion (p. 375). Fiction and play are thus brought to the fore as necessary to understand current changes in the religious landscape. Unlike Cusack and Plate, however, who focused on fiction as a source for religious communities' formation and practice (cf. also Davidsen 2012, 2016), in the case of *TLM*, *TLM2* and other LEGO transmedia products (including Ninjago, Elves and Chima), play's relevance lies mainly in narratives, concepts and ideas, and less in the ritual and social aspects of religion.[11] Although playing with brick sets is also part of the (trans-)mediatization of LEGO (cf. Undheim 2018a), the narrative imagination opens up the playful approach to religion in the first place.

In the book *Drawing on Tradition*, Jolyon Baraka Thomas (2012) points out:

Play—like religion—often relies on ideation of other worlds, frequently involves submission top imagined strictures and rules, and furthermore features imputations of particular potency to certain agents and attributions of unique significance to specific events. (p. 17)

Thomas demonstrates how anime and manga producers and audiences alike participate in processes that recreate religion, writing: "In some cases, the verisimilitude of fictive worlds – regardless of their fidelity to formal religious cosmologies – is so entirely convincing that that figments become facts and chimera incarnate" (2012, p. 155). This seems similar to the creative processes Lynn Schofield Clark (2003) noted when she interviewed American teenagers and their families about their TV habits. She discovered that what they watched on TV influenced and reinforced the informants' conceptualization of whether or not there are superhuman agents[12] with relevance to their lives, and how, and with what kind of relevance. For example, while some of her participants found comfort in representations of guardian angels in *Touched by an Angel*, others were more intrigued by the *X-Files* and

Buffy the Vampire Slayer. This returns us to the mediatization processes Hjarvard described, where the media produces banal religion

"All Puns Are Intended, My Friend. Intended by God."[13]

Though in other settings combining humor with religion can cause trouble, humor is a central pop culture element in the LEGO Movies. In her book *Laughing Gods, Weeping Virgins*, Gilhus (1997) noted that in the recreated "Eastern" spirituality of the "West," the "laughter of the holy men of the East is seen as a token of their self-realization and liberation. We want to share the joke to receive part of their supposed superhuman knowledge" (p. 122). Laughter resulting from some esoteric or superhuman insight has its very own appeal, perhaps reminiscent of the sometimes-cryptic intertextuality of dense insider jokes or puns that only a few catch.

Cusack (2010) also has noted the importance of humor, particularly what she finds to be the "confrontational use of humor and irreverence" (p. 146). She argued, "The humorous and irreverent nature of the teachings of many invented religions [...] is closely linked to rebelliousness and to the sensibilities of youth culture, although they may appeal to all ages" (p. 147). Although *TLM's* humor includes a number of puns on religion and spirituality (the prophecy, for instance), it is not irreverent, always cleverly balancing on ambiguity.[14] In this sense, the film's use of humor may be similar to what Thomas identified in his fieldwork in Japan and called "tongue in cheek religion." According to Thomas (2015),

> tongue in cheek religion reflects the anxiety that an outside observer might mistake one's ritual behavior for being "really religious." The practitioner of *tongue in cheek religion* mocks and parodies her ritual activity even as she engages in it. She knows that her actions look devout; she winks at her audience and flaunts this knowledge. Her performed awareness of her behavior distinguishes *her* activity from (what she or others

may see as) the unreflective, sheep-like actions of the pious. This performance allows the practitioner of *tongue in cheek religion* to laugh at religion but do religious stuff anyway. The practitioner of *tongue in cheek religion* is not an adherent. She is never a *follower* of tradition. She irreverently draws on tradition in bright, bold graffiti.

TLM's self-aware, meta-reflective playfulness, particularly in light of the irreverent use throughout of the monomyth as "Hollywood gospel," seems to perfectly balance "tongue in cheek religion" ("The prophecy, I made it up"; "I know it sounds like a cat poster, but it's true"), but it is always good-hearted and ambiguous enough to work either way.

In an interview, Phil Lord and Chris Miller, the (co-)writers/producers/directors behind the two LEGO Movies, demonstrated this ontological tension and the role of humor in solving or easing it (Wilner 2014):

> "What's interesting about LEGO is it's constantly reminding you that it's a facsimile of something else," Miller says. "It's a reproduction of the Taj Mahal or a police car or whatever. That's stimulating to us artistically; I think it'll always be a hallmark of our work. It's real, we're trying to really hook you, and we're trying to convince the audience to invest emotionally in this moment, and then the very next moment we slap everybody and say, 'Just kidding! This is all fake.'"

Returning to *TLM2*, the scene with the so-called Shimmer and Sparkling Spa wonderfully presents the notion of self-awareness and "tongue in cheek." After a number of action-filled scenes, our group of Apocalypseburg heroes arrive at *Planet Sparkles* and *The Palace of Infinite Reflection*, where they are to receive a SPA makeover. Welcomed by the vampire Balthazar and his crew with the greeting "Namaste," an impressed Unikitty exclaims "Ooh! Sounds spiritual!" The self-proclaimed "attractive and non-threatening teen vampire" replies: "It is sooo spiritual!" With an obvious nod to not only the makeup and wellness industry but to the pop-cultural idealization of Vampires as young girls' love interests, the joke self-consciously satirizes its own ambiguity.[15]

Another concept that may clarify this particular use of humor, also in jokes with religious content, is "metamodernism." According to Timotheus Vermeulen and Robin van den Akker (2010), the cultural industry has responded to what we often call "postmodernism" by "increasingly abandoning tactics such as pastiche and parataxis for strategies like myth and metaxis, melancholy for hope, and exhibitionism for engagement" (p. 5). A key term for metamodernism is "oscillation" (Kersten and Wilbers 2018). Vermeulen and van den Akker (2010) stress that this is not an oscillation as balance, but as a wide, swinging pendulum: "Each time the metamodern enthusiasm swings towards fanaticism, gravity pulls it back toward irony; the moment its irony sways toward apathy, gravity pulls it back to enthusiasm" (p. 6). Thus, metamodernism (as quoted by Ceriello 2018) is

> A continuous oscillation, a constant repositioning between attitudes and mindsets that are evocative of the modern and postmodern but are ultimately suggestive of another sensibility that is neither of them. A discourse that negotiates between a yearning for universal truths but also an (a)political relativism, between a desire for sense and a doubt about the sense of it all, between … sincerity and irony, knowingness and naivety, construction and deconstruction. (p. 201)

Linda C. Ceriello (2018) has applied metamodernism's theoretical perspectives to identify and analyze trends among those often grouped as SBNR ("spiritual but not religious"). She highlighted fictionalized representations of "mystical encounters," especially as transmitted through film and television, as sites for self-reflexive negotiations over being secular and spiritual at the same time. Metamodernism can in this regard elucidate what she called the "boundary-blurring ontology" (p. 200), which seems characteristic of SBNR millennials. In a recent YouTube video, Logan Rees (2019) applied metamodernism to explain the success of the movie directors/producers/(co-)writers Lord and Miller, whose filmography includes the LEGO Movies and the Academy Award winning *Spider-Man: Into the Spider-Verse* (2018). According to Rees, because the audience is hyper-aware of Hollywood filmmakers' tropes, Lord and Miller treat their audience as if they're "in the directors' chair with them, in on every joke, and aware of every twist and turn" (4:25–4:33). As Rees (2019) explains,

> As a metamodern audience, we wouldn't have been satisfied if Emmet had just become the special and saved the day,—he had to realize that the prophecy itself was arbitrary but choose to find meaning in it anyway. (5:23–5:33)

As a reaction against the postmodernism's cynicism and sarcasm, metamodernism evokes some of the same reactions of the ontological tensions that Johannsen identified in the literary project of some Norwegian freethinkers' *fin-de-siècle* romanticism. The playful, humoristic, but never mean-spirited mash-up of non-specified, free-floating religious references that already are part of a pop-cultural, globalized repertoire make it possible to balance this tension between satire and sincerity. And the questions thus remain: Is it a Christian message? A spiritual one? Or one that is interfaith? Are we just playing with religion or is this serious? This is all left to the individual viewer to judge. The fact that the symbols and religious references are there, though, entices the viewers own interpretative and creative process. As Thomas (2015) concludes in his reflections on his Japanese material:

> The irreverent humor of *tongue in cheek religion* gives them a chance to play at religion without formally adopting a religious identity. Everybody benefits, and nobody has to be "religious" who does not want to be.

The self-awareness of the tongue in cheek, combined with what Thomas (2015) describes as "just in case religion," captures this neo-romantic strand of metamodernism, and the constant oscillation between sincerity and irony. In a global market, with a potential audience that includes all kind of religious and non-religious affiliations, religion is also potentially dangerous. Institutionalized religions often carry identity markers that stress difference and borders (cf. Undheim 2016, 2017). For a company like LEGO, it is therefore important to avoid religious markers that may spark controversy and upset potential customers. The non-specific, Unikitty-sweet frosting on the Space temple/wedding cake that is built "right at the center of the Universe" is thus more palatable than a "matrimonial ceremony" held in a church. Still, a strand of optimistic romanticism appears when the cynical, eternal Bat-chelor Batman is tricked into falling in love. Unnoticeable, like Hjarvard's banal religion, the references to temples, prophecies, heroes and martyrs are still "religion in the sense that it evokes cognitions, emotions or actions that imply"—or, in this case, perhaps more precisely, play on—"the existence of a supernatural agency" (Hjarvard 2011, p. 128). This vagueness also allows for glocalization in different ways than more religion-specific references would have done.

Can we say that *TLM*, *TLM2* and the LEGO Universe(s) are religious, then? That depends. To some, LEGO can tell the story of Jesus, the son and savior; to others, a story of Moses leading his people to the Promised Land; and to others still, one of a failed, gnostic creator-god. Some may find a message encouraging them to explore unknown realms or to believe in themselves and creating their own worlds. In the spirit of LEGO, how you put the pieces together is up to you.

LEGO's approach to religion is not unique. Popular culture and other toy-brand supersystems have similar tendencies. LEGO's multimedia and global reach make it remarkable and perhaps comparable only to Disney as purveyor and producer of "banal religion" on a global scale. The dominant tendency is indeed absence of religion or secularity. Nevertheless, a non-specific, vague and almost unnoticeable kind of "spiritual secularity" emerges through tongue-in-cheek puns, play and chaotic pop-cultural mash-ups.

And for the question of Vitruvius' prophecy: Is it true, even if it is made up? Or is it just "hippie, dippie baloney," as Lord Business claims? Of course the prophecy can be true, even though it is made up. This brings us back to Cusack's argument: Invented religions are in many ways the most authentic religions of our age. If you ask the Internet, it will happily tell you that the name of our hero, Emmet, is Hebrew for Truth. Is this the true, hidden message of the creators of the movie? Whether it is or not, you can nevertheless choose for yourself what that means to you. You even can be "ironic and sincere at the same time" (Vermeulen and van den Akker 2010),[16] After all, it is a mind game, and you can come and play it, if you choose.

Notes

1. I wish to thank the editors, Sharon R. Mazzarella and Rebecca Hains, for inviting me to write this chapter, and for their generous, patient and very constructive engagement in this process. Some of the theoretical approaches and material I have discussed elsewhere (e.g., Undheim 2016, 2017, 2018a, b). I here build on these previous publications, yet with a focus on new material (two Lego movies) and some new conclusions on how we can understand the relationship between LEGO and contemporary religious change based on these movies in particular. As always, my expert consultants, Magnus and Johannes, deserve great thanks for sharing their knowledge and curiosity with me.
2. A wonderful scene later in the movie juxtaposes Vitruvius with both Gandalf and Dumbledore in some kind of subtle and funny "superior wizard" contest.
3. What Linda Woodhead has called the "inadequacy approach" (2010, cf. Kraft 2014).
4. For a critique of the so-called World Religion paradigm, see, e.g., Cotter and Robertson (2016).
5. For apocalyptical and eschatological discourses in popular culture, see Lied (2012, p. 185; 2017).
6. Even though Chima sets are no longer in productions, the fact that the episodes still air can be seen as an example of the ongoing mediatization of this specific understanding/interpretation of the concept of Chi. For more about this as "religion," see Undheim (2017).
7. In a podcast interview, *Maltin on the Movies*, the writers Phil Lord and Chris Miller credit the Hageman brothers with the idea of "a metauniverse of some kind" (Maltin and Maltin 2019, at approx. 40 minutes). The Hageman brothers, i.e. Dan and Kevin Hageman, wrote almost all the seasons of the TV series *Ninjago*, from 2011 to 2018. They are also credited as screenwriters for *TLM*, together with Phil Lord and Chris Miller. The notion of a multiverse takes a different, but not less interesting turn in Lord and Millers Academy Award winning "*Spider-Man: Into the Spider-Verse.*"
8. For critical evaluations of the concept, and of the "mediatization of religion" theory, see Lövheim (2011) and Lied (2012).
9. "I don't see Star Wars as profoundly religious. I see Star Wars as taking all the issues that religion represents and trying to distill them down into a more modern and easily accessible construct—that there is a

greater mystery out there. [...]. I put the Force into the movie in order to try to awaken a certain kind of spirituality in young people—more a belief in God than a belief in any particular religious system. I wanted to make it so that young people would begin to ask questions about the mystery" (Moyers and Lucas 1999, cf. Campbell 1988, p. xiv). Note now how the ideas of Campbell have resurged in the popular multimedia phenomenon Jordan Peterson (Pothast 2019).

10. In the words of Cusack (2013), "Paganism is important, as it is an invented tradition that has gained a profile as a *bona fide* religion" (p. 371).

11. That does of course not mean that these aspects are irrelevant. Online fan communities are certainly one kind of group formation where the boundaries between fandom and religious devotion may be blurred (cf. e.g., Anker 2017). The production of "commentaries" that are both interpretations and elaborations of the already existing narratives takes on both literary, but also highly multimodal forms, as the endless homemade videos uploaded on YouTube demonstrate.

12. The notion of "superhuman agents," also called "superhuman beings," is a category that encompass gods as well as other intermediary beings such as demons, angels, djinns, elves and monsters (cf. Gilhus 2016).

13. Tweet (Peel 2019) quoting from an interview with Phil Lord and Chris Miller.

14. "We try to avoid any mean-spirited humour and just have it be fun," Miller says. "Just from a psychological standpoint, it's really helpful having films with a joyful message and positivity, so we try to do that with all our movies, really" (Wilner 2014).

15. Cf. Hjarvard (2011, p. 129): "Another example of banal religion is Stephenie Meyer's Twilight series about teenage romance that is centred on encounters with supernatural phenomena such as vampires and werewolves and invested with Christian Puritan beliefs."

16. Jerry Saltz, "Sincerity and Irony Hug It Out," *New Yorker Magazine*, May 27, 2010, quoted in Vermeulen and van den Akker 2010.

References

Anker, T. (2017). Med himmelen som tak Ungdom, religion og fandom. *Prismet, 68*(1–2), 133–148. http://dx.doi.org/10.5617/pri.4771.

Bado-Fralick, N., & Norris, R. S. (2010). *Toying with God: The world of religious games and dolls*. Waco, TX: Baylor University Press.

Bado, N., & Norris, R. S. (2015). Games and dolls. In J. C. Lyden & E. M. Mazur (Eds.), *The Routledge companion to religion and popular culture* (pp. 261–280). New York: Routledge.

Caleb. (n.d.). The Lego Movie is a true story. How to break free from cultures mold! *Gamerfaith*. Blogpost. Retrieved from http://gamerfaith.com/lego-movie-religious/.

Campbell, J. (1988). *The power of myth*. New York: Doubleday.

Ceriello, L. C. (2018). Toward a metamodern reading of spiritual but not religious mysticisms. In W. B. Parson (Ed.), *Being spiritual but not religious past, present, future(s)* (pp. 200–218). New York: Routledge.

Clark, L. S. (2003). *From Angels to Aliens: Teenagers, the media and the supernatural*. New York, NY: Oxford University Press.

Cotter, C. R., & Robertson, D. G. (Eds.). (2016). *After world religions: Reconstructing religious studies*. London: Routledge.

Cusack, C. M. (2010). *Invented religions: Imagination, fiction and faith*. Farnham, UK: Ashgate.

Cusack, C. M. (2013). Play, narrative and the creation of religion: Extending the theoretical base of "invented religions". *Culture and Religion, 14*(4), 362–377. https://doi.org/10.1080/14755610.2013.838797.

Davidsen, M. A. (2012). The spiritual milieu based on J. R. R. Tolkien's literary mythology. In A. Possamai (Ed.), *Brill handbooks on contemporary religion: Vol. 5. Handbook of hyper-real religions* (pp. 185–204). Leiden, The Netherlands: Brill.

Davidsen, M. A. (2016). From Star Wars to Jediism: The emergence of fiction-based religion. In E. van den Hemel & A. Szafraniec (Eds.), *Words. Religious language matters: The future of the religious past* (pp. 376–389). New York: Fordham University Press.

Feldt, L. (2016). Contemporary fantasy fiction and representations of religion: Playing with reality, myth and magic in His Dark Materials and Harry Potter. *Religion, 46*(4), 550–574. https://doi.org/10.1080/0048721x.2016.1212526.

Forbes, B. D. (2005). Introduction: Finding religion in unexpected places. In B. D. Forbes & J. H. Mahan (Eds.), *Religion and popular culture in America* (pp. 1–20). Berkeley, CA: University of California Press.

Gilhus, I. S. Sælid. (1997). *Laughing Gods, weeping virgins: Laughter in the history of religion*. London: Routledge.

Gilhus, I. S. S. (2009). Hva er religion i dag? Religionsbegrep og religionsvitenskap. In A. Bruvoll, H. Bringeland, N. Gilje, & G. Skirbekk (Eds.), *Religion og kultur: Ein fleirfagleg samtale* (pp. 19–31). Oslo: Universitetsforlaget.

Gilhus, I. S. (2016). What became of Superhuman Beings? In P. Antes, A. W. Geertz, & M. Rothstein (Eds.), *Contemporary views on comparative religion: Essays on comparative religion presented to Tim Jensen on the occasion of his 65th birthday* (pp. 375–387). Sheffield: Equinox.

Gilhus, I. S., & Mikaelsson, L. (2000). Multireligiøse aktører og kulturens refortrylling [Multireligious agents and the re-enchantment of culture]. *Sosiologi I Dag, 30,* 3–22.

Gilhus, I. S., & Sutcliffe, S. (2013). Conclusion: New Age spiritualities—"Good to think" in the study of religion. In S. J. Sutcliffe & I. S. Gilhus (Eds.), *New age spirituality: Rethinking religion* (pp. 256–262). Durham, NC: Acumen.

Hjarvard, S. (2004). From bricks to bytes: The mediatization of a global toy industry. In P. Golding & I. Bondebjerg (Eds.), *European culture in the media* (pp. 43–63). Bristol, UK: Intellect Books.

Hjarvard, S. (2011). The mediatisation of religion: Theorising religion, media and social change. *Culture and Religion: An Interdisciplinary Journal, 12*(2), 119–135. https://doi.org/10.1080/14755610.2011.579719.

Jewett, R., & Lawrence, J. S. (1977). *The American monomyth.* Garden City: Anchor Press.

Johannsen, D. (2016). On elves and freethinkers: Criticism of religion and the emergence of the literary fantastic in Nordic literature. *Religion, 46*(4), 591–610. https://doi.org/10.1080/0048721x.2016.1210394.

Kersten, D., & Wilbers, U. (2018). Introduction: Metamodernism. *English Studies, 99*(7), 719–722. https://doi.org/10.1080/0013838x.2018.1510657.

Kraft, S. E. (2014). New Age spiritualities. In J. R. Lewis and J. A Petersen (Eds.), *Controversial new religions* (pp. 302–314). Oxford: Oxford University Press.

Lied, L. I. (2012). Religious change and popular culture: With a nod to the mediatization of religion debate. In S. Hjarvard & M. Løvheim (Eds.), *Mediatization and religion: Nordic perspectives* (pp. 183–201). Göteborg: Nordicom.

Lied, L. I. (2017). *Den som ler (aller) sist... Religion going public.* http://religiongoingpublic.com/no/arkiv/2017/den-som-ler-aller-sist. Accessed on July 10, 2019.

Little Light Studios. (2015, February 11). *The Lego Movie makes God an evil tyrant*. Blogpost. Retrieved from https://www.littlelightstudios.tv/lego-movie-makes-god-evil-tyrant/.

Lövheim, M. (2011). Mediatisation of religion: A critical appraisal. *Culture and Religion: An Interdisciplinary Journal, 12*(2), 153–166. https://doi.org/10.1080/14755610.2011.579738.

Maltin L., & Maltin, J. (2019, January 18). *Interview with Phil Lord and Chris Miller*. Maltin on Movies [Audio podcast]. https://open.spotify.com/show/0Nv1eqfXlU79TuONfQTbpo?si=KXqHTs1wSDO986vOYP4oww. Accessed on July 10, 2019.

Moyers, B., & Lucas, G. (1999). Of myth and men. *Time.* http://content.time.com/time/magazine/article/0,9171,23298,00.html. Accessed on July 10, 2019.

Newsome, K. (2014, February 25). *The Lego Movie: One of the most anti-Christian movies ever*. Blogpost. Retrieved from https://kevennewsome.com/2014/02/25/the-LEGO-movie-one-of-the-most-anti-christian-movies-ever/.

O'Neil, T. (2014, February 26). 5 ways "The Lego Movie" hints at a Christian worldview. *The Christian Post.* https://www.christianpost.com/news/5-ways-the-lego-movie-hints-at-a-christian-worldview.html. Accessed on July 10, 2019.

Peel, J. [@jeremy_peel] (2019, February 17). *All puns are intended, my friend. Intended by God.* @philiplord on this excellent podcast. https://twitter.com/jeremy_peel/status/1097126252341809152. Accessed on July 10, 2019.

Perchlik, T. M. (2014, May 2). *Lego Movie theology*. Rev. Thomas Perchlik's Weblog. Blogpost. https://thomasperchlik.wordpress.com/2014/05/02/lego-movie-theology/. Accessed on July 10, 2019.

Plate, B. (2010). Religion is playing games: Playing video Gods, playing to play. *Religious Studies and Theology, 29*(2), 215–230. https://doi.org/10.1558/rsth.v29i2.215.

Pothast, E. (2019, March 22). The barely hidden flaws in Jordan Peterson's scholarship. *Medium.* https://medium.com/s/story/jordan-peterson-is-a-very-poor-researcher-whose-own-sources-contradict-his-claims-464633558b75?fbclid=IwAR1VILU2Lv0_M96ykisJzWPb4HJX3My0aP-oyY0tAfbQse7LKTpaHJJ7Yac. Accessed on July 10, 2019.

Rees, L. (2019, April 3). *How Lord & Miller make Bad Movies good | Spider-Verse analysis*. Fandom Entertainment. https://www.youtube.com/watch?v=smmmnpmUZ0Y. Accessed on July 10, 2019.

Rothstein, M. (2014). Religion, ikke-religion, hyper-religion. *Dīn. Tidsskrift for religion og kultur, 1,* 134–155. http://ojs.novus.no/index.php/DIN/article/view/721. Accessed on July 10, 2019.

Skjoldli, J. (2017). *World Youth Day: Religious interaction at a Catholic festival.* Unpublished PhD, University of Bergen.

Thomas, J. B. (2012). *Drawing on tradition: Manga, anime, and religion in contemporary Japan.* Honolulu: University of Hawaii Press.

Thomas, J. B. (2015). Tongue in cheek, just in case. *Sacred Matters Magazine.* https://sacredmattersmagazine.com/tongue-in-cheek-just-in-case/. Accessed on July 10, 2019.

Undheim, S. (2016). Spiritual Lego: Temples, rituals and New Age in Ninjago and Chima. In A.-V. Kärjä (Ed.), *Holy crap! Intersections of the popular and the sacred in youth cultures* (pp. 48–58). Helsinki, Finland: International Institute for Popular Culture.

Undheim, S. (2017). The sacred power of Lego-Chi: Mediatized spirituality in "Lego, Legends of Chima". *Young: Nordic Journal of Youth Research, 25*(1), 66–86. https://doi.org/10.1177/1103308816668921.

Undheim, S. (2018a, June 8). Magical bricks: Religion, spirituality and modern magic in the toy box. *Religion Going Public.* http://religiongoingpublic.com/archive/2018/magical-bricks-religion-spirituality-and-modern-magic-in-the-toy-box. Accessed on July 10, 2019.

Undheim, S. (2018b). Lego-religion in the classroom: The potential use of children's popular culture in the teaching of religion and ethics. *Zeitschrift für Religionskunde - Revue de didactique des sciences des religions, 6,* 52–66. http://religionskunde.ch/images/Ausgaben_ZFRK/Rubriken/2018_06_3_Undheim_ZFRK_6-2018.pdf. Accessed on July 10, 2019.

Vermeulen, T., & van den Akker, R. (2010). Notes on metamodernism. *Journal of Aesthetics Culture, 2*(1), 1–14. https://doi.org/10.3402/jac.v1i0.5677.

Weiss, J. (2014, February 12). Underlying religious themes in "The Lego Movie" take viewers on wild, mythic ride. *Huffington Post.* https://www.huffpost.com/entry/lego-movie-religious-themes_n_4775830. Accessed on July 10, 2019.

Wilner, N. (2014, February 6). Philip Lord and Chris Miller: How to build a different kind of Toy story. *Now.* https://nowtoronto.com/movies/features/phil-lord-and-christopher-miller/. Accessed on July 10, 2019.

Woodhead, L. (2016). Intensified religious pluralism and de-differentiation: The British example. *Society, 53,* 41–46. https://doi.org/10.1007/s12115-015-9984-1.

Woodhead, L. (2010). Real religion and fuzzy spirituality? Taking sides in the sociology of religion. In S. Aupers & D. Houtman (Eds.), *Religions in modernity: Relocating the sacred to the self and the digital* (pp. 31–48). Leiden: Brill.

6

The Accursed Second Part: Small-Scale Discourses of Gender and Race in *The LEGO Movie 2*

Matthias Zick Varul

The LEGO Movie (2014; hereafter *TLM*) is a cultural phenomenon in many respects. As a uniquely successful combination of blockbuster family movie and extended commercial for the LEGO product range, *TLM* cross-franchised the movie industry, from *Lord of the Rings* to *Harry Potter* and, above all, the Marvel Universe. It rejuvenated the LEGO brand by dramatizing the tension between the basic principle of freely recombining generic bricks and ever-more detailed and scripted building sets in a self-deprecating way, getting away with freely helping itself to fans' ideas (Goggin 2018). It also made a political statement, which was often mistaken for an outright anti-capitalist critique by reviewers both sympathetic and, like *Fox News*, otherwise. Since its release in 2014, *TLM* gained further significance because it inadvertently anticipated the rise of a wall-building, big-business rogue to the US presidency. In hindsight, *TLM*'s main conflict is clear: It is neither pro- nor contra-capitalism in its politics, but, rather, presents liberal-creative capitalism against authoritarian racket capitalism (Varul 2018).

M. Z. Varul (✉)
Rottenburg, Germany

© The Author(s) 2019
R. C. Hains and S. R. Mazzarella (eds.), *Cultural Studies of LEGO*,
https://doi.org/10.1007/978-3-030-32664-7_6

While the first movie dealt with the liberal fear of dictatorial order, *The LEGO Movie 2: The Second Part* (hereafter *TLM2*) addresses the mirror fear of chaos. The latter was not just what drove the movie's villain Lord Business' irrational quest for absolute order. (His evil project was to use super-glue to freeze the neatly compartmentalized and orderly LEGO worlds/sets in a moment of perfection.) Fear of chaos is also the more deeply seated fear that has accompanied liberal-bourgeois society from the Enlightenment onward (Schumacher 1972), making it a mainstay of its cultural diet from the gothic novel to the apocalyptic disaster movie.

The first movie's cliff-hanger ending suggests that it is the latter genre that the sequel will adopt. The story of *TLM2* unfolds as follows: Aliens from the Planet Duplo have technologically evolved and now engage in sustained attacks on Bricksburg from their home constellation, the Systar System, which is centered around a temple and governed by the shape-shifting Queen Watevra Wa'nabi. These attacks create a *Mad Max*-like scenery of destruction and desolation. In the general atmosphere of doom, only the hero of the first movie, Emmet Brickowski, has maintained his positive outlook, still listening to the song "Everything Is Awesome" on his portable. His companion Lucy, who has reverted to her previous streetfighter persona of Wyldstyle, nags him about his lack of "grit" while he presents her with a family home that he has created for the two of them, which an alien attack destroys shortly after. Led by General Sweet Mayhem, who unlike the characters from *TLM* is not a minifigure, but rather a mini-doll, an alien commando abducts Lucy and a sample of other Bricksburgers, including Batman. Enraged, Emmet finally develops the grit he so far lacked and sets out in hot pursuit. Meanwhile, Queen Watevra Wa'nabi tries to convince the abductees that her actual aim is peace between the Systar System and Bricksburg. She reveals that she in fact admires the Bricksburgers and intends to seal the peace by marrying Batman. She manages to convince all the abductees except Lucy.

On his rescue mission, Emmet gets into trouble before reaching the Systar System, but Rex Dangervest saves him. Rex is a hypermasculine space-hero modeled on *Jurassic World*'s Owen Grady while also heavily referencing Indiana Jones and other cinematic heroes, and Emmet tries to be more like him—an effort that Dangervest actively encourages. The two join forces to destroy the Systar System's central temple, hoping to prevent the marriage Batman has been talked into by Queen Watevra, since they assume it is a ritualistic device to trigger the final apocalypse. Lucy, who managed to escape, joins them, but soon discovers that Watevra's intentions are sincere after all and that her aim is indeed peace and harmony. However, she cannot prevent Emmet from using the techniques of destruction he has learned from Rex Dangervest to smash the temple. This act then actually does trigger "Armamageddon" [sic!]—which, it turns out, was precisely what Dangervest had intended from the outset. In the end, Lucy and Emmet manage to eliminate Rex Dangervest, who in a last twist outs himself as Emmet's time-traveling future self. When Emmet chooses not to adopt his destructive persona but to remain true to himself (and Lucy), Rex dissolves into thin air, and the apocalypse is averted.

The first movie's most surprising twist came when it turned out that the animated action of the LEGO figurines was but a reflection of a live-action plot about a LEGO-set-collecting businessman and his son, Finn, who interferes with his father's intricate creations. In the second movie, the twist has become a premise. The audience already knows that the animated action is allegorical (which, by the way, justifies reading both of the movies as veritable morality plays[1]). The father causes the above-mentioned cliff-hanger ending when he allows not only Finn access to the LEGO bricks in the basement, but also Finn's preschool-aged little sister, Bianca. Just as Finn did with his father's LEGO sets, Bianca interferes with Finn's creations, which plays out as an invasion of monsters made of Duplo blocks (LEGO's preschool line) at the end of the first movie. In the second movie, the children are a little older and also play with LEGO mini-dolls, found in a number of LEGO's girl-oriented sets. (See also Chapter 11, "'I Just Don't Really, Like, Connect to It': How Girls Negotiate LEGO's Gender-Marketed Toys," by Hains and Shewmaker in this volume for more detail on mini-dolls and girl-oriented LEGO sets.) The ensuing LEGO/Duplo/Minidoll war of the worlds results from the siblings' constant bickering and, mainly, Finn's destructive behavior toward Bianca. The real-life cause of *Armama*geddon is their mother having had enough and ordering all the LEGO parts to be dissembled and put away in boxes in the basement. The final reconciliation is manifested by brother and sister building a hybrid LEGO/Duplo city out in the sunny garden of their seemly suburban home and Finn being more supportive toward and sharing with his little sister.

On the "ideological" level, it might at first appear that the film is mainly concerned with gender relations and a critique of aggressive masculinity. Most reviewers take this message as so obvious they do not spell it out. For example, Simran Hans (2019) in the British *Guardian* talks of a "placid moral message" about sibling harmony, while Manohla Dargis (2019) in the *New York Times* notes, "There's a tidy message here: Be nice to your kid sister, which is supernice advice especially because the movie was produced, directed and written almost entirely by men." Possibly assuming *USA Today* readers need a more concrete explanation, Brian Truitt (2019) elucidates:

> Apocalypseburg is a manly Lego "Mad Max" wasteland come to life, while Watevra's landscape and Planet Duplo have a girl-friendly vibe, and new characters wonder why Lucy's heroism has taken a backseat to Emmet's. Batman's testosterone-riddled personality, like in his spinoff flick, also is mocked: One tune is all about how Gotham City doesn't spawn great boyfriends.

Against this first impression, in this chapter, I argue that the "message" is not unambiguously clear: Just as in the first movie, Emmet as the male "Chosen One" again appropriates Lucy's achievements and integrates them into his own agency. And just as in the first movie, in the end, Lucy's inescapably stereotypical feminine inner nature is "revealed." As I will demonstrate, the movie's message is a call for a more empathic and liberal attitude toward gender difference, but not for equality. Further, I will argue that, in its subtext, the movie also conducts a discourse on race in which, in the figurine of Watevra, gender stereotypes are merged with racialized ones. Against this background, Emmet's character development emerges as a straightforward "white savior" plotline (Vera and Gordon 2003). Finally, I will make the case that what we are presented with in the guise of a harmlessly trivial family entertainment doubles as an everyday-metaphysical statement concretizing cosmological-anthropological foundation myths from *TLM*, slating into the continuity of ideological reworkings of European masculinities, balancing middle-class existence as Becoming between Chaos and absolute Being. The *Second Part* as Batailleian *part maudite* therein refers to the amorphous, threatening other of the middle-class male white self—anxieties assuaged by way of minimalization and cuteification.

The means to achieve this remarkable feat range from "the bleedin' obvious" to the very subtle. An example for the former would be the happy ending, with aerial shots of the large middle-class home containing the now-content nuclear family after sibling harmony is restored without a serious challenge to gender roles. An example of the latter is how the Lutheran symbol of the heart is used to juggle cultural references from the deep racism of Joseph Conrad's (1997) *Heart of Darkness* (Achebe 1977) to social-conservative concerns for balance of family and business life in *The Habits of the Heart* (Bellah et al. 1985), ending in the most literal and probably also most painless heart attack of movie history.

Gender: Restoring the Habits of the Heart

Right at the start, *TLM2* denounces the first movie's domestication of female protagonist Wyldstyle back into Lucy—turning from a battle-hardened, assertive Gothamian into a vulnerable, emotionally dependent LEGO Friends-type girl. Before abducting Lucy to the Systar System, General Sweet Mayhem exposes how Emmet, by sheer luck, received all the credit for the first movie's happy ending, while she, Lucy, did all the fighting, constructing and thinking for him. Lucy tries to defend Emmet's record, but for obvious reasons fails miserably. In the sequel, Emmet starts off as the useless parasite on female work that he is, while Lucy recovers her streetwise confidence in confronting the challenges of post-apocalyptical life.

Further, with Rex Dangervest as villain, the film denounces toxic masculinity. In Rex's last attempt to bring Emmet into line with traditional machoism, the film ridicules the conspiracy discourse of the ultra-misogynic "pickup artists": Rex asks Emmet to stay outside *The Matrix*—a reference to the "pickup artists'" blue-pill/red-pill rhetoric. Rex is subsequently deleted in a combination of a quaintly literal "heart attack" and remorseful insight: When Lucy launches one of the Systar System's heart-shaped missiles at him, he acknowledges his defeat and even expresses relief that Emmet is to grow up into someone better than him.

But despite all this, the second movie manages to repeat the taming-of-the-shrew of the first, this time in fact blaming female attitudes for Emmet's detour through hypermasculinity. The film implies that Lucy's nagging about his need "to get tough" and "battle-ready," her going on about "grittiness," is what makes him susceptible to Rex Dangervest's proposals. As he learns that violence and smashing up things increase (or rather establish) his sexual attractivity to Lucy, he undergoes a development from boyhood to manhood by way of participation in war, which alters the relation to our central symbol here, the heart. As Tina Modelski (1991, p. 62) illustrates with reference to a key scene in Stanley Kubrick's 1987 *Full Metal Jacket*: "When Rafter Man, the Mama's boy turned gung-ho killer, critically wounds the young female sniper, he boasts, 'Am I a heart-breaker, am I a life-taker?'" Modelski argues that this scene is emblematic of how cinematic representation firmly intertwines "activities of breaking hearts and taking lives—that is, sexual domination and wartime aggression" (p. 62). In *TLM*, Emmet shows no such manifestation of masculinity, as he is not involved in physical combat—unlike Batman, who is admired by his then-girlfriend Wyldstyle. The relation is possessive, which emerges when Batman more or less gifts her to Emmet, illustrating the "ideological workings of a system in which women, far from being in a position to *give* the gifts, *are* the gifts, 'indispensable intermediaries' between men" (Modelski 1991, p. 48). Subsequently, it is due to Lucy as transmitter of expectations as to what constitutes a "real man" (namely being capable of violence toward objects and people) that Emmet comes under pressure to justify Batman's gift by adjusting to those expectations. After all, according to Marcel Mauss' classical 1924 essay on the gift, which names both military services and women as integral parts of a *"système de prestations totals"* (Mauss 1950, p. 151), the gift carries the giver's spirit and forces a return from the recipient by the power resting in the gifted object. In this context, Lucy's martial capacities can be understood to be inculcated by her relationship to Batman and not intrinsic to her personality—a mere surface, just like her leather jacket and black hair dye.

After being ridiculed for not being a real man by Sweet Mayhem and driven by Lucy's disappointment, Emmet falls for Rex Dangervest's proposition to transmogrify into ... Rex Dangervest. Rex also seems driven by sensitivities vis-à-vis women in arms, the fear of the castrating *Flintenweib* Klaus Theweleit (1987) detects in the writings of the fascist militiamen of interwar Germany. Presenting Wyldstyle as constantly tense and enervated, the movie seems to buy into the notion that unlike men, women cannot be at ease with being forceful—that is, that she had unnaturally adopted a masculine role. The statement is repeated when General Sweet Mayhem, who herself turns out to have adopted a military persona out of character, tells Lucy: "You care – I knew there was some sweetness under that darkness."

Throughout this transformation, Emmet manages to keep the audience on his side. *TLM2* achieves this by utilizing what Goggin (2018) has analyzed as LEGO's "power of cuteness." Even more than his templates from live-action movies, Emmet/Rex gets away with it by still being the little boy underneath, underlined by a cultivated immaturity in all matters not to do with fighting or technology. Chris Pratt (giving voice to both Emmet and Rex) has proven an apt carrier for this "charming" combination of physical and sexual prowess and emotional vulnerability that makes him needy for female support (e.g., when having dad-issues as Peter Quill in *Guardians of the Galaxy 2*). Interestingly, too, Emmet is not completely cleansed of the toxically masculine side of the Rex Dangervest persona after the latter's demise. Dangervest may not be actualized as Emmet's future self, but by implication, he remains a potential version of Emmet, a dormant option, an implicit threat. In the closing scenes, Emmet forgiving Lucy for her nagging as he himself just triggered Armamageddon is an instance of what Ben Pitcher (2013) has called the "cultural politics of being a knob": the hypermasculine (and racist, as I describe below) tendencies play out under the premise that, in our day and age, they cannot be meant seriously and hence must be excused as ironic by default.

Also, a closer look at Emmet's pre-masculinist stage shows that, from the outset, he is not at all written as a feminist new man. When Emmet guides Lucy through his vision of domestic bliss, which he set up by building a suburban home for the two of them outside Apocalypseburg, he narrates: "Living room [...], dining room, TV room, Planty's room and Kitty-cat room" and also shows her porch with the inevitable double-decker porch swing: spaces for leisure and relaxation. But there are conspicuous absences: no room implying housework, such as a kitchen or pantry; Lucy will have discovered these in the rebuild by now. Here, and even more clearly on the level of real-life behind the LEGO world, the movie takes for granted conventional ideas about the division of labor in the modern nuclear family, particularly the still-dominant notion that women are singularly suited to child care and, because of that, also to domestic chores and especially food work (e.g., Began et al. 2008). In the parallel world of *TLM2*'s real Family, whose meta-story plays out in the LEGO world, we find a 1950s-model nuclear family, which the Father summarizes by calling to the Mother: "Honey, where are my pants?"—the origin of *TLM*'s running gag in Bricksburg's popular pre-apocalyptic sitcom revealed. When bell hooks (1984, p. 103) emphasizes the importance of "revolutionary parenting," it is partly because men as boys, unlike girls, have not been taught to do housework. Unable to look after themselves, they rely on techniques to invite and exploit mothering from women.

To fulfill this latter role, in *TLM2*, Wyldstyle again reverts into Lucy—which had been disclosed as her real name in *TLM* (significant also as the name given to the oldest female human skeleton found—a link Luc Besson's 2014 film *Lucy* makes explicitly). In the sequel, her streetfighter persona begins to crumble when her original turquoise-pink lollipop hair is revealed (implying Finn had coated it black with permanent marker to make her more compatible with his set of figurines). She finally collapses when she admits that she was in the band that recorded "Everything is Awesome," the happy song which she subsequently had come to loathe.

Hence the ridicule Emmet is exposed to is a ruse. *TLM2* is deeply committed to precisely the nuclear-family model which generations of sociology students have been taught to dismiss: that outlined by Talcott

Parsons (1956). Here men and women, husbands and wives, fathers and mothers are conceptualized (counterfactually) as equal in power (especially vis-à-vis the children, as can be seen by the authority Real Mother exerts over the two warring siblings, making them box up their beloved toys). But they are differentiated by function: Men are "instrumentally" orientated toward the outside world, i.e., economic work and business, while women are "expressively" orientated toward stabilizing the harmony of family life. *Plus ça change*—both in Hollywood's and LEGO's suburbias, such as the world of LEGO Friends (for the latter, see Johnson 2014).

The moral of the story in terms of gender relations, then, seems to be that Lucy should have accepted Emmet's vision for her as inhabitant of the LEGO Friends universe (which the other abductees happily bought into when introduced to the Edenic suburbia in the outskirts of the Systar System). Her revelation occurs when she, after combat, saves General Mayhem, who turns out to be the all-American woman on a mission to reconcile the masculine Bricksburg and the feminine Systar System—an allegorical moral quest to preserve the habits of the American heart.

According to Robert Bellah and his co-authors of the 1985 sociological bestseller *Habits of the Heart*, those habits, formed in the nineteenth century, were still largely endorsed by the time of writing (Bellah et al. 1985). They had, however, become problematic not just because of (but as they admit in their view *also* because of) the rise of feminism, which increased participation of women in the labor market, but also because of a crisis of values which leads to "lack of fit between the present organization of the self and the available organization of work, intimacy, and meaning" (p. 47). In this respect, *The LEGO Movie 2* works as psychological relief. The suggestion is one of social conservatism focusing on conventional domestic life and burdening women with the mission of holding male individualism in check. According to *Habits of the Heart*, nineteenth- and twentieth-century American clergymen

saw the future of a free society dependent on the nurturing of family mores, passed on to children by mothers and exerted by wives to restrain husbands. (Bellah et al. 1985, p. 88)

This moral agenda from the nineteenth century, now taken up by the twenty-first-century blockbuster, in effect calls for a tempering of feminism to protect the family sphere as expressive-individualistic counterweight to the utilitarian-individualistic business sphere:

> One resolution would be to see that the obligations traditionally associated with "woman's sphere" are human obligations that men and women should share. There is anxiety, not without foundation, among some of the opponents of feminism, that the equality of women could result in complete loss of the human qualities long associated with "woman's sphere." (p. 111)

TLM2 embraces this project based on notions of femininity as defined by the dated social psychology of the mid-twentieth century. The "nod to gender parity" mentioned in the *Los Angeles Times* review (Chang 2019) is a nod and a wink to contained-yet-sustained male privilege.

Anti-conquest: Brightening Up the Heart of Darkness

Unlike the gender theme, *TLM2*'s racialized discourse is not immediately obvious. But by the mere fact that it takes part in the space-invasion genre, it cannot help commenting on the fear of the racialized Other. As John Rieder (2005) shows, in alien invasion plots, the theme of "race" is all but inevitable against the background of colonial history:

> For enslavement, plague, genocide, environmental devastation, and species extinction following in the wake of invasion by an alien civilization with vastly superior technology—all of these are not products of the fevered imaginations of science fiction writers but rather the bare historical record of what happened to non-European people and lands after being "discovered" by Europeans and integrated into the capitalist world economy from the fifteenth century to the present. (p. 373f.)

The system broken up by the revolt of brickolarians in *TLM* was precisely what Frantz Fanon (2002) in his 1961 *Les damnés de la terre* identified as a fundamental reality of colonialism, namely "*un monde compartimenté*," a compartmentalized world. Now that the walls are torn down (in the movie, not in the real world), the pent-up anger of the colonized and excluded may turn against the metropolis. The monsters from Planet Duplo who invade Bricksburg in the closing scene of *TLM* (announcing "We're here to destroy you") represent Finn's little sister, Bianca, who had also been newly permitted access to the Father's LEGO collection in the basement. Historically, Europeans have infantilized and feminized colonized Africans to construct whiteness as adult masculinity, a pattern continued in post-colonial commodity racism (e.g., Auerbach 2002). In reverse conclusion, *TLM2* excludes the female infant by racializing her through her avatar in the LEGOverse.

The leader of the invaders, the shape-shifting Queen Watevra Wa'nabi, is the only main character with an immediately recognizable, emphatically Black voice.[2] From the beginning, she is racialized along the lines through which classical American literature constructs Black characters as alien: an "estranging dialect" and spelling (here also of the name with internal apostrophe) "contrived to disfamiliarize" (Morrison 1992, p. 52). Her problems in applying correct semantics are functional in the plotline (her honest assertion of goodwill and peacefulness come across as insincere), but they also play to everyday-racist assumptions regarding a presumed Black language deficiency (Essed 1991, p. 202).

Following the genre's logic, the threat of alien invasion here, too, is interwoven with ideas of colonial revenge. In the US context, there further is a strong element of dealing with the "Africanist presence" (Morrison 1992) created by slavery which is the frequent focus for the cinematic construction of whiteness (Vera and Gordon 2003). The parallel concern from a European perspective would be postcolonial people of color's presence in the wake of demised empires. In both contexts, popular culture articulated new fears concerning this "exotic" immigration (e.g., in Barry Sonnenfeld's 1997 *Men in Black*; see Vera and Gordon 2003, pp. 180–181). In all these constellations, forced or voluntary non-white presences in the United States and Europe are interpreted as equivalent of (and revenge for) colonialist invasion, subjugation and genocide.

There are two fundamental ways the (former) colonizers can position themselves with respect of this fear of postcolonial revenge, and they are rooted in the main currents of Victorian attitudes toward imperialism: conquest (imperialism) and anti-conquest (liberalism). The imperialist response is a military one. It is the dominant theme in science-fictional movies into the 1960s: the military sorting out the invaders. A later example would be Roland Emmerich's 1996 *Independence Day*, in which remnants of Earth's air forces under the command of the US President defeat alien invaders. In *TLM2*, this strategy is represented by Emmet's quest to not only liberate Lucy and the other abductees, but also (under Rex Dangervest's influence) annihilate the civilization of the Systar System.

Anti-conquest, in contrast, rejects the imperialist call to arms. This tradition, as Mary Pratt (1992) has analyzed it, is not necessarily anti-colonial and does not fundamentally challenge assumptions about European superiority. It is simply another approach to translating that assumed superiority into supremacy. The Other is domesticated not by force but by intercourse (commercial and sexual, trade and marriage). Films like *Avatar* represent this strategy. It, too, rests on assumptions about racial otherness and superiority—a brother- and sisterhood of woman- and mankind, in which white Europeans play the part of the elder brother and their racial Other that of the little sister (a metaphorical arrangement literalized in *TLM2*). In *Avatar*, the imperialist drive to exploit the planet's mineral resources blocks the potentially harmonious relations between the natives (the Na'vi) and the colonists from Earth, who destroy the central holy place of the Na'vi, a giant tree which concentrates and channels the spiritual energies of life there. The plot consists mainly of a conversion story of the protagonist Jake Sully, a marine in the service of the occupying forces, from imperial stormtrooper to leader of the native insurgence. Two female characters guide his transformation: the princess of the Na'vi, Neytiri, and the exo-anthropologist Dr. Grace Augustine. The promise to the white audience is identification not with a victorious conqueror but with the more benevolent but no less problematic figure of the "white savior"

(Newitz 2009; Djèlí Clark 2013) who is absolved of colonial guilt by siding with and presiding over the aliens/non-white other. Emmet's destruction of the Duplo Temple can be seen as an allusion to that of the Na'vi's Hometree, and Emmet's conversion to white savior parallels that of Sully.

Flattering and convenient for the liberal white self, the anti-conquest strategy nonetheless requires trust and the readiness to take a leap into the unknown. Seeking alliances seems risky and is laden with the fear of disappointment, as reflected in novels about failed White saviors like J. M. Coetzee's (2004 [1980]) *Waiting for the Barbarians* or Henning Mankell's (1990) *Eye of the Leopard.* Reactionaries love to taunt liberals with prospect of failure: Just as in Steven Spielberg's (1977) *Close Encounters of the Third Kind* the open-minded flock to the landing site of the alien spaceship to find enlightenment, in *Independence Day* hippies gather to greet the alien visitors from the top of a Los Angeles skyscraper—only here they are vaporized to the sniggers of xenophobic viewers, as Mike Davies (1998) notes:

> When the aliens turn to Los Angeles however, who could identify with the caricatured mob of hippies, new agers, and gay men dancing in idiot ecstasy on a skyscraper to greet the extraterrestrials? There is a comic undertone of "good riddance" when kooks like these are vaporized by the earth's latest ill-mannered guests. (p. 277)

TLM2 begins with a cuteified version of Emmerich's scenario. While the other Bricksburgers rush to take up arms, Emmet quickly assembles a brick heart, which he presents to the Duplo monsters as token of peace. Unlike Emmerich's L.A. hippies, Emmet survives the futile attempt: The monsters just attack and eat the heart, not Emmet himself.

Establishing a plausible white-savior plotline involves symbolic work on two fronts. The first is in the portrayal of the natives as naïve and misguided but essentially of goodwill, so that they are at once needy and receptive of white support and leadership. The second is a representation of and dissociation from the evil white villain. Hernán Vera and Andrew M. Gordon (2003) have shown up the paradigmatic role of a "divided white self" (pp. 16–32) in the Civil War movies from the unabashedly racist *Birth of a Nation* (1915) down to the outspokenly liberal *Glory* (1990) which all "work toward a final reconciliation or reunification of the split white self through marriage or family reunion" or "through sacrificial death in battle" (p. 17). The split white self in *TLM2* consists of Emmet and his alter ego and role model Rex Dangervest—the reconciliation achieved is, as we will see, one of the most interesting twists in the movie.

The journey Emmet undertakes in this movie mirrors that of Jack Sully in *Avatar*, but before turning from imperialist conqueror into white savior, he has to turn from petty-bourgeois love'n'peace hippie into imperialist conqueror, and he accomplishes a temporary hypermasculinist conversion as discussed above. Unlike *Avatar*, *TLM2* spares the white protagonist the inconvenience of having to move away from home and marry into an alien tribe (after all, Emmet is destined for lollipop Lucy); this task is left to Batman, who Queen Watevra tricks into marriage with her skillful exploitation of his narcissism. Also, Batman much better fits the bill of Marine veteran Jake Sully in terms of manliness.

Emmet's role regarding the alien Queen is more fundamental and paternal: The heart Emmet presented to the Duplo monsters in *TLM*, whose apparent destruction seemed to disprove his anti-conquest approach toward the alien invasion, turns out to have survived and inseminated a civilizing process: *TLM2* reveals the heart to have been Queen Watevra's "original form." Therefore, he is her accidental creator. For this reason, the Other was never dangerous, simply misunderstood in the mystic quest to overcome alienation from the Creator. Again, the narrative places blame on the object of stereotyping: As mentioned, Watevra failed to make her peaceful intentions credibly clear due to language deficiency. All she and her people wanted was the love and respect of the white man, whom they admired and have taken inspiration from since the beginning. The Heart of Darkness is not altogether dark and threatening, but of an entirely different hue.

Above I facetiously referred to the film's central symbol as a "Lutheran" heart. Yet the workings of *TLM2*'s symbolism *are* surprisingly straightforward traditionally Christian. The messianic imagery is hidden in plain sight: Emmet as savior offers up at once his body and blood in eucharist (the heart is a fleshy container of blood, after all), and the participants are rewarded with a second coming of Emmet after a period of strife culminating in Armamageddon. Even Emmet's destruction of the Systar System's holy site, which triggers Armamageddon, has precedent in Gospel: Just as we never see Emmet commit acts of violence before or after this episode, Jesus's rampage in the Temple was His only turn to violence. One could say that *TLM2* thus takes the white-savior motive to new religious heights, and it also offers one of the cleverest solutions processing the trope of the split white self.

As mentioned, Vera and Gordon (2003) have shown that in the construction of "sincere fictions" of whiteness, the story is as often about attempts to reconcile a rift in the respective white, European, colonizing communities as it is about their identities in relation to people of color, Africans, the colonized. Mostly, the split is externalized, as in the Civil War movies mentioned and more recent films like *Avatar* and *District 9*, where it affords a clear break by revenge killing (Rieder 2011). Even *Black Panther* falls into this category, with CIA agent Everett K. Ross empowered to innocent whiteness by way of contrast with Boorish arms trafficker Ulysses Klaue. I mention Ross here as he is another good example of that split's inner component: Like most white saviors (or, in this case at least, a white ally), Ross is invested in the colonialist power structure and undergoes a slow transformation that enables him to engage in an anti-conquest level. (As Pratt [1992] describes it, these are "strategies of representation whereby European bourgeois subjects seek to secure their innocence in the same moment as they assert European hegemony" [p. 7].) But unlike Black Panther T'Challa's antagonist N'Jadaka (Killmonger Stevens), Ross is redeemed by his choice to support Wakanda against the likes of Klaue. N'Jadaka, who kills Klaue, can only find redemption in death, although his guilt mainly consists of doing dirty work as black-op in the very organization in which E. K. Ross is a commanding officer. As in *TLM2, Black Panther* at least partly achieves white innocence by application of the power of cuteness: Ross is played by a boyish Martin Freeman, who brings a lot of the Hobbit and Arthur Dent into this role.

TLM2 perfects this method and unites the external and internal rifts: The white villain and the inner imperialist are the same person.

Dangervest is, as discussed above, just a future self of Emmet. When Emmet decides not to become Rex, the latter simply disappears, but not without the consolation that Emmet's maturation into a postcolonial guiding elder brother was only possible because he passed through an identificatory stage with him: "You're gonna grow up to be better than me… but kinda thanks to me, so… I'm also great"—he can go out with "no regrets." Thus, revenge-killing and reconciliation of the split white self converge.

In terms of conquest–anti-conquest dialectics, *TLM2* attempts a reversal of the way Joseph Conrad's 1902 *Heart of Darkness*, the urtext of colonialist angst, foretells European character development. Conrad's novel culminates in an account of the moral and psychological decay of the colonial goods trader Mr. Kurtz, whom the narrator traces up the River Congo to discover that the once-commercial-genius succumbed to the call of the jungle and started engaging in obscure practices of brutality, driven by what he sums up in his famous final words "The horror! The horror!" (1994, p. 100), after concluding his tract for the fictional International Society for the Suppression of Savage Customs with the infamous line, "Exterminate all the brutes!" (p. 72). But he had begun it with the quite-different assertion that European colonizers "must necessarily appear to them [savages] in the nature of supernatural beings" so that by "the simple exercise of our will we can exert a power for good practically unbounded" (p. 72). The latter is revealed (in hindsight) to be the exact case for the inhabitants of the Systar System, who admire the Bricksburgers and especially Emmet as quasi-gods. The Kurtzian madness of Dangervest turns the situation into an imperialist quest with the aim of exterminating their civilization. With Dangervest's demise, the original proposition is re-installed, establishing the relation with the racialized other on the basis of goodwill and trust—but still as an unequal one. Even if *TLM2* here goes beyond Conrad,[3] it still remains within the logic of *Heart of Darkness*, albeit brightened up and cuteified.

Order and Chaos

Gendered and racialized discourses interweave to concretize *TLM*'s metaphysical proposition: that contemporary capitalism is a locus of struggle to enhance creative potential through maintaining a balance between organizational authority and individual expression. These are presented as emanations of archaic principles of order and chaos—the former as white and masculine rationality and the latter as its emotional/irrational Other. It is no accident that the Mother as Ar*mama*geddon poses this Other as threat of total decomposition into dark chaos, unstructured and undefined space, as unbuilt and dispersed LEGO. Rather, it fits perfectly well into the Platonic Demiurgic cosmology and Erotic anthropology on which already the first movie operates. As I have previously suggested, such a logic is central to the ideological workings of *TLM*, in which human activity and productivity are understood as resulting from a constant struggle against disintegration and decay along the lines of Plato's allegoric rendering of the Eros myth:

> In the Symposium, god Eros (Ἔρως), and with him the drive that defines Man, love-as-desiring-ambition, is son of Penia (Πενία – Want, Poverty) – and Poros (Πόρος – Wealth). Earthbound Eros struggles to become similar to his father: rational, beautiful, powerful and rich while he is continuously dragged back down into the amorphous mires of his maternal origins. (Varul 2018, p. 727)

This allegory prefigures the gendered assumptions about order and chaos right into modernity. The maternal, feminine principle is, in the bourgeois imagination, associated with both immature infantility and the "uncivilized" natives, who are presented in alternatingly or simultaneously feminizing and infantilizing ways. *TLM2* taps into this tradition. Male destructivity in this scheme is presented as creativity frustrated by the resistance of the amorphous female/native against attempts to create form and order. In the first movie, male destructivity is one of total order that annihilates the created by freezing it in place, arresting any further development which it can only perceive as decay.

Master building turns into master taxidermy. In the second movie, the frustration is turned into total destructivity, the smashing-up of all competing forms that threaten the fragile adolescent male ego. Against the background of such implicit ontology, it is significant that Watevra Wa'nabe as the culmination of the threateningly gendered and racialized other is a shape-shifting monster (one of the shapes—uniquely for both LEGO Movies—being a feminine body): Penia as she teeters on the brink of amorphousness. That she can turn into every shape she wants (hence the name) negates the masculine sharp-edgedness of the original LEGO brick, and it threatens to dissolve this most masculine of all shapes: the ultimate horror of the hyper-male (Theweleit 1987).

When first introduced, Watevra is in a horse-shape, and she makes it clear that her current form is only for the benefit of her previous guest. Then, to demonstrate her transmogrificational abilities, she turns into a monstrosity most horrifying to the hyperman: a Lovecraftian, cthulhu-esque form. This shocks and disgusts Batman, as always-in-shape beacon of public order. H. P. Lovecraft describes a young artist's representation of the monster as a figurine in *Call of the Cthulhu* as follows:

> If I say that my somewhat extravagant imagination yielded simultaneous pictures of an octopus, a dragon, and a human caricature, I shall not be unfaithful to the spirit of the thing. A pulpy, tentacled head surmounted a grotesque scaly body with rudimentary wings; but it was the *general outline* of the whole which made it most shockingly frightful. (Lovecraft 2008, p. 204)

The general description fits Watevra in that state, but with its translation into Duplo bricks, the blatant racism and misogyny behind Lovecraft's monster (e.g., Wisker 2018) pull down onto a level of cuteness. This is only a quantitative reduction, however, not a qualitative change of perspective. Although, as Gina Wisker (2018) argues, some women writers succeeded in appropriating and subverting Cthulhu, the cuteification into a small-c Duplo cthulhu simply tempers the shape-shifting potential into a manageable inconvenience, without challenging the basic propositions about race and gender. The orderly, sharp-edged shape of the brick as basic LEGOverse element anticipates all the ordered and well-set constructions, playing to the white male self-image of clipped sharpness (cutting into the principle of Penia and causing considerable pain to the real-life Mother as she steps onto one of the bricks left on the floor). But its material, plastic, puts a question mark behind every achieved state. As Roland Barthes (1957, p. 171) points out, "*le frégolisme du plastique est total*": Plastic is the ultimate quick-change artist. What is already a property of the substance as unprecedented artificial material of the twentieth century transfers to the ready-made bricks, in which the "master builders" take one object apart to build another with the speed Leopoldo Fregoli changed his persona on stage. LEGO's fregolism culminates in Watevra Wa'nabe.

As a shifting outline of unreliable substance, gendered and racialized, Watevra finds another cultural precedent which proved unsettling to European bourgeois masculinities: Pablo Picasso's *Les demoiselles d'Avignon*, depicting prostitutes in cubistic manner (assembled from or dissembled into flattened ashlars), two of them wearing African masks. The picture was credited with the disturbing effect that we see repeated in Batman's reaction to Watevra's cthulhu-esque form. While his shock does not transmit to the audience, the emancipatory menace, which despite the patriarchal reception of Picasso's painting can be transformed into and appropriated as by feminist audiences (Chave 1994), is also lost. It is infantilized, reduced from a real menace with liberating potential to a silly quirk to be put up with, as one can rely on the fact that on the way from LEGO Duplo to LEGO Friends, it will be contained. In the movie, this process of domestication is sped up by the marriage of Watevra to Batman, sharp-edged from mask to abs, to restore of psycho-cosmic balance (especially since Batman, as Bruce Wayne in disguise, can represent Poros/Wealth also in terms of class vis-à-vis Penia/Poverty).

In the middle-class utopia the movie envisages, a mix-and-match approach achieves a balance in diversity. This approach relishes in harmonizing opposites but remains committed to the anchoring in assumptions about masculinities, whiteness and order on the one hand and femininity, blackness and disorder on the other. What is more, it even maintains the need for the potential of excess white masculinity as an unrealized corrective. The "*Second Part*" in the movie title thence corresponds to Georges Bataille's (1967) *part maudite*—the accursed part or share, excess, luxury, waste, ultimately death. The excess before, above and beyond rational production is represented by the Systar System and its queen, expending excess energy in luxurious waste and mechanized warfare, which is precisely where Bataille sees the point in which unchecked growth will be seen a curse. The rejection of the imperialist response—conquest, search-and-destroy and suppression—is justified *not* by a critique of the white hypermasculinity that drives it, but by a hint that it would end in a victory of the accursed *Second Part*. A successful overreach in the Erotic quest for the Absolute would not result in the envisaged world of total control and order, but in its opposite: a relapse into total chaos. In the first movie, the checks and balances suggested remained slightly abstract: an appeal to the principle of *bricolage* (in quite explicit allusions to Claude Lévi-Strauss' 1962, *pensée sauvage*, i.e., the wild-style thinking, which Mary Douglas 1967, referred to as "Emmet engineering"…) and borrowings from the Navajo Coyote trickster myths to counter the uninhibited ascend of the Erotic/Faustian *ingénieur* (Varul 2018). In the second movie, the chaotic/messy principle of Coyote has been concretized by way of gendering and racialization. As mentioned, Cthulhu as materialization of the innermost essence of racist and sexist fear has been cuteified to become the transient vision of Watevra as a cthulhu, but only as a trade-off for the cuteification of toxic masculinity. The gendered and racialized stereotypes are miniaturized in scale, so they can be instrumentalized for a suggestion of liberal balance in the quest to reestablish the American habits of the heart, harmonizing economic and social liberalism, utilitarian/instrumental and emotional/expressive individualism, public and private life—without a serious challenge to privilege.

Notes

1. On the signifying role of the allegorical (as differentiated from the symbolical) and its inevitably political character, see Walter Benjamin's (1978) analysis of it from the Baroque play onwards.

2. In *TLM2*, the LEGOverse is still predominantly white. The only Black characters are not functional to the plotline: Retired basketball players Sheryl Swoopes and Gary Payton have short cameo appearances.
3. Chinua Achebe (1977) highlights that unlike Albert Schweitzer, Joseph Conrad did not concede an even unequal relationship between elder and younger brother but at most one of very distant kinship.

References

Achebe, C. (1977). An image of Africa. *The Massachusetts Review, 17*(4), 782–794.

Auerbach, J. (2002). Art, advertising and the legacy of Empire. *Journal of Popular Culture, 35*(4), 1–23.

Barthes, R. (1957). *Mythologies*. Paris: Éditions du Seuil.

Bataille, G. (1967). *La Part maudite*. Paris: Éditions du Minuit.

Began, B., Chapman, G. E., D'Sylva, A., & Bassett, B. R. (2008). "It's just easier for me to do it": Rationalizing the family division of foodwork. *Sociology, 42*(4), 653–671.

Bellah, R. N., Madsen, R., Sullivan, W. M., Swidler, A., & Tipton, S. M. (1985). *Habits of the heart: Individualism and commitment in American life*. New York: Harper & Row.

Benjamin, W. (1978). *Der Ursprung des deutschen Trauerspiels*. Frankfurt am Main: Suhrkamp.

Chang, J. (2019, February 5). Review: "The LEGO Movie2" is funny but falls short of the first. *Los Angeles Times*. https://www.latimes.com/entertainment/movies/la-et-mn-the-lego-movie-2-the-second-part-review-20190205-story.html. Accessed on July 16, 2019.

Chave, A. C. (1994). New encounters with les demoiselles d'Avignon: Gender, race, and the origins of cubism. *Art Bulletin, 76*(4), 597–611.

Coetzee, J. M. (2004 [1980]). *Waiting for the barbarians*. London: Vintage.

Conrad, J. (1994 [1902]). *Heart of darkness*. London: Penguin.

Dargis, M. (2019, February 6). "The Lego Movie 2: The Second Part" Review: Everything is not awesome. Everything is an ad. *The New York Times*. https://www.nytimes.com/2019/02/06/movies/the-lego-movie-two-the-second-part-review.html. Accessed on July 16, 2019.

Davis, M. (1998). *Ecology of fear: Los Angeles and the imagination of disaster*. New York: Metropolitan Books.

Djèlí Clark, P. (2013, December 28). Oh come all ye white saviors. *Mediadiversified.* https://mediadiversified.org/2013/12/28/oh-come-all-ye-white-saviors/. Accessed on July 16, 2019.

Douglas, M. (1967). The meaning of myth, with special reference to "La Geste d'Asdiwal". In E. Leach (Ed.), *The structural study of myth* (pp. 49–69). London: Tavistock.

Essed, P. (1991). *Understanding everyday racism: An interdisciplinary theory.* London: Sage.

Fanon, F. (2002 [1961]). *Les Damnés de la terre.* Paris: Éditions La Découverte & Syros.

Goggin, J. (2018). "How do those Danish bastards sleep at night?": Fan labor and the power of cuteness. *Games and Culture, 13*(7), 747–764.

Hans, S. (2019, February 9). The Lego Movie 2 review—Another block-solid success. *The Guardian.* https://www.theguardian.com/film/2019/feb/09/the-lego-movie-2-review. Accessed on July 16, 2019.

hooks, b. (1984). *Feminist theory: From margin to center.* Boston, MA: Southend Press.

Johnson, D. (2014). Chicks with bricks: Building creativity across industrial design cultures and gendered construction play. In M. J. P. Wolf (Ed.), *LEGO studies: Examining the building blocks of a transmedial phenomenon* (pp. 107–130). London: Routledge.

Lévi-Strauss, C. (1962). *La Pensée sauvage.* Paris: Plons.

Lovecraft, H. P. (2008). *Necromonicon.* London: Gollancz.

Mauss, M. (1950). *Sociologie et anthropologie.* Paris: Presses Universitaires de France.

Modelski, T. (1991). *Feminism without women: Culture and criticism in a "post-feminist" age.* London: Routledge.

Morrison, T. (1992). *Playing in the dark: Whiteness and the literary imagination.* Cambridge, MA: Harvard University Press.

Newitz, A. (2009, December 18). When will white people stop making movies like "Avatar"? *io9.* https://io9.gizmodo.com/when-will-white-people-stop-making-movies-like-avatar-5422666. Accessed on July 16, 2019.

Parsons, T. (1956). The American family: Its relations to personality and to the social structure. In T. Parsons & R. F. Bales (Eds.), *Family: Socialization and interaction processes* (pp. 3–33). London: Routledge & Kegan Paul.

Pitcher, B. (2013). The cultural politics of being a knob. In P. Bennett & J. Mcdougall (Eds.), *Barthes' Mythologies today: Readings in contemporary culture.* London: Routledge.

Pratt, M. L. (1992). *Imperial eyes: Travel writing and transculturation*. London: Routledge.

Rieder, J. (2005). Science fiction, colonialism, and the plot of invasion. *Extrapolation, 46*(3), 373–394.

Rieder, J. (2011). Race and revenge fantasies in Avatar, District 9 and Inglorious Basterds. *Science Fiction Film and Television, 4*(1), 41–56.

Schumacher, J. (1972 [1937]). *Die Angst vor dem Chaos. Über die falsche Apokalypse des Bürgertums*. Frankfurt am Main: Makol Verlag.

Theweleit, K. (1987). *Male fantasies, volume 1: Women, floods, bodies, history*. Minneapolis: University of Minnesota Press.

Truit, B. (2019, February 4). Review: Everything is still pretty awesome in super-fun "Lego Movie 2." *USA Today*. https://eu.usatoday.com/story/life/movies/2019/02/04/lego-movie-2-sequel-review-everything-still-pretty-awesome/2723313002/. Accessed on July 16, 2019.

Varul, M. Z. (2018). The cultural tragedy of production and the expropriation of the brickolariat: The LEGO Movie as consumer-capitalist myth. *European Journal of Cultural Studies, 21*(6), 724–743.

Vera, H., & Gordon, A. M. (2003). *Screen saviors: Hollywood fictions of whiteness*. Lanham, MD: Rowman & Littlefield.

Wisker, G. (2018). Speaking the unspeakable: Women, sex and Lovecraft, Angela Carter, Caitlín R. Kiernan and Beyond. In S. Moreland (Ed.), *New directions in supernatural horror literature: The critical influence of H. P. Lovecraft* (pp. 209–234). Cham: Palgrave Macmillan.

Part II
Creativity in the LEGO Universe

7

Master Building and Creative Vision in *The LEGO Movie*

Jonathan Rey Lee

The well-worn adage "play is the work of the child" suggests that play is not mere fun but is—to borrow a constructionist expression often employed by LEGO—*serious* fun. Literally capitalizing on this vision of child development, the creative toy industry relies on the interpenetration of education and fun to simultaneously market its toys to parent and child consumers. LEGO has arguably been the company to most successfully navigate this paradox, maintaining cultural status as a creative icon while achieving immense financial success as a branded, mass-market toy. To accomplish this, LEGO has cultivated an elaborate ideology for how its construction toys materially mediate creative vision in ways that complement rather than contradict fun-driven toy play. This culture-shaping narrative is perhaps best encapsulated in the image of the Master Builder, a figure that blurs work and play to produce an ideology of creative vision problematically inflected by an ethos of *mastery*. Following Amy Ogata's (2013) claim that "Things, especially those for children, are designed according to social scripts, and

J. R. Lee (✉)
University of Washington, Seattle, WA, USA
e-mail: jlee105@ucr.edu

© The Author(s) 2019
R. C. Hains and S. R. Mazzarella (eds.), *Cultural Studies of LEGO*,
https://doi.org/10.1007/978-3-030-32664-7_7

these are often the key aspects of signification" (p. xvii), this chapter deconstructs the cultural construction of LEGO toy play as mediated by the representation of Master Building and creative vision in *The LEGO Movie* (hereafter referred to as *TLM*).

Throughout its history, LEGO has linked creativity and mastery by using multiple referents of "Master Builder" to align professional designers and aspiring child builders. One telling instance was the LEGO Master Builder's Academy (MBA), a mishmash of instructional playsets and supplementary texts wrapped up in a club mentality that playfully appropriated the metaphor of school. Blurring rhetorics of work and play, this multimodal product line extolled the virtues of serious fun from the converging perspectives of adult professional and playing child. For instance, the MBA featured series of "blocumentary" videos with professional Master Builders that echoed shared sentiments that working for LEGO is not only fun but might also help renew the playful spirit of the adult's inner child. Conversely, a 2013 advertisement features a testimonial from a boy who argues that a functional education in LEGO cultivates a mastery that makes play more fun. Framed in aspirational language, the child apprentice can leverage these sets to become more like the professionals, as "Not only do the LEGO Master Builders have the coolest job in the world, but they also know the best tips and tricks for making models that look good and stay together" (LEGO 2013). Together, the adult striving to make work playful and the child striving to professionalize play move toward an ideal of creative mastery as a joyous, life-giving endeavor only enhanced by disciplined cultivation.

Exemplifying serious fun, creative mastery blurs work and play. While creativity is sometimes portrayed as escape from social drudgeries, theories of the creative process often emphasize that cultivating creativity takes *work*. One such theory, proposed by Mihaly Csikszentmihalyi and adopted by the LEGO Foundation Systematic Creativity report (discussed later), outlines the creative process in five stages: preparation, incubation, insight, evaluation and elaboration. While the central stage of *insight* represents the culturally familiar notion of creative spark, the rest define creativity as work. Preceding the spark, preparation and incubation lay conceptual foundations for exploring a problem in need of a creative solution. And following the spark, evaluation and elaboration develop the creative idea into an applicable solution. Taken together, these stages represent a vision of creativity as a labor-intensive and intentional process of cultivation, a vision well-suited for the child development focus of the creative toy industry.

In similar fashion, the playful narrative of *TLM* (Lord and Miller 2014) does serious ideological work in simultaneously critiquing and advocating LEGO's distinctive creative vision. Building on extant scholarship on the film, the vast majority of which critiques the film's commodification, this chapter further deconstructs the ideology of creative play the film attributes to the LEGO medium. To this end, this chapter loosely adapts the aforementioned stages to (1) outline a preparatory history of LEGO's creative vision as told in two LEGO Foundation research reports, (2) unpack the narrative tension between creative visions that constitutes the space of incubation of *TLM*, (3) dig deeper into the film's metaphor of vision or insight, (4) evaluate the revolutionary potential of *TLM* protagonist Emmet's collectivist value system, and (5) elaborate on the ethics of applying a hierarchical language of mastery to creative vision.

Preparation

Despite the something-out-of-nothing connotations of the word *creativity*, creativity necessarily emerges from ongoing material and cultural practices. Indeed, the first stage of the creative process—preparation— basically amounts to immersion in an environment already laden with meaning. Likewise, the kind of creative play LEGO facilitates is rooted in a broader ideology of creative play that inflects all aspects of LEGO from design to marketing to play. As preparation for the following analysis, this section explores theories of creativity as synthesized in two research reports—*Defining Systematic Creativity* (Ackermann et al. 2009) and *Cultures of Creativity* (Gauntlett and Thomsen 2013)— published by the LEGO Foundation, a nonprofit institution and 25% shareholder in the LEGO Group that aims "to reveal and realize every child's potential, and to empower children to create a better future, based on their natural creativity, curiosity, and playfulness" (Gauntlett and Thomsen 2013, p. 4). Despite being distinct from the LEGO toy company, the LEGO Foundation's work provides a theory of cultivating creativity via material construction systems that helps articulate many unspoken assumptions behind LEGO's design and marketing.

The LEGO Foundation's core tenet—and, indeed, the very reason for its existence—is the notion that *creativity can be cultivated*, an idea consonant with Ogata's (2013) picture of creativity in Postwar American culture. Despite an occasional recurrence of naturalistic language in describing children's creative *potential*, the reports consistently reject the idea that creativity itself is inborn, listing among myths to be debunked that "creativity represents the innate spirit of the individual" (Ackermann et al. 2009, p. 25) and that "Creativity is something you are born with" (p. 27). Consequently, the reports emphasize that nature needs nurture, stressing the importance of a "stimulating, supportive culture which both inspires ideas and helps them to flourish" (Gauntlett and Thomsen 2013, p. 5). As the LEGO Foundation aims to promote rather than merely theorize the cultivation of creativity, these reports survey various theories to outline the main features necessary for establishing the aforementioned "stimulating, supportive culture."

Shifting the research focus from the playing child to the cultivating context raises questions about how social institutions contribute to creativity's cultivation. Significantly, while the LEGO Foundation's reports express no qualms about corporations cultivating creativity, they express pessimism about other social institutions, including education:

> This report argues that societies often fail to properly nurture and sustain the cultures of creativity which are vital to their future. Young children arrive at school with a creative mindset, but this is often eroded or even erased by conventional educational practices. We are failing our children if we do not recognise the crucial role of playing, making and sharing in the development of both the individual human being, and the innovative society. (Gauntlett and Thomsen 2013, p. 5)

Interestingly, the LEGO Foundation's reports offer not a critique of educational institutions, but an alternate pedagogical model that scavenges from educational theory. Thus, this passage continues by advancing an ideal of "lifelong kindergarten" that abstracts a philosophy of play-based education away from the institutional context of Friedrich Froebel's kindergarten system: "There is one place of learning which does foster creative, risk-taking, collaborative activities: kindergarten. The notion of the 'lifelong kindergarten' offers the possibility of a space where everyone can tinker, experiment, and play" (Gauntlett and Thomsen 2013, p. 6). This separation of the kindergarten spirit from actual schooling lacks grounding in any coherent critique of educational institutions. Instead, it seems to spring from an understandable desire to frame the cultivation of creativity in terms that fit foundation work and commercial products.

Consequently, the reports construct a theory of creative development suited to cultivation by LEGO. This LEGO-centric theory begins with drawing a link between the culture-shaping potential of the medium and brand and the aforementioned "stimulating, supportive" cultures of creativity. For instance, in listing ten ways the "LEGO System lends itself very well to both learning and creativity" (Ackermann et al. 2009, p. 11), the Systematic Creativity report attributes to LEGO characteristics that pertain more to a culture than a medium, such as "A belief in the potential of children and adults and their natural imagination," "A belief in the value of creative play," and "A supportive environment" (p. 12). Although attributing belief to a system of inanimate objects might seem strange, the report later explains: "The system also involves an ethos which is just as important, although less tangible" (p. 19). In other words, the reports argue that LEGO can cultivate creativity precisely because LEGO—the object system as well as the brand—is ideological.

In particular, the ideology of the LEGO system connects creativity to material construction systems: *materiality*, *construction*, and *systematicity* constituting three prominent threads in these reports. To establish the primacy of material systems as tools for thinking, the Cultures of Creativity report draws on Merlin Donald's theory that social evolution requires tools for externalizing thought via *cultural memory systems*. Although LEGO clearly differs from such systems, the argument here is one of analogy: LEGO is a material system for creative play in the same way that writing and other media technologies are material systems for cultural memory. Thus, the reports cite multiple theories that provide a foundational role for construction play. This can be seen in the allusion to the spirit of "tinkering" behind Froebel's "gifts," the geometric educational toys of his own design that played a prominent role in his kindergartens. Similarly, the reports commend Seymour Papert's theory of constructionism, "the idea that we build knowledge through making things, or 'learning by making'" (Gauntlett and Thomsen 2013, p. 11), and "the notion of constructivism, from Jean Piaget, which suggests that the world we engage with is actively constructed in our minds" (pp. 11–12).

Rather than emphasize the process of learning by making itself, however, the LEGO Foundation reports shift emphasis toward the design of object systems to construct a theory of *systematic creativity* that suggests creativity is best cultivated not by cultures such as educational institutions, but by systematic tools:

> The "tools as confining" myth rests on the notion that systematic tool use is contrary to the nature of creativity, which must be "free." According to this view, materials should be malleable (like clay!), and user-friendly. Contrary to belief, however, materials with an integrity (a "logic" of their own) are often more useful in boosting a maker's creativity - provided, of course, that the maker invests the time and applies the discipline required to become a fluent user of that tool. (Ackermann et al. 2009, p. 26)

Clearly, any theory of creativity that privileges logically rigorous materials over fluid materials like clay, and material systems over interpersonal interactions, is well-suited to promoting LEGO. In short, this theory emphasizes the systematicity LEGO already possesses, becoming a self-fulfilling promise in which tools define rather than confine creativity. Describing mastery as "fluency," this passage construes creativity as not only making meaning, but also as learning to decode the extant meanings already built into the material design of systematic tools. This emphasis on tools reframes the cultural problem of creative development as fundamentally a design problem, paving the way for the creativity toy industry to offer commercial products as creative aids.

In this vein, these reports culminate in a powerful claim about LEGO's potential to fulfill the Foundation's stated mission of realizing children's creative potential:

> As we know, the LEGO System is all about giving people a tool to explore their world and to invest it with meaning. [Ivan] Illich's arguments speak powerfully to the LEGO ethos: giving people the tools to make what they want to make, not what others have made for them, and being able to give something meaning themselves, rather than being told what to think. (Ackermann et al. 2009, p. 48)

To put it bluntly, this claim to neutral facilitation of individual creativity contradicts the reports' premise of that creativity must be cultivated. As the reports argue, LEGO can only cultivate creativity because the brand is ideological, systematic, and already laden with meanings. While it would be an overstatement to say that LEGO tells its players what to think, it is also misleading to suggest that LEGO only gives "people the tools to make what they want to make, not what others have made for them" (Ackermann et al. 2009, p. 48). Tools, after all, are cultural artifacts that are never value-neutral. And LEGO is more laden with representational and socializing content than most tools. Moreover, LEGO has always sent strong ideological signals about play through a vast network of paratexts ranging from instruction manuals and product art to advertisements and fan clubs to a burgeoning transmedia empire. While it is fair to say that LEGO can and does cultivate creativity, the reality is that such cultivation is heavily implicated in ideological constructions worth calling into question.

Incubation

Despite targeting children, *TLM* is in many ways better situated to articulate LEGO's vision of creative vision than are the LEGO Foundation reports. The reports—completely abstracted from the design, circulation, and play of any actual LEGO products—theorize creativity for a primarily inward-facing, organizational audience.

In contrast, *TLM* provides a consumer-facing narrative that engages LEGO toys' long cultural history, steeped in the "commodification of creativity" (Fanning 2018). Carefully rendered to mimic stop-motion animation of actual LEGO toys, *TLM* is a light-hearted toys-to-life adventure with a fairly archetypical plot: An ordinary working man (Emmet) in blandly dystopic society (Bricksburg) stumbles across a magical object (the Piece of Resistance) to fulfill ancient prophecy of a chosen one (the "Special"); joins a group of ragtag freedom fighters (Master Builders); and climactically thwarts the schemes of a dystopian overlord (Lord Business). However, the twist comes when the animation cuts to live-action footage, which suggests that Emmet's heroic struggle with Lord Business is the toy-mediated attachment plea of a young boy to his hobbyist father. (I discuss this twist further in forthcoming work.) In this chapter, I consider how *TLM*'s postmodern breaking of the fourth wall reframes the archetypical adventure plot as a meditation on the medium itself, allegorizing an ideology of creative vision. To begin to unravel this allegory, in this section, I argue that the narrative tension between the creative freedom advocated by the Master Builders and the creative control advocated by Lord Business constitutes a space of *incubation*, the stage of the creative process in which nascent ideas churn together to catalyze a moment of insight.

To narrate this incubational tension, *TLM* plays its toy story against familiar filmic conventions, particularly the nonconformists-rebel-against-dystopian-society genre (think *The Matrix*). Taking countercultural imagery to parodic extremes, the film associates its freedom fighters via a mishmash of countercultural styles: Vitruvius' tie-dye with hippie culture, Batman's music with grunge, and Wyldstyle's aesthetic with graffiti (of which wildstyle is a genre). Notably, these countercultures all have strong art-making traditions, reflecting a cultural association of creative production with individual self-expression: "Positioned against the critique of social conformity, creativity stood for an admirable individuality" (Ogata 2013, p. 187). However, the LEGO versions of these countercultural identities express personal tastes rather than revolutionary practices, adopting an individualist model of creative freedom that fractures the revolutionary movement.

This revolutionary failure is allegorized in one of the most extensive building scenes in the film, in which the Master Builders collaboratively build a submarine (Fig. 7.1) to flee Lord Business' henchmen. The emergent patter fails to synthesize into a conversation, as each builder individually pursues a personal aesthetic that admits no variety, flexibility, or change. Thus, Batman attempts to monopolize the dark-colored bricks because "I only work in black … and sometimes very, very dark gray," while Benny constructs the same kind of retro spaceship he builds in every situation. Even Wyldstyle undermines her claim to be fighting to tear down walls that impede collaboration by asserting her freedom negatively as freedom *from* interference, exclaiming to Benny, "Eww, get your retro space stuff out of my area." After all, tearing down walls is one thing; building bridges is another, as the film demonstrates when their submarine breaks apart underwater as an allegorical demonstration of their lack of cohesion. While the film doesn't question their

Fig. 7.1 Screenshot of the submarine constructed by the Master Builders during *TLM*. The individual styles of the different builders include the scuba bear and rainbow (Unikitty), the retro space undercarriage and satellite dishes (Benny), the noir front section and back fins (Batman), the blue and purple side paneling (Wyldstyle), and the dreamcatcher (Vitruvius)

intentions, this dénouement suggests that the Master Builders' individualist ethos has insufficient creative potential to bring about the revolution.

At the same time, the film also rejects Lord Business' singular, authoritative vision of creative control. To illustrate this, the film surrounds Lord Business with symbols of corporate power, as it associated the Master Builders with countercultural images. His villain outfit sports a necktie-shaped cape and coffee cup horns, suggesting his alter ego is not far removed from his cover identity as President Business, "President of the Octan Corporation and the world." Although Lord Business wields significant military power in the form of a robotic police army, his power is largely economic and cultural, as Emmet unwittingly reveals: "And Octan, they make good stuff: music, dairy products, coffee, TV shows, surveillance systems, all history books, voting machines." Along these lines, Joyce Goggin (2017) argues that the film enacts the complex social interpenetration of financial interests and the surveillance state that produce a *lego-ification* of workers as interchangeable parts in decidedly unfree labor system. She further notes (2018) that "while *The LEGO Movie* lampoons the kinds of corporate profit-generating strategies for which the LEGO Group is known—that is, unabashed commercialism, the marketing of bricks in playsets—the film also generates profits from what it criticizes" (p. 759). As capitalism is known for commodifying even anti-capitalist sentiments, the film's visions of creative failure show how, when enmeshed in the institutional power of creative industries, creativity easily becomes another instrument of conformist world-building.[1]

In other words, *TLM* construes Lord Business' tyranny as making as well as taking, as constructive as well as destructive. Shaping all aspects of society from city architecture to cultural tastes, this creative control produces genuinely remarkable new things. Thus, the stakes of the film are not creativity versus non-creativity, but what power dynamics will define the creative culture. Critiquing its authoritarian underpinnings, the film names Lord Business' terrifying brand of tyranny *micromanagement* (his robotic minions are "micromanagers"), the paternalistic belief that strong top-down management is necessary to construct a "perfect" society. In the parallel real-world narrative, this emerges as a distorted relational politics in which the father regulates his child's play to the point of exclusion. In the dystopian narrative of the adventure plot, this emerges as an attempt to violently regulate creative freedoms.

As Wyldstyle explains, "President Business was confused by all the chaos, so he erected walls between the worlds and became obsessed with order and perfection," a sentiment which he willingly echoes, saying: "All I'm asking for is total perfection." Rationalizing totalitarian control, this model of perfection subsumes creative production under the established creative order just as it lego-ifies creative workers by reducing them to interchangeable roles within the labor system. Continuing the film's material allegories, this vision ultimately coalesces in weaponized stasis: "The film's true villainous object is not the instruction manual, but the Kragle, the weaponized glue that Lord Business plots to use to freeze the LEGO-verse in a state of permanent stasis" (Mittell 2014, p. 272). While the threat of permanent stasis—arising here from the non-LEGO medium of glue—clearly entails death for LEGO characters, it also means death for a medium defined by the possibility of infinite recombination. Thus, the film portrays Lord Business' tyranny not only as a crime against human—or, rather, minifigure—rights, but also as a crime against LEGO itself.[2]

Unlike archetypical dystopian rebellion narratives, perhaps the most pointed part of these critiques is the close parallel between the creative visions of the Master Builders and Lord Business. Even the playful anarchy of Cloud Cuckoo Land, the most chaotic and bizarre LEGO realm in the film, reflects Business' authoritarianism, as shown in the following exchange between a bewildered Emmet, a skeptical Wyldstyle, and an effusive Princess Unikitty:

Emmet: So, there's no signs or anything. How does anyone know what *not* to do?
Unikitty: Here in Cloud Cuckoo Land, there are no rules! There's no government, no babysitters, no bedtimes, no frowny-faces, no bushy mustaches, and no negativity of any kind!
Wyldstyle: You just said the word "no" like a thousand times.
Unikitty: And there's also no consistency!

Although diametrically opposed in temperament, Lord Business and Princess Unikitty alike author restrictive rule systems to enact visions of sociality that mimic their individual desires. In a stereotypically gendered response, Business acts out his frustration with others by trying to control them, whereas Unikitty consistently represses and denies her anger until she is finally pushed to the breaking point in the final climactic battle. Yet, underlying these divergent responses is a structurally similar idealism that maintains purity via exclusion. To be fair, Unikitty's vision of playful anarchy is much more benign. While her utopic vision is exclusionary, she exerts power to defend other's freedoms and promote sociality, as reflected in her unironic battle cry: "You need to be more friendly!" Still, such sentiments do not produce genuine change, as they reinforce a strongly binary logic in which creative freedom and creative control are fundamentally irreconcilable.

Consequently, the film does not resolve with the beleaguered freedom fighters climactically overthrowing the dystopian power—indeed, this conflict is not the pivot on which the fate of their world will swing. Instead of being a site of natural selection in which the strong overcome the weak, the tension between creative freedom and creative control constitutes a space of incubation where contradictory ideas intermingle to create newness. The irreconcilable binary operates as a dialectic from which a moment of insight emerges to redefine the LEGO vision of creativity.

Insight

From classical muses and Romantic geniuses to contemporary tech innovators characterized as "visionaries," much of creativity's cultural history draws on visual metaphors of *insight*. Often described as a "flash" or "Eureka moment,"[3] insight encompasses both *vision* (seeing reality in new or transformative ways) and *visions* (potentially divine glimpses transcending everyday reality). Together, vision and visions comprise the central metaphors underlying *TLM*'s translation of the ideology of creativity from material play into the filmic medium. Through a series of moments of insight narrated via visual metaphors—especially the product catalog visualization of Master Building—the film deconstructs the surface reality of the LEGO world through its reliance on the LEGO Foundation's definitional ideology, while simultaneously elucidating the creative potential of a world predicated on play.

Vitruvius articulates the framing doctrine of creative vision when he promises Emmet that "all you have to do is believe and then you'll *see* everything," a promise later fulfilled when Emmet returns from his encounter with The Man Upstairs, saying "I can see everything! I am a Master Builder." Despite being named after a Roman architect, Vitruvius builds very little and lacks a clear building style. Indeed, his only clear contribution to the submarine is a relatively superfluous dreamcatcher "in case we take a nap" (see Fig. 7.1). Every other part is recognizably associated with the other builders except a single section of Old West-style rock face that is potentially explained by a collision with said rock face during the construction process. Instead, his most intentionally crafted creation is the first scene's prophecy, a fabrication in the form of a divine vision. Appropriately, Vitruvius constructs this vision in the moment of his blinding, an allusion to the blind prophets of myth. Blurring the line between *vision* and *visions*, a common irony in classical mythology is that the sighted are often figuratively blind whereas the blind have a special vision that penetrates to the essence of things. Similarly, whereas blindness characterizes the Master Builders' failure to defeat Lord Business, Vitruvius recognizes that victory requires a new vision, embodied in the unlikely figure of the uncreative Emmet, who despite being sighted is initially blind to his society's dystopic nature. Vitruvius' prophecy, then, is not itself a moment of insight but the creation of a space of incubation—one which ultimately contributes to Emmet's development into a creative hero.

Inspired by Vitruvius, Emmet becomes the film's second visionary—not by learning to master-build, but by being open to the perception of a new reality. Emmet ostensibly becomes "the Special" by finding the fabled Piece of Resistance, but this explanation collapses after Vitruvius reveals he had fabricated the prophecy. The narrative twist that exposes the real-world context surrounding the LEGO storyline reveals the Piece of Resistance to be a non-magical, everyday object.

Emmet's encounter with the Piece is special, but not because of the potency of the Piece itself. Rather, Emmet—an otherwise highly conformist thinker—somehow recalls flashes of the outside world when confronted with an object whose origin lies outside the LEGO medium. In Platonic terms, Emmet remembers the long-forgotten world of forms. Thus, in a backhanded compliment, Vitruvius marvels that Emmet can see The Man Upstairs because his "mind is already so prodigiously empty that there is nothing in it to clear away in the first place." While this statement seems rather insulting, it also makes clear that Emmet's creativity lies not in the generation of ideas (Emmet himself acknowledges, "I never have any ideas"), but in his openness to alternate realities—his creativity is *vision*. Or, rather, his creativity is in his *visions*, the perspective he gains on his reality by perceiving it from the "outside" framing reality.

In this context, the film's most important portrayal of creative vision is arguably the alignment of Master Building in the diegetic world of the film with Master Building in the extradiegetic world of LEGO products. Literalizing the idiom that knowledge is power, in these narratives, visions of reality allow "chosen ones" to transcend the physical laws they are born into. Like Plato's allegory of the cave, a story of realizing one's everyday reality to be a shadow of a truer realm of forms, the Master Builders gain power over their reality only when they learn to perceive it according to the LEGO toy's brand logic.

In a pivotal early scene that introduces Master Building to viewers and Emmet alike, Wyldstyle builds a "Super Cycle" (immortalized in Set #70808, *Super Cycle Chase*) out of the alleyway. As she begins her build, the camera (see Fig. 7.2) takes on a dreamlike quality as it focuses in on close-ups of different parts of the alley, using special effects to highlight particular elements, whose name and part number appear on the screen as a technical readout. As a particularly visual way of expressing Master Building, this presentation construes creativity *as* vision, a vision governed by a corporate logic of product codes akin to the visible computer codes in *The Matrix*.

This consumer-facing visual presentation aligns the diegetic LEGO world's magic with the reality of LEGO play presumably familiar to most viewers. Consequently, the creativity narrative that unfolds for

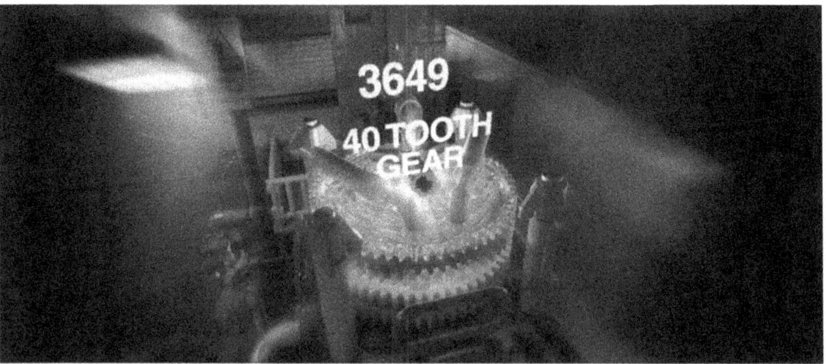

Fig. 7.2 Screenshot of *TLM* showing the first scene where Wyldstyle engages Master Building vision

the characters is materially connected with creativity narratives pertaining to the playing child as well as the knowledge economy of material LEGO products. The Master Builders' abilities exhibit a supernaturality derived from the vision of a greater reality, namely the reality of the cataloguing of LEGO elements (the part number in Fig. 7.2 is accurate) as synecdochal for real-world Master Building. Here, the ideal of "systematic creativity" returns in a taxonomic perspective that clearly illustrates the systematicity of the LEGO system and its highly combinatoric model of creativity. It is, therefore, ironic that to achieve this understanding the Master Builders must adopt a perspective that deconstructs their essential identity—not a fabricated identity, like the one deconstructed in *The Matrix*—as elements in an interchangeable medium.

Thus, *TLM* presents LEGO mastery as a kind of re-vision that reveals the medium's corporately designed potential to facilitate certain kinds of connections. In other words, these animated toys gain agency over their world by adopting a vision that reveals the LEGO toy's inanimateness as product. Rather than weaving new possibilities from nothingness or from somethings designed to be fluid (like the clay dismissed in the Systematic Creativity report), this model of creative vision demands reading the possibilities designed into the medium and permuting those fixed possibilities in new ways. This consumer-facing film then invites viewers to share its paradoxical vision, a transcendent perspective in which toys come to life by embracing their status as objects within a corporately designed toy system. And, in its postmodern irony, the film further invites users to reflect on their complicity within the consumer culture that the film simultaneously critiques and advances. This invitation becomes even more fraught given the politics of incorporating fan work into the film, a practice Goggin (2018) critiques from a fan studies perspective. Such problematics demonstrate that for all the cultural mystique surrounding moments of insight, genuinely new ideas may very well reinforce or even sustain prevailing ideologies, including corporate commodification of creativity.

Evaluation

While creative insight does produce new ideas, newness does not necessitate revolutionary potential. To move beyond the unresolvable narrative tension between creative freedom and creative control, *TLM* requires a transformation in the value systems themselves. Newness is not enough, as influential theorist of creativity Margaret Boden (2004) notes: "Because creativity *by definition* involves not only novelty but value, and because values are highly variable, it follows that many arguments about creativity are rooted in disagreements about value" (p. 10). The creative process, therefore, continues beyond the moment of insight with the lengthier, more deliberate process of *evaluation*, the reflective negotiation between the creation of new ideas and the value they provide. Despite the term's misleading connotations, I understand evaluation to be not just assessing a new idea's worth, but also adapting the idea to mesh with material and conceptual realities. Evaluation, in other words, is *valuation* in which new ideas interface with and potentially transform existing value systems. Consequently, I suggest the distinctiveness of *TLM*'s vision of creativity lies in Emmet's valuative reparative work. Emmet does not tip the scales to make one vision of creativity win. Instead, his most creative act is to reframe creative vision according to a collectivist ethos that the film advances as constitutive of the LEGO brand and toy.

When the Master Builders' submarine breaks apart as a material metaphor for their collaborative efforts' fractiousness, Emmet reveals his previously unnoticed contribution: a double-decker couch, which saves them three times, as (1) this lone piece of surviving wreckage prevents them from being stranded in an ocean without a vessel; (2) its unassuming character allows them to pass undetected beneath Lord Business' henchmen; and (3) the surprising character of these first two escapes convinces the previously reticent pirate Metalbeard to return to their aid. In all instances, "the one thing that stayed together" serves as material allegory for the restorative potential of Emmet's collectivist ethos, refracted through Emmet's dream that "everyone could watch TV together and be buddies." Precisely because this design is ridiculed throughout the film, its affective rather than effective design pioneers a revolutionary value system in which collectivity supersedes functionality.

For all its newness, the couch is only the most tangible manifestation of the collectivist ethos in which Emmet's true transformative potential lies. In his humility, he criticizes and eventually unites the Master Builders, saying: "Guys, you're all so talented and imaginative but you can't work together as a team. I'm just a construction worker, but when I had a plan and we were all working together—I mean—we could build a skyscraper." Calling into question the opposition between creative freedom and creative control, this speech leverages Emmet's history of conformity within the construction arm of Lord Business' civilization-making machine to reconfigure creative construction as interactive and participatory. In so doing, Emmet sows the seeds for rethinking the revolutionary struggle's oppositional logic as an opportunity to reunite and repair the social bonds threatened by Lord Business. This transforms creativity from a form of individual expression to a form of collectivist world-making,[4] a view that echoes the claim in the LEGO Foundation's *Systematic Creativity* report that "LEGO bricks are a social tool, fostering connection and collaboration" (Ackermann et al. 2009, p. 10).

Interestingly, Emmet only indirectly catalyzes this change as he is absent during the film's revolutionary climax, in which the citizens of Bricksburg unleash their creative potential. Instead, Wyldstyle catalyzes this moment—not by becoming the revolutionary savior she had hoped to be, but by inspiring others to their collective creative awakening. This scene unfolds immediately following Emmet's self-sacrificing fall from Octan Tower, when the Master Builders lament his presumed loss and for the first time recognize that "Emmet had ideas." This lament catalyzes an epiphany for Wyldstyle, who realizes in the very moment when she appreciates him most that Emmet might not have been so unique after all. This insight reinterprets creativity as an ordinary rather than a privileged position, echoing the *Systematic Creativity* report, which argues that "creativity is grounded in everyday abilities" (p. 17). Upon this recognition, Wyldstyle hijacks Lord Business' media network to make an impassioned plea to the citizens to wake up, embrace their creative potential, and fight back. Unlike some dystopian narratives in which the citizenry is unable to awaken to non-conformist thought, *TLM's* optimistic narrative suggests that creative potential is never lost. To the contrary, Lord Business schemes to deploy his gluey superweapon precisely because LEGOverse's diverse worlds otherwise readily yield new ideas.

This moment is also significant because the citizens' clever war machines headlined *TLM* playsets teased piecemeal several months before the film debut to build hype, piquing fans' interest with sets narratively and stylistically evocative of fan production.[5] As playsets, the war machines are 2-in-1 sets that, reminiscent of Transformers toys, can be constructed in everyday forms or reconfigured war machine forms. These sets therefore operate as material metaphors for an ideology of the (potentially dormant) creative potential of the everyday, while capitalizing on Emmet's collectivist ethos through their seemingly haphazard repurposing of extant materials. In a blend of conformity and nonconformity, the citizens engage in a revolutionary *bricolage*, turning the signifiers of their roles within the authoritarian society into expressions of identity and resistance. Collapsing the binary between the countercultural signifiers associated with the Master Builders and the conformist signifiers associated with Lord Business, these sets' dominant aesthetic is a whimsical reinterpretation that plays on doubled significations.

Take, for example, the *Ice Cream Machine* (Set #70804) shown in Fig. 7.3, which features elements for alternately building an ice cream truck and a flying ice cream assault vehicle. The set includes three

Fig. 7.3 Reverse package image of the *Ice Cream Machine* set (#70804). The same set of elements are used to build the alternate models featured in the two upper panels. The minifigures are shown and named in the center lower panel

minifigure characters—Ice Cream Jo, Ice Cream Mike, and Cardio Carrie—identified via a grammatically hybrid mix of proper names and descriptive content. This naming of hybrid identity departs from typical LEGO naming conventions, which usually feature either generic characters in non-narrative themes, or named characters in sets with licensed or proprietary story-oriented (e.g., LEGO Friends and LEGO Elves) content. Although reducing individuals to social roles underpins the dehumanization of Lord Business' consumer economy, as reflected in the lego-ification of interchangeable names, these names do not disavow the characters' conformist roots. Instead, this hybridization weaponizes generic identity in their anti-conformist resistance. Yet this resistance is more collectivist than that of the Master Builders, as evinced by promotional images for each of these 2-in-1 war machines depicting a pair of thematically aligned resistance fighters aiding a third character who does not share their identity. Taking this further, whereas the ice cream truck maintains a clear architectural separation between consumer and purveyor, the rebuilt war machine literally opens space for Carrie to fight *alongside* the ice cream duo (see rightmost panel). As when the citizens click together unlikely combinations of pieces to initiate their creative awakening, such architecture constitutes a material allegory for newfound social *connection*, linking this collectivist ethos with the fundamental character of the LEGO medium.

Similarly, these 2-in-1 war machines' design relies on the visible transformation of social signifiers into weapons of resistance, drawing on LEGO's complicated relationship between form and function. In a mechanically realistic world where function depends upon internal mechanisms rather than surface presentation, a giant ice cream cone could not suddenly become a cannon, no matter how it was pointed. In LEGO, however, form defines function, such that looking like a cannon is the sole criterion for *becoming* a cannon. As LEGO elements become what they appear, acts of vision could be said to bestow the affordances of LEGO sets. Because the hybrid significance of the cone/cannon depends on visual interpretation, LEGO comes seemingly close to the Foundation reports' stated ideal of "giving people the tools to make what they want to make, not what others have made for them, and being able to give something meaning themselves" (Gauntlett and Thomsen 2013, p. 48). Yet, these interpretations are not freely created by ex nihilo imaginative leaps. Here, the significance of the cone/cannon[6] is not infinite, but rather dual, enmeshed in two heavily ideological visual rhetorics: the Bricksburg dystopia's consumer culture and the citizens' creative resistance via countercultural *bricolage*.

While world-making in LEGO amounts to re-visioning, visual design heavily constrains the possibilities of re-visioning. The paradigm shift required to reconceptualize an ice cream truck as a war machine is a leap between two paradigms already well-established by design conventions (utility vehicles and war machines being two recognizable types of LEGO vehicles). The revolutionary awakening, therefore, entails an extradiegetic leap from the conformist mindset cultivated by Lord Business toward a creative mindset cultivated instead by the extradiegetic influence of LEGO. Thus, just as generations of political philosophers have based theories of social ethics on what it means to be human, this social revolution ultimately hinges on what it means to be LEGO.

Paralleling the citizens' awakening, Emmet returns from the human realm with his own conformity-turned-resistance style of Master Building that weaponizes his identity as a construction worker. No longer acting as the ill-fitting Special of a fabricated prophecy, Emmet returns as one of the citizens who has unlocked his everyday creative potential. Characteristically, Emmet finds power in blending in with the collective. He sets himself apart, however, by resolving the film's central tension in a way neither the Master Builders nor the citizenry can: By inviting his nemesis to share his collective ethos. "You are the Special," Emmet tells Business, "And so am I. And so is everyone." Where anyone else might see a warzone, Emmet reevaluates the moment of violent collision as a space of incubation, saying "You might see a mess … what I see are people inspired by each other and by you. People taking what you made and making something new out of it." While the framing narrative construes this statement as an appeal to familial reconciliation, within the LEGO world this statement reimagines the prevailing social order as a collaborative makerspace. This is a moment of genuine revolution—one that does not merely redistribute power but rather reimagines an entire social order. At the same time, this new social order is defined by an ethos inextricable from branded toy play.

TLM therefore sells a distinctive brand of consumer ethics that critiques an individualist streak running through LEGO's own deployment of mastery. With violence played for comic effect, the primary sin in this ethos is to refuse collaboration. Despite drawing on familiar genre conventions, the film's overarching theme is an ethics of toy play that reflects collaborative and participatory culture for which "taking what you made and making something new out of it" becomes a rallying cry.

Elaboration

The creative process is actualized when "elaborated" (a process that refers more to labor—*elabor*ation—than verbal explication) in real-world contexts. Similarly, *TLM's* narrative regarding this creative ethos becomes significant as it unfolds through the film's circulation through a children's culture in which branded LEGO toys take a significant part. While a much more substantive study would be required to trace such rhetoric's direct consequences on actual play within particular cultures, I wish to conclude by elaborating a few potential problematics built into how the collectivist ethos is tied to the branded LEGO medium.

A common refrain in both popular and scholarly critiques of *TLM* is that for all its ostensibly anti-capitalist theming, the film amounts to a feature-length toy commercial. Dalia Grobovaite (2017) argues that *TLM* promises "both the liberation from the culture industry hegemony and further integration by use of its products" (p. 70). Despite promoting creativity and imagination, "the idea of creativity and imagination appears to be limited to the use of the brick, namely the Lego brick" (p. 57). This timely critique reveals the contradiction behind an ethics of play that is simultaneously collectivist and proprietary. With *TLM* and its sequel telling stories of interpersonal miscommunication being mediated by LEGO, the medium very much becomes the message. While the collectivist ethos may seem congenial when abstracted from its rhetorical context, its omnipresent corporate entanglements complicate this ethic. As the ethos that drives the MBA demonstrates, LEGO attempts to bridge cultural, generational, and gendered divides using a model of affiliation based on brand identification. Also following the principles of market segmentation, however, LEGO often segregates its products according to these same cultural, generational, and especially gendered divides. (For more on LEGO's use of gender stereotyping in its products, see also Chapter 11 by Hains and Shewmaker and Chapter 12 by Merskin in this volume.) Consequently, the brand often sends messages contradicting its own collectivist ethos, both identifying the brand against other forms of toy play and segregating forms of play within its own brand.

While differentiating a target market according to identity politics is problematic enough when considered separate but equal, the language of "mastery" implies that such separations are not likely to be equal. While mastery certainly can be pursued by a collective, cultural ideals of mastery are often hierarchical in ways that promote individualism or pit one collective against another. In the film, the pursuit of mastery hopelessly entangles play with questions of power and agency. In the adventure plot, the Master Builders and Lord Business are violently locked in a perpetual and unhelpful struggle. Similarly, in the real-world narrative father and son have a fractured relationship as long as they vie for control over the LEGO world. While this political sense of mastery is more prevalent in the film than in LEGO at large, mastery implies control in ways that problematize the LEGO philosophy of play. Control is in many ways antithetical any collaborative or explorative spirit to play. Indeed, even the most workmanlike educational toys are designed for exploration and discovery, evoking a sense of apprenticeship rather than mastery. And yet the LEGO Foundation research reports characterize LEGO as a "medium for mastery," echoing the Master Builder Academy advertisement's implication that mastering building techniques makes the medium more fun. While the persistent promise of mastery is clearly intended to entice aspiring builders to new creative heights, the rhetoric of mastery aligns play and power in ways that problematize the cultivation of collaborative creative spaces.

Even when the LEGO brand does not directly express mastery as power over (or as asserting independence from) others, it implies a form of agency predicated on human power over passive matter. This is worrisome in several respects. Although I have drawn elsewhere on the critical potential of LEGO to argue that "questioning—not mastery—ought to be the attitude through which material relationships with and within the world are composed" (Lee 2014, p. 96), the vision of mastery behind Master Building can promote an overly simplistic view of the emergent relationships between human and non-human actants. While creativity expressed in a medium necessarily emerges from the interaction between the creativity of the individual maker and the affordances of the medium, emphasizing mastery can overstate the originality of the maker and understate the agential force of the medium and its messages. The LEGO medium is not a collection of passive elements for neutrally unleashing developmental potential but is an active force in cultivating creative cultures.

Ironically, giving the medium too little credit can simultaneously give it too much power by obscuring its ideological force. By actively taking on the work of cultivating creativity, LEGO constructs a vision of creative vision that serves a corporate enterprise. LEGO cultivates creative impulses according to a distinctly LEGO-like vision of creative vision. This situates LEGO itself as mediating and branding creative culture, an incredibly ambitious claim that needs to be interrogated precisely because it is likely true.

Notes

1. Indeed, the Master Builders' creativity literally fuels the Business empire as the captured Master Builders are plugged into a "think tank" that harnesses their creative energies to produce the designs for everything Business constructs.
2. Glue being a crime against LEGO is a rhetoric that runs through certain segments of the LEGO fan community.
3. Serendipitously, a key figure in popularizing the myth of the Eureka moment is none other than Roman architect Vitruvius.
4. The clearest real-world example of this is Olafur Eliasson's (2005) *The collectivity project*, an interactive art installation that has passersby collectively construct their ideal city.
5. See Goggin (2018) for further discussion of the appropriation of fan work in the film.
6. This element (in gray) was originally a drill bit for a mining set. Although this element demonstrates a rather remarkable flexibility in signification, it is important to note that it has always had representational content heavily determined by its contextual use.

References

Ackermann, E., Gauntlett, D., & Weckström, C. (2009). *Defining systematic creativity*. Billund: LEGO Learning Institute. https://www.legofoundation.com/en/learn-how/knowledge-base/defining-systematic-creativity/. Accessed on June 21, 2019.

Boden, M. A. (2004). *The creative mind: Myths and mechanisms* (2nd ed.). London: Routledge.

Eliasson, O. (2005). *The collectivity project* [Interactive installation]. Exhibited at Tirana, Albania.

Fanning, C. (2018). Building kids: LEGO and the commodification of creativity. In M. Brandow-Faller (Ed.), *Childhood by design: Toys and the material culture of childhood, 1700–present* (pp. 89–105). New York: Bloomsbury Visual Arts.

Gauntlett, D., & Thomsen, B. S. (2013). *Cultures of creativity*. Billund: The LEGO Foundation. https://www.legofoundation.com/en/learn-how/knowledge-base/cultures-of-creativity/. Accessed on June 21, 2019.

Goggin, J. (2017). 'Everything is awesome': The LEGO movie and the affective politics of security. *Finance and Society, 3*(2), 143–158.

Goggin, J. (2018). "How do those Danish bastards sleep at night?": Fan labor and the power of cuteness. *Games and Culture, 13*(7), 747–764.

Grobovaite, D. (2017). Politics of bricolage and the double-sided message of *the LEGO movie. Canadian Journal of Media Studies, 15,* 57–78. https://cjms.fims.uwo.ca/issues/15-01/Grobovaite.pdf. Accessed on June 21, 2019.

Lee, J. R. (2014). The plastic art of LEGO: An essay into material culture. In D. M. Weiss, A. D. Propen, & C. E. Reid (Eds.), *Design, mediation, and the posthuman* (pp. 95–112). Lanham: Lexington Books.

LEGO. (2013). *It's a great day for building* [Advertisement]. Retrieved from https://www.youtube.com/watch?v=_sKfsq5TJSw. Accessed on June 21, 2019.

Lord, P., & Miller, C. (Directors). (2014). *The LEGO movie* [Motion picture]. United States: Warner Bros. Pictures.

Mittell, J. (2014). D.I.Y. disciplinarity—(Dis)assembling LEGO studies for the academy. In M. J. P. Wolf (Ed.), *LEGO studies: Examining the building blocks of a transmedial phenomenon.* New York: Routledge.

Ogata, A. F. (2013). *Designing the creative child: Playthings and places in Midcentury America.* Minneapolis: University of Minnesota Press.

8

Toyetics and Novelizations: Bringing *The LEGO Movie* to the Page

Joyce Goggin

Novelizations get short shrift in scholarly work and are largely ignored in both literature and film studies, where one might expect them to have received at least passing attention. Various factors influence the lack of interest in novelizations, including their medial status as transcriptions of film versions of what were initially text-based narrative properties, such as novels, plays or scripts. Indeed, research on novelizations has lagged behind even in adaptation studies, a rapidly developing quasi-discipline that addresses narrative transposition from one medium or platform to the others, as well as the logic and processes through which such transpositions operate. And while adaptation studies continue to widen the scope from text adapted into film to include remakes, prequels and sequels, as well as adaptations from comic books and graphic novels to video games and even toys, novelizations continue to receive little attention.

J. Goggin (✉)
University of Amsterdam, Amsterdam,
The Netherlands
e-mail: J.Goggin@uva.nl

R. C. Hains and S. R. Mazzarella (eds.), *Cultural Studies of LEGO*,
https://doi.org/10.1007/978-3-030-32664-7_8

This chapter is intended as a serious contribution to the study of novelizations as well as to LEGO studies, albeit from the perspective of somewhat non-serious objects. In what follows, I will discuss novelizations of 2014's *The LEGO Movie* (*TLM*) and 2017's *The LEGO Batman Movie* (*LBM*), as well as the industry's history, authors and audiences. By exploring the phenomenon of novelizing LEGO movies from various critical perspectives, my goal is to shed light on a cluster of concerns, such as the role that the cultural capital of novelizations plays in their reception; the role of gender in the writing of novelizations; the pedagogical aims of these texts; and some of the reasons why both authors and readers might be attracted to textual versions of the LEGO movies.

Novelizations and the Question of Gender

Before shifting my focus to LEGO movie novelizations, a brief directed discussion of novelizations, their history and their status is in order. As noted above, novelizations are largely disregarded and even disdained; hence, virtually everyone who writes on the topic begins with the common complaint that "the phenomenon of novelization is remarkably widely underresearched (sic.), even within adaptations studies" (van Parys 2009, p. 1). According to one scholar, "[w]hile praise is regularly heaped on the opposite form of adaptation—films based on novels— novels based on films remain marginalized" (Mahlknecht 2012, p. 139).[1]

A quick perusal of standard reasons for the perennial lack of interest in studying novelizations suggests that one of the primary causes for their neglect is connected with the history of novelizations as tie-in products "written quickly on commission and issued to cross promote a screen release"—commonly the release of popular Hollywood movies—or to extend films' popularity after their release (Murray 2012, p. 152). Given that the generally accepted function of novelizations is promotion, they are also disparaged as being commercial rather than artist-driven; hence, as Linda Hutcheon (2006) explains, novelizations are seen as "simply commercial grabs, unmitigated commodifications, or inflationary recyclings" (p. 119). So while novelizations are understood as a sort of by-product or form of extended advertising, their perceived lack of originality contributes to their undervaluation, given that their plots derive from or serve as transcriptions of already-known commodities. These factors combined have resulted in broader observations such as that made by Simone Murray (2012), namely that as prose reworkings of a produced screen play, novelizations have "typically occupied the very lowest rung on the literary ladder" (p. 152).[2]

However intuitive or studied such standard assessments of novelizations may be, the first examples indeed were written to coincide with or follow quickly after the release of movies. The earliest of these novelizations appeared in 1911 in monthly fan magazines as serialized short-story editions of American films, most notably in *Motion Picture Story Magazine* and *Photoplay* (Mahlknecht 2012, p. 138). In other words, right from their beginnings, novelizations have been associated with the sensational movie magazines in which they appeared, and their short-story format doubtless also contributed to the perception that novelizations are dumbed-down versions of simplistic narratives that began as popular culture products.

Whatever part the cultural status of the first novelizations may have played in their initial public perception, *Motion Picture Story*'s success with this new entertainment genre prompted *Motion Picture Classic*, *Moving Picture Stories*, and *Photo Play* to follow suit. Along with novelizations of single films, these publications also began publishing text versions of film series, such as *What Happened to Mary* (Edison 1912–13), which was simultaneously novelized in *The Ladies' World*. This publication strategy was duly noted and followed up with *The Adventures of Kathlyn* (Selig Polyscope 1914), *The Perils of Pauline* (Eclectic 1914) and *The Exploits of Elaine* (Pathé 1914) (Newell 2017, p. 28; Van Parys 2009, pp. 306–307). Given these titles, it is hardly surprising that, according to Kate Newell (2017), the magazines that published these serialized novelizations of women's (mis)adventures developed into celebrity tabloids targeting female fans. Therefore, in keeping with the "increased focus on female spectatorship" in the film and associated industries as they developed, a long-standing and deep relationship between women and novelizations took hold from the early days of narrative cinema (p. 28).

If, therefore, it is safe to attribute at least some of novelizations' lowly status to their historic association with women, this ranking is arguably connected with the production and reception women's writing, and writing associated with women more generally. Indeed, in 1856—long before the publication of the first novelizations—George Eliot enthusiastically polemicized against "Silly Novels by Lady Novelists" (1856/2006). In this famous essay, she complained that women who penned frivolous novels in the nineteenth century were distinguished by "the particular quality of silliness that predominates them," while women's fiction, according to Eliot, was known as a combination of "the frothy, the prosy, the pious, or the pedantic" (p. 301). So just as novelizations have been disdained because of their association with women's movies, women's writing and women readers, so too have popular novels since the genre's early days.

The quintessence of the cheap narrative property by and for female readers that Eliot so gleefully disparaged would arrive on the scene a century after her essay in the form of the Harlequin Romance. Founded in 1949, the company began as a "reprint operation [...] issuing cheap versions of material that it had acquired from a wide variety of sources" and then novelized, including detective stories, Westerns and even pornography (Radway 1991, p. 39). Key to Harlequin Enterprise's success was the appointment of the company founder's wife Mary Bonnycastle as chief editor, who directed the company to focus on "stories that ended well and were in good taste" (p. 39). Bonnycastle also discovered that British firm Mills & Boon, which had been publishing romances since 1908, published her favorite novels. She promptly acquired the paperback rights to some of their romances, banking on the intuition that there was an untapped market of female readers who loved romance novels (Harlequin, n.d.). By 1984, Harlequin had come to define the market in formulaic romances and claimed a readership of some 16 million women in North America. It has now sold well over 6 billion books (pp. 39–40).

In the present context, it is notable that Harlequin Enterprises also makes an appearance in *LBM*, as a minifigure rendition of Marvel comics character Harley Quinn. In *LBM*, Harley Quinn is a rogue as well as a nurturing female. She soothes the Joker's ego when Batman's constant rejections bruise it, telling him, "You're too good for Batman. He needs to open his eyes and see what it feels like when you're not around." She later goes undercover as a "Phantom Zone" laundry company worker which—however coincidentally—ties in neatly with both women's traditional domestic role and Harley Quinn's namesake novels, originally marketed with laundry detergent.[3] As one of *LBM*'s main characters, Harley Quinn gets a full page in Beth Davies' (2017) Level 2 novelization, *Rise of the Rogues*, where readers learn that Harley loves the Joker's "silly pranks" and that "[h]er colourful costume and bright make-up are nearly as eye-catching as the Joker's" (p. 16). Given this description, it is also tempting to draw a connection between the character's appearance (bright make-up that does not outshine the male lead's) and her propensity for silly jokes to the stereotypes associated with women that I have outlined thus far.

Eliot's (1856/2006) scathing critique of female authors of frivolous fiction includes another significant detail: she suggests that women may have begun writing frothy formulaic stories "because they had no other 'lady-like' means of getting their bread" (p. 302). Although one may judge "the commodity to be a nuisance," writes Eliot, one was also "glad to think that the money went to relieve the necessitous, and we pictured to ourselves lonely women struggling for maintenance of wives and daughters devoting themselves to the production of 'copy' out of pure heroism,—perhaps to pay their husband's debts, or to purchase luxuries for a sick father" (p. 302). For Eliot, however, while "empty writing" (as she calls it) may once have been "excused by an empty stomach," and while women may previously have produced "copy" out of a combination of necessity and limited opportunity, Eliot quickly supplants this notion with her theory that women had since begun writing "under totally different circumstances […] in elegant boudoirs, with violet-coloured ink and a ruby pen […] inexperienced in every form of poverty except of poverty of brains" (pp. 302–303).

However doubtful Eliot's notion that writing frivolous fiction became a lucrative profession for women in the nineteenth century may be, much evidence suggests that women are now writing commercial copy such as novelizations simply to earn a living, rather than to secure large fortunes or pursue lofty aesthetic goals. In an essay on recession-era chick flicks' characterization of female "hack" writers, Pamela Thoma (2014) argues that since the 2008 financial crisis, there has been a "relocation of public to domestic femininity through an emphasis on women's self-work and through the trope of writing as both a creative activity and a safe and lucrative form of employment" (p. 108). Since then, according to Thoma, writing as represented in popular Hollywood film has become a socially approved form of women's entrepreneurial labor, because writing from the home "blur[s] the lines between paid marketplace labor and unpaid reproductive or domestic labor." Thus, writing becomes "allied and closely associated with gendered domestic labor" (p. 110).

Likewise on the production side, Thoma (2014) among many others has pointed out that creative workers in the current neoliberal "talent-led economy" often use their own homes or cafés as production sites, from which they do various forms of writing or "piece work" as casual, part-time labor (p. 125). This means working without the benefit of a physical company office space. It is revealing here to note that the Web page of Erin Soderberg, a LEGO junior novel writer, states: "I have this very nice office, filled with books and a (sort of) tidy desk, and a soft and squishy rug" (Soderberg, n.d.), under a photograph of what appears to be a room in her own home, further domesticated with the "soft and squishy" tag (Soderberg, n.d.). The author, Erin Soderberg, then explains that inspiration comes to her in many places, and that she uses "whatever resources are available (like a pizza-sauce-filled paper plate at the arcade during a kid birthday party) [...] because [t]he fact is, writing is a job you can do anywhere!" Under a photo of the author correcting a manuscript while seated on a sofa with a dog nestled between her outstretched legs, we read, "When I'm working from home, I have furry company sitting on my lap most days." Similarly, LEGO novelizer Anna Holmes notes on her Amazon.com profile that she now writes and "lives in the beautiful Pacific Northwest with her husband and two spoiled cats," again bringing domesticity to her writing practice, and seeming to indicate that she works at least in part from the home (Holmes, n.d.). Likewise, novelizer Meredith Rusu who specializes "in titles based on television and movies such as LEGO [...] lives in New Jersey with her husband and two young sons who provide much of the inspiration for her writing. When she isn't working, Meredith enjoys karaoke, spending time with family, and going on the occasional adventure or two" (Rusu 2019), again bringing domestic warmth and inspiration to the picture that Rusu paints of her writing career.

Newell has also noted that many of the novelizers she surveyed work from home were "not able to make a living from just the 'one off,'" and worked on a casual, contract-to-contract basis (K. Newell, personal communication, May 6, 2019). Indeed, the job of novelizing LEGO movies and toys, which is virtually the exclusive domain of women, is almost always casual and flexible. This typically also means that these workers' situation is precarious and frequently involves labor without benefits such as healthcare coverage (Thoma 2014, p. 125). Unsurprisingly, then, one woman who writes LEGO novelizations describes her career path as having consisted almost exclusively of casual employment, having picked up jobs as "a waitress, a malt-maker, a tour guide on a boat, a book editor, a cookie inventor, a movie extra, and [she] also worked for Nickelodeon" (Soderberg, n.d.). Similarly, Anna Holmes—author of *Emmet's Awesome Day* (2014)—informs visitors to her writer's page that she "has held many strange jobs, including teaching high schoolers how to outwit the SAT, polishing boots and lacing corsets, and what a friend described once as 'being a library elf'" (Holmes, n.d.).

As Thoma (2014) argues, recent aspirational movies and chick flicks often represent female authors engaged in "devocationalized commercial forms of writing that are sanctioned for women," such as blogging, self-help and other forms of life writing, rather than portraying women working with "literary forms associated with the masculinized figure of the writer as artist" (p. 125).[4] These genres, to which I would add novelizations, fall under the kinds of pink-collar labor that sit well with postfeminist popular culture, wherein women supposedly participate willingly in an "expanding global media industry, effectively modeling an abiding interest in the production and consumption of the texts in which her work appears" (p. 125). It is therefore also conjectured that contemporary popular culture "tacitly tutor[s] women in the gendering of labor or the various kinds of work society expects from them in a labor market deeply segregated horizontally by occupation and vertically within occupations" (p. 124).

"Everything Is Awesome"? Novelizations and LEGO

So, where novelizations of the LEGO movies are concerned, many aspects of what I have just been discussing come sharply into focus. For example, I have argued that under-valued genres of writing such as "silly novels," Harlequin romances and novelizations have been associated with female authors since their beginnings, and that this continues to be the case in the present. It is, therefore, not surprising that virtually all LEGO novelizations are written by women, including *The LEGO Batman Movie* Junior Novel by Jeanette Lane, Davies' *The LEGO Batman Movie: Rise of the Rogues*, Anna Holmes' *Emmet's Awesome Day*, and Kate Howard's *LEGO: The LEGO Movie: Junior Novel* (2013). I began by arguing that since the nineteenth century and throughout the twentieth, trivial genres have been associated with women readers and writers, and that in contemporary, postfeminist popular culture, "commercial writing becomes the entrepreneurial labor of choice for women," according to Thoma (2014, p. 130). Indeed, all of this is abundantly illustrated by the authors' profiles just cited, from their histories of casual, creative labor to their engagement with what is supposedly the "lowest rung on the literary ladder," and the ways in which their domestic lives, children and pets merge with their professional lives—writing space, story lines, inspiration—so that the two become profoundly interwoven. Based on this brief history of women and "trivial" genres of writing, and given the sheer number of female novelizers of LEGO, it appears that the craft has become a small cottage industry for women. In this section, I want to continue to explore theories and arguments as to why this might be the case.

Concerning the reception and audience appeal of women's fiction, it is commonly assumed that women enjoy strongly emotive narratives, be they romantic boy-meets-girl stories or sentimental stories focused on marriage, children and domesticity. Thoma (2014) has also observed that contract-to-contract women's writing is often the focus of chick flicks "precisely because it allows for the expression of feelings," including "the production of emotional intimacy" (pp. 119, 128). Such forms of labor often also amount to a kind of self-work or self-improvement (on the part of the author and/or readers) and frequently includes the performance of nurturing, caring labor on behalf of others, such as caring for children (McGee 2005, pp. 139–193). The cluster of tasks that I am describing here falls under the heading of "affective labor," or labor that is frequently immaterial, "even if it is corporeal and affective, in the sense that its products are intangible: a feeling of ease, well-being, satisfaction, excitement, passion – even a sense of connectedness or community" (Hardt 1999, p. 96).[5] Seen in this light, it is interesting to note that Erin Soderberg, who writes for LEGO under pseudonym "Beth Davies," describes writing for children as an endeavor to create characters who are "extra close and supportive of one another" and "there for each other no matter what" (Soderberg, n.d.).[6]

While *TLM*'s target audiences are wide and varied—including children, their parents, AFOLs [adult fans of LEGO], and fans of all ages of popular franchises featured in the movie, such as Batman, Teenage Mutant Ninja Turtles, the Simpsons, and so on—the novelizations appeal primarily to children. This is why Davies' (2017) *The Rise of the Rogues*, a Level 2 category junior novel, includes a "Guide for Parents," as well as various tips for using the book, such as "praise, share and chat" to ensure "a valuable and shared reading experience" (pp. 46–47). While undertaking such nurturing tasks with children is not women's exclusive domain, it is unsurprising that women would write novelizations intended to instruct and entertain children. Soderberg explains that her own interest in writing LEGO novelizations was borne from her intuition that "movie novelizations—and other books based on popular brands, TV shows, and movies—is a great way to encourage kids to read for fun" (B. Davies, personal communication, May 13, 2019).

Affective labor also includes nurturing in the form of life coaching and helping people to develop "awesome" productive personal habits, through self-realization, self-help and self-motivation.[7] In this regard, LEGO junior novelizations such as *Emmet's Guide to Being Awesome* by "Ace" Landers and *Keeping it Awesomer with Emmet* by Meredith Rusu also end up remediating Emmet Brickowski's feel-good *Instructions on How to Fit in, Have Everybody Like You, and Always Be Happy!* from the film, which include,

Step 2: Greet the day, Smile and say: Good morning city!
Step 3: Get some morning exercise.
Step 4: Take a shower, and always be sure to keep the soap out of your eyes!
Step 5: Brush your teeth.
Step 7: Comb your hair.
Step 8: Wear clothes.
Step 9: Share a meal with the special people in your life.
Step 10: Greet your neighbors.
Step 11: Obey traffic signs and regulations.
Step 16: Always return a compliment.
Step 19: Don't touch any weird objects.

The novelizations that adapt this particular aspect of *TLM* are focalized through Emmet (*Keeping it Awesomer* even comes with an Emmet minifigure), who explains "how to find your inner awesome," discusses "finding the true you" and "the power to be special," and introduces junior readers to the "Master Builders" who showed him how to believe in himself (Wyldstyle, Vitruvius, Batman, Unikitty and so on). Therefore, if *TLM* presents tongue-in-cheek renditions of self-help manuals that promote laudable practices such as paying attention to personal hygiene, the novelizations do so with perhaps a little less cynicism and considerably more focus on influencing young readers with what one reader describes as "inspirational messages for kids" (Amazon.com, n.d.). Given the current neoliberal trend to propose self-help techniques such as mindfulness training to deal with the stress of constant work precarity and as a remedy for the erosion of social safety nets around the globe, grooming children to take self-help advice from *TLM* is a somewhat remarkable if questionable undertaking.

When considering the potentially profound effects of LEGO novelizations on impressionable young readers and their personal habits, one might also keep in mind that, although novelizations are criticized for simply promoting the movies they adapt in order to sell more product, they are also said to "provide more details, especially about adapted characters' inner lives, but in the process they also help foster audience/reader identification with those characters" (Hutcheon 2006,

p. 118), which again relates to the LEGO novelizations' pedagogical aim or purpose. Accordingly, one author of LEGO novelizations writes that "young readers, especially, need to develop reading habits, and sometimes it's easiest to do that when you're spending time with characters and worlds you already know and love" (Personal communication, May 13, 2019). Therefore, one may also conclude that these products help children develop healthy reading habits and improve their reading skills—a potentially positive aspect of novelizations.

That said, writing LEGO novelizations, at least for the author just quoted, incentivizes children to read because of their own strong, affective bonds with LEGO and a beloved movie, no matter how commercialized that love may be. While assisting children in their development of useful skills and wholesome habits through entertaining copy may be the goal, LEGO novelizations are thus also a means of extending the brand's reach. *The LEGO Batman Movie Junior Novel* is a prime example of how a novelization can do both: The cover informs readers that it is "Based on the hit movie!" while the first page states, "Batman was a dark, brooding Super Hero who fought the evilest of villains in order to rid the famous city of crime" (Lane 2016, p. 3). The cover cues readers to connect the text with the film it promotes, and the text fills junior readers in on Batman's backstory in the unlikely event that they are unfamiliar with the Batman franchise. The title page states that this junior novel was "adapted by Jeanette Lane, based on the screenplay by Seth Grahame-Smith and Chris McKenna & Erik Sommers, with additional material by Jared Stern & John Whittington, based on LEGO Construction Toys," thereby further connecting the author as adaptor of the film, the original screenplay, and finally the interlocking blocks on which all of the above are based, to LEGO and the company's fiscal goals. (Refer to Chapter 3 in this collection by McAllister and LaGroue for a discussion of the role of novelizations in the broader world of LEGO merchandising.)

As already noted, critics also argue that novelizations are unimaginative, slavish copies of the underlying "original" narrative property, and certainly many readers seem to be seeking a faithful prose copy of a favorite film. For example, one reader commenting on Jeanette Lane's *LEGO Batman Movie Junior Novel* wrote, "this book was not the best junior novel I have ever read. Nothing like the movie but the beginning was kinda the same. I did not like the part that Joker did not bring back the Phantom Zone with him [...]. I am obsessed with LEGO Batman and i (sic.) got so excited when i (sic.) saw this book in the kindle store. Finished it the same day i (sic.) bought it but was disappointed." Similarly, another reader commented, "I read this to my five year old and he followed along fine. My only criticism is that the plot does not match the movie [...]. He kept asking me if there was another Lego Batman movie out that we didn't have." On the other hand, readers of Kate Howard's (2013) *The LEGO Movie Junior Novel* gave the novelization a positive rating, based on her novelization's faithfulness to the movie: "This is just like the movie. We liked the movie so much, we bought the junior novel to read." In sum, these comments suggest that some readers indeed want an exact copy in prose of a narrative property they know from another medium, such as film or TV.

But while some of the more negative aspects of novelization (commerciality, lack of originality) are captured in these readers' comments, some readers also confirm the notion that "[n]ovelizations of films, including what are called 'junior' novelizations for younger viewers, are also often seen as having a kind of educational—or perhaps simply curiosity—value" (Hutcheon 2006, p. 118). Indeed, although much commercial value can be squeezed out of narrative properties by recycling them across media platforms such as film, video games, remakes and so on, children are also likely aided in developing reading skills by returning to familiar stories that they have taken in aurally and/or visually, transposed into text form. So whether or not one agrees with the notion of children being cajoled into reading "another great book about batman (sic.) for the starting reader," readers continue to post comments about how children love these books: "Can't get enough! Great read for my 9 year old!"

"A very cute little book:
Cute for any lego (sic.) fan!"[8]

In this final section, I focus more concertedly on the relationship between affect and LEGO, in particular where the notion of toyetics is concerned, and cuteness as a particularly emotive or affect-inducing aesthetic. First, the term "toyetic" was coined by Bernard Loomis, a development executive for Kenner Toys who also worked for Mattel in the 1960s. He reportedly used the word for the first time in telling Steven Spielberg that the upcoming *Star Wars* movie was not "toyetic" enough, when he was considering acquiring the license to create toys to promote the film. The term is now used to describe the "suitability of a media property, such as a cartoon or movie, for merchandising tie-in lines of licensed toys, games and novelties," and it is also understood in reverse, as in the case of the current craze for toy-driven feature films (Orr 2009).

As a star product featured in video games, TV shows and movies, LEGO is a toyetic triumph. Interestingly, however, some of LEGO's success in this regard is attributable not to company executives and filmmakers, but rather to fans who first tapped the bricks' toyetic potential in homemade "brickfilms." Lars C. Hassing and Henrik Hassing made the first Super 8, stop motion animation brickfilm entitled *Journey to the Moon* [*En rejse til månen*] in 1973 (released on YouTube in May 2013). A second brickfilm, *LEGO* (1980) by Fernando Escovar, was released on YouTube on April 2, 2007. From 1985 to 1989, Lindsay Fleay of Perth, Western Australia worked to create *The Magic Portal* from LEGO bricks, plasticine, and cardboard characters in stop motion animation and live action. The most significant moment in early brickfilms, however, was a music video for UK dance act Ethereal and their song "Zap" on Truelove Records, produced and released in 1989. Shown throughout the MTV network and on other music channels, that brickfilm marked an important moment for The LEGO Group, which began officially commissioning brickfilms in 1987.

In the late 1990s, digital cameras facilitated brickfilms' production, and the Internet made it possible for brickfilmers to distribute their work more rapidly and to wider audiences. (For an exploration of one subset of this type of online distribution of fan-made films featuring LEGO bricks, see Chapter 9 in this volume: "LEGO Porn: Phallic Pleasure and Knowledge" by Brownlee.) The founding of Brickfilms.com in 2000 consolidated the brickfilming community, linking pages where the films could be downloaded or streamed. At the same time, LEGO Studios released boxed sets with which children could make their own brickfilms, since which time The LEGO Group have openly and actively encouraged the production of fan brickfilms to help the company advertise new themes. More concretely, the makers of *TLM* tapped fan labor and creativity in producing the film. With a contest later publicized in a video, Chris Pratt (Emmet Brickowski) explained the following:

> It's truly amazing how many LEGO fans there are around the world who love to create short films using LEGO bricks. The filmmakers of *The LEGO Movie*, Chris and Phil, thought it would be fun to challenge the rebrick community—that's LEGO's official social media platform—to come up with an original brickfilm between fifteen and thirty seconds with the winning entry being featured during *The LEGO Movie*. (The LEGO Movie—Fan Made Films 2014)

Also in the lead-up to the film, The LEGO Group launched other contests for children aged seven to twelve, including one to build a LEGO vehicle that looked like something else, for which the winner was awarded $1000 and a spot for the vehicle in the movie. There was likewise a contest for the creation of LEGO minifigures that appeared in the film's official trailer and, in another contest, children were challenged to build the "biggest, wildest and most awesome space-ship model ever!" Given *TLM*'s simple plot (i.e., a LEGO minifigure changes up his environment to fight off a bad guy) and the number of contests that fed the film with fan-made characters and scenarios, much of the film's intellectual property resulted from various "labours of love" (Goggin 2018).

While certainly not claiming to write LEGO junior texts out of love alone, one novelizer explained that, when offered the opportunity to write *TLM* novelizations, she "obviously jumped on the chance!" and further stated that she has "always found LEGO to be an incredibly cute, clever and funny brand, and it's really exciting to get an early look at the script and casting" (Personal communication, May 13, 2019). What I want to suggest here is that LEGO is able to rely on remarkably strong brand loyalty and fan engagement, which in turn is grown, encouraged and tapped in order to create new outputs, to increase fan identification with the toy, and to further deepen continued involvement with the brand as child fans become AFOLs. (See also Chapter 10 in this volume: "'It's All About the Brick': Mobilizing Adult Fans of LEGO" by Jennings.)

Supporting all of the above is the look and feel of the LEGO product, from the bright colors to the diminutive minifigures. I would argue that a large part of this brand appeal is attributable to cuteness, as well. A distinguishing feature of many toys such as dolls (Goggin 2017a, pp. 218–230), what cuteness is and does as an aesthetic look and practice—the effects it produces on the level of affect or the warm, cuddly emotion that cuteness is capable of awakening in those interacting with it—has been the focus of a growing body of scholarship on the topic.

Serious work on cuteness began with ethologist Konrad Lorenz's 1943 essay, "Innate Forms of Experience" [*Die angeborenen Formen möglicher Erfahrung*] containing his "child schema" which outlines a set of physical features and behavioral characteristics shared by young children and baby animals. These include "a relatively large head, predominance of the brain capsule, large and low-lying eyes, bulging cheek region, short and thick extremities, a springy elastic consistency, and clumsy movements," all of which Lorenz claimed would trigger an involuntary desire to nurture in adults (Lorenz 1950/1971, pp. 154–162).

Where cuteness and LEGO is concerned—from children's loyalty to the brand, to novelizers' excitement about writing prose versions of the movies—this aesthetic feature of the product is key to its ability to act as an "innate releasing mechanism" [IRM]. According to Lorenz (1950/1971), cuteness triggers involuntary responses, and cute objects foster emotional bonds in subjects responding to it. The importance of cuteness, and indeed the interlocking brick manufacturer's awareness of the power of cuteness to stimulate certain responses, is made clear in *LBM* when orphan Dick Grayson (Michael Cera), looking for a father figure in Batman, asks: "Should I get experimental surgery to make my eyes larger and more vulnerable-looking?" While the character's idea is that larger eyes would make him "more vulnerable-looking" and cuter as per Lorenz's schema, his intuition that bigger eyes will have the desired effect also falls into line with Lori Merish's (1996) assertion that "the cute is always shopping for a mother"—that is, the appeal of cuteness supposedly arouses maternal instincts, particularly in women, for things and creatures considered vulnerable (p. 196).

In *Our Aesthetic Categories: Zany, Cute, Interesting*, Sian Ngai (2012) writes that "certain kinds of work have always been affective women's paid and unpaid caring work in the household, and jobs in the services sector implicitly or explicitly based on that work, such as health care, retail, and teaching" (p. 10). The development of what is referred to as the dematerializing economy—that is, an economy that relies increasingly on the production and marketing of experience and affect (movies, videogames, gambling, travel), rather than the production of goods—coupled with neoliberalism's attack on the social safety net, including the responsibilization of the individual beginning in the 1970s, has caused a sizable shift to "precarious labour, immaterial and affective labour [...] within the over-arching frame of post-Fordist regimes of production" (McRobbie 2010, p. 60). This shift, which has occasioned what "is often referred to as the feminization of work" and includes "the growth of freelance or precarious self-employment" and "new forms of micro-entrepreneurialism associated with the growing cultural and creative and media sectors of advanced capitalism," has impacted women both positively and negatively (pp. 62, 65). On the one hand, there is increased opportunity for women, such as those who write for LEGO, to work on a causal basis, and women report that this kind of subcontracting is conducive to their lifestyles, making it possible to write in the "furry company" of the family dog or "spoiled cats," as the two authors I quoted previously reported. And, as McRobbie notes, in spite of the "high degree of uncertainty or precariousness in their freelance of micro-entrepreneurial activities," many express work satisfaction and "passionate commitment" (p. 71) to jobs such as writing LEGO novelizations. Given the brand loyalty and the pull of cuteness at LEGO's command, working for the company feeds into fandom, overriding concerns about contingency and trumping the desire for large monetary rewards. As one novelizer wrote, while she had always enjoyed the brand, there were other perks: It's exciting to get an early look at "pre-release film images when you work on novelizations" (Personal communication, May 13, 2019). In other words, cuteness and toyetics produce excitement and affect, which becomes—at least in part—its own "awesome" reward for novelizers of the LEGO movies.

Conclusion

In this essay, I set out to explain why the majority of LEGO novelizations are written by women, based on my intuition that the predominance of women producing them relates to the texts' nature and purpose, as well as to traditional gender roles in several fields of endeavor, such as teaching children and certain types writing (arguably including novelizations). It is a truism that such so-called trivial genres of literature are associated with women writers and readers, and this has been the case for centuries. Indeed, the genre is most commonly associated with frivolous "silly" novels for women is the Harlequin Romance, personified in *LBM* in the character Harley Quinn.

Given that novelizations are likewise seen as a genre so negligible as to be almost completely ignored in scholarship on literature, film and adaptation, it seems both natural and unfortunate to associate it, at least in the case of LEGO adaptations for junior readers, with women. Equally unfortunate, however, is how we tend to look past some of novelizations' positive aspects, such as the powerful incentive they hold out to children to read, and the encouragement they provide to keep reading. Indeed, in attempting to recall my own experience novelization of *The Parent Trap* (1968) that I read as a child, I remember being drawn along by my impressions of the film, and not being able to put the book down because my attention was focused so intently through those impressions together with the fascination of "reading" the movie.

While neoliberalism has much to answer for in terms of worker precarity, the dissolution of employee benefits, and the elimination of professional work spaces in favor of e-commuting and working in the home, freelancing and micro-entrepreneurship have upsides. Where women are concerned, copywriting and novelization which can be done in the home facilitates domestic labor and caring for children; but one should equally be concerned about the potential of freelance writing careers to re-relegate women to the private sphere.

Finally, many people are, of course, drawn to cuteness and suceptible to its capacity to produce affect by triggering caring behaviors. Although feminist theory has debunked Lorenz's insistence that women are particularly drawn to cuteness as a function of their supposed maternal instincts, and although critics such as Ngai (2012) have argued that cuteness can equally trigger sadistic impulses, cuteness undeniably acts as an emotional stimulus. Precisely this capacity has led to the cute aesthetic's global spread, along with its rhetorical force and its power to move people which can be harnessed for less-than-salutary ends. Indeed, while working from home alongside puppies and kittens (as the novelizations' authors mention on their Web sites) has a cute factor that may ease work-related stress, or the stress of not having work, it can also be a key factor in convincing fans—such as fans of LEGO—to labor for meager or scant rewards. What is more, as Lazzarato (n.d.) has explained, immaterial labor "produces the 'cultural content' of the commodity, [and] involves a series of activities that are not normally recognized as 'work'" which define and fix "cultural and artistic standards, fashions, tastes, consumer norms, and, more strategically, public opinion." In other words, while a toy and the stories it generates may seem innocuous, its power to shape opinion and to influence people from a very early age can be enormous.

Therefore, the critique I set out to deliver in this chapter turns out to be rather more complicated than a LEGO junior novel. As LEGO studies take off amid the brand's runaway success; as the bricks become more than just a toy to generations who grew up playing with LEGO; as children become AFOLs; and as the cuteness of LEGO, its aesthetic and affective appeal becomes ever-more-deeply imbricated in our daily lives in the form of endless products and entertainments, there are many important avenues for research and scholarship on LEGO left to explore.

Notes

1. For a strong new contribution to studies of the novelization genre, please see Jan Baetens' (2019) *Novelization: From Film to Novel.*
2. According to Mahlknecht (2012), "novelizations consist of work done for hire. This automatically denies the genre access to an idealized notion of literature according to which a work of art if the motivation for creating it comes from the author himself or herself" (p. 150).
3. When, in 1971, Harlequin hired W. Lawrence Heisey, former "soap salesman" for Proctor and Gamble, he included "sample copies [of Harlequin Romances] in boxes of Bio-Ad laundry detergent" (Radway 1991, pp. 40–41).
4. Although compiling a comprehensive list of who writes novelizations by gender is beyond the scope of this chapter, a quick survey reveals that higher-end novelizations aimed at the adult market are somewhat more frequently penned by male authors. Typical titles of novelizations written by men include *The Omen*, *Star Wars*, *Taxi Driver*, and *American Gigolo.* See Verevis (2017).
5. According to Maurizio Lazzarato immaterial labor "is defined as the labor that produces the informational and cultural content of the commodity. The concept of immaterial labor refers to two different aspects of labor. On the one hand, as regards the 'informational content' of the commodity, it refers directly to the changes taking place in workers' labor processes in big companies in the industrial and tertiary sectors, where the skills involved in direct labor are increasingly skills involving cybernetics and computer control (and horizontal and vertical communication). On the other hand, as regards the activity that produces the 'cultural content' of the commodity, immaterial labor involves a series of activities that are not normally recognized as 'work'—in other words, the kinds of activities involved in defining and fixing cultural and artistic standards, fashions, tastes, consumer norms, and, more strategically, public opinion" (Lazzarato, n.d.).
6. According to Soderberg, whenever she writes "stories or novelizations that are based on someone else's characters, [she] use[s] a pseudonym – [she doesn't] want anyone to get the false impression that [she] created these movies or characters. [She is] only using them (with permission) for a short while" (E. Soderberg, personal communication, May 13, 2019). That said, however, Soderberg's choice to publish her LEGO

novelizations under a pen name may also be related to Mahlknecht's (2012) claim that novelizers "frequently use pen names, lest their more ambitious work should suffer contamination" (p. 150).

7. For more on this topic specifically in relation to *The LEGO Movie*, see Goggin (2018) and Goggin (2017b). There is a considerable body of work on women and the performance of self-actualization in popular film, novels and television. For more on this topic in the specific case of Elizabeth Gilbert's *Eat, Pray, Love*, see Goggin (2018) and Goggin (2017b). For work on precarity, neoliberalization and affective capitalism, consult William Davies' excellent *Happiness Industries*, 2015.

8. This is taken from readers' comments at Amazon (n.d.).

References

Amazon.com. (n.d.). https://www.amazon.com/Emmets-Awesome-Day-Lego-Movie/product-reviews/1407155695/ref=cm_cr_dp_d_show_all_btm?ie=UTF8&reviewerType=all_reviews. Accessed on July 17, 2019.

Baetens, J. (2019). *Novelization: From film to novel*. Columbus: The Ohio State University Press.

Corporate Harlequin. (n.d.). https://corporate.harlequin.com/. Accessed on July 25, 2019.

Crume, V. (1968). *The parent trap*. New York: Scholastic Book Services.

Davies, W. (2015). *The happiness industry: How the government and big business sold us well-being*. London and New York: Verso.

Davies, B. (2017). *The LEGO Batman Movie: Rise of the rogues*. London: Random House.

Eliot, G. (2006/1856). Silly novels by lady novelists. In *The Norton anthology of English literature* (8th ed., pp. 1342–1349). New York: W. W. Norton.

Goggin, J. (2017a). Affective marketing and the kuteness of kiddles. In J. Dale, J. Goggin, J. Leyda, A. McIntyre, & D. Negra (Eds.), *The aesthetics and affects of cuteness* (pp. 216–235). New York: Routledge.

Goggin, J. (2017b). "Everything is awesome": *The LEGO movie* and the affective politics of security. J. Morris & N. Boy (Eds.), *Special Issue: Finance and Society, 3*(2), 143–158. https://doi.org/10.2218/finsoc.v3i2.2574.

Goggin, J. (2018). "How do those Danish bastards sleep at night?": Fan labour and the power of cuteness. S. Giddings & A. Harvey (Eds.), *Special Issue: Ludic Economies*, 1–18. https://doi.org/10.1177/1555412018760918.

Goggin, J. (2019). "Everything is awesome": Spreadable stories and *the LEGO movie*. Forthcoming. In J. Fehrle & W. Schäfke (Eds.), *Adaptation in the age of media convergence*. Amsterdam: Amsterdam University Press.

Hardt, M. (1999). Affective labour. *Boundary 2, 26*(2), 89–100.

Holmes, A. (n.d.). *About Anna Holmes*. https://www.amazon.com/Anna-Holmes/e/B00NB2IAL0?ref=dbs_p_pbk_r00_abau_000000. Accessed on July 17, 2019.

Holmes, A. (2014). *Emmet's awesome day*. New York: Scholastic.

Howard, K. (2013). *LEGO: The LEGO movie: Junior novel*. New York: Scholastic.

Hutcheon, L. (2006). *Adaptation*. London and New York: Routledge.

Lane, J. (2016). *The LEGO Batman Movie: Junior novel*. New York: Scholastic.

Lazzarato, M. (n.d.). *Immaterial labour*. http://www.generation-online.org/c/fcimmateriallabour3.htm. Accessed on July 17, 2019.

Lorenz, K. (1971). Part and parcel in human and animal societies (R. Martin, Trans.). In *Studies in animal and human behaviour* (Vol. 2, pp. 115–195). Cambridge: Harvard University Press.

Mahlknecht, J. (2012). The Hollywood novelization: Film as literature or literature as film promotion? *Poetics Today, 33*(2), 137–168.

McGee, M. (2005). *Self-Help, Inc.: Makeover Culture in American Life*. Oxford: Oxford University Press.

McRobbie, A. (2010). Reflections on feminism, immaterial labour and the post-Fordist regime. *New Formations, 70,* 60–76.

Merish, L. (1996). Cuteness and commodity aesthetics. In R. G. Thompson (Ed.), *Freakery: Cultural spectacles of the extraordinary body* (pp. 185–206). New York: New York University Press.

Murray, S. (2012). *The adaptation industry: The cultural economy of contemporary literary adaptation*. New York and London: Routledge.

Newell, K. (2017). *Expanding adaptation networks: From illustrations to novelization*. London: Palgrave.

Ngai, S. (2012). *Our aesthetic categories: Zany, cute, interesting*. Cambridge: Harvard University Press.

Orr, C. (2009, November 5). *Toyetic*. Retrieved from The New Republic website https://newrepublic.com/article/70952/toyetic.

Radway, J. A. (1991). *Reading the romance: Women, patriarchy, and popular literature*. Chapel Hill and London: University of North Carolina Press.

Rusu, M. (2019). *About Meredith Rusu*. https://meredithrusu.com/about-author-meredith-rusu/. Accessed on July 17, 2019.

Soderberg, E. (n.d.). On writing. *Erin Soderbergh: Books for kids (and fun adults!)*. http://erinsoderberg.com/on_writing. Accessed on July 17, 2019.

The LEGO Movie—Fan Made Films—Official Warner Bros. UK. (2014, August 11). https://www.youtube.com/watch?v=XSSZJxDsjew. Accessed on July 17, 2019.

Thoma, P. (2014). What Julia knew: Domestic labor in the recession-era chick-flick. In D. Negra & Y. Tasker (Eds.), *Gendering the recession: Media culture in an age of austerity*. Durham and London: Duke University Press.

Van Parys, T. (2009). The study of novelisation: A typology and secondary bibliography. *Literature/Film Quarterly, 37*(4), 305–317.

Verevis, C. (2017). Film novelization. In J. Grossman & R. B. Palmer (Eds.), *Adaptation in visual culture* (pp. 3–19). London: Palgrave.

9

LEGO Porn: Phallic Pleasure and Knowledge

Shannon Brownlee

In the canonical *Hard Core: Power, Pleasure, and the "Frenzy of the Visible,"* Linda Williams (1989) argues that pornography does not simply give pleasure; it is a discourse of *knowledge* about pleasure. In particular, she sees porn as a predominantly patriarchal discourse that investigates the mysteries of the female body's sexual experiences and pleasures. Pornographic moving images centered on LEGO, most of which are stop-motion animation featuring LEGO minifigs and other bricks, may seem too frivolous to convey or perpetuate knowledge, but we can learn a lot about both LEGO and pornography from them. However, this is not a pornography that is primarily concerned with the secrets of the female body. It is phallic and phallocentric. Grounded in the direct analogy between sexual penetration and the penetration of one LEGO brick by another, LEGO porn uses metaphors, allusions and the technical specificities of bricks to explore this theme of penetration. The results are often funny, sometimes disturbing, and they distance us both from conventional live-action porn and from much animated porn in ways that are—sometimes—smart and illuminating.

S. Brownlee (✉)
Dalhousie University, Halifax, NS, Canada
e-mail: Shannon.Brownlee@Dal.Ca

© The Author(s) 2019
R. C. Hains and S. R. Mazzarella (eds.), *Cultural Studies of LEGO*,
https://doi.org/10.1007/978-3-030-32664-7_9

History and Definitions of Cinematic and LEGO Porn

Although animated porn is almost as old as live-action cinematic porn (Capino 2018), because the latter is so much better known and is clearly a crucial reference point for animated porn (Saunders 2019, p. 250), its story bears telling. From the 1910s through the 1960s, stag films were short, silent, usually black-and-white, sometimes narratively incoherent films made by men (and the women they hired) solely for men; they were mostly live-action, although some included cartoon sequences (Penley 2006, p. 106; Williams 1989, p. 70). They were almost exclusively aimed at a heterosexual male audience, although they often featured girl-on-girl action[1] for the purposes of male titillation and very occasionally showed sex acts between men presented "in the context of heterosexual hegemony" (Waugh 1996, p. 310). Nonetheless, Constance Penley (2006) notes that American stag films also often made jokes at the expense of the main male character (p. 103) and emphasized female agency (p. 105). A major shift in cinematic porn history came in the 1960s, when beaver films (in which female strippers displayed their genitalia) and feature-length exploitation films paved the way for the so-called Golden Age of porn that began with *Deep Throat* (Gerard Damiano 1972). *Deep Throat* integrated feature-length, coherent narrative with explicit sexual acts; it was shot with sound and color and was first screened in a legal cinema to heterosexual couples as well as men on their own. Higher budget, narrative porn subsequently dominated the 1970s and continued through the 1980s and beyond, although budgets started to decrease around 1982 when features changed over to video from celluloid (Alilunas 2016). Since then, home video and, later, Internet distribution slowly coincided with another radical change in porn form. Tristan Taormino (2013) maps out the typical heterosexual, single-couple format of today: "two minutes of fellatio, two minutes of cunnilingus (this is *optional*), two to three minutes of the first intercourse position, two to three minutes of the second position, two to three minutes of the third position, external cum shot" (p. 258, emphasis in original). There are variations. Feature-length porn is still produced—"Feature" is a well-stocked category on adultdvdempire.com—although it is the exception rather than the rule, and some narrative endures in shorter formats such as the PropertySex subgenre, in which randy real estate agents hearken back to the pizza delivery boys of yore. Overall, though, the narrative, feature-length porn of the 1970s and 1980s was "merely an entr'acte" (Schaefer 2002, p. 4) in the history of a cinematic form that is usually only minimally narrative and much shorter than feature length.

It is difficult to determine when LEGO porn entered the picture. Perhaps people built figures out of the first interlocking LEGO bricks and made them perform sex acts; perhaps the introduction of minifigures in 1978 inspired LEGO sex play; perhaps these experiments were filmed on 16 and 8 mm home movie cameras. We can only speculate that pornographic moving images featuring LEGO *proliferated* with the ubiquity of consumer-grade analogue and digital video production technologies. John Baichtal (2011) facetiously but maybe not inaccurately links the filming of LEGO sex play to online distribution: "Lego minifigs have been forced to hump one another by 8-year-old boys since day one, but with the wonders of the internet, these lewd fantasies have been turned into videos, web sites, and photos." The oldest LEGO-based pornographic moving images located during this research were posted to YouTube on December 26, 2006 (hellsvenom299 2006a, b), but the form may have existed before.

Although varied, LEGO porn is recognizable as an amateur genre that follows certain broad patterns. The vast majority of pornographic moving images featuring LEGO are stop-motion animation,[2] and most use minifigs as "porn stars." I have written elsewhere about the aesthetics of amateur stop-motion LEGO animation (Brownlee 2016), and LEGO porn conforms to general principles. Movement may be fairly sophisticated, though it is often extremely rudimentary, with frame rates of 1 or 2 per second. The professionalism of focus, lighting and camera mobility all vary from film to film. Sound often consists solely of a music track, which is simple to lay down once the images have been captured, but may be a more complicated composition of dialogue (and grunting and moaning), music and sometimes other sound effects. These more complicated soundtracks approximate the multi-track design of professional narrative cinema, although they still usually sound amateur in their simplicity and/or relatively low-quality recording. Dialogue is perhaps more common in LEGO porn than in other forms of LEGO animation because the voice is so effective at communicating pleasure and arousal. None of these features, however, is unique to LEGO porn.

Like other genres of amateur filmmaking as well as pornographic film, LEGO porn is an extremely ephemeral kind of cinema. By far, the largest repository of LEGO-based pornographic moving images is on YouTube, but the site removes videos regularly for violating its Nudity and Sexual Content Policies (2018): During this research, several videos have become inaccessible. Several others, although not discernibly different in content, are age-restricted although, ironically, the voice acting of many LEGO porn films suggests they have been made by prepubescent children or teenagers. It is not clear how YouTube applies its sexual content policies to LEGO porn, but we can guess that removals and age restrictions result from user complaints and flags. While LEGO porn can be found on other sites such as Vimeo and Pornhub and does not appear to be subject to such censorship there, the vast majority of the form today is framed by YouTube's apparently fairly arbitrary application of policies and is thus an unstable archive.

Defining the form is a correspondingly debatable process. Pornography is notoriously difficult to define, and this chapter does not aim to get entangled in these debates. Williams (1989) defines hardcore cinematic porn pragmatically as "the visual (and sometimes aural) representation of living, moving bodies engaged in explicit, unusually unfaked, sexual acts with a primary intent of arousing viewers" (p. 30). This is broadly useful even though in animated porn the unreal bodies and frame-by-frame creation of movement undermine the "living" and "unfaked" nature of the acts. Nonetheless, Williams's (1989, p. 70) and Penley's (2006, p. 106) seamless integration of animated sequences in their discussions of predominantly live-action porn suggests that this liveliness and realness may not be so important after all. Furthermore, in some ways, animated porn simply takes the excess of live-action porn to its logical conclusion. As Capino (2018) states: "The sexual plenitude of live-action's pornotopia is surpassed by animation's superhuman capacity for producing bodies, sexualities, and desires." Although animated porn is "paradoxical" in its "lack of bodies and sexuality," it is "real enough to become the subject of angry protests and serious lawsuits" (Capino 2018). As far as LEGO porn is concerned, the Urban Dictionary (2017) provides the only current definition, and a thin one at that: "Images of Lego minifigures engaging in sexual maneuvers and positions." This is not entirely accurate: Video uploaders also apply tags and titles like "lego porn" to films that feature live-action humans or larger LEGO figures built of a range of bricks rather than minifig elements. In general, though, there is a pragmatic consensus that LEGO porn is the representation of sex acts involving LEGO, and it is not legally important or socially prominent enough to have come under scrutiny and for its definition to have been refined.

There is also a general consensus about the social value of LEGO porn in the discourse surrounding it: It is puzzling, perverse and troubling, but also fascinating and amusing. A post on Mommyish.com includes a series of standalone images and screen captures from higher-quality LEGO porn videos, and the introduction encapsulates a common attitude to LEGO porn:

> I've started looking at Lego porn, and I am addicted. I may need to go to a meeting, perhaps a sub-chapter of Sex Addicts Anonymous. Once you delve into this amazing Lego porn, you'll probably become an addict too. And then you'll be looking at it all the time in the bathroom on your iPhone, and everyone will be ashamed of you, and you'll probably lose your most important relationships.
>
> So check out this Lego porn at your own risk. If you fall down a slippery shame spiral and become sexually attracted to Legos, that's really not my problem because I told you not to. If you need help with your addiction, you're going to have to seek out other Lego lovers that are into freaky freak plastic porn because they are the only people that can help you now. (Ramos 2017)

While titillation here is facetious rather than palpably authentic, usually it is more straightforwardly demonized. For example, user comments on the compilation video *Inside the world of Lego porn* (beautiful pics 2017) include "Uhhh I'm highly concerned for people who search this stuff up..........." (TT theGE 2018) and "i regret searching this up" (Crappy Productions 2018). DeathLord402 (2016) comments in his reaction video that "I literally want to kill myself" after stumbling on LEGO porn and that "even sadder" is the fact that people probably think LEGO porn is hot. And YouTube vlogger AngryChimp (2016) states: "I don't understand the point. Do people really get off on this stuff? Is there someone, some sad man wanking somewhere over some LEGO porn or some Minecraft porn? I'm guessing there must be." But he also states (2017) that his first video about LEGO porn is the most popular on his channel; clearly LEGO porn fascinates, even if it is seen as a travesty.

The fan culture around LEGO porn, then, is ambivalent: Arousal is vilified and projected elsewhere, while disgust, outrage and amusement are avowed by the writer or speaker. The primary confessed intent of LEGO porn is also to amuse and/or disgust rather than to arouse, as LEGO pornographers most frequently categorize their videos on YouTube in the "Comedy" or "Entertainment" genres. However, while user comments sometimes confirm that the joke finds its audience, more frequently they proclaim outrage. Nonetheless, it seems hard to imagine that the responses of real, living people are not more ambivalent and complex than single-line comments or single-word tags suggest. It is important to see these tags and comments less as authentic and exhaustive testaments to the ways people really feel and more as performative moments in a discourse that surrounds images (and sounds) of LEGO sex. In this discourse, the configuration of emotions and responses is different from Williams's "living, moving bodies" in "explicit, unusually unfaked, sexual acts with a primary intent of arousing viewers," (p. 30) but arousal is still part of the discourse. It is simply disclaimed, perhaps disavowed, while what remains is an intensely emotional response of disgust or amusement or both.

This is reminiscent of the discomfort that more famously surrounds "cloppers," a subset of adult male fans of the television show *My Little Pony: Friendship is Magic* (*MLP*). Cloppers create and/or consume erotica featuring the show's equine characters and are commonly accused of pedophilia and "pornifying" (Jones 2015, p. 122) the series. Animated porn has recast children's characters such as Snow White and Mickey

Mouse in sexual scenarios throughout its history (Capino 2018), but the clopper phenomenon is particularly revealing for its contemporaneity, similarities and differences from LEGO porn. First, although very few adult *MLP* fans engage with this erotica, many complain that "this marginal activity gets so much attention due to its distastefulness it becomes read as representative of all adult, male *MLP* fans" (Jones 2015, p. 122). LEGO porn is far more marginal to LEGO fandom than cloppers' work is to the discourse around *MLP* fandom, so adult fans of LEGO (AFOLs) are not subject to the same accusations of perversion, and the more unilaterally horrified responses to cloppers contrast with common hilarity in response to LEGO porn. This difference may be due in part to a technical difference between the two forms. *My Little Pony* porn is often technically reminiscent of live-action porn insofar as the 2D animation allows pornographers to portray the characters in a range of sexual positions and to add sexualized attributes such as breasts to the ponies; it thus falls into a long line of animated porn that takes advantage of the malleability of cel animated shapes and movements (Capino 2018) and, more recently, of computer-generated animation (Saunders 2019, pp. 243–244). On the other hand, as we will see in the next section, LEGO porn is constrained by the materiality of bricks that were not designed for representing sexual acts. Indeed, the resistance and limitations of the LEGO medium are central to its pornographic applications. Nonetheless, responses to both *MLP* and LEGO porn attest to similar rather hysterical disgust with the juxtaposition of adult sexuality and a child's toy.

LEGO Sex

Against this cultural backdrop, the texts of LEGO porn videos follow certain trends. LEGO porn contains many of the key features of its live-action cinematic counterparts such as money shots (shots of ejaculation) and porn sound conventions (moans, sex-oriented dialogue and porn groove music), but there are also idiosyncratic aspects of the subgenre, some of them related to but not determined by the shapes of LEGO bricks and minifigs. For example, money shots are common in LEGO porn, as filmmakers use bricks, modeling clay, cotton balls and other props to represent semen; however, these shots are not nearly as ubiquitous as they are in live-action porn. I focus on a few particularities of LEGO porn. The first and most important is the direct sexual analogue to the fundamental principle of LEGO: the penetration of one brick by another. This analogy plays out in phallocentric terms, which raises questions about heteronormativity and the places of gender and sexual diversity in LEGO porn and LEGO culture more broadly. In addition, minifigs' size, shape and stiffness—pun intended—seem to have an impact on the popularity of certain positions and sex acts over others as well as popular ways of photographing them, and the use of sound attests to a range of both sexual knowledge and nostalgia. Different LEGO pornographers relate to these topics in different ways, but these are the main forces that shape the subgenre of LEGO porn.

The video *(18 + ?)Lego porn* by Minifigure Torture (2018) encapsulates the analogy between the LEGO studs' penetration of grooves and the interpenetration of bodies during sex. It features LEGO Brick Suit Girl and LEGO Brick Suit Guy from Minifigure Series 18. Instead of the regular minifig body, the characters are "dressed" as upended 2×3 bricks, with studs on the front and grooves in the back. Minifigure Torture has stuck them together, male behind and female in front, and animated them so that Brick Guy's rocking motion pulls Brick Girl off her feet and then sets her down on the ground again. This explicit sex scene is intercut with live-action footage of two human hands putting together and taking apart, in the same rhythm, standard 2×4 bricks of the same colors as Brick Girl and Guy. The sound here is not the moans or porn groove music that dominates most LEGO porn soundtracks but the sound of bricks being pulled apart and put together, underscoring the materiality of LEGO rather than sexual acts. As the scene goes on, the smile on Brick Girl's face changes to a look of consternation, while Brick Guy continues to smile. Finally, Brick Girl falls face forward onto the ground, a tube of grey modelling clay stretching from Brick Guy's crotch area into Brick Girl's anal area, connecting them in what reads as a money shot. We then cut to the hands pulling apart the 2×4 bricks with a similar tube of modeling clay between them, and the video ends. This video maps LEGO onto sex more directly than others, to the extent that the assembly of standard LEGO bricks produces ejaculate, but the metaphor is one of the foundational pleasures and jokes of LEGO porn.

When the analogy between brick and sexual penetration is less overt, the fundamental logic and irony of much LEGO sex come to the fore. LEGO sex scenes are very predominantly phallocentric, but penises are usually implicit. In their absence, penetration seldom actually takes place, and animated movement is the only visual sign of sex. Moaning, dialogue and other sounds can play a crucial role here in making the sexual content explicit, especially when the animation is rudimentary. In these cases, the lack of contact and penetration seems to concretize Jacques Lacan's (1999) famous claim that "there's no such thing as a sexual relationship" (p. 12), no immediate or natural sexual relationship, just signification and fantasy. We can only speculate that the ambivalent enjoyment of LEGO porn may be a space to acknowledge sexual alienation, safely disavowed through comedy. These videos, haunted by penetration but incapable of actualizing it, highlight both the absurdity of LEGO sex and potentially of sex more generally.

In about a quarter of LEGO porn videos, on the other hand, filmmakers work imaginatively—a Lacanian may say desperately—to overcome the absence of LEGO minifig penises and thus create work that is indubitably phallocentric. Sometimes filmmakers make penises out of modeling clay or some similar material; at other times, they use LEGO pieces such as antennae with rounded tops (part 3957[3]). Occasionally, builders are even more exacting. For example, in *LEGOPORNO*, John Carlsen (2018) takes the minifigs apart in order to make them more anatomically accurate, after a fashion. He sandwiches LEGO part 3700, a 1×2 brick with a hole in its face, between the male minifig's legs and torso; it holds a bar that protrudes out of his front and into the hole of LEGO part 2444, a 2×4 plate with a hole below it that is sandwiched between the female minifig's legs and torso. The holes and antenna disappear after sex. The irony here is that the insistence on anatomical completeness distorts the figures into inhuman shapes: Sex makes the human form grotesque, and normalcy is only restored afterward. Although John Carlsen's video is an extreme example, most videos clearly convey the idea that a penis on a minifig is unnatural but important. If LEGO porn were entirely determined by the shape of LEGO minifigs rather than phallocentric logic, one could expect pornographers to use the convenient minifig hands as tools of penetration, but they almost never do. Nonetheless, LEGO porn phallicism is not that of po-faced patriarchy but of often puerile delight and hyperbole. The penis is privileged but bizarre: 75% of the time it is invisible, and when it is visible, it is potent but farcical.

Another grotesquerie in the interests of sexual precision is the way many LEGO pornographers use the top set of grooves in the backs of minifigs' legs as bodily orifices into which penises, tools and even light sabers (MiniHeroes182 2010) can be thrust. Although dialogue will occasionally indicate that the hole represents an anus (e.g., sickmcc 2009; Темный свет 2017), it is usually not clear whether these grooves are anuses, vaginas (when the minifigs are female) or both—or some LEGO orifice that has no exact equivalent in human anatomy. Or, more precisely, the holes *both* represent human orifices *and* offer a fantastical, LEGO-specific plenitude of permeability: porn stars with *four* holes! LEGO is literally polymorphous, its shapes adaptable, and in a sexual context, this enables a kind of infantile polymorphous perversity that exceeds the phallicism of the subgenre without genuinely undermining it. All of these manipulations of the minifig, from the miming or building of penises to the use of grooves in the legs, attest on the one hand to a desire to present sex as anatomically accurately as possible, especially through the heteronormative synecdoches of male as penis and female as "hole," and on the other hand to hyperbolize through the adaptability of LEGO. It attests to an anatomical curiosity explored through the distorting lens of LEGO and to a curiosity about the sexual and anatomical potential of LEGO itself.

Although minifig morphology does not dictate the sexual acts of LEGO porn, the convenient and visible orifices in the backs of minifig legs likely influence the fact that rear-entry sex is the most common sexual position in LEGO porn. About three-quarters of LEGO porn videos feature this position, while less than half feature the second most common position, fellatio. Another reason for its popularity is likely the fact that minifigs bend forward at the hips, while their legs do not spread laterally. Minifigs' "stiffness," so different from the fluidity of cel and computer-generated animated porn stars, thus provides an image of phallic rigidity while also limiting the acrobatics of sex acts. Animating rear-entry sex is also clear and simple: The figure in front, bent over to greater or lesser degrees, does not need to move (e.g., MADxMovies 2009). The effect is that rear-entry sex creates an impression of passivity in the figure in front, even of reluctance or lifelessness. The grimace on Brick Girl's face near the end of Minifigure Torture's *(18+?)Lego porn* is an explicit image of the power imbalance that is coded into many of the scenes. This power imbalance is also gendered: Cunnilingus, as Taormino notes about live-action porn, is optional—in LEGO porn, quite rare. LEGO porn thus shows a preoccupation with phallic pleasure and active penetration that is underpinned, though not determined, by the design of LEGO minifigs.

The other side of the phallic metaphor is that occasionally LEGO sex is represented as a destructive force. In such videos, the process of taking apart LEGO bricks after a build is parallel to the "petite mort" of orgasm. Narratives end in chaos; landscapes end in rubble; and sexuality is linked to the death drive, to the dissolution of the autonomous self through sex: Taking apart LEGO is a metaphor for sexual experience and a way of performing what is otherwise personal, internal and sometimes even invisible. Williams (1989) argues that the lack of visible evidence of *female* orgasm is the concern of much porn, but in LEGO sex, it is primarily male orgasm that elicits visual metaphor. At times, the destructive frenzy is concentrated in the minifig itself: In johanessmorra's *Lego Porn* (2009), for example, a threesome ends with a minifig's head popping off. In hazabaza96's *LEGO porn...* (2010), the male figure rides his female partner from the back too hard, punting her like a pool ball across the room and popping her head, torso and legs apart; her pathetic cries for help drive home the gendered violence. At other times, the violence exceeds the bodies and wracks the whole LEGO world (e.g., bmxassholes 2008; Satyramaniacal 2010). We could connect destructiveness to Leo Bersani's (1987) argument that sexuality is the movement "between a hyperbolic sense of self and a loss of all consciousness of self" (p. 218). However, the recurrence of gendered violence and lack of consent and the reinscription of male sexuality as stereotypically, inherently violent also bear out Bersani's criticism of the heteronormative-patriarchal *devaluation* of sexual passivity (p. 217) and self-shattering. Ultimately, phallic violence in LEGO porn mostly affirms the integrity of the penis at the expense of the penetrated character or world.

The ubiquity of penetration and uncoupling, both literal and metaphorical, is patently phallocentric, but the gender landscape of LEGO porn is not simple. LEGO's own prioritization of male minifigs over female shapes this gender landscape, although the extent of the prioritization is debatable. We must usually determine LEGO minifigs' gender identities based on normative markers such as hairstyles, costume, makeup and, where applicable, identifiable character from a known story world such as *Harry Potter*. Relying on such markers is unsatisfying: A short-haired, cosmetics-free LEGO minifig could realistically be a cisgender woman, or a cisgender male could have long hair. In practice, though, gender markings are generally used and understood very normatively. To complicate matters, there is disagreement about whether minifigs without clear gendered features are gender neutral/fluid or simply unmarked males. In his impressive compendium of LEGO minifigs through the decades, Jesus Diaz (2013) reads the first minifigs, who lacked either long hair or facial hair, as male. On the other hand, Maia Weinstock (2012), David Pickett (2012) and Ramblingbrick (2016) have done meticulous studies of the gender breakdowns of LEGO minifigs, and all "gave TLG [The LEGO Group] the benefit of the doubt and counted as gender neutral any minifigs lacking definitely masculine (facial hair) or feminine (lipstick, eyelashes, cleavage) traits" (Pickett 2012). Despite this conservatism, all three find that LEGO has statistically favored male minifigs. Pickett finds that only 8.9% of minifigs released between 1989 and 1999 were definitively female while 33.4% were definitively male. Weinstock finds that 15% of minifig heads on BrickLink.com in 2012 were female while 57% were male. And Ramblingbrick's study of LEGO City shows that between 6 and 13% of minifigs released between 2011 and 2014 were female, while 23–47% were male. These findings reinforce Baichtal and Meno's (2011) more general claim that male minifigs outnumber female 18:1 (p. 57), presumably counting "neutral" minifigs as male. I myself read "neutral" minifigs as unmarked males, in part because the company has clearly not earned the benefit of the doubt that Weinstock, Pickett and Ramblingbrick grant it. No doubt some individual LEGO fans do genuinely interpret the "neutral" figures as such—and even assign genders in contradiction to the normative markers of hair, makeup and costume. Nonetheless, the male bias in LEGO minifigs is indisputable even if it is not unvarying or uncomplicated.

This is no doubt a contributing factor of one of the more surprising and yet disregarded aspects of the subgenre: its representation of same-sex sex acts. Sex scenes with multiple female minifigs are extremely rare, even in threesomes with a male minifig involved. This is striking in light of the ubiquity of girl-on-girl scenes in live-action porn through the ages. I have located only a handful of LEGO pornographic moving images that feature sex between women, usually very briefly. Significantly, this rare form of LEGO sex appears in *gang bang lego loving sluts* (paulaskitchen 2008), the only LEGO porn video I have found whose authorship is explicitly coded female: Two female minifigs introduce themselves as "the only lesbians in the village" who are "not ashamed" and demonstrate their intimacy with pride. This video is unique on other counts, as a female minifig uses a strap-on to penetrate a male minifig, who seems to enjoy the experience, and a range of female sexual subjectivity (including enjoyment of heterosexual sex and bestiality) is explored. Although it is not always appropriate to connect filmmakers' gender identities directly with the content they produce, in this case it is not too simplistic to say that the filmmakers, credited within the video as Paula Scott and Rebecca Shutt, represent lone female, feminist voices in a subgenre that is otherwise phallocentric and sometimes misogynist. That said, LEGO pornographers almost never fall into the porn cliché of girl-on-girl action aiming to titillate a heterosexual male viewer.

Almost a third of the videos sampled, however, included intercourse between what I read as two or more male-coded minifigs. About half of these are undeniably same-sex scenes, with two or more participants clearly marked as male through costuming, voices, titling, or because they involve identifiable characters such as Darth Maul; the other half involves "gender neutral" figures who can plausibly be interpreted as male. Still others (e.g., MegaBallsackface 2012) show heterosexual minifig couples voiced by boys and thus come across as same-sex sex acts on the auditory level. None of this suggests that LEGO porn is an untapped gay cinema resource—far from it. First, just as we need to differentiate lesbian porn made by and for lesbians from girl-on-girl sex filmed for heterosexual male viewers, we also need to distinguish porn by and for gay men from merely fortuitous same-sex sex acts in LEGO porn. Even when the same-sex scenes are not unintentional or unre-marked, some videos (e.g., sickmcc 2009) frame the same-sex sex acts as rape or punishment rather than a source of pleasure between consent-ing participants. Gay practices may also be framed as a joke: Half the videos that uploaders have categorized as "Comedy" contain same-sex sex acts, while other more neutral categories, such as "Film & Animation" and "People & Blogs," feature less same-sex sex. The significance of this categorization can be overstated, since some of the videos categorized as comedies predominantly involve heterosexual sex, but there are a few, such as *Lego gay porn* (tooking tolet 2015), whose categorization as a comedy is clearly homophobic. On the other hand, sex between male minifigs is usually presented without comment about the genders of the performers. It would be excessive to praise LEGO porn for the naturalization of gay sex, but this is one (presumably unin-tentional) result of the largely homosocial environment of the LEGO minifig world. One can only hope that a few gay viewers find pleasure and affirmation in such scenes.

The next major marker of LEGO porn relates to the small size of the LEGO minifig and has an impact on the kinds of knowledge that circulate in this subgenre. In live-action porn, the production of knowledge often takes the form of close-ups on faces in orgasm or organs in action. However, staging a close-up on a minifig is techni-cally difficult, as it may require special equipment such as a macro lens. Only the highest quality LEGO animation of any genre features close-ups, and when it does, it is often prompted by specific, live-action visual reference. For example, high-quality animated LEGO remakes of live-action film material may feature close-ups, although even here, the camera often frames LEGO minifigs from a slightly greater distance than it frames their live-action counterparts (see 22 Bricks 2017; Toscano Bricks 2015; WideSquare Media 2018).

A less professional-looking LEGO remake such as Squash the Brickfilmer's version of the trailer for *The Force Awakens* (2014) demonstrates the difficulty of achieving crisp focus when a LEGO minifig is close to the camera. Consequently, LEGO porn is predominantly a pornography of full-body—and often fully clothed—sex acts. In the absence of the close-up, these full-body configurations speak more to sexual positions and broad trends than to the specifics of particular actions. This is part of the reason that sexual positions are so significant in this subgenre. While live-action porn often magnifies anatomical details, LEGO porn has the opposite effect, pulling the camera away from the action and satisfying a different kind of curiosity.

Another feature of LEGO porn is its self-reflexivity and nostalgia. LEGO porn sometimes features a porn shoot (e.g., DamDam Andros 2018; Satyramanical 2010), shows characters watching porn (e.g., ItalicSix 2013; Meush 2013) or includes parodies of adult content warnings (e.g., HenDeadly 2007; vincentino1977 2008). It may even be self-referential in ways that have nothing to do with porn; for example, minifig performers may bow to the camera as if they were in a stage play (e.g., johannessmorra 2009; vincentino1977 2008). Second, the prevalent use of porn groove music, associated primarily with Golden Age porn, distances LEGO porn from contemporary conventions while nostalgically referencing the 1970s. This nostalgia is reinforced by the fact that LEGO porn is so often funny. Nina K. Martin (2006) notes that the porn of the 1970s often integrated comedy; however, as narrative has dwindled in porn, so has comedy. Instead, porn is now "deeply invested in seriousness, and much of porn's lack of humor relates to cultural understandings of patriarchal power, a power that is rigorously maintained by equating the sight/site of the penis with awe. Porn conventions emphasize not only the size of the penis, but its requisite, and often perpetual hardness" (Martin 2006, p. 193). Comedy has not entirely disappeared from porn: The Adult Video News Awards or "porn Oscars" include categories such as Best Parody and Best Comedy, but these are often associated with nostalgia and an older audience (Meikle 2015, p. 128). However, while humor is not as ubiquitous as it was in the 1970s, LEGO porn keeps the tradition alive. Although it is deeply invested in patriarchal power and the supremacy of the penis—and no man is harder than a LEGO man—it is a subgenre that giggles knowingly. And it knows not only contemporary online porn, with its ubiquitous money shots and lack of narrative structure, but also the humor and music of the 1970s.

All of these issues, from phallocentrism and violence to the difficulties of the close-up, the distorting lens through which LEGO can represent sexuality, and the currency of 1970s porn come together in Satyramaniacal's exceptionally elaborate, 5-and-a-half-minute *Lego Porno* (2010). This video highlights trends in LEGO porn by conforming to some and departing from others. Its animation is minimal, moving at about 1 frame per second, but the set builds are large and detailed. The video begins self-reflexively with the filming of an infomercial for sexual lubricant in the factory that makes the product. A group of partygoers outside the factory finds their way inside; two heterosexual couples pair off to have sex although, unusually, later the two women have sex with each other. While one of the couples has sex, we cut to what appears to be a close-up. Overcoming the technical limitations of the minifig, here a large, disembodied female genital area is constructed of red LEGO plates inside and yellow plates outside with green tree limb elements for pubic hair (the visual pun on "bush" worthy of Radley Metzger's 1976 *The Opening of Misty Beethoven*). It is penetrated by a large yellow LEGO penis which, after a few thrusts, spews cotton ball ejaculate. This money shot exploits the potential of the LEGO medium to exceed what live-action porn can do: Because the LEGO vagina stays open, the LEGO penis can move in and out of it while ejaculating, circumventing live-action's need for external ejaculation as "proof" of male pleasure. The sequence is also carnivalesque, as an octopus, a horse and several minifigs emerge from the vagina before the camera dollies in on it to end the shot. These carnivalesque elements demonstrate how LEGO sex exceeds the sex acts of live bodies and also works metaphorically to represent pleasure—here, atypically, female pleasure as well as male—as the images of fireworks and bells ringing do in *Deep Throat*. We cut back to the couple having sex, implying that, although they are fully clothed, the close-up in some way represented their experience.

When the gigantic genitals make a reappearance in the climax of the video, however, they are not implicitly connected to any minifig performer but rather disembodied, almost godlike forces. In the final sequence, a robot arm runs amuck, first raping the female couple having sex and then destroying the factory set. Washed out of the factory on a sea of cling film lubricant and cotton ball semen, the robot penetrates the leg grooves of various minifigs, accompanied by the sounds of Grieg's "In the Hall of the Mountain King." The gigantic penis then stabs downward from the sky, creating further chaos and destruction and spewing more ejaculate. This stabbing motion is live-action rather than animated: We even see a hand holding its base. When the shaft breaks, the hand picks up the diminished head and continues to stab the LEGO scene below. The sequence ends with the hand throwing down the gigantic LEGO "balls" followed by a bottle of Jack Daniels (still quite full). If the gigantic penis was a close-up before, here it is a monstrous, independent element. This is confirmed when we cut to the male minifig whose penis the "close-up" appeared at first to show: The gigantic vagina appears at the window and draws all the furniture up into itself with a sucking sound. With a male voice, the vagina announces itself as "Vaginor" and promises to "get" the minifig. As it consumes chairs, factory equipment and another minifig on a motorcycle, the camera shakes to heighten the effect. Finally, the male minifig is sucked into its opening, and the film ends with his gurgling the words, "Please, mother, noooooooo." The close-up is turned inside out; the sexual organs overwhelm and consume the bodies of which they seemed at first to be only a part.

The Oedipal implications of gigantic, vengeful male and female genitals are not subtle, but they do capture the hyperbolic approach to sex common in much LEGO porn. This video is out of the ordinary for its inclusion of girl-on-girl action and a metaphorical representation of female pleasure. Its use of Grieg rather than porn groove music is also unusual, while the inclusion of rape is less unusual but still not absolutely typical. Most curiously, the ventriloquism of the giant vagina perfectly captures the impetus that Williams (1989) sees to be central to so much porn: the patriarchal will-to-knowledge that urges the female body "speak" its pleasures to male spectators. Here, that speech is literal, comic, threatening and overtly a product of *male* authorship. At the same time, the video's exploration of the destructive power of sexuality and the varied and creative uses of LEGO as a medium of sexual representation are all exemplary of LEGO porn. The brutality of both the rapist robot arm and the deadly gigantic penis reflects the main preoccupation of LEGO porn—phallic power—while also proclaiming this power to be ludicrous.

Conclusion

One question perpetually asked of porn concerns its social value. LEGO porn does not offer the utopian model of healthy, varied, steamy, consensual performed sex for which feminist pornographers such as Tristan Taormino and Courtney Trouble are justifiably praised. Nonetheless, it is useful for its unreality, its self-referentiality and its excesses. Rebecca Saunders (2019), writing about amateur, computer-generated pornography, argues that the technical imperfections of the form "open up a space for critique" (p. 247) of mainstream, live-action pornography. In LEGO porn, it is specifically the technical limitations imposed by the bricks that, at times, distance us from its own naked phallicism. This phallicism is not specific to this subgenre, nor is it entirely determined by LEGO's sexually analogous studs and grooves. In LEGO porn, we see the influence of a live-action industry still predominantly bankrolled by and created for heterosexual men in which the pleasures and subjectivity of women are often secondary and/or presented for the scrutiny of a heterosexual male spectator. But we also see the performative nature of porn, the unreality of porn bodies, the sometimes-puerile nature of phallic obsession and the way a homosocial world (in this case, the world of LEGO) contributes to imbalances of power and pleasure. Although I doubt most consumers of LEGO porn think deeply and critically about it, as it is framed as a perverse but throwaway form, the mixed outrage, amusement and fervent denial of arousal in their reactions suggest that it does, at least, provoke conflicting and intense emotions. And perhaps reflection can begin with ambivalence, especially when wrapped up in an entertaining package such as LEGO porn that, as Bethany Ramos writes, is curiously addictive.

Acknowledgements Many thanks to Jade Nauss for sharing her extremely insightful comments, expertise and great sense of humor with me. Her comments about polymorphous perversity and childhood sexual play were especially helpful.

Notes

1. I distinguish between girl-on-girl action primarily intended for the pleasure of a heterosexual male viewer and lesbian porn usually made by and for lesbians which "directly address[es]" lesbians and "solicit[s] lesbian identifications" (Henderson 1992, p. 175).
2. Pornographic *still* images featuring LEGO are more diverse. Many are photographs of LEGO minifigs that could be stop-motion film stills. However, there are also many photos of naked humans surrounded by LEGO and drawings featuring figures that look more or less like LEGO minifigs. Although these are predominantly amateur productions, professional artists have also entered the fray, both intentionally and unintentionally (see made by virgins 2009; Miranda 2011; Summer 2014).
3. For the sake of precision, where possible I refer to LEGO design or element numbers to identify specific bricks. These numbers allow LEGO users to identify individual bricks both in LEGO's official shop and on third-party sites such as BrickLink.com.

References

22 Bricks. (2017, August 12). *Lego IT trailer side by side comparison* [Video file]. https://www.youtube.com/watch?v=dq145hfDJ1A. Accessed on August 25, 2018.

Alilunas, P. (2016). Shot live on videotape: The televisual era of adult film, 1978–1982. *Post Script, 35*(3), 6–18. http://www.tamuc.edu/academics/colleges/humanitiesSocialSciencesArts/departments/literatureLanguages/publications/postScript.aspx. Accessed on May 3, 2018.

AngryChimp. (2016, July 1). *Looking at—LEGO PORN* [Video file]. https://www.youtube.com/watch?v=YZ_l6bFk1Gc. Accessed on May 5, 2018.

AngryChimp. (2017, March 9). *Lego porn is awesome* [Video file]. https://www.youtube.com/watch?v=PdrdoP5PWIc. Accessed on May 5, 2018.

Baichtal, J. (2011). *Lego porn*. Boing Boing. https://boingboing.net/2011/11/01/lego-porn.html. Accessed on June 5, 2018.

Baichtal, J., & Meno, J. (2011). *The cult of LEGO*. San Francisco, CA: No Starch Press.

beautiful pics. (2017, July 23). *Inside the world of Lego porn* [Video file]. https://www.youtube.com/watch?v=0LZ1MncIS6Q. Accessed on May 11, 2018.

Bersani, L. (1987). Is the rectum a grave? *October, 43*, 197–222. https://doi.org/10.2307/3397574.

bmxassholes. (2008, May 25). *Lego porn movie* [Video file]. https://www.youtube.com/watch?v=mJtTl6M6PV8. Accessed on August 3, 2018.

Brownlee, S. (2016). Amateurism and the aesthetics of Lego stop-motion on YouTube. *Film Criticism, 40*(2), 1–21. https://doi.org/10.3998/fc.13761232.0040.204.

Capino, J. B. (2018). *Filthy funnies: Notes on the body in animated pornography.* PAF. http://www.pifpaf.cz/en/filthy-funnies-notes-on-the-body-in-animated-pornography. Accessed on June 7, 2019.

Carlsen, J. (2018, June 3). *LEGOPORNO* [Video file]. https://www.youtube.com/watch?v=bp5LqAHA0Eo. Accessed on July 30, 2018.

Crappy Productions. (2018). Msg 3. Message posted to https://www.youtube.com/watch?v=0LZ1MncIS6Q. Accessed on July 25, 2018.

DamDam Andros. (2018, February 23). *Porn Lego* [Video file]. https://www.youtube.com/watch?v=rCo4mIVFSQo. Accessed on May 9, 2018.

Damiano, G. (Director). (1972). *Deep throat* [Motion Picture]. USA: Bryanston Pictures.

DeathLord402. (2016, May 18). *LEGO PORN?* [Video file]. https://www.youtube.com/watch?v=JQpSjD2QQy8. Accessed on July 31, 2018.

Diaz, J. (2013, June 26). *Exclusive: The evolution of the minifig.* Gizmodo. https://gizmodo.com/exclusive-the-evolution-of-the-minifig-5070884. Accessed on August 10, 2018.

hazabaza96. (2010, May 24). *LEGO porn….* [Video file]. https://www.youtube.com/watch?v=fsos9G-NoDg. Accessed on July 30, 2018.

hellsvenom299. (2006a, December 26). *Lego porn 1* [Video file]. https://www.youtube.com/watch?v=_IrvnO0G1jk. Accessed on July 31, 2018.

hellsvenom299. (2006b, December 26). *Lego porn 3* [Video file]. https://www.youtube.com/watch?v=TZ-No0iAj2E. Accessed on July 31, 2018.

HenDeadly. (2007, July 15). *Brick banging! (lego porn!!!)* [Video file]. https://www.youtube.com/watch?v=xE2CZyGqdT0. Accessed on May 17, 2018.

Henderson, L. (1992). Lesbian pornography: Cultural transgression and sexual demystification. In S. Munt (Ed.), *New lesbian criticism: Literary and cultural perspectives* (pp. 173–191). London: Harvester Wheatsheaf.

ItalicSix. (2013, May 5). *Lego porn* [Video file]. https://www.youtube.com/watch?v=bNXH5e3zR-8. Accessed on July 23, 2018.

johannessmorra. (2009, February 20). *Lego porn* [Video file]. https://www.youtube.com/watch?v=xUAqrnVxbJQ. Accessed on August 3, 2018.

Jones, B. (2015). My Little Pony, tolerance is magic: Gender policing and Brony anti-fandom. *Journal of Popular Television, 3*(1), 119–125. https://doi.org/10.1386/jptv.3.1.119_1.

Lacan, J. (1999). *The seminar of Jacques Lacan Book XX: On feminine sexuality, the limits of love and knowledge, 1972–1973* (A. Miller & B. Fink, Eds.). New York, NY: W. W. Norton.

Lego porn. (2017, October 15). *Urban dictionary.* https://www.urbandictionary.com/define.php?term=Lego+porn. Accessed on July 25, 2018.

made by virgins. (2009, December 26). Lego porn. *eBaum's World.* http://www.ebaumsworld.com/pictures/lego-porn/80867632/. Accessed on July 15, 2018.

MADxMovies. (2009, August 16). *Lego porn* [Video file]. https://www.youtube.com/watch?v=Sxr1YrnlpM8. Accessed on July 30, 2018.

Martin, N. K. (2006). Never laugh at a man with his pants down: The affective dynamics of comedy and porn. In P. Lehman (Ed.), *Pornography: Film and culture* (pp. 189–205). New Brunswick, NJ: Rutgers University Press.

MegaBallsackface. (2012, May 15). *Lego porno, by Anthony* [Video file]. https://www.youtube.com/watch?v=EgIt542Y6ZY. Accessed on July 31, 2018.

Meikle, K. (2015). Pornographic adaptation: Parody, fan fiction and the limits of genre. *Journal of Adaptation in Film & Performance, 8*(2), 123–140. https://doi.org/10.1386/jafp.8.2.123_1.

Metzger, R. (Director). (1976). *The opening of Misty Beethoven* [Motion Picture]. USA: VCA Pictures.

Meush. (2013, December 15). *MEUSH—Lego porn* [Video file]. https://www.youtube.com/watch?v=k0HsCHJpOUg. Accessed on November 25, 2014.

Minifigure Torture. (2018, April 23). *(18 + ?)Lego porn* [Video file]. https://www.youtube.com/watch?v=2Om7DNfZBZo. Accessed on May 6, 2018.

MiniHeroes182. (2010, July 16). *Star Wars porn* [Video file]. https://www.youtube.com/watch?v=lE0B9o_xTqw. Accessed on July 31, 2018.

Miranda. (2011, February 1). X-rated Lego: Pixxxel. *Clutter Magazine.* https://www.cluttermagazine.com/news/2011/02/x-rated-lego-pixxxel. Accessed on July 15, 2018.

Nudity and sexual content policies. (2018). *YouTube Help*. https://support.google.com/youtube/answer/2802002?hl=en. 2018. Accessed on July 15, 2018.

paulaskitchen. (2008, February 19). *Gang bang lego loving sluts* [Video file]. https://www.youtube.com/watch?v=DT19PtpQkj0. Accessed on August 3, 2018.

Penley, C. (2006). Crackers and whackers: The white trashing of porn. In P. Lehman (Ed.), *Pornography: Film and culture* (pp. 99–117). New Brunswick, NJ: Rutgers University Press.

Pickett, D. (2012, May 15). *Part II: Historical perspective on the LEGO gender gap*. The Society Pages. https://thesocietypages.org/socimages/2012/05/15/part-ii-historical-perspective-on-the-lego-gender-gap/. Accessed on June 5, 2018.

Ramblingbrick. (2016, September 28). *Living with DiverCITY: Changing depictions of gender roles with LEGO minifigures in the post-Friends era*. Ramblingbrick.com. https://ramblingbrick.com/2016/09/29/living-with-divercity-changing-depictions-of-gender-roles-with-lego-minifigures-in-the-post-friends-era/. Accessed on July 15, 2018.

Ramos, B. (2017, July 31). *10 naughty Lego positions for adults only*. Mommyish.com. https://www.mommyish.com/lego-porn/. Accessed on August 8, 2018.

Satyramaniacal. (2010, February 14). *Lego porno* [Video file]. https://www.youtube.com/watch?v=k2LbZntVRXo. Accessed on May 10, 2018.

Saunders, R. (2019). Computer-generated pornography and convergence: Animation and algorithms as new digital desire. *Convergence, 25*(2), 241–259. https://doi.org/10.1177/1354856519833591.

Schaefer, E. (2002). Gauging a revolution: 16 mm film and the rise of the pornographic feature. *Cinema Journal, 41*(3), 3–26. https://doi.org/10.1353/cj.2002.0010.

sickmcc. (2009, March 7). *Lego porn* [Video file]. https://www.youtube.com/watch?v=aJA-GxhT664. Accessed on July 30, 2018.

SquashtheBrickfilmer. (2014, November 30). *LEGO Star Wars: The force awakens in LEGO* [Video file]. https://www.youtube.com/watch?v=k7XQuVxdyXk. Accessed on August 25, 2018.

Summer, M. (2014, June 11). *Nudity meets LEGO in a revealing world first*. Lost At E Minor. https://www.lostateminor.com/2014/06/12/nudity-meets-lego-world-first/. Accessed on July 15, 2018.

Taormino, T. (2013). Calling the shots: Feminist porn in theory and practice. In T. Taormino, C. P. Shimizu, C. Penley, & M. Miller-Young (Eds.), *The feminist porn book: The politics of producing pleasure* (pp. 255–264). New York: The Feminist Press.

Темный свет. (2017, April 4). *Porno Lego* [Video file]. https://www.youtube.com/watch?v=xxfvBiRrYCo. Accessed on July 30, 2018.

tooking tolet. (2015, July 15). *Lego gay porn* [Video file]. https://www.youtube.com/watch?v=Uuo015lAVJk. Accessed on July 30, 2018.

Toscano Bricks. (2015, February 5). *Fifty shades of grey Lego trailer comparison* [Video file]. https://www.youtube.com/watch?v=Nm3dqeCt0RA. Accessed on August 25, 2018.

TT theGE. (2018). Msg 1. Message posted to https://www.youtube.com/watch?v=0LZ1MncIS6Q. Accessed on July 25, 2018.

vincentino1977. (2008, December 30). *Lego porno* [Video file]. https://www.youtube.com/watch?v=q8ae5MOTTNQ. Accessed on July 30, 2018.

Waugh, T. (1996). *Hard to imagine: Gay male eroticism in photography and film from their beginnings to Stonewall.* New York: Columbia University Press.

Weinstock, M. (2012, February 20). *My dear Lego, you are part of the problem.* Annals of Spacetime. Retrieved from http://annalsofspacetime.blogspot.com/2012/02/my-dear-lego-you-are-part-of-problem.html. Accessed on July 15, 2018.

WideSquare Media. (2018, May 25). *LEGO Thomas and friends | Percy's ghost scene remake | scene comparison* [Video file]. Retrieved from https://www.youtube.com/watch?v=QqnFc8gv0UM. Accessed on August 25, 2018.

Williams, L. (1989). *Hard core: Power, pleasure, and the "frenzy of the visible"* (Expanded paperback ed.). Berkeley: University of California Press.

10

"It's All About the Brick": Mobilizing Adult Fans of LEGO

Nancy A. Jennings

As I entered the home of firefighter and paramedic Rodney Dicus, I soon learned about his true love of LEGO. Our first stop, his front office, was filled from floor to ceiling with LEGO Minifigures and Funko Pops, still in their boxes and neatly stacked. His desk was a workstation for his Minifigure creations, complete with a magnifying glass lamp and tools to place small objects onto the tiny Minifigure elements. He showed me his latest work-in-progress at his desk before we headed downstairs. As I rounded the corner at the bottom of the steps, my eyes widened and I gasped at the sight: wall-to-wall LEGOs, ceiling-to-floor bins of sorted LEGOs and narrow passages to walk to workstation benches along the walls. He beamed with pride, and I was filled with surprise and joy. I had truly found an Adult Fan of LEGO (AFOL).

LEGO celebrated the 60th anniversary of its plastic bricks in 2018 continuing with its mission of "inspiring and developing the builders

N. A. Jennings (✉)
Department of Communication, University of Cincinnati,
Cincinnati, OH, USA
e-mail: jenninna@ucmail.uc.edu

© The Author(s) 2019
R. C. Hains and S. R. Mazzarella (eds.), *Cultural Studies of LEGO*,
https://doi.org/10.1007/978-3-030-32664-7_10

of tomorrow" (Jensen 2015). The term "LEGO" was formed as an abbreviation of two Danish words, "leg godt," which translates to "play well" (Mortensen 2017)—and indeed, people young and old continue to play well with LEGO. In 60 years, the "builders of tomorrow" have grown up. Now, people of all ages "play well" with LEGO and with each other, creating communities of builders and LEGO fans around the world. Mobilized by their love of LEGO, these fans find themselves at the intersection between their passion for the brick and their potential exploitation in various forms of free labor for the brand. (For more on the brand's exploitation of fan labor, see Chapter 8 in this volume by Joyce Goggin.) In this chapter, I examine the various user communities and roles of AFOLs, particularly in relation to fandom studies. Beyond this, I explore how LEGO adroitly mobilizes its adult fans in various ways, including as brand ambassadors to promote LEGO through community building; as consumers to make more and bigger purchases; and as co-creators in new product development.

Fan Studies and Fan Communities

Fan studies has a short (barely 30 years) yet prolific history. Booth (2018) submits that in the past three decades, fan scholarship has led to the growth of two journals, multiple published monographs and edited anthologies, and much more. Yet within that time, fan studies has transformed in research and methodological approaches (Sandvoss et al. 2017) and crossed many academic disciplines' boundaries. Let's consider how fan studies inform each other by exploring their various systems and considerations, since this refines my approach to the study of AFOLs.

Parasocial Relationships and Fans

Horton and Wohl first introduced the concepts of parasocial interactions (PSI) and parasocial relationships (PSR) in 1956. Although scholars often use the terms interchangeably, PSI focuses more on short-term exchanges, and PSR centers on more long-term bonding and affection. In this chapter, I explore PSR as it relates to fans and fandom. From a scholarly perspective, the traditional understanding is that viewers can build PSRs with on-screen personalities, leading to a sense of friendship and companionship. As such, the literature defines PSR as a one-sided interpersonal relationship that resembles real-world relationships, particularly in terms of social support (Hartmann et al. 2008). People construct PSRs similarly to how they make real-life, interpersonal relationships: both actively, such as talking about characters with others, and passively, such as by observing on-screen personalities and learning about their thoughts, behaviors and values (Perse and Rubin 1989). While an individual may hold a PSR with personae, such relationships can also bring people together through a shared connection for an object of affection, whether it be a person, activity or thing. Jenkins (2018) draws a distinction between fans and fandoms and proposes that the word "fan" describes "anyone who forms an intense affective bond with a particular property" (p. 16), while a fandom extends to a broader community of fans that "claim a common identity and a shared culture" (p. 16). As such, PSR serves as a foundation for the development of fans and fandoms (Jennings 2018). With toy fans, the object of affection is, in fact, a non-person whose fandom grows from a shared liking and passion for collecting, playing, displaying and connecting with others who share the same interests and passions.

Waves of Fan Research

Fan studies has progressed through three waves of research movements with divergent goals, reference points and methodological approaches (Sandvoss et al. 2017). Each wave contributes to a richer understanding of fans and fandom, serving as points of inspiration for my approach to studying AFOLs.

The first wave focused on power and consumption, treating fandom as "an act of subversion and cultural appropriation against the power of media producers and industries" (Sandvoss et al. 2017, p. 2). As such, scholars in this wave regarded fans as composing a subculture with a political purpose: to disrupt the media industry. Jenkins (1992) has suggested that the early understanding of a fan described professional sports teams' followers' unbridled and excessive enthusiasm (particularly baseball fans), but eventually, fans were understood to include other entities and personae, as well, including avid theater-goers and the devotees of television shows, movies and celebrities. Early fan studies scholars defended fan communities and examined fan practices' most active sites, such as conventions or cons and fan fiction, to show another side of fandom that contrasted with fandoms' portrayal by the media and non-fans. Employing an ethnographic approach, first-wave fan scholars gained insider status, leading to a kind of activist research described as "Fandom Is Beautiful" (Sandvoss et al. 2017, p. 3). Mainstream media often associated fans with negative traits: Jenkins (1992) claimed that early news reports characterized fans as "psychopaths whose frustrated fantasies of intimate relationships with stars … take violent and antisocial forms" (p. 13). As such, fans were ostracized and marginalized as subcultures to mainstream society.

This contrasts with second-wave scholarship, which "highlights the replication of social and cultural hierarchies within fan cultures and subcultures" (Sandvoss et al. 2017, p. 5). Second-wave scholars employed French sociologist Pierre Bourdieu's (1984) approach concerning cultural capital, suggesting a structure and social positioning within the fandom itself based on "who is a fan of what and how" (Sandvoss et al. 2017, p. 5). As such, scholars developed typologies and systems of fandoms, leaning away from the first-wave orientation of fandom as a place of political resistance. However, these typologies ignored the growing practice of the everyday fan—individuals who love a show, watch every episode, love to talk about it, and form PSR with characters, but do not engage in other fan practices. Gray et al. (2007) suggested that this more subdued behavior is "fandom in one of its most common forms" (p. 4). Indeed, with a shift from broadcasting to narrowcasting, fans as a specialized and devoted consumer have become cherished by the industry and serve as a "centerpiece of media industries' marketing strategies" (Gray et al. 2007, p. 4). Fandoms have moved from the eccentric forms of political resistance to ordinary spaces for social community building.

With this transformation, fan studies' third wave began to shift the focus once again. Third-wave scholars "have explored the *intra*personal pleasures and motivations of fans" (Sandvoss et al. 2017, p. 6). Fans form intrapersonal relationships with one another, finding others with similar interests in and love of the fan object. Moreover, the Internet's rapid explosion facilitated the growth of online communities, making it easier for individuals to locate other fans and build online networks. Fans build community and relations from shared PSRs with a fan object. This approach to fan studies has inspired a spectrum of psycho-analytic and critical studies to explore "how we relate to ourselves, to each other, and to how we read the mediated texts around us" (Sandvoss et al. 2017, p. 7).

Cutting across these waves, I navigated my research approach to study AFOLs. First, incorporating first-wave methods, I engaged in ethnographic participant observation of AFOLs. Second, I identified second-wave positionalities of the AFOL culture. Third, I explored third-wave interpersonal relationships among AFOLs. As such, this research involved a multi-method approach. First, I conducted a lengthy (three- to four-hour) interview with a founding member of a LEGO user group (LUG) in Kentucky. I took detailed notes during the interview and added reflective notes after the interview. In addition, the founding member responded to text and messages with follow-up questions and clarifications of content. Second, I attended a LEGO convention known as Brick Universe which was held in Dayton, Ohio. At Brick Universe, I observed and noted different types of participants at the conference including artists, vendors, contest participants and visitors to the conference. I also spoke informally with many of these individuals and engaged in conference activities, such as building with LEGOs. Third, I attended a sponsored LUG community event and a regular meeting of a LUG at a local comic book store in the greater Cincinnati area. For the community event, LUG members brought LEGOs for store visitors to build. The event focused on providing a space for families to build together. Children who completed a design received an engraved LEGO brick to keep. Following the commu-nity event, LUG members gathered for a monthly meeting where I continued to make observations. Finally, I examined LEGO Group documents which established guidelines for LEGO fan communities. LEGO Group is the privately held company in Denmark that manufactures LEGO materials.

Adult Fans of LEGO (AFOLs)

Toys and play conjure images of childhood, innocence and fun. Sutton-Smith (1986) has suggested that, historically, toys became "personal possessions and the first form of private property for children" (p. 120) signifying a child as "an owner, a consumer, and an achiever" (p. 127). Children form PSR with their toys and these affections can become a source of contention with their parents when children are "unwilling to outgrow" their toys (Sutton-Smith 1986, p. 126). Bond and Calvert (2014) have added that children's PSR dissipate or fade over time, such that children experience parasocial breakups with beloved characters and objects. However, for some, the breakup never occurs, leading to an ongoing one-sided bond. Heljakka (2017) has suggested that adults who continue to hold bonds with toys face the fear of being referred to as infantile or regressed adults. While some would argue that adults who love toys are holding on to the past and are guided by nostalgia, Heljakka (2017) has submitted that playing with, creating and collecting toys provides opportunities to share this passion with other like-minded individuals. Moreover, Geraghty (2018) has argued that "nostalgia for childhood should be viewed as an integral part of keeping in touch with the fan self and as an anchor to a personal history which can be remade, recreated, and remolded at the touch of a button or the purchase of a new toy" (p. 161). Such is the case with AFOLs and their online and offline communities.

Even though LEGO's plastic bricks have been around for 60 years, the adult fan community of LEGO only began emerging in the 1990s. Two significant factors contributed to the rise in LEGO's adult fan community: (1) the introduction products, particularly LEGO Mindstorms and LEGO Star Wars, that appealed to an older audience and (2) the Internet's community building capabilities, which enabled people to connect and find like-minded fans both near and far

(Antorini et al. 2012). Fan studies research also suggests that digital technologies including social media networks, online discussion groups and mobile media have contributed to the normalization of fandoms in general, making fans a part of everyday life rather than members of outsider, ostracized communities (Sandvoss et al. 2017). As such, LEGO fan communities known as LEGO user groups grew from 11 in 1999 to over 150 groups in 2012 (Antorini et al. 2012). Today, Reddit/Lego (https://www.reddit.com/r/lego/) has over 382,000 subscribers, and over 300 AFOL communities exist worldwide (https://lan.lego.com/clubs/overview/).

Mobilizing as User Groups and Ambassadors for the LEGO Group

Currently, the LEGO Group recognizes three types of fan communities: (1) Recognized LEGO User Groups (RLUGs); (2) Recognized LEGO Online Communities (RLOCs); and (3) Recognized LEGO Fan Media (RLFMs) (Thomsen 2017). In common practice, the "R" is dropped from the title, and the communities refer to themselves as LUGs, LOCs and LFMs. The LUG and LOC are the most similar to each other, in that they engage the fan community in either a local physical space (LUGs) or online (LOCs). The LFMs include physical and online magazines, blogs, YouTube channels and the like. Two common threads exist with each of these communities: (1) the presence and active participation of a LEGO ambassador and (2) an obligation to keep confidential information from the LEGO Group to themselves (Thomsen 2017). A LEGO ambassador is a community member of 18 years or older who functions as the single point of contact between the LEGO Group and the community. First, the ambassador brings information to the community members, ensures that all related reporting to the LEGO Group occurs in a timely manner and complies with guidelines and policies established by the LEGO Group including the Fair Play Policy, Brand Values, Novelty Policy and IP Guidelines. In addition, the ambassador is expected to be a positive role model with the fan community and with other ambassadors by acting in a respectful, constructive manner (Thomsen 2017). Second, the LEGO Group is actively concerned with their trademark and maintaining LEGO brand values, even among fan communities—particularly with recognized communities. Violations of brand values by community members and ambassadors may result the community or ambassador losing "recognized" status. The expulsion of an ambassador is particularly devastating for the community, since the community itself therefore also loses its recognized status (Thomsen 2017).

According to the LEGO Group, LUGs typically have 20–50 active members that meet regularly, build with LEGOs together and host public community events (Thomsen 2017). Each LUG has an organizational structure and supports initiatives from the LEGO Group, such as distributing and completing LEGO Group surveys and reporting on community events. Similarly, the LOC focuses on forums and online discussion or presence that is "perceived as valuable by the Community" (Thomsen 2017) but has no required number of participants or forums or steady online traffic. The LRM, on the other hand, should publish on a regular basis (weekly for online sites) and maintain a steady traffic flow. The LFM also shares announcements and press releases from the LEGO Group and their partners. Moreover, the LEGO Group's established guidelines for LUGs distinguish what constitutes acceptable practice of LEGO Group IP assets. LUGs must meet four requirements to be considered for "recognition" from LEGO: (1) existing for one a minimum of one full year; (2) having an active community; (3) being known and having a positive reputation within the AFOL community; and (4) maintaining compliance with the LEGO Rules and Guidelines (Thomsen 2017).

Protection of the LEGO trademark and intellectual property is particularly important to the LEGO Group. As such, the LEGO Group imposes three guidelines about use of LEGO IP assets, particularly regarding LUGs' naming rights. First, when LUGs host an event, they often create an event design and print it on t-shirts. Specific rules govern this practice: LEGO characters, primarily LEGO Minifigures and LEGO DUPLO figures, may be used on event t-shirts; however, t-shirt bearing these designs may only be used in connection to the event, and no sales to the general public may be made. The quantity of t-shirts ordered and prepared should reflect the number of t-shirts "reasonably expected to be used at the event" (The LEGO Ambassador Network, n.d.). LUGs may only sell overstock to members for a maximum of 90 days after the event ends. Moreover, they may produce no additional t-shirts. While LUGs may use LEGO Minifigures' images on t-shirts, use of the LEGO logo is prohibited, and the LUG may not suggest that the LEGO Group sponsors, endorses or is affiliated with the event. Moreover, while the t-shirt may feature a LEGO character, promotional materials such as banners, posters or signs may not (The LEGO Ambassador Network, n.d.). Finally, the t-shirt design must be "family-friendly" and appropriate for all ages. Second, the LEGO name and trademark may not be used in the LUG name or the LUG's organized event name. Additionally, the LEGO name and trademark may not be part of the LUG or LUG event's Web site domain name (The LEGO Ambassador Network, n.d.). Alternatively, LUGs often use the term "brick" in the naming of an event, such as "Brickfair." Finally, LUGs may refer to themselves as a "Recognized LEGO User Group," and non-commercial LUGS may use depictions of the LEGO brick or the LEGO studs in their logo—but not the LEGO logo, LEGO Minifigures, or other LEGO characters (The LEGO Ambassador Network, n.d.).

Interestingly, the LEGO Group acknowledges the AFOL community's value as "high-level consumers of LEGO products" and LEGO brand promoters through their public events, community activities and creations with LEGO bricks and elements (The LEGO Ambassador Network, n.d.). Here, the LEGO Group recognizes a tension between AFOLs as consumers and as brand diplomats. AFOLs' parasocial relationship with LEGO is a double-edged sword: They are heavy consumers because they buy a lot of product (Austin 2018) and often buy higher-priced sets and materials (Wolff-Mann 2015), which is good financially for LEGO (see more in the "Type of Toys and AFOLs" section below); and they foster interest in LEGO (possibly including purchases by non-AFOLs) by "selling" the brand to others through their creative builds and displays, particularly at LEGO conventions such as Brick Universe. To be clear, AFOLs do not represent LEGO officially, even as a recognized community, despite their deep passion, interest and investment in the product. However, in order to maintain the "recognized" status, these communities must follow the LEGO brand values. The LEGO Group submits that the LEGO brand is "more than simply our familiar logo. It is the expectations that people have of the company towards its products and services" including six key values: (1) imagination, (2) creativity, (3) fun, (4) learning, (5) caring, and (6) quality (Jensen 2016). As a LEGO ambassador and subsequently a recognized LEGO community, the LEGO Group imposes these expectations on group members in their activities. For instance, the requirement of a "family-friendly" t-shirt design would embody these values.

Currently, 310 RLUGs exist globally. Europe has the greatest concentration, with 182 RLUGs (https://lan.lego.com/clubs/overview/). In addition, 67 RLOCs exist globally, which may also be RLFMs. One example of a RLOC/RLFM is *Blocks Magazine*, a monthly LEGO fan magazine available online and in print from England. *Blocks* features a different LUG each month, and most recently, OKI LUG—the AFOL community with which I engaged the most for this study—took the spotlight.

OKI LUG. In 2009, Rodney Dicus and his mother, Ethel Dicus, formed OKI LUG. Rodney is currently the president of OKI LUG, and he and his mother have been collecting LEGO for over 40 years. Since 2009, OKI LUG's membership has grown from nine to 34 AFOLs (Wharfe 2018). Based in Florence, Kentucky, this LUG serves members in the Ohio, Kentucky and Indiana tri-state area. According to Dicus, members meet monthly, with ten business meetings and two family member parties over the course of the year. During my visit to a business meeting, executive committee members presented various reports while LUG members discussed and voted on upcoming events and opportunities.

Every OKI LUG business meeting also features LEGO building, such as a demonstration by a club member or a pre-meeting "build and take" activity (a quick LEGO build with provided materials that can be taken home) that is open to the public. In other cases, the meeting may involve a themed build challenge in which members bring built original constructions focused on a particular theme, such as the Christmas/holiday theme for the November 2018 meeting. Finally, LUGs will often hold a "parts draft" at the end of a meeting, as did the OKI LUG at the meeting I attended. In a parts draft, members agree on a particular set to be "parted out" among the participating members so that members may accumulate more LEGO elements of a certain type within the set without purchasing the entire set multiple times.

OKI LUG is very active, participating in LEGO fan cons including Brickworld Chicago and Brickfair, Virginia, and building displays for events hosted by organizations such as the Cincinnati Museum Center, EnterTRAINment Junction and the Boone County Fair in Kentucky (Wharfe 2018). OKI LUG also collaborated with the Cincinnati Museum Center to host building classes for 7–10-year-old and 11–14-year-olds girls. In addition, for the past seven years, OKI LUG has hosted their own Kentucky Brick Expo, bringing out displays for public enjoyment (Wharfe 2018). In August 2018, OKI LUG brought a large group build that debuted at Brickfair 2018 to the UC Health Stadium, home of the Florence Freedom, a professional baseball team. The build was a Harry Potter Quidditch Pitch complete with Hagrid's hut. For 3 days in Florence, KY, OKI LUG members hosted tables where ballpark visitors could build with LEGO and marvel at the Quidditch display (Wharfe 2018). Later, the OKI LUG moved the Quidditch display to a comic book store where members often have business meetings and where LEGO sets are sold.

Mobilizing as Collectors, Artists, Designers and Everyday Players

Not all toy fans share the same motivations. Heljakka (2017) identifies four categories of toy fans: (1) toy collector, (2) "toying" artists, (3) toy designers, and (4) "everyday players" (p. 94). Toying artists and toy designers share a motivation to play with toys as part of their professional and leisure activities. As professionals, toy artists use toys and toy parts as their chosen materials for creating art. Toy designers also engage in a creative process with a different result—to make or modify toys or toy pieces to provide a different form of play for others. As such, toying artists and toy designers share a passion for creativity and involve the toy as a primary component of their art or design. Toy collectors vary slightly in that they see the value of toys "both as investments and as objects of research" (Heljakka 2017, p. 94). They see the beauty of the toy, much like the artists and designers, yet they are also interested in collecting, organizing and displaying toys as an art form. Collectors take pride in their treasure-hunting skills and capturing of rare and limited-edition toys. The everyday player, however, is the toy fan who enjoys the toy for the toy's sake. The toy fulfills no professional need, but rather satisfies the ordinary, common pleasures of joy through play. LEGO collectors, artists, designers and "everyday players" can be found from LEGO cons to AFOL community meetings.

LEGO artists—that is, artists who use LEGO as their medium—approach their art with many different approaches. While attending Brick Universe, I observed the work of LEGO artists Jonathan Lopes, Rocco Buttliere, Paul Hetherington and Raymond Griffith, who accompanied their art displays and mingled and interacted with convention visitors. LEGO artists displayed three-dimensional constructions of buildings, characters and scenes as well as wall art and even airbrush LEGO caricatures. Artwork included custom created images, portraits, corporate logos and interactive builds. At the convention, artwork could be seen in protected, chained areas, similar to artwork in a museum.

LEGO artwork and builds can take months of work and feature many thousands of elements (Seyd 2015). Some artists specialize in different areas and prefer to use different elements. At Brick Universe, I observed that Hetherington often populates his builds with minifigures, such as a creation resembling a Lady Gaga stage show with her "Little Monsters." By contrast, Buttliere, an architect, started building 1:650 scale models of global landmarks, and he displayed a few at Brick Universe, including landscapes of central London, lower Manhattan and the Chicago North Loop. While many LEGO artists use brick elements in their work, others take inspiration from the bricks in their drawings. LEGO artist Griffith, whom I also observed at Brick Universe, creates airbrush caricatures of customers, transforming the shapes of their heads to resemble a minifigure's cylindrical shape—"a fun, exaggerated drawing of you…But a little squarer than usual" (Funny Figs LLC, n.d.).

Many LEGO artists played with LEGOs as a child. Buttliere described his journey from childhood hobbyist to adult LEGO artist and reflected that his LEGO hobby was not taken seriously in his high school years, but his professors at the Illinois Institution of Technology took his builds and designs far more seriously (Meet Rocco 2018). Buttliere has spoken highly of the support he receives from the LEGO fan community and from fellow LEGO artists and professionals (Meet Rocco 2018). Similarly, Hetherington played with LEGOs as a child, gave up LEGO in his pre-teen years and gravitated back to LEGO building as an adult (Seyd 2015). Both Hetherington and Buttliere consider themselves AFOLs, and Hetherington is an active member of a Vancouver, Canada LEGO club (Seyd 2015).

Since many LEGO artists require specific colors, sizes and styles of bricks, they often become LEGO collectors, as well. Hetherington estimated that in 2015, he owned between one and two million pieces, sorted and stored in plastic drawers in his home (Seyd 2015). Interestingly, the collecting process for LEGO takes on different forms, from searching for specific elements to searching for rare or special edition sets. For example, in their quest for the right number of specific pieces to complete a build (such as a blue 2×2 brick or a plain minifig head), LEGO artists may collect individual elements and keep them sorted in different containers like Hetherington. For these collectors, the sheer volume of elements gathered and sorted for building use constitutes the collection's value. Aside from volume, collections may be comprised of specific sets and elements. In this case, the collector may have a passion for a particular theme, such as Castles or LEGO Friends, and may search for as many sets within the theme that they can find. For example, LEGO has developed several different castle sets since the first castle, which the company produced in Europe in 1978 and made available in the United States in 1981 (375 Castle, n.d.) Within theme, subthemes or factions often exist. Following the castle sets, nine different factions of castle sets existed between 1984 and 1998 and eight additional subthemes appeared from 1998 to 2013 (Castle, n.d.). Collectors particularly value these historical sets and pieces that LEGO no longer produces. The sets' and pieces' condition also matter to the collector. Has the set's box ever been opened? How many sets did LEGO produce and when? The older and the fewer sets produced, the rarer and more valuable the items. Heljakka (2017) identifies several acronyms that describe the collected items' condition, including (1) MIB = "Mint" in its original box; (2) NRFB = "never removed from box"; and (3) MWMT = "mint with mint tags." These conditions add further value to the items.

Individuals' LEGO collections can grow quite large and span products from over 60 years. Michael LeCount, a former teacher and founder of Sheffield's Bricks and Bits, owns one of the UK's largest and oldest collections. He and his family recently purchased a second home in Sheffield just to house the 4000 LEGO sets in his collection (Needham 2018). Meanwhile, in the United States, Daryl Austin, a father of three, he has spent over $45,000 on LEGO toys (Austin 2018). Speaking of his LEGO collection, Wayne Hussey, AFOL and Brickcon Director, has argued: "We haven't wasted the money. We've invested the money" (Gibson 2013). Indeed, as reported in 2015, the average value of a LEGO set in "pristine condition" has appreciated 12% compared to the S&P 500 at 4.2% and gold at 9.6% (Wolff-Mann 2015). Collectors drive up rare sets' prices. For example, the Star Wars Ultimate Collector's Millennium Falcon sold for $510 in 2007, but it was worth $4041 in 2015 (Wolff-Mann 2015).

Just as the Internet contributed to the rise of LEGO fan communities, it has likewise made collecting easier through a variety of online stores and outlets. On eBay, shoppers can browse an entire section dedicated to LEGO building toys, but for AFOLs, the most well-known and preferred online shopping experience is Bricklink. Launched in 2000, Bricklink is the world's largest online marketplace for LEGO shoppers and sellers. There, anyone can search online catalogues for items, and registered members can post wanted-item requests and sell their own LEGO pieces and sets (Antorini et al. 2012).

Some toy designers make or modify toys to develop new sets or new pieces when items they need aren't available. This is the case with LEGO, particularly among AFOLs. The LEGO company employs toy designers, but AFOLs often generate new ideas and can inspire complimentary products, as well. LEGO has even been known to hire AFOLs as designers; by 2012, for example, the company had hired at least 20 AFOLs (Antorini et al. 2012). AFOLs create and utilize software to generate designs and My Own Creations (MOCs), which are instructions for new sets that can be made from packaged LEGO sets. In 1995, James Jessiman released a freeware computer-aided design (CAD) program that allows users to create and document designs with LEGO elements prior to actually constructing a design (Antorini et al. 2012). Currently, Bricklink supports a freeware program called Studio 2.0, in which users can build and render designs from LEGO elements. The program is integrated with Bricklink's catalog so that that users can check the availability of elements, and it offers an in-app instructions maker so that designers can edit and create instructions for their designs (Studio 2.0 2018). In addition, designers can submit their MOCs to an online database called Rebrickable (https://rebrickable.com/), where people can search for and locate building instructions and a full parts list for each shared design.

While the common perception of AFOLs may be as "everyday players" who play with LEGO for the pure joy, AFOL communities also include designers, collectors and artists. This is the case within the OKI LUG, whose members collaborated to design Minifigures for the group's large Harry Potter Quidditch display. OKI LUG members had decided that the display should have an equal distribution of Quidditch match attendees from each Hogwarts house, but LEGO only makes Slytherin and Gryffindor Minifigures—not Hufflepuff or Ravenclaw. To represent the latter two houses, an OKI LUG member designed a vector of the appropriate school uniform, which a company custom-printed onto Minifigure torsos. By so doing, OKI LUG could boast over 800 Minifigures in their display—with at least 200 Minifigures representing each Hogwarts house.

The resulting Quidditch display itself was treated like the work of art that it indeed was. For example, when the OKI LUG members transported and re-constructed the Quidditch display to the comic book store where they have their meetings, they placed the display carefully in the store roped it off like cherished artwork in a museum—to be seen, not touched. During the LUG's rebuild and placement of the Quidditch display, I discovered that the comic book store displayed other LEGO artwork, which had also been created specifically for the store by OKI LUG members and the store owner. Large wall art of two different comic book covers adorned the store's walls, and OKI LUG members provided a large Bob the Builder model and two Disney Minions displays for the store that day, as well. Although these AFOLs may not earn a living from their designs and artwork, they actively engage in these aspects of the toy fandom and willingly share their ideas and creations with others.

The categories of designers, artists, collectors and everyday players often overlapped among AFOLs and revealed another type of fan: a toy historian. During my visits with OKI LUG members at community events and their business meeting, I observed AFOLs moving between roles, sharing their designs or art one moment and talking about their own collections the next. Furthermore, as I listened to them discuss LEGO, it became clear that a knowledge of the LEGO history and toy lines provided them with the means to further engage with one another and share their passion for LEGO. A dedicated AFOL has a working knowledge of that history, perhaps because they, too, are a part of that story. Many AFOLs started playing with LEGO as a young child—such as Dicus, who started at the age of 7 years. While some, such as Dicus, never stop playing with LEGO toys, other experience what is known in the fan community as a "dark age"—a time, usually in the teen years, when "playing with LEGO" is not popular with peers, and many stop playing to "fit in." After this "dark age"—for example, as young adults—many AFOLs return to LEGO play and engagement.

As a LEGO fan for over 40 years, Dicus grew up with LEGOs. He not only knows the history but also carries it with him in his collection and in his heart. As we discussed LEGO, Dicus described in detail the changes in design in different generations of Minifigures and readily relayed for me the history of when and how LEGO sets first came to the United States. He had working knowledge of the toy line from his experiences with the toy product, which informed his art and designs. For example, Dicus described a display he created for Fur Reality, a furry convention held in Cincinnati, OH in 2014 (Weird Review 2014). Within his display, he incorporated into a village scene a number of animals as Minifigures. The animals appeared as members of the community, driving vehicles, walking on the sidewalks and having lunch. Dicus explained that LEGO had manufactured these animal-headed characters in a discontinued line called FABULAND (LEGOLAND FABULAND, n.d.), now considered rare among collectors. Dicus revealed that prior to the 2014 convention, in his 40 years of collecting LEGO, he had never used these rare pieces in his artwork. He had kept his FABULAND characters in storage, and the furry convention provided a perfect opportunity to share this piece of LEGO history with others (Weird Review 2014). He thus shared not only his love of LEGO but also his knowledge of LEGO history and rare collection pieces with those who visited his artwork. This anecdote about Dicus's historical knowledge, design ability and passion for collecting exemplifies the convergent nature of the toy fan roles.

Mobilizing and Co-creating with LEGO

For brands, fans convergent knowledge, passion and experience can make for the perfect storm—as has been the case for the LEGO Group's AFOLs. As indicated in my discussion earlier in this chapter of the waves of fan studies, the study of fandom is rooted in concerns about power and subversion of the industry's strength and identity. Yet, over time, the industry came to embrace the fan as a source of revenue and inspiration. Fandoms have become more normalized and accepted, giving them their own source of power. Moreover, fandoms can be creative and innovative, as suggested with AFOLs: They are designers, artists, collectors, historians and everyday players who play with the brand and product in new ways. Consequently, corporations face a conundrum: either embrace the fans (their product's dedicated consumers) or alienate them (with costly litigation to protect the brand name). LEGO faced such a situation with AFOLs in the late 1990s with the introduction of new series (Star Wars and LEGO Mindstorms) that adult users found particularly appealing and with the rise of the Internet, which helped AFOLs connect in previously unimaginable ways (Antorini et al. 2012).

The relationship between AFOLs and LEGO sits at the intersection between fan studies, product development and brand management. For years, LEGO relied, as do most toy companies, on internal research and designers to create new products and product lines. With the launch of LEGO Mindstorms, the first LEGO robotics toolkits, the LEGO Group recognized AFOLs' creativity and volume and forged new relationships to involve the user community in product development (Antorini and Muñiz 2013). Labeled as co-creation, Zwick et al. (2008) propose that this process involves "new possibilities for value creation that are based on the expropriation of free cultural, technological, social, and affective labor of the consumer masses" (p. 166). Moreover, Hatch and Schultz (2010) suggest that co-creation extends beyond product development and into brand marketing practices, as well. To better facilitate co-creative practices, LEGO began reviewing AFOL input and collaborating with AFOL community users (Antorini et al. 2012). In 2005, the LEGO Group established the LEGO Ambassador Programme to facilitate a closer relationship and better engagement with AFOLs around the world (Mortensen 2012). Since then, AFOL user communities have grown in number, size and strength.

Co-creation can be valuable to corporations and consumers. Antorini and Muñiz (2013) have claimed that user engagement can be advantageous to the company in at least 3 ways: (1) reducing the economic risks of launching new products that may not be of interest to consumers; (2) lowering development costs by using the labor of the community users to generate ideas and test prototypes; and (3) reducing product failure by being responsive to consumers. Similarly, Hatch and Schultz (2010) suggested that co-branding can create dialogue within organizations and with stakeholders outside organizations, provide two-sided points of contact for consumers and stakeholders within organizations and create further transparency with the consumer by sharing the organization's culture—although that carries its own risks, as well.

Through the LEGO Ambassador Program and their LEGO Group AFOL Engagement Department, AFOLs and the LEGO Group forge relationships and interact with one another. The 2018 AFOL Designer Program provided an example of co-creation between AFOLs and LEGO. Through this program, Bricklink and the LEGO Group supported a competition with AFOL designers for realization of their creativity in a limited edition 60 Years Anniversary set (Bricklink Team 2018).

AFOLs submitted over 400 designs, created in Studio 2.0, through a portal available to registered members on Bricklink.com (Bricklink Team 2019). LEGO design team members reviewed the submissions and selected 16 finalists from nine different countries (Bricklink Team 2019). Beginning in February of 2019, the finalists' designs were displayed for crowdfunding consideration, with 13 successfully crowdfunded (Bricklink 2019), Bricklink acquired IP rights from the designers of the funded designs in exchange for 10% of total sales revenue (Bricklink Team 2018). This competition lived up to the expectations of co-creation and greatly benefitted the LEGO Group and Bricklink. Furthermore, earning a portion of the sales revenues presented a direct financial benefit to the winning designers, and selected designers could expect their reputations to be elevated among the AFOL community and the LEGO Group—another reward with value. These sets' rarity could also prompt collectors to see them as valuable investments, as the pre-order phase set the maximum order per set at 2500. At the time of this writing, one set—Löwenstein Castle—had already sold out (Malloy 2019), making the 2500 sets produced even more valuable on the secondary market.

These relationships do prompt some concerns, however. The sponsors will benefit more from the co-creation competition than will the AFOL designers, placing the financial advantage in the hands of the LEGO Group and Bricklink. After all, LEGO has a vested interest in celebrating events such as their bricks' 60th anniversary, and by relying on the free labor of AFOLs to design sets of interest to AFOLs, the brand is actually reducing its own costs. Furthermore, LEGO will benefit not just from free design labor, but also from free marketing labor: The AFOLs who design the sets will be invested in promoting and sharing information about the designs to support the crowdfunding campaign's success. So, too, will the LUGs to which they belong. Then, following the sets' actual production, the AFOLs and their LUGs will actively review the sets and share comments about them—which also functions as a form of marketing labor from which the brand benefits. Although there is no easy remedy for the concerns that LEGO exploits fan labor in product development and marketing, recognizing the give and take of co-creation is important.

Conclusion

When I asked Dicus, "What draws you to LEGO?" he said, "It's all about the brick." This sentiment reflects the heart and soul of a pure AFOL. The joys of play, the shared friendships with fellow AFOLs, the sense of community, the beauty of the art, the intricacy of the design—all exist because of the brick. LEGO's mission ("inspire and develop the builders of tomorrow") and vision ("inventing the future of play") both speak to human possibility, which is brought to life through the children that play with LEGO and those that grow up to be AFOLs. They continue to inspire, develop, build, invent and play. Corporate co-creation, marketing and fandom stigma play important roles in understanding the AFOL community. However, putting aside the stigma of adults playing with toys and corporations' potential questionable use of free labor, at the end of the day, it's still all about the brick—what it represents, what it supports and what it stirs in the minds and dreams of others.

References

375 Castle. (n.d.). *Brickipedia*. https://lego.fandom.com/wiki/375_Castle. Accessed on November 2, 2018.

Antorini, Y. M., & Muñiz, A. M. (2013). The benefits and challenges of collaborating with user communities. *Research-Technology Management, 56*(3), 21–28. https://doi.org/10.5437/08956308X5603931.

Antorini, Y. M., Muñiz, A. M., Jr., & Askildsen, T. (2012). Collaborating with customer communities: Lessons from the LEGO Group. *MIT Sloan Management Review, 53*(3), 73–79. https://sloanreview.mit.edu/. Accessed on November 9, 2018.

Austin, D. (2018, April 9). Confession: I'm a grown man who has spent over $45,000 on LEGO toys. *Huffington Post*. https://www.huffingtonpost.com/entry/grown-man-45000-dollars-legos_us_5ac39e72e4b00fa46f86b180. Accessed on November 10, 2018.

Bond, B. J., & Calvert, S. L. (2014). Parasocial breakup among young children in the United States. *Journal of Children and Media, 8*(4), 474–490. https://doi.org/10.1080/17482798.2014.953559.

Booth, P. (2018). Introduction. In P. Booth (Ed.), *A companion to media fandom and fan studies* (pp. 1–10). Hoboken, NJ: Wiley.

Bourdieu, P. (1984). *Distinction: A social critique of the judgment of taste.* Cambridge, MA: Harvard University Press.

Bricklink. (2019, June 7). *Today we unbox one of our 13 AFOL Designer Program finalists, Wild West Saloon!* [Facebook post]. https://www.facebook.com/bricklink/. Accessed on July 12, 2019.

Bricklink Team. (2018, September 12). *Your design can become a limited edition 60 Years Anniversary set!* https://www.bricklink.com/v2/community/newsview.page?newsid=44. Accessed on November 11, 2018.

Bricklink Team. (2019, February 1). *Crowdfunding is officially open!* https://www.bricklink.com/v2/community/newsview.page?newsid=46. Accessed on June 8, 2019.

Castle. (n.d.). *Brickipedia.* https://lego.fandom.com/wiki/Castle. Accessed on November 2, 2018.

Funny Figs. (n.d.). *About Funny Figs.* http://funnyfigs.com/. Accessed on November 11, 2018.

Geraghty, L. (2018). Nostalgia, fandom and the remediation of children's culture. In P. Booth (Ed.), *A companion to media fandom and fan studies* (pp. 161–174). Hoboken, NJ: Wiley.

Gibson, J. (2013, January 7). *AFOL: A blocumentary* [Video file]. https://www.youtube.com/watch?v=e0gtavrtKxQ. Accessed on May 3, 2018.

Gray, J., Sandvoss, C., & Harrington, C. L. (2007). Introduction: Why study fans? In J. Gray, C. Sandvoss, & C. L. Harrington (Eds.), *Fandom: Identities and communities in a mediated world* (pp. 1–18). New York: New York University Press.

Hartmann, T., Stuke, D., & Daschmann, G. (2008). Positive parasocial relationships with drivers affect suspense in racing sport spectators. *Journal of Media Psychology, 20*(1), 24–34. https://doi.org/10.1027/1864-1105.20.1.24.

Hatch, M. J., & Schultz, M. (2010). Toward a theory of brand co-creation with implications for brand governance. *Journal of Brand Management, 17*(8), 590–604. https://doi.org/10.1057/bm.2010.14.

Heljakka, K. (2017). Toy fandom, adulthood, and the ludic age. In J. Gray, C. Sandvoss, & C. L. Harrington (Eds.), *Fandom: Identities and communities in a mediated world* (pp. 91–105). New York: New York University Press.

Horton, D., & Wohl, R. R. (1956). Mass communication and para-social interaction: Observations on intimacy at a distance. *Psychiatry, 19,* 215–229. https://doi.org/10.1080/00332747.1956.11023049.

Jenkins, H. (1992). *Textual poachers: Television fans and participatory culture.* New York, NY: Routledge.

Jenkins, H. (2018). Fandom, negotiation, and participatory culture. In P. Booth (Ed.), *A companion to media fandom and fan studies* (pp. 13–26). Hoboken, NJ: Wiley.

Jennings, N. A. (2018). Why do kids think Dora the Explorer is their friend? In N. A. Jennings & S. R. Mazzarella (Eds.), *20 questions about youth and the media* (2nd ed., pp. 125–135). New York: Peter Lang.

Jensen, M. V. (2015, February 12). *The LEGO Group.* https://www.lego.com/en-us/aboutus/lego-group. Accessed May 3, 2018.

Jensen, M. V. (2016, February 22). *The LEGO brand: Brand values.* https://www.lego.com/en-us/aboutus/lego-group/the_lego_brand. Accessed November 9, 2018.

LEGOLAND FABULAND. (n.d.). *LEGO history.* https://www.lego.com/en-us/themes/lego-history/articles/legoland-fabuland-89ed9a-0951314507915def5b1dbdcb0a. Accessed on November 10, 2018.

Malloy, C. (2019, April 22). *LEGO Löwenstein Castle set from BrickLink's AFOL Designer Program* [Review]. https://www.brothers-brick.com/2019/04/22/lego-lowenstein-castle-from-bricklinks-afol-designer-program-review/. Accessed on June 8, 2019.

Meet Rocco Buttliere of Landmark | Landscape in northwest suburbs. (2018, September 18). *VoyageChicago.* http://voyagechicago.com/interview/meet-rocco-buttliere-landmark-landscape-northwest-suburbs/. Accessed on October 31, 2018.

Mortensen, T. F. (2012, January 9). *Timeline 2000–2010.* LEGO. https://www.lego.com/en-us/aboutus/lego-group/the_lego_history/2000. Accessed on November 10, 2018.

Mortensen, T. F (2017, October 17). *The LEGO Group history.* https://www.lego.com/en-us/aboutus/lego-group/the_lego_history. Accessed on January 15, 2019.

Needham, J. (2018). Inside the utopian, brick-loving world of LEGO's adult fandom. *Wired.* http://www.wired.co.uk/article/lego-60-anniversary-afol-community-adult-lego-fans. Accessed on May 3, 2018.

Perse, E. M., & Rubin, R. B. (1989). Attribution in social and parasocial relationships. *Communication Research, 16*(1), 59–77. https://doi.org/10.1177/009365089016001003.

Sandvoss, C., Gray, J., & Harrington, C. L. (2017). Introduction: Why still study fans? In J. Gray, C. Sandvoss, & C. L. Harrington (Eds.), *Fandom:*

Identities and communities in a mediated world (2nd ed., pp. 1–26). NY: New York University Press.

Seyd, J. (2015, March 6). *LEGO artistry is awesome: Real life master builder creates amazing scenes from traditional toy.* North Shore News. https://www.nsnews.com/community/lego-artistry-is-awesome-1.1784922.   Accessed October 31, 2018.

Studio 2.0 [Application Software]. (2018). https://studio.bricklink.com/v2/build/studio.page?utm_content=subnav. Accessed on November 11, 2018.

Sutton-Smith, B. (1986). *Toys as culture.* New York, NY: Gardner Press.

The LEGO Ambassador Network. (n.d.). *Guidelines for the use of LEGO Group intellectual property assets by recognized LEGO user groups ("RLUGs").* https://lan.lego.com/applications/core/interface/file/attachment.php?id=2081. Accessed on October 3, 2018.

Thomsen, K. E. (2017, June 14). *The LEGO ambassador network—Rules and guidelines* [Electronic mailing list message]. https://lan.lego.com/topic/9-the-lego-ambassador-network-rules-and-guidelines/. Accessed on May 3, 2018.

Wharfe, C. (2018, October). OKI LUG. *Blocks (48),* 80–81. https://www.blocksmag.com/. Accessed on March 19, 2019.

Weird Review. (2014, October 17). *Interview with Rodney Dicus at Fur Reality 2014* [Video file]. https://www.youtube.com/watch?v=ysiYcNGgmvI. Accessed on November 11, 2018.

Wolff-Mann, E. (2015, December 28). LEGO sets have been a better investment than gold since 2000. *Money.* http://time.com/money/4162059/lego-investment-compare-gold-return/. Accessed on November 10, 2018.

Zwick, D., Bonsu, S. K., & Darmody, A. (2008). Putting consumers to work: Co-creation and new marketing govern-mentality. *Journal of Consumer Culture, 8*(2), 163–196. https://doi.org/10.1177/1469540508090089.

Part III

The Politics of Representation in the LEGO Franchise

11

"I Just Don't Really, Like, Connect to It": How Girls Negotiate LEGO's Gender-Marketed Toys

Rebecca C. Hains and Jennifer W. Shewmaker

LEGO has become a contested site of children's culture. Once regarded as a toy for all children, LEGO's rebranding as a "boys' toy" and, later, the development of a separate line of LEGO toys for girls raised concerns about gender equity and inclusion. Given the brand's reputation as a toy line that benefits children through STEM play, LEGO's gender segregation and gender-stereotypical marketing practices are laden with cultural significance and meaning.

But how did LEGO morph from a *children's* toy to a *boys'* toy in the first place? A brief history informs that question. LEGO began as a line of wooden toys by master carpenter Ole Kirk Kristiansen in Denmark, 1932. After investing in a plastic injection-molding machine in 1946,

R. C. Hains (✉)
Department of Media and Communication,
Salem State University, Salem, MA, USA
e-mail: rhains@salemstate.edu

J. W. Shewmaker
Abilene Christian University, Abilene, TX, USA
e-mail: jws02b@acu.edu

R. C. Hains and S. R. Mazzarella (eds.), *Cultural Studies of LEGO*,
https://doi.org/10.1007/978-3-030-32664-7_11

Kristiansen began producing plastic toys, and the company introduced interlocking plastic bricks 1949. These products began to retail in international markets in 1956, reaching the United States and Canada in 1961. The brand's many successes required business expansions throughout the 1950s and 1960s and an ever-growing workforce in an increasing number of international locations ("Wooden Toys," n.d.; Mortensen 2017). So, in 1963, to help guide the brand and its hundreds of employees, company head Godtfred Kirk Christiansen (Ole's son) articulated ten product characteristics. The first was, "Unlimited play potential." The second: "For boys and girls" (Mortensen 2017).

Through the 1970s, the brand hewed closely to that second characteristic. The LEGO Group ran full-color advertisements depicting boys *and* girls playing creatively with brightly colored LEGO blocks. In the 1980s, however, the LEGO Group strayed from this mission, transforming into a "boy brand" (Hains 2015). Then, from 1992 to 2003, LEGO released a series of ill-fated girls' products that little resembled their core products, like Scala, which offered dollhouses and Barbie-like dolls (Feloni 2014; "LEGO Scala" 2010). Taken together, these offerings' characteristics reveal institutional beliefs contradictory to the directive that being "for boys and girls" was a core LEGO characteristic. The brand's leadership presumed that girls lack interest in complex building and gender-counterstereotypical themes. As noted in this book's introduction, by 2004, LEGO was on the brink of bankruptcy and responded in part by streamlining their offerings in a way that excluded girls (Feloni 2014; Wieners 2011).

After four years of market research to avoid repeating past failures, the LEGO Group released LEGO Friends in January 2012. The LEGO Group asserted that Friends—with pastel colors and stereotypically feminine topics—reflected what girls actually wanted. LEGO Group CEO Jorgen Vig Knudstorp called this "the most significant strategic launch we've done in a decade," noting, "We want to reach the other 50 percent of the world's children" (Mortensen 2017).

But market research about consumer preferences generally yields results reflecting consumers' marketplace socialization, offering ideas about what will be good for a company's profitability and its shareholders—nothing more. The LEGO Group's market research seems to have assumed girls' consumer socialization as an unproblematic given, and—perhaps to avoid a perceived risk of damaging their standing as a boy brand—it is unclear whether the team researched ways of bringing boys and girls together in play, such as by emphasizing community and agency in their themes, which advertising research has suggested as an alternative to developing separate, gendered sets of advertisements to market the same products to boys and girls (Bakir et al. 2008).

LEGO Friends received a mixed reception, however. For example, a *CNet* article titled "Lego for girls: Wait, what?" asked, "Is the firmament crumbling? Or do girls need different colored bricks?" (Matyszczyk 2011). An article in *Jezebel* mused, "A commercial that shows girls building creative models with plain Lego bricks would have been cheaper, but we've reached the point where girls see blocks in primary colors and think they're not for them" (Hartmann 2011). And a couple of years later, when illustrator Maritsa Patrinos first heard about LEGO Friends, she created a comic strip depicting a LEGO representative introducing LEGO Friends to a woman, who—baffled and uninterested in the girlish themes—explained that including more girls in LEGO could be as simple as changing a minifigure's hairpiece (Hains 2014). The strip resonated with readers and quickly went viral.

Mads Nipper, Executive Vice President of Marketing at the LEGO Group, defended LEGO Friends by citing the company's aforementioned market research. In a press release, Nipper stated, "of the current active LEGO households in the U.S., only 9% of them report that the primary user of the product in that household is a girl," with similar statistics in other nations, and explained that a global market research project with 3500 participants had informed their decisions (Nipper 2012).

In response, SPARK—objecting to the "distorted notion that, in order to buy LEGO, girls need messages about the value of shopping, clubbing, baking, and tanning"—countered that the brand had long abandoned girls, evidenced by the overall lack of girls in its commercials and in its playsets. "This was never an effective marketing strategy for selling LEGOs to girls, and it is disingenuous to suggest that it was. That only 9% of regular LEGO users before the Friends line were girls is thus not surprising. You had stopped selling to girls" (SPARK 2012).

In 2011, immediately following the announcement of the upcoming release of LEGO Friends, SPARK launched an anti-Friends petition, garnering more than 68,000 signatures. The petition and its many signers' comments documented growing cultural concerns about LEGO's gender segregation and its separate-but-not-equal approach to girls.

A wealth of scholarship on gendered marketing and its implications supports such concerns. For example, research indicates that increased exposure to gender-stereotyped media is associated with increased stereotypical behavior (Coyne et al. 2016) and that gender-stereotyped beliefs can lead to less gender stereotype flexibility (Hilliard and Liben 2010), limiting a child's play behavior and interests (Bakir and Palan 2010; Hilliard and Liben 2010). Advertisements for children overwhelmingly present gendered associations, typically linking pastel colors, cooperation and indoor play with girls, while associating bold, neon colors, competition and outdoor play with boys (Auster and Mansbach 2012; Kahlenberg and Hein 2010). In fact, LEGO has specifically been noted as a brand whose marketing messages position boys as active, capable agents and girls as passive, novice, social caregivers (Reich et al. 2018). These authors found that LEGO's marketing focused on boys used active words such as "build," "investigate" and "explore" while those directed at girls were passive, such as "relax," "primp" and "hang out" (Reich et al. 2018). As children build their understanding of gender and identity, marketing plays a part in that formation. Portrayals of what it means to be a boy or a girl will shape the child's perception of normative behavior, interests and abilities (Shewmaker 2015). Gendered marketing practices put children at risk of internalizing rigid, negative stereotypes about their own gender. When this occurs, the consequences for children, particularly the girl child, can be serious, as belief in gender stereotypes can harm self-esteem, hinder academic performance, limit play and narrow vision of the roles and opportunities available in life (Coyle and Liben 2016; Coyne et al. 2016; Fine and Rush 2018; Liben et al. 2001).

Given these concerns, in this chapter, we seek to better understand girls' negotiations of LEGO toys following the brand's evolution from inclusive to gender-segmented and gender-stereotypical. Building upon previous research (Hains and Ostrow 2017; Shewmaker and Hains 2016), and drawing upon our respective backgrounds in media studies and psychology, we investigate young girls' negotiations of a range of LEGO sets.

Methodology

In this chapter, we explore the findings of a qualitative research study we conducted with twenty girl participants in late 2018 and early 2019 at two sites: one, a mid-sized city in rural Texas, and the other, the suburb of a large city in Massachusetts (with ten participants in each location). Using word of mouth and snowball sampling, and with the mediation of their parents, we recruited participants between the ages of six and eleven with a self-reported interest in LEGO. All participants came from White, middle-class families.

We asked each participant a series of questions about her LEGO interests, then handed each participant large, laminated, full-color photos of eight LEGO boxed sets and asked some questions about which of the LEGO sets depicted they were most interested in. Then, we invited the girls to engage in free play with all of the pieces (and instructions) from those eight sets. After the participants concluded their free play, we invited them to give us a tour of their creations using iOS devices we provided. Next, we asked a few questions about gender, such as whether they felt that all LEGO sets are meant for boys and girls alike or whether some are for boys and some for girls. If a participant responded with the latter option, we followed up with the question, "How can you tell which is which?" We saved the gender questions for last to avoid inadvertently leading the girls into certain types of play during the free play portion of the interview. In total, we spent between 30 minutes and one hour with each girl.

We selected the eight LEGO sets used in this study to represent a range of gender-stereotypical marketing tactics. Applying the criteria mentioned above regarding gender-associated characteristics in marketing to children, we selected three femininely gender-stereotyped sets, all featuring packaging dominated by pastel colors:

- LEGO Friends: Olivia's Speed Boat 3937 (Ages 5–12, 65 pieces, featuring one female mini-doll with a speed boat and other beach accessories),

- LEGO Friends: Olivia's Inventor's Workshop 3933 (Ages 5–12, 81 pieces, depicting a female mini-doll in a STEM-oriented workshop),
- LEGO Friends: Snow Resort Hot Chocolate Van 41319 (Ages 5–12, 246 pieces, featuring two female mini-dolls).

Two sets gender-stereotyped as masculine, with packaging dominated by bold primary colors—red, blue and yellow:

- LEGO City: Pizza Van 60150 (Ages 5–12, 249 pieces, with one male and one female minifigure) and
- LEGO City Juniors ("Easy to Build"): Mountain Police Chase 10751 (Ages 4–7, 115 pieces, with two male minifigures).

And three sets less gender-stereotypical sets:

- LEGO Safari 4637 (Ages 4+, 152 pieces, with one male and one female minifigure on a safari; packaging features yellow, pale blue and only minimal dark blue and red),
- LEGO Ideas: Research Institute 21110 (10+, 165 pieces, with three female minifigures in paleontology, astronomy and chemistry scenes, but in a box predominantly featuring black, white, red and blue—typical "boy" colors),
- LEGO City: Fun at the Beach 60153 (Ages 5–12, 169 pieces, a "people pack" which—although in typical blue LEGO City packaging—is dominated by minifigures (7 male, 7 female and 1 ambiguous, ranging from children to grandparents) and features leisure-oriented beach-themed accessories/activities and animals, which are common characteristics of LEGO sets targeting girls (Hains and Ostrow 2017).

With many gender-stereotypical LEGO sets we could have chosen from, we made these selections in part by identifying sets in some ways comparable, despite falling into different categories (gendered feminine, gendered masculine or gender-inclusive). These were:

- LEGO Friends: Snow Resort Hot Chocolate Van and LEGO City: Pizza Van

- Both feature food service vans,
- Both feature two characters (one with a male and a female, one set of two females),
- Both have a similar number of pieces;

- LEGO Friends: Olivia's Workshop and LEGO Ideas: Research Institute

  - Both depict female characters only (one a single female, one three females),
  - Both show these characters engaged in STEM work; and

- LEGO Friends: Olivia's Speedboat and LEGO City: Fun at the Beach

  - Both are set at the beach,
  - Both include some similar beach-themed accessories, such as sand castles and beach umbrellas,
  - Both include recreational water vehicles—a speedboat in the Friends set and a kayak and a stand-up paddleboard with sail in the City set.

Data Analysis. We engaged a research assistant and a professional transcriptionist to produce our transcripts. Then, we analyzed these transcripts for emergent themes and coded them, allowing us to identify patterns across our data set, rather than simply within one data item (Boyatzis 1998; Braun and Clarke 2006). By inductively deriving themes through a data-driven "bottom-up" process, developed primarily on the direct content of the answers rather than prior research (Braun and Clarke 2006), we allowed for the possibility that themes would emerge in the participants' answers that we could not predict or expect.

Findings

In this section, we will review several key themes that emerged in our analysis of the interviews with our participants. Note that the girls in our study (all of whom we refer to using pseudonyms) could easily describe for us the characteristics of LEGO toys that indicated whether or not the company intended them for girls or for boys—effortlessly citing variables such as the color schemes of the packaging and products; the mix of male and female characters included in the packages; the characters' roles within the playsets; and the types of activities portrayed within the playsets as indicating whether they were meant primarily for girls, primarily for boys or for boys and girls alike.

Girls' Negotiations of Gender-Stereotyped LEGO Sets

Predictably, some of our participants were drawn to certain sets, but not others, because of how LEGO had gendered them. Several participants indicated that they would be uninterested in certain sets that were "boyish" or "for boys."

For example, the Mountain Chase Police Set—which many of our participants recognized as clearly being meant for boys—solicited many expressions of disinterest from our participants.

- "Well, I'm not really interested in police" (Samantha, 8).
- "I just don't really, like, connect to it, I don't really…well I would get it but I wouldn't choose it" (Mia, 9).

Similarly, seven-year-old Sophia said she would choose to play with neither the Safari, City Pizza Van, nor the Mountain Chase Police sets, "Because they're boyish." When asked what made these sets seem boyish, she replied, "Because there's mostly boys in them.…Well, also because it's boy trucks."

Meanwhile, the Research Institute set—which we selected for seeming relatively gender-neutral—caught some participants' attention for its exclusive inclusion of female minifigures. For example, although science is stereotypically coded as a boys' theme, and although Sophia was averse to any theme we shared that she found "boyish," she remarked of the Research Institute: "I like it because it has girls."

Some participants, however, offered oppositional readings to the implicit gender directive that LEGO's gendered playsets offer to children. For example, knowledge that LEGO intended some sets for girls or boys specifically did not necessarily limit all of our participants' perspective on which sets children might like to play with. Chloe—who, at age nine, was a bit older than Isabella and Samantha—noted that she feels it's okay for children to play with toys meant for the other sex: "I feel like some are more for boys, and some are more for girls… but I feel like girls can play with the boys and boys can play with the girls, if they want." Similarly, Hana (age seven) indicated that although some LEGO sets are meant for boys and some are meant for girls, she thinks LEGO is "for everyone," drawing upon an example from another children's toy brand to make her case:

Hana: Well, boys are supposed to not like My Little Pony. And our friend, James, likes My Little Pony. So I think it's for everyone. Everyone can use it.

Nora (age ten) said that there "shouldn't be a set made just for girls or just for boys," but she was aware that LEGO often did market their play sets in gendered ways. "The kids don't really care about that," she said. "They just play with it no matter what."

Researcher: [So] LEGO does make some sets for girls and some for boys? How do you think kids can tell which is which?
Nora: The characters.
Researcher: Oh, it's the characters?
Nora: Yes.
Researcher: So tell me more.
Nora: Because personally, I like playing with most of the girls [LEGOs]. I don't know why, I just do. Whenever I go over to some of my friends-who-are-boys' houses, if they [play] with LEGOs, they're usually playing with boy LEGOs.
Researcher: Meaning the characters are boys?
Nora: Yes. They're also, like, different-colored sets, like blue, dark blue, black, gray, because the LEGO companies think that's what boys' colors should be. But my brothers, I'm pretty sure my [15-year-old] brother's favorite color is purple. […] Also, my favorite color is light blue. So I don't think that the LEGO company should be like,

"Oh, these people should like this color, so we're just going to put it on what we think should be a boys' kit and what we think should be a girls' kit."

When asked in the interviews to identify with whom they engaged in LEGO play, the girls mentioned siblings, friends, cousins and sometimes parents. Interestingly, the majority of the girls who mentioned parents only mentioned playing LEGO with their father. Nine-year-old Ella said of her father, "If we're playing, he'll help us sometimes." The interviewer asked her, "Anyone else in your family do LEGOs?" Ella responded, "My mom doesn't really." When asked about who LEGO toys are for, Madison (age 10) responded "Certain kinds of people, 'cause they have to be patient. They have to be patient to build things….my mom can't do LEGOs because she's not patient." Ten-year-old Abigail discussed playing with LEGO sets and pieces that her dad had saved from his childhood. Then she noted, "my mom didn't play with LEGO."

Girls' Negotiations of Female LEGO Minifigures and Mini-Dolls

As LEGO's female mini-dolls tend to have more stereotypically feminine characteristics than their female minifigure counterparts, it is useful to consider how our participants responded to the design of the LEGO sets' female characters.

The Research Institute features three female minifigures. LEGO markets this set as being for ages 10 and up, and it comes across as more gender-inclusive or gender-neutral due to its sedate color scheme. Also, conveying that science is a serious pursuit, the three minifigures that come with the Research Institute have relatively serious expressions on their faces. This is a gender-nonconforming decision, as smiling and maintaining a pleasant countenance are gender-stereotypical (and sexist) cultural expectations of girls and women. For eight-year-old Alyssa, however, these minifigures' lack of smiles was off-putting. Although she called the set's T-Rex fossil "cool," she decided that she would not be interested in playing with the Research Institute set. Her reason was, "This one I don't like because these two [minifigures] are the only ones that frown."

In contrast, LEGO offers mini-dolls that present in gender-stereotypical ways, encompassing not only their facial features and hairstyles, but also their apparel. Thus, ten-year-old Ella noted that she generally prefers LEGO's mini-dolls over their minifigures because of the level of detail found on their clothing. "Their clothes are more realistic," she explained. "Like this one, for example […] her shirt is more realistic. Like, instead of it just being a jacket with a zipper down the middle, they have pockets, and there's fur. You can tell she's wearing gloves, and her shoes have pompoms." Her interest in these details may reflect an interest in fashion that, like fashion doll play and dress-up play, is generally gendered as a feminine pursuit and which LEGO is hailing in the way it styles its mini-dolls.

In a similar vein, Abigail (age ten) mentioned that changing the clothing of minifigures and mini-dolls appealed to her in her LEGO play. She said she enjoyed that "you can change the people if you don't like their outfit. That's fun. Kinda like a fashion show!"

Not all participants seemed to prefer gender-stereotypical characteristics in minifigures and mini-dolls, however. For example, nine-year-old Hailey objected to the gender-stereotypical shaping found across female LEGO characters' bodies. She critiqued LEGO's female minifigures, which are created with blocks that are the same shape as the male minifigures, for being painted to look as though they have a bust and a smaller waist. She explained:

Hailey: One of my opinions about them is that personally, I don't really like the female LEGO original characters 'cause it's like, why do they have a square body, but it looks like they have, like, indents on them to make them look like they're not this guy?

Researcher: Oh, the way that they're painted? [i.e., with curves to give the female minifigs the illusion of a stereotypically feminine tapered waist]

Hailey: Yeah.

Researcher: To have a curvy body? [Hailey nods.] And you don't like that?

Hailey: Yeah. This [referencing the torso she used for a female character in her build] actually goes to a boy's outfit, I just snapped them together 'cause…like why? She [pointing to one] would be skinny. She [pointing to another] would be more like me. She's actually probably a future version of me.

Researcher: What does the future version of you look like? Like if you were to describe it in words?

Hailey: Probably have glasses. I mean, my body shape will probably look like hers [gesturing to the minifigure she built], not like this [indicating one painted to have a more hourglass shape].

Researcher: Not like that?

Hailey: No.

Researcher: [Indicating the minifigures] What about like, these?

Hailey: I could *never* be like this. I could never be that skinny.

Researcher: Why do you say that?

Hailey: 'Cause the way my body is now, I'm like, I'm fine with that. I mean, I do wanna be a little bit healthier. But still. I love my body! And I don't wanna be this skinny!

These remarks bring to mind LEGO design director Rosario Costa's explanation for the decision to create mini-dolls. As Wieners (2011, n.p.) explained:

> The key difference between girls and the ladyfig [mini-doll] and boys and the minifig was that many more girls projected themselves onto the ladyfig [mini-doll]—she became an avatar. Boys tend to play with mini-figs in the third person. "The girls needed a figure they could identify with, that looks like them," says Rosario Costa [...] The Lego team knew they were on to something when girls told them, "I want to shrink down and be there."

LEGO introduced only one new body type, however—one that is even less realistic for many girls and women than those minifigures, given the contrast between demographic weight trends and the mini-dolls' tall-and-thin proportions. The research that girls wish to project themselves on to mini-dolls seems to hold true for Hailey, but as her body type deviates from the tall, thin beauty ideal that the mini-dolls reflect, she is in many ways partially excluded from the target audience for these play sets. In her interview, this seems to cause her to reassert that she is fine with her body and doesn't want to be that thin—but even the curves painted on the female minifigures' torsos remind her that her shape is outside the ideal, which may constitute a form of stereotype threat. Research has established that when a stereotype exists about a person's social identity—such as their gender—and they are aware of it, that awareness alone can lead to negative consequences, such as changes in academic performance, behaviors and success (Spencer et al. 1999; Steele and Aronson 1995; Martens et al. 2006).

Participants' Reception of Other Characteristics of LEGO Sets

While some of our participants indicated that they preferred LEGO sets intended for girls and eschewed sets meant for boys, gender variables were not the only factors involved in their engagement with LEGO toys. Many such themes emerged in our analysis of our transcripts. Those we will address here are: (1) an interest in generative play; (2) an interest in science; and (3) an interest in action-oriented play.

Our participants did not tend to discuss these themes in gendered ways. In fact, these comments arose before the interviewers introduced questions of gender. It is of interest, then, to note that each of these three themes defies gender stereotypes about girls' interests and aptitudes.

Generative play. Girls consistently talked about being attracted to LEGO based on its generative nature. Participants used terms such as "create," "build" and "make" across several different discussions regarding their interest in the toy—active terms that are contrary to the gender stereotype (often found in children's toy marketing) that girls prefer passive activities.

- "I like building stuff with them and I don't know, there's so many different things you can do with them, so it's fun to see how many different ways you can do it and stuff" (Chloe, 9).
- "Just the creativity of all the stuff that you get to build [and] imagine…" (Emma, 11).
- "Getting to use your creation and sometimes building things that look cool and using them and stuff" (Madison, 10).

- "I just play and kinda create my own thing with LEGOs" (Olivia, 7).
- "With LEGOs, you can just build anything. You can build ramp stuff, you can build a wall, you can build a boat out of stuff that you're not supposed to build a boat with…different kinds of stuff.… Yeah, you can build whatever you want. Like if LEGO pieces go to a set and you lost the instructions and the set's broken, you can just take it apart and build whatever you want" (Mia, 9).
- "I really like to make forts and that's kinda like making a tiny version of a fort" (Alyssa, 8).

Our participants also verbalized about generative problem-solving as they played. When seven-year-old Olivia couldn't find a piece called for in an instruction booklet, she sought out alternatives. "[This piece] is white, but we can use it," she said. "Is it the same size as this? Yeah, it's the same size as this. We need two of these." She added, "This is just like that [piece], so we don't have to use the same color. We can just use this one."

Similarly, Mia, age nine, talked of problem-solving while she engaged in free play. "Well, I cannot find two green pieces," she remarked, "and I don't really have to have them […] 'Cause sometimes you have to, like, use other pieces for it to work."

Personal interest in science. Another emergent theme was an interest in science. In reviewing the eight LEGO packaging photos we shared with them, several participants said that they would want to play with Olivia's Invention Workshop or the Research Institute because they liked science. Sophia (age seven) indicated she would play with these sets because they're "kinda science-y… and I like science." Other comments about these two sets included:

- "Ooooo, science! I love science!" (Abigail, 10).
- "I like science a lot, so that would be fun" (Chloe, 9).
- "[I like that it] has a board and a telescope and robots and potion stuff" (Emily, 7).
- "I like this one [Olivia's Inventor Workshop] because it has a little robot, and like, I usually like things like these little bottles" (Alyssa, 8).

Eight-year-old Lily was also drawn to the science-oriented LEGO sets, and she played with several pieces from the Research Institute and Olivia's Inventor Workshop together. When she first saw the Research Institute playset, she described what the various characters on the box were doing, saying: "She's looking at the stars, she's just investigating, she's putting, like, liquid into a different chemical into another vial, and then there is this big chair. And this for, like, examining stuff."

For her build, seven-year-old Hana used pieces from the Research Institute, Olivia's Inventor Workshop and other sets, as well. During her free play time, she built a science classroom filled with characters and pretended one of them was a 10th-grade science teacher, as follows:

Today we're gonna learn about science, like always. [voicing different characters] *Ok, you first. What do you think today is about?* Um, I think we're going to be learning about science. *Correct!* […] *Today we're gonna be learning about how parrots change their feathers. You first.* Um, I think it's because of the air? And how they, how the temperature is? *Well, that's part of it.* I think it's how warm their blood is. *Um, no. You?* I think it's because of what music they're listening to? *Definitely not!* I think it's because the sun, they're always in the sun and the sun is always on their feathers. And…*Yes! You are correct! Yes, that is correct. Now we're going to be drilling into this ruby and seeing what's inside.* [drilling noises] *It looks like rock, but it's actually a precious metal, see?* [shows student characters] Oh, so pretty! Nice! Nice! Cool! I think my pet likes it! You're doing very well as a teacher in training. *Now, we're gonna learn about explosions.* What? *Let's see what happens when I put the gem in the top of this! You there, stand up! Or sit up. Guess it won't stand up. But I'll put some gasoline in it and then it'll blow up. 5, 4, 3, 2, 1…* [explosion noise].

She continued in this vein for several minutes, play-acting science class as an exciting activity.

Interest in action-oriented play and vehicles. Action-oriented play interested many of our other participants, as well, with the vehicles in the LEGO sets we shared proving to be appealing. These included the van and scooter in the City Pizza Van; the van in the Friends Hot Chocolate Van; and the water vehicles in the City Day at the Beach People Pack and Olivia's Speedboat.

Isabella (age seven): I like…the boat and the…and I like, the…water and then I like this one because of the dolphin and he's on the boat.
Mia (age nine): I love the beach. […] I like to canoe and sail and I like to hang out.
Alyssa (age eight): It's really cool how they made the [Pizza Van] truck. It made the wheels look like real wheels. I also like the scooters. And they have helmets there like the normal [helmets] I have at home.
Hana (age seven): I like this one because it has the little motorcycle and the pizza. The pizzas and the van. And I like how it shows, it actually has the little pizzas in it, and the sliding tops.
Emma (age eleven): There's just a lot of action in this one [the Mountain Chase Police set]. [It] looks more fun to play with.
Lily (age ten): [Wrapping up her free play]: I just need to put this other stuff […] and the motorcycle. There! And, a kayak. Okay, she has a motorcycle and a kayak. Okay, I'm ready.

A few participants did note that they liked the Friends Hot Chocolate Van, which LEGO marketed as a girl product, but not the similar City Pizza Van, marketed as a boy's product, but it was unclear whether this preference was due to the gender-stereotypical marketing used in these sets or other factors. For example:

Mia (age nine): If I got to choose between the cocoa and the pizza, I'd choose the cocoa, 'cause I love snow too, so…and I like to be warm when there's snow. So I like to drink hot cocoa. The pizza van, I like pizza, but if I got to choose, I'd choose this one (pointing to hot cocoa van).

Likewise, seven-year-old Emily noted that she would like to play with the Hot Chocolate Van, but not the Pizza Van. She said that the Pizza Van "kinda looks silly." When asked what about it looked silly, she remarked, "The people in the truck"—which, as a LEGO City set, consisted of minifigures, rather than the mini-dolls characteristic of Friends sets, such as the Hot Chocolate Van.

Ella (age nine) mentioned that Olivia is her favorite Friends character because "she's always doing something really fun," then explained:

Ella: I think she was in the yacht set. She does a lot of boating. Like, she was in this boat set.
Researcher: Do you like boating?
Ella: My dad does boat races and stuff.
Researcher: Yeah? That's cool. Do you ever go, like, kayaking or anything in the harbor?
Ella: Mm-hmm. We used to go to my mom's friend's house, and we would kayak out to an island for a day.
Researcher: Oh, that's nice. So you share some of those interests that Olivia's stories show.
Ella: Mm-hmm [affirmative].

At the end of the free play period of her interview, seven-year-old Emily enthusiastically described the slide she created while playing with the pieces we provided to her.

So, here's what I'm making. And I'm…climb up on. And this should help them because it has little bumps and so they can like, grab, grab, and then grab all the way to the top. And then I'm adding this little fence to get them up. And now, I'll show you how you do it! So here's my person, and I will climb her up. She can jump…[makes LEGO person go down slide] Wooo!

Emily's build facilitated her portrayal of an active, energetic girl who was having fun playing in an outdoor setting—counter to stereotypical representations of girls as passive, inactive and located in interior settings. Many of the girls were physically active during their play sessions, moving around the play area, spinning in their chair or standing, reaching and moving about to get to specific pieces.

Discussion

In analyzing our interviews with our study's participants, we found that the girls could quite easily identify which LEGO products targeted girls and which targeted boys. This is unsurprising, given the cultural context in which gender and its associated stereotypes are so often used as an organizing category for children's material and media culture. When discussing which of the LEGO sets we shared most interested them, some participants made selections that adhered to these stereotypes, while others did not. In conversations about the gendering of LEGO sets, the older participants (ages 10 and 11) seemed more likely to exhibit gender stereotype flexibility or the ability to see that not all gender stereotypes are applicable to all people. Some of those girls expressed resistance to the idea that certain LEGO sets should be meant for one gender only. Instead, many of the older girls moved easily among the sets and figures gendered masculine and feminine. As Bakir and Palan (2010) note, the degree to which a child develops gender stereotype flexibility is important in determining whether or not the type and extent of gender content—such as gender-specific toys—will be significant to those children. Children who indicate more gender stereotype flexibility are more likely to play with playmates of the other sex, engage in activities typically associated with the other sex, and endorse interest in careers that are not stereotypically considered for their own gender (Coyle and Liben 2016; Liben et al. 2001). Gender stereotype flexibility benefits children by allowing them more freedom to develop relationships with playmates of the opposite gender and to view their own prospects from a wider perspective. On the other hand, when girls and boys are consistently shown and told that they should be interested in only specific, narrow areas, then many of them will begin to demonstrate those interests (Hilliard and Liben 2010), potentially limiting their understanding of their own agency and ability to succeed in a variety of careers and social relationships (Coyne et al. 2016; Reich et al. 2018).

Some of our participants also offered remarks about the characteristics of female minifigures and mini-dolls, from a range of perspectives: Some wished for the minifigures to be more gender-conforming, for example, while others expressed concern about the body types of both kinds of female LEGO figures. The girls demonstrated an awareness of and thoughts concerning the different kinds of body types represented in the LEGO figures.

It is interesting to note that of the girls who played LEGO with a parent, the majority mentioned playing with their father. Some specifically noted what they saw as a lack of interest on the part of their mother. Given that these parents were children in the 1980s, after LEGO had begun using gendered marketing strategies (Hains 2015), it is possible that the low level of noted LEGO interest on the mothers' part is due to the heavily male-focused marketing strategies used during their own childhoods.

Contrary to what LEGO's market research suggested (Mortensen 2017), we also found that the characteristics of LEGO play that our participants seemed to most enjoy defied gender stereotypes. These included (1) generative play, or an interest in building/creating/making things; (2) an interest in science, reflected by the popularity among our participants of the Olivia's Workshop set from the LEGO Friends line and the Research Institute featuring three female minifigures; and (3) an interest in action-oriented play and vehicles, with many girls expressing enthusiasm about and engaging with features such as the vans, scooter, speedboat, kayak and sledging slide. The girls in our study often demonstrated physically active forms of LEGO play, moving around the area with the vehicles or objects they had built. The majority were not still or passive while playing. These findings provide an interesting contrast to the narratives that LEGO promotes to girls, focused on passive and caretaking roles (Reich et al. 2018). While the marketing narratives identified in Reich et al.'s study (2018) encouraged girls' interest in beauty and shopping, those themes were not prominent in the play behavior of the girls in this study.

Although the current study had the strengths of including multiple data collection sites, multiple reporters and a variety of school settings represented, we would like to note that the sample is somewhat limited as all of the children came from White, middle-class families. We recommend that future research examine these variables from a more intersectional perspective within diverse populations.

Conclusion

While the girls in this study appeared to understand the gender associations of specific marketing strategies such as color, type of minifigure and themes such as active and passive play, they also defied these in many ways. For example, they generally noted interest in science and action-oriented play and vehicles. Rather than using the passive narratives that LEGO marketing seems to promote to girls, the participants in our study engaged in active play and used words such as "build" and "create" to describe their interest in and use of LEGO. In fact, the generative, problem-solving nature of LEGO was the aspect most noted for liking to play with the toy. Most girls in our study demonstrated play behaviors that moved freely between the different sets offered, regardless of the sets' gendered characteristics. In discussing their preferences in the interviews, some girls used the gendered marketing associations to determine which toys they said they would choose to play with. However, when provided the opportunity to play freely with all of the pieces from the various sets we showed them during their interviews, those who engaged in generative play showed little concern about which pieces came from which set. Instead, girls generally demonstrated the ability to create and build without constraint based on gender-stereotypical associations. This was especially true of the older girls in our sample.

In sum, our findings suggest that girls readily understand and may adopt the gendered marketing associations of LEGO toys, which are so clearly visible in the toys' packaging. But when girls have a chance to play with LEGO bricks and characters away from the context of their original packaging, they are able to demonstrate active, generative, creative play, defying gender stereotypes about girls and their interests.

References

Auster, C. J., & Mansbach, C. S. (2012). The gender marketing of toys: An analysis of color and type of toy on the Disney Store website. *Sex Roles, 67*, 375–388. https://doi.org/10.1007/s11199-012-0177-8.

Bakir, A., Blodgett, J. G., & Rose, G. M. (2008). Children's responses to gender-role stereotypes in advertisements. *Journal of Advertising Research, 48*(2), 255–266. https://doi.org/10.2501/S0021849908029X.

Bakir, A., & Palan, K. M. (2010). How are children's attitudes toward ads and brands affected by gender-related content in advertising? *Journal of Advertising, 39*(1), 35–48. https://doi.org/10.2753/JOA0091-3367390103.

Boyatzis, R. E. (1998). *Transforming qualitative information: Thematic analysis and code development*. Thousand Oaks: Sage.

Braun, V., & Clarke, V. (2006). Using thematic analysis in psychology. *Qualitative Research in Psychology, 3*, 77–101. https://doi.org/10.1191/1478088706qp063oa.

Coyle, E. F., & Liben, L. S. (2016). Affecting girls' activity and job interests through play: The moderating roles of personal gender salience and game characteristics. *Child Development, 87*(2), 414–428. https://doi.org/10.1111/cdev.12463.

Coyne, S. M., Linder, J. R., Rasmussen, E. E., Nelson, D. A., & Birkbeck, V. (2016). Pretty as a princess: Longitudinal effects of engagement with Disney Princesses on gender stereotypes, body esteem, and prosocial behavior in children. *Child Development, 87*(6), 1909–1925. https://doi.org/10.1111/cdev.12569.

Feloni, R. (2014, February 20). These are the disastrous Lego kits that almost ruined the company. *Business Insider.* https://www.businessinsider.com/legos-worst-failures-2014-2. Accessed on July 25, 2019.

Fine, C., & Rush, E. (2018). "Why does all the girls have to buy pink stuff?" The ethics and science of the gendered toy marketing debate. *Journal of Business Ethics, 149*(4), 769–784. https://doi.org/10.1007/s10551-016-3080-3.

Hains, R. C. (2014, December 23). *LEGO Friends comic goes viral: An interview with illustrator Maritsa Patrinos.* https://rebeccahains.com/2014/12/23/lego-friends-comic-goes-viral-an-interview-with-illustrator-maritsa-patrinos/. Accessed on July 25, 2019.

Hains, R. C. (2015, July 9). The problem with separate toys for girls and boys. *The Boston Globe Magazine.* https://www.bostonglobe.com/magazine/2015/02/27/the-problem-with-separate-toys-for-girls-and-boys/2uI7Qp0d3oYrTNj3cGkiEM/story.html. Accessed on July 25, 2019.

Hains, R. C., & Ostrow, C. (2017, August 9). *Toy marketing and gender stereotypes: A critical content analysis of 40 children's retail web sites.* Paper presented at the Annual Meeting of the Association for Education in Mass Communication and Journalism, Chicago, IL.

Hartmann, M. (2011, December 15). Lego targets girls with pink blocks, cute figures, and no creativity. *Jezebel.* https://jezebel.com/lego-targets-girls-with-pink-blocks-cute-figures-no-5868334. Accessed on July 25, 2019.

Hilliard, L. J., & Liben, L. S. (2010). Differing levels of gender salience in preschool classrooms: Effects on children's gender attitudes and intergroup bias. *Child Development, 6*, 1787–1798. https://doi.org/10.1111/j.1467-8624.2010.01510.x.

Kahlenberg, S., & Hein, M. (2010). Progression on Nickelodeon? Gender-role stereotypes in toy commercials. *Sex Roles, 62*(11–12), 830–847. https://doi.org/10.1007/s11199-009-9653-1.

LEGO Scala—Interesting and Sweet. (2010, November 27). *The Brick Blogger.* http://thebrickblogger.com/2010/11/lego-scala/. Accessed on July 25, 2019.

Liben, L. S., Bigler, R. S., & Krogh, H. R. (2001). Pink and blue collar jobs: Children's judgments of job status and job aspirations in relation to sex of worker. *Journal of Experimental Child Psychology, 79*(4), 346–363. https://doi.org/10.1006/jecp.2000.2611.

Martens, A., Johns, M., Greenberg, J., & Schimel, J. (2006). Combating stereotype threat: The effect of self-affirmation on women's intellectual performance. *Journal of Experimental Social Psychology, 42,* 236–243. https://doi.org/10.1016/j.jesp.2005.04.010.

Matyszczyk, C. (2011, December 19). *Lego for girls: Wait, what?* CNet. https://www.cnet.com/news/lego-for-girls-wait-what/. Accessed on July 25, 2019.

Mortensen, T. F. (2017, October 17). *The LEGO Group history.* About the LEGO Group. https://www.lego.com/en-us/aboutus/lego-group/the_lego_history/. Accessed on July 25, 2019.

Nipper, M. (2012, January 20). *LEGO Group commentary on attracting more girls to construction play.* About the LEGO Group. https://www.lego.com/en-us/aboutus/news-room/2012/january/lego-group-commentary-on-attracting-more-girls-to-construction-play. Accessed on July 25, 2019.

Reich, S. M., Black, R. W., & Foliaki, T. (2018). Constructing difference: Lego® set narratives promote stereotypic gender roles and play. *Sex Roles, 79*(5–6), 285–298. https://doi.org/10.1007/s11199-017-0868-2.

Shewmaker, J. W. (2015). *Sexualized media messages and our children: Teaching kids to be smart critics and consumers.* Santa Barbara: Praeger.

Shewmaker, J., & Hains, R. C. (2016, August 7). *Gendered marketing and promotion of stereotypes in girls aged 8–11 years.* Poster presented at the Annual Meeting of the American Psychological Association, Denver, CO.

SPARK. (2012, January 20). *Our letter to Lego.* SPARK Movement. http://www.sparkmovement.org/2012/01/20/our-letter-to-lego/. Accessed on July 25, 2019.

Spencer, S., Steele, Claude M., & Quinn, D. (1999). Stereotype threat and women's math performance. *Journal of Experimental Social Psychology, 35*(1), 4–28. https://doi.org/10.1006/jesp.1998.1373.

Steele, Claude M., & Aronson, J. (1995). Stereotype threat and the intellectual test performance of African Americans. *Journal of Personality and Social Psychology, 69*(5), 797–811. https://doi.org/10.1037/0022-3514.69.5.797.

Wieners, B. (2011, December 15). LEGO is for girls: Inside the world's most admired toy's effort to finally click with girls. *Bloomberg Businessweek.* https://www.bloomberg.com/news/articles/2011-12-14/lego-is-for-girls. Accessed on July 25, 2019.

Wooden Toys. (n.d.). http://www.miniland.nl/Historie/houten%20lego%20eng.htm. Accessed on July 25, 2019.

12

Mia Had a Little Lamb: Gender and Species Stereotypes in LEGO Sets

Debra Merskin

From children's earliest moments, animals are part of their lives. Present in forms such as stuffed toys, games and picture book characters, they are important symbolic carriers of meaning.[1] In their various capacities, animals "may function as a meaning system through which children make sense of both themselves and their surrounding environments" (Melson 2001, p. 15). Despite these facts, many studies of children's popular culture give no attention to the role of animals in their fantasy and play activities. It is one of the least studied aspects of child development (Melson 2001; Merskin 2018; Tipper 2011). This oversight is significant, however, as ignoring symbolic animals obfuscates the human impact on real animal lives.

LEGO building sets are one of the many children's products that include representations of animals. As other chapters in this volume indicate, LEGO toys convey messages about aspects of identity such as gender and religion, yet animals' assigned roles within the LEGO

D. Merskin (✉)
University of Oregon, Eugene, OR, USA
e-mail: dmerskin@uoregon.edu

R. C. Hains and S. R. Mazzarella (eds.), *Cultural Studies of LEGO*,
https://doi.org/10.1007/978-3-030-32664-7_12

universe have received little attention. One notable exception is Van Pelt's (2017) analysis of the farming motif in LEGO sets, wherein he connected this theme to an ideological concept of agricultural idealism that views animals as tools and as expendable parts in sanitized environments. As Van Pelt noted, LEGO farms are small farms, which feature no fertilizers or pharmaceuticals, and whose animals appear not intended for eating, but for use in the appropriation of eggs, milk, wool and other parts of their bodies. This is unrealistic in the age of the preponderance of concentrated animal feeding operations (CAFOs) and factory farming. Although Van Pelt noted that "LEGO Farm sets are toys, not a direct representation of reality," he argued that the message children receive from such fantasy sets is worth considering: "Will children grow up eating chicken and hamburger, not realizing that chicken and hamburger were once living birds and living cows? This kind of sheltered upbringing is not healthy. It leads to a parent having awkward conversations at the dinner table, such as 'Mommy, why does daddy say he likes his steak bloody? Where does the blood come from?'" (2017, pp. 146–147).

This type of question comes from the omission of what actually happens to animals on farms. Drawing on Hall's (1997) theory of re-presentation, one could predict that constructed scenarios such as farm sets and toys display the world as it is, or, in some cases, as idealized. Re-presentations construct meaning, in this view, a preferred reading, that is consistent with the status quo. These sets are, as Van Pelt (2017) found, "misleading" in terms of "ambiguity … about where our food comes from," the absence of sense of the economic, environmental or labor-related issues of farming, as well as the unrealistic sense of small farming as common and sustainable. More so, such LEGO sets offer a sense that farmed animals are happy creatures gladly participating in the farmed life. They "don't make the connection from farm to fork," which "is actually a teachable moment for the proactive parent, not a moment to avoid the messy details of the food system" (p. 148). Ultimately, this is an opportunity missed: Like the parent–child co-reading of books, playing with toys offers parents and other adults an opportunity to engage with children around issues that go beyond the object.

Building upon Van Pelt's (2017) work, as well as gender and animal studies research in children's play and media, this chapter explores the significance of the roles assigned to animals in illustrative LEGO playsets. I add to this the intersectional dimension of species as a conceptual frame (Hovorka 2012) that is a central aspect of the LEGO experience, as learning by playing is an important pedagogical tool. Crenshaw's (1989) theory of intersectionality guides this study as a way of revealing multidimensionality of identity that includes species, as I posit animals are the most silenced of marginalized beings. Rather than just considering animals as not-human, I argue that the complexity of their lives, whether they are male or female, young or old, and of what species, matters, to them and to us. This is tricky business, given histories of oppression experienced by people of color in which they were regarded as animals, treated as animals, considered, like animals, as property, or in discourse devalued as animals. Bringing actual animals into the fold of compassion does not mean disregarding that treatment or symbolism. I am not suggesting that we are all the same. What matters is centering the concept of the living being in considering moral inclusiveness and treatment. As Alice Walker (1988, p. 13) wrote: "The *animals* of the world exist for their own reasons. They were not made for humans any more than black people were made for whites or women for men." Thus, both gender and species are intersectionally related in the toyified re-presentations of animals (such as dairy cows). The intersection of multiple identities leads to intersecting oppressions.

Gender, as used in this chapter, is defined as "cultural or social binaries that narrowly categorize individuals according to socially agreed upon characteristics that are either feminine or masculine" (Merskin 2018, p. 123)—for example, ascribing certain colors to masculine (blue) or feminine (pink), as well activities viewed as "natural" for men (work; success) and women (caretaking; beauty). "Gender development is a critical part of the earliest and most important learning experiences of the young child" (Peterson and Lach 1990, p. 188). But gender does not exist apart from other identity markers such as race, class and sexuality, and it is often taught using animals as symbolic stand-ins for humans. Yet studies of children and play often render animals invisible. Thus, intersectionality is a useful theoretical lens to examine LEGO playsets. It helps us unpack how the invisibility of species, alongside stereotypical re-presentations of gender, can also operate as an educational tool. According to intersectionality theory, discrimination doesn't occur "along a single categorical axis" (Crenshaw 1989, p. 140), but rather among multiples. Intersectionality, as part of feminism, should also include which species someone belongs to, for animals teach not only about human behavior but also about the animals themselves. Furthermore, feminism must include an analysis of species privileging if it truly means what it aspires to in terms of ending oppression and discrimination on the basis of difference. As Hovorka (2012) stated in a study of gender roles and species positionality in Botswana, "identities are emergent properties not reducible to naturally given biological essences or socially constructed role expectations. Emphasis lies on how identities or relations occur in intersections rather than on stable or given understandings of social difference" (p. 876).

Hall's (1997) theory of representation as re-presentation accompanies this perspective. Re-presentation helps us understand how difference, however defined, is used to construct identity "not [as] an essence, but a positioning" (1990, p. 226). Thus, media and popular culture construct and position the Other in ways that create oppositional types that appear normal and natural until we interrogate them. Hall argued that gender and race's re-presentation aligns with dominant culture. I extend this argument to include species' identities and roles. As animals are increasingly known to us more in their symbolic rather than real forms, concealing their lived experiences in the world, the present study matters.

Understanding Toys, Play and Gender

In this section, I briefly examine play and toys' nature, particularly as related to gendering. I then discuss the importance of animals in children's emotional development before moving into a textual analysis of LEGO sets that feature animals.

Playtime Matters

All beings appear to engage in play (Bekoff and Byers 1998; Burghardt 2005). Playing involves following rules. It teaches order, affords freedom and helps keep children fit and active. In fact, "it's so familiar to us, so deeply ingrained in the matrix of our childhood, that we take it for granted" (Ackerman 1999, p. 4). Yet, how one plays, with what and whom, and what one learns through play varies across time and culture. According to Postman (1982/1994, p. 3), there was a time "when there were no children." He means that childhood is a social construct, for in earlier historical eras, adults and those we now consider children had less separation in their dress, work and living spaces. Historically, children had utility in terms of contributing to household income and upkeep, and they "shared the same games with adults, the same toys, the same fairy stories. They lived theirs together, never apart" (p. 15). During industrialization in the United States, and the rise of child labor laws, children began spending more time at home and had more hours to fill (Katz 2013). Thus, childhood per se is a relatively modern construct that accompanied mass production, consumerism, increases in leisure time and the rise of screen cultures (Postman 1982/1994).

Imaginative and physical play are essential components of children's healthy cognitive and physical development (Ginsburg 2007). In fact, the United Nations High Commission for Human Rights, Part 1, Article 31 declared that every child has the right "to rest and leisure, to engage in play and recreational activities" ("Convention on the Rights" 1989, p. 9). Engaging with each other or with objects such as toys affords children opportunities to perspective-take, or engage in a "theory of mind," such that "the individual imputes mental states to himself [sic] and others" (Premack and Woodruff 1978, p. 515). As an empathy-building exercise, imaginative play encourages self-regulation (Berk et al. 2006; Hirsh-Pasek et al. 2009) and enhanced creative flexibility and performance (Russ and Fiorelli 2010).

Vygotsky's (1933/1966) theories of child development view play as a positive force that is biologically and culturally constituted. Make-believe play has three components through which "children create an imaginary situation, take on and act out roles, and follow a set of rules determined by those specific roles" (Bodrova and Leong 2015, p. 374). Vygotsky posited that imaginative pretend play and social interaction contribute to children's abstract-thinking abilities—for example, pretending a broomstick is a horse.

Pretend play, particularly through the ages of 2 ½–7 years, offers cognitive benefits related to language acquisition and use (Kaufman et al. 2012). In addition, play is important in maintaining strong parent–child bonds, in stress reduction (Potasz et al. 2013), and in children's healthy social, psychological and physical well-being (Ginsburg 2007; Singer 1994). Free playing time with toys allows individual creativity and intelligence to flourish apart from modern scheduling's confines and curricular limitations. Play thus is "an exemplification of the child's fundamental need to make sense of the large, the looming, and the loud in her world by forming manageable units and exploring these strange objects over and over again" (Singer 1994, p. 9). Playing also affords an opportunity to learn about gender roles.

Gender Socialization and Toys

How do children learn about gender through play? Since "children are not passive observers" and look to the world around them for examples, (Shaw 1998, p. 24), it is unsurprising that adult–child interaction can influence children's adoption of stereotypical concepts. When parents relay information such as gender roles in picture books (DeLoache et al. 1987) and toys (Kollmayer et al. 2018; Weisgram and Bruun 2018), they can easily reinforce stereotypes about people, places, things and animals. Preexisting stereotypes in the mind of the reader who is helping the child interpret the pictures perpetuate these assumptions. For example, in one study, when mothers described nature book characters and pictures to toddlers, they used pronouns such as "his," "he" and "him," when in fact nothing in the book indicated whether the character was male, female, masculine or feminine (DeLoache et al. 1987). Similarly, adult readers are also likely to gender-stereotype animals, who are often central characters in stories, games and toys.

Some independent children's brands are pushing back in light of this stereotyping. For example, the Jill and Jack Kids clothing catalog has a popular line of t-shirts that state "Half of all T-Rexes were girls" (https://www.cafepress.com/jillandjackkids/12715021), and Boy, Wonder is introducing clothing for boys featuring animals such as kittens and butterflies (Melsky 2019).

Important sources of inspiration and interpretation for children's imaginative play include parental involvement such as talking with them about what they are interested in, as well as reading to them or telling them stories (Shmukler 1981; Singer and Singer 2005), and, of course, toys. As I discuss in the next section, toys are mechanisms that re-present, drawing on Hall (1997), as they carry forward the essence of someone or something, give meaning to it (i.e., stand in for the real).

Toying Around

Play objects/toys are as old as humankind. Some of the oldest, more than 4500 years old (Bronze Age), come from southern Siberia, carved in soapstone resembling both human-type dolls and an animal head (Medrano 2017). Modern construction toys, such as classic Lincoln Logs or LEGO building pieces, are in essence gender-neutral. Product descriptions and advertising, however, can indicate a toy's gender orientation and the skills necessary to engage with it. In a study of four- to seven-year-olds, Spinner et al. (2018) showed their participants images of children playing with counter-stereotypic or stereotypic toys. When the researcher read aloud product packaging words, they found that children who saw counter-stereotypic pictures were more open in their answers. When asked, children often said that other boys and girls could like either toy, but their individual preferences reflected gendered readings.

Spinner et al. (2018) also showed their preschool participants print advertisements in child-targeted magazines that revealed "gender-typed toy play by peers" (p. 314). The researchers examined gender flexibility, such as "open-minded attitudes around gender roles" in playmate and toy preferences (p. 315). While children's responses to the ads evidenced change, such as being more willing than in the past to say it was fine for either boys or girls to like gendered toys, when it came to their own preferences they remained stereotypic, as did the advertisements. Gender-normative language, behaviors and stereotypes continue to dominate media re-presentations of toys (Blakemore and Centers 2005; Leaper et al. 2002; Murnen et al. 2016; Thompson and Zerbinos 1995). Television programs and commercials tend to emphasize traditional feminine roles, colors and passive, private space activities for girls, whereas those targeting boys feature traditional masculine roles, colors, active, public space activities (Browne 1998; Merskin 2002).

This matters in terms of limiting children's conceptions of self and identity, as well as in the types of skills particular toys encourage. For example, "traditionally masculine toys like blocks and puzzles … encourage visual and spatial skills, while traditionally feminine toys encourage communication and social skills" (Klass 2018). Toys' gendering and play made national attention when, in January 2014, seven-year-old Charlotte Benjamin wrote a now-famous letter to LEGO saying the brand offered more boy LEGO figures and very few girl figures, and that LEGO presented girls as essentially passive; whereas boys had adventures, worked in interesting jobs and "saved people … even swam with sharks" (qtd. in Wade 2014). Based on a literature review, Gutwald (2017) states of one LEGO theme in particular: "There is some solid evidence that LEGO Friends is supporting and expressing implicit biases and stereotypes associated with gender and that both boys and girls will take up these attitudes as they play" (p. 110).

LEGO sets potentially frame children's play experience within their product titles, such as "Cargo Train," "Farm Adventures," "Steam Train, "Family Pets" and "Mia's Tree House." Whereas the original LEGO toys required complete imaginative play, today's sets have particular characters and construction outcomes in mind. The company has strategically created products for preschoolers all the way up to teen years that cultivate brand loyalty. According to LEGO systems President Søren Torp Laursen, "We are a single brand company with a unique play system and play material, yet numerous play patterns beyond building. Every time we sell a LEGO set, we engage children in a way that positively reinforces our entire brand and business" ("LEGO systems"

2016). This reinforcement, of course, has implications for how children learn about themselves and others, including animals, through LEGO play. In the Zimmerman (2017) study cited earlier, a girl-targeted ad for LEGO Friends Café had a female narrator and emphasized cooperation, whereas the boy-and-girl-targeted ad was Crayola Color Explosion Glow Dome. In their study of the online promotion narratives of LEGO building sets, Reich et al. (2017) found consistently gendered messages about play. Furthermore, studies indicate that the toys communicate that caring for and about animals is a femininely gendered activity (Gutwald 2017; Wainman and Grant 2017).

Gender is taught not only through the marketing of human characters in toys, but also through animals included in the play experience. The intersectional aspects of gender's construction alongside the construction of "appropriate" species and gendered species roles are "illustrate[d] [by] human and nonhuman animal othering as necessarily wrapped up with gender–species relations of power" (Hovorka 2012, p. 875). In the Botswana study mentioned earlier, Hovorka (2012) noted that particular species and genders are associated, such as women with chickens and men with cattle, reflecting acceptable spheres of activity and visibility in patriarchal culture. She noted: "In addition to ideological and institutional marginalization, women are othered and men privileged through their associations with particular nonhuman animal species, as mediated largely through agricultural roles, expectations, and practices" (p. 878).

Gendering Animals

As anthropologist Claude Lévi-Strauss (1966) pointed out, "animals are good to think" (p. 89). Many times, this thinking *about* (as opposed to with) has to do with a social norms and values. Thus, "the most important lesson taught by animal books…," for example, "was about the proper structure of human society" (Ritvo 1985, p. 80) (i.e., humans at the top), that animals were created for human use (and within that, that some species sought "or at least accept[ed] without protest, human companionship and exploitation" (p. 81). While famous child researchers such as Piaget and Bowlby studied children from multiple viewpoints and created important typologies of development, studies either ignored or dismissed the intimate relationships children have with animals, real and imagined. The fact is animals matter to children. Tipper (2011) argues:

> Situated, emplaced, embodied, relational engagements with animals are a part of what it means to live as a child and attending to them may well enhance our understanding of children's everyday experience. If we wish to fully understand how children engage in relationships, or experience issues such as place, generation, embodiment and discipline or rules, then we need to attend to animals. (p. 160)

Animal toys figure early and often throughout childhood. From plush crib companions to on-screen friends, "children's worlds are full of animal characters on television, in children's books, movies, and advertising that is aimed at children" (Karniol et al. 2000, p. 378). While, by a certain age, children begin to recognize that the television/movie/book world is one of fantasy and make-believe, "they tend to anthropomorphize animal characters and develop affective reactions to them" (Bodrova and Leong 2015, p. 378). Curiously, Spinner et al. (2018) used My Little Pony in their experiment as the toy associated with femininity (for boys, they used a car), but the authors do not discuss the pony is as a species. This speaks to the essential invisibility of animals as animals in research on children, play and gender.

In their interactions with children, adults (such as parents) who interpret books, toys, movies and other forms of mass communication impart not only gendered, but also speciesist stereotypes. For example, Arthur and White (1996) presented 60 preschool and elementary children (evenly divided groups of girls and boys) with cards that contained drawings of a bear. The researchers found children assigned gender-neutral bear characters an age and gender based on size (larger bears presumed to be adults). The assumed-to-be-male child bears were most often in the company of adults in the books. In the pictures, some bears were involved in stereotypically gendered activities, such as showing affection between large and small bears, watching television, while some were neutral. The researchers asked children to create stories about the bears and to name them. The biggest differences in the children's gender assignment were between the youngest (four- to five-year age range) and the older groups. Younger children typically assigned their own gender to the bear, consistent with theories of development that say younger children see the world primarily in terms of themselves. The two older age groups reflected stereotypes, however. The older children were more likely to label as "male" bears shown alone, and as "female" those engaged in showing affection, with boys stereotyping animals more often girls. The results suggest that children learn gender-based stereotypes early in life, indicating the importance of creating children's books and activities that counter cultural training.

For centuries, animal-rich stories and rhymes such as "Three Little Pigs," "Little Bo Peep," "Three Blind Mice" and Aesop's fables have given children access to animals' symbolic lives and "delineated the characters and passions of men [sic] under the semblance of Lions, Tigers, Wolves, and Foxes" (Bewick 1885, p. iv). "Three Little Kittens" and "The Three Bears" teach children not only about themselves, as seen in the adventures and experiences of anthropomorphized animals, but also (accurately or inaccurately) about different species' qualities and characteristics. Through games, songs and activities, children learn different animals' names, often acquiring the alphabet with associations such as "A" is for "Aardvark" or "W" is for "Whale."

Research suggests that gender is one of the first categorizations in children's perceptions of animals (Merskin 2018; Tipper 2011). A variety of methods of cueing gender exist in animal figures such as colors, clothing, names, hair length and voices. Patt and McBride (1992), for example, found that children used masculine pronouns significantly more than feminine or neutral pronouns to refer to animals or people when gender is unknown. "The animals within [children's] stories are also gendered, both in appearance and mannerism and also by the interpretations of those who read the books out loud to children, explaining interactions, scenes, and answering questions the child might have" (Merskin 2018, pp. 114–115).

Children can also learn about other intersectional aspects of identity, such as race, class, age and species, from toys or media that depict animals. As Hains (2014) has noted, Disney has tended to substitute animals for people of color in its children's animated films, particularly those set in nations outside of Europe: Movies such as *The Jungle Book* (1967, set in India) and *The Lion King* and *Tarzan* (1994 and 1997, respectively; both set in Africa) used animals but no people of color, while in *The Princess and the Frog*, the title characters—Disney's first African-American princess and the racially ambiguous prince with whom she partnered—spent much of their on-screen time in animal form. As King et al. (2011) discuss, such films' racialization of animals is deeply problematic. *The Lion King* promotes racist themes about Latinos and Black people, "endowing whites with superiority" (King et al. 2011, p. 61), while *Tarzan* "clearly articulat[es] a vision of white supremacy, little changed from the heights of Jim Crow and the white man's burden" (p. 61). These films are, of course, represented in the marketplace with licensed children's toys.

Seeing animals as extensions of ourselves is a powerful and important step toward becoming empathetic. Yet, in play literature, Melson (2001, p. 11) points out, "Nowhere can animals be found in the voluminous literature on children's play and peer relationships." They often, particularly for very young children, stand in for human characters. Given children's natural, nearly instinctive interactions with real and imaginary animals, those that appear as toys also have the potential to influence their understandings of themselves and the species re-presented. Drawing from this literature, the present study investigates how the relationship between animals and human figures is constructed/re-presented, particularly as that relationship intersects with gender. In addition, this study deconstructs how the "importance of animals in children's lives" (Morrow 1998, p. 218) is conveyed through LEGO playsets.

Method

I analyzed forty-one playsets that appeared on September 26, 2018 under the Product Type Tab at the LEGO web site with "animals" (https://shop.lego.com). In my analysis, I considered re-presentations of gender roles for both human and animal characters. As the semiotics of toys such as LEGO focuses on the codes and contexts upon which meaning-making depends, I used textual analysis to ascertain what was present in and absent from each set, and why.

At the time of this study, LEGO presented a variety of sets under the "animals" designation, including some that are no longer available. In this chapter, I use illustrative examples to identify animals in the sets by their species and also by what their species means in terms of children's gender identity development, with consideration for the potential implications for lived experiences of real animals. Drawing upon LaDow's (1976) content analytic method, I read each set for the following:

- Main character of set (gender);
- Other human characters;
- Race of human characters;
- Human character roles;
- Animal species;
- Species role(s).

In my analysis, a few characters seemed intentionally ambiguous in terms of skin tone and sex, and rather than attempting to categorize such characters, I made a note of their ambiguity.

In reading each set for the human characters' races, I considered the characters' skin tones as they appeared in the photographs presented on the LEGO Shop Web site. If a character had what appeared to be a pale peachy or neutral skin tone, I coded this as re-presenting Whiteness. If characters had skin tones in deeper shades of brown, I coded these characters as likely being meant to belong to other ethnic/racial groups. I also attended to contextual cues, such as stereotypical roles and clothing (such as for LEGO's "Eskimo" characters) or situational elements (re-presenting characters situated in India, for example, with brown skin tones). While there are limitations to this approach, and it is possible that I categorized some specific characters in different ways than the LEGO brand might have intended to categorize them—or in ways that others examining the sets might read differently—in the course of my analysis, overarching patterns appeared that inform this chapter in meaningful ways.

Findings and Discussion

To begin, let's consider gender and race representation of human characters within these sets. In my analysis, I found that the gender of human characters was fairly equal in the sets sampled for this study. Of 81 human characters, 46% (38) were male (adult and child); 38% (31) were female (adult and child); and 15% (12) were either unidentifiable as male/female or were fantasy characters, such as goblins and skeletons. To ascertain each character's gender/sex identity, I referred to clear markers such as clothing, clothing colors and character names. Among the girl-targeted sets, the LEGO Friends theme has five named girl characters: Olivia (who has light brown skin/dark red hair), Andrea (who appears to be Black), Emma (who appears to be White and brunette), Mia (who is White, with bright red hair), and Stephanie (who appears White and blonde). These characters repeat across assorted Friends sets, as do characters from the Disney Princess and Elves sets by LEGO, who also feature a range of skin tones signifying racial diversity.

In contrast, the LEGO sets in my sample that featured primarily boy/male characters (which are too numerous to list) had no repeating characters and appeared predominantly White or—unlike the Friends, Disney Princess and Elves sets—featured LEGO's neutral yellow skin tone, which previous studies have suggested actually functions to signified an unmarked Whiteness (Johnson 2014).

Examples of sets from my sample that seemed to target boys and featured a majority of male characters—most of which appear to be White—include the "Cargo Train"; "Jungle Exploration Site"; "Around the World," which includes animals from a range of global cultures, as well as three characters that appear White, an Inuit character (possibly male, but ambiguous because its hair is not visible), and a Black woman who appears to be a tour guide; "Arctic Supply Plane" features four explorers in LEGO's neutral yellow skin tone, one clearly male (due to his beard), one clearly female (due to her lipstick), and others whose genders were ambiguous in the site's photos (because their hair and facial features were obscured by their winter gear). "Steam Train" featured a male train driver with dark hair and dark eyes and a female child with dark hair and green eyes; both appeared on the Web site's photographs to have darker skin than most of the characters in the other boy-oriented sets I sampled.

Human Gender Roles

In the LEGO sets I sampled, the characters had clearly differentiated gender roles, particularly in terms of their occupations. Twenty-six male characters had clear occupational markers such as uniforms, named characters and contextual cues. These male characters were assigned active roles: ride operators, cargo and regular train drivers, police officers, jungle explorers, forklift operators and shopkeepers. They also had relatively few animals in comparison with the girl characters.

In contrast, while the vast majority of female LEGO characters are presented as caregivers/users/superiors of animals, only two girl characters—Doc McStuffins from the TV show of the same name and Mia from the Friends theme—had clear occupations: as a doctor for stuffed animals and a farmer, respectively. In "Mia's Farm Suitcase," Mia wears gender-neutral overalls in her role as a farmer, but a bow in her hair marks her as traditionally feminine and cute. Note that in this set, the animal figures are babies (a brown foal and a white lamb), as well, enhancing the set's cute and gendered factor. As intersectional studies of gender and species such as Hovorka (2012) demonstrate, women are more likely than men to be shown with easy-to-care-for, reproductively prolific animals.

Consider the following LEGO sets, for example, all from themes that target girls:

- In LEGO Friends: "The Big Race Day" features Stephanie, Mia and Vicky along with Vega the cat, Dash the dog and Twister the rabbit; in "HeartLake," Mia and Stephanie run a combination store and pet clinic/grooming salon, joined by Mimi the bird, Harry the hamster, Lady the poodle, Bubble the turtle and Mini the bunny; "Mia's Tree House" offers human characters Mia and Daniel with Mimi the bunny, and Cinnamon the bird; and "Friendship House" has three human figures (Olivia, Emma and Andrea) and three named pets (Dash the dog, Rumble the hamster and Cinnamon, which in this set is the bunny's name).

- LEGO Elves offers "Azari and the Goblin Forest Escape," featuring fire elf Azari with pegasus/horse Bolt; and "Rosalyn's Healing Hideout," featuring pale-skinned, light-haired water elf Naida Riverheart with her baby water dragon, Lula; darker-skinned, blue-black-haired healer elf Rosalyn Nightshade with Sapphire, her adult female dragon; the goblin Rimlin; and Lil' Blu, a baby bear.

- In LEGO's Disney themes, "Tangled" features the blonde Rapunzel and a white pony, Maximus (also blonde), and "Cinderella's Enchanted Evening" likewise features a blond princess with a white pony. Meanwhile, "Sofia the First Magical Carriage" features the titular princess (a light-skinned brunette) with a flying purple horse/pegasus named Minimus the Great and a squirrel named Whatnaught. "Doc McStuffins' Pet Vet Care" offers Doc McStuffins, the African-American girl character from the animated TV show by the same name, with three plastic versions of stuffed animals that come alive on the show: Hallie, the hippo; Findo, a dog; and an unnamed cat.

- The LEGO sets sampled incorporate a wide array of animals: "farm" animals (e.g., cows, chickens, pigs, etc.); "exotic" animals (e.g., tigers, leopards, hippopotami, hedgehogs, etc.); and aquatic animals (e.g., dolphin, whales, penguins, several species of fish, etc.) The most common animal characters were dogs, horses, cats, birds and rabbits/bunnies. Some sets ("Jungle," "Rosalyn's Healing Hideout," "The Farm Cottage") included both baby and mother animals. Only a few sets, all associated with named girl characters, gave animals names.

Of all the sets sampled, only "Mia's Tree House" (mentioned above with other LEGO Friends sets) includes both a boy character and named animals. The preponderance of girl sets is consistent with stereotypical gendered and speciesist roles, featuring traditional pastel colors (such as buildings with pastel roofs), subservient animals and girls in caretaking/domestic/nurturing roles.

The differences between LEGO's cute, caregiving-oriented sets for girls and the active, occupation-oriented sets oriented sets for boys are consistent with other research, which argues that in popular culture, "boys act and girls appear" (Murnen et al. 2016).

Gendered Animals

Are the animals themselves in these LEGO sets gendered? My analysis indicates that through association, yes, they are. Some sets with a geographic focus show stereotypic charismatic megafauna ("Jungle Exploration Site," "Around the World" or "Arctic Supply Plane"), such as zebra, lions, bears, leopards and crocodiles. These are in essence boy-targeted, with the assumption girls might also play with them—but girls are not their primary target audience.

In contrast, LEGO's girl-targeted sets, particularly those from the Friends theme, tend to feature the softer species, baby animals or mother/baby pairings. (Examples include "Friendship House," "HeartLake City Pet Center," and "Mia's Farm".) These girl-targeted sets may also feature anthropomorphic touches, such as bows and barrettes in the hair of animals to connote femininity. For example, the LEGO Friends Buildable Hedgehog Storage set offers the option of a pink or blue bow for the hedgehog, allowing the child to customize it, depending on interests and gender.

Some LEGO sets may be read as gender-neutral, however, such as one set in particular, "Cargo Train," which can also be read as supportive of animal agriculture—similar to what Van Pelt (2017) found in the study of LEGO Farm. The products' accompanying text says: "Move heavy goods – and animals!"—normalizing the idea of animals as objects that, along with things, are naturally to be transported. The set also describes that it is the child's "job to make sure the cargo is in the right place at the right time to keep the city running smoothly"; thus, a cattle wagon and cargo wagon are included. The only animal figure in this set is a brown cow.

Animals' Roles

With the exception of some of LEGO's fantasy-type or girl story narratives, in my analysis, I found that the animals in the sampled LEGO sets are clearly objectified. Human characters have dominant caretaking roles, while the animals are on farms, at the vet's office, or in stables, meant to be cared for by the set characters and, through play interaction, by children.

Giving animals roles as pets and as farmed creatures suggest inequity, serving as mechanisms for learning/teaching about gender and species dynamics and occupations. In these sets, LEGO uses animals as objects of human care by girls and/or to signify place (such as farm, adventure, nationhood/culture). It is a dynamic of dominance, even if one of affection. As Tuan (1984) argues, our affection for animals, particularly those we consider "pets," is inseparable from our power over them. In these intimate relationships, besides using animals for food and furs, we also use them as companions.

As mentioned earlier, few animals in the sets were named, and those that were only appeared in girl-targeted sets, as described earlier. On the one hand, this is an example of presenting girls as, and encouraging them to be, closer to animals than are boys. On the other hand, names such as Dash, Rumble and Vega are relatively gender-neutral, which allows children to decide whether a cat is male or female, for example. At the same, the lack of names, as well as few breed distinctions, also contributes to an overall invisibility of animals as individuals which does not generate empathy, give identity, or "se[t] it apart from the rest of its nameless species" (Raymond 2016).

While ideally a child playing with these sets will become empathetic and engaged and interested in the lives of animals, when some of the animal characters are presented in fantastic colors—such as blue raccoons, red dogs and pink cats—children may be less likely to see them as connected to real animals.

Overall, then, LEGO constructs the dynamic between animal and human figures in much the same way as in society constructs does in real life. The land of LEGO sets maintains species hierarchy, with humans on top, animals below—and with male characters and their animals of occupational/economic importance making them superior to girls and their animals, who are largely confined to domestic/caregiving roles.

Conclusion

According to Konzack (2014, p. 10), "rather than presenting a toy for children to play with [LEGO] presents a play world in which the audience must lend themselves to the illusion, and for a given time believe, that it is more real than reality itself." The friends, family members and workers in the sets are thus idealized, living apart from reality in perfect HeartLake houses, riding stables, veterinary clinics, having global adventures and working in transport services. Goldstein (1994, p. 2) points out that "play does not occur in a vacuum." While play may mirror social life, "it is always a distorting mirror. … So, children enact the gender roles they see around them … if these did not matter to adults, they would not matter to children." The same can be said of imitating what they hear and see in regard to animals, i.e., which are to be loved and pampered and which are to be used and, potentially, abused, depending on species. At the same time that gender is inscribed on the playsets by presenting traditional gender roles, it is also reinforced on the basis of which, if any, animals are present—and, if they are, by the multiple, intersecting identities of the animals represented in the sets.

Consistent with van Pelt (2017), in this study of multiple LEGO sets, human and animal characters most often were paired in agricultural or husbandry settings, especially with girls. The girl characters were often accompanied by animal pets (even in fantasy settings, with dragons serving as pets to the elf characters) or small farm animals, such as pigs. The intersectional aspects of identity communicated by the LEGO sets include the dynamics of traditionally gendered activities (male active, rational/female passive, emotional), lack of named animals except when associated with girls, and a focus on mother and baby animals when paired.

These markers serve to reinforce stereotypes about humans and other animals in terms of species and normalization of dominion, as

Hovorka (2012) noted about women's relationship/portrayal aligned with smaller, less "important" animals. As such "positionality is discursively bounded and reinforces ideas about when, where, and how they can be and are recognized and valued" (p. 881). Furthermore, associating boy characters with "important" work and/or adventures also positions them closer to agriculture as an economic value.

Finally, the intersection of gender and species is evident in the association of reproductively valued animals such as female chickens, rabbits and pairing of mother/child animals as a natural/normal role. The consistent portrayal in the sets of hegemonic dynamics thereby misses an opportunity, at crucial developmental stages for children, to re-present more gender-neutral understandings of occupations and roles as well as to develop empathy for animals.

This chapter offers a peek into the land of LEGO sets examining intersections of gender and species re-presentations. Given the global brand reach and influence of this toy manufacturer, a huge opportunity exists not only to entertain children, but also to nurture their sense of self and other identity development, teach them about the real-world applications and implications of the re-presentations in toys, as well as to cultivate realistic views of animals. Animals are not merely as objects to be used: They are individuals to be appreciated and embraced in a compassionate worldview.

Note

1. While humans are animals, this chapter uses the term "animal" to describe other than humans for ease of writing and understanding.

References

Ackerman, D. (1999). *Deep play*. New York: Vintage.
Arthur, A. G., & White, H. (1996). Children's assignment of gender to animal characters in pictures. *Journal of Genetic Psychology Research, Theory, & Human Development, 157,* 297–301. https://doi.org/10.1080/00221325.1996.9914867.

Bekoff, M., & Byers, J. A. (Eds.). (1998). *Animal play, evolutionary, comparative, and ecological perspectives*. Cambridge, UK: Cambridge University Press.

Berk, L. E., Mann, T. D., & Ogan, A. T. (2006). Make-believe play: Wellspring for development of self-regulation. In D. G. Singer, R. M. Golinkoff, & H. Hirsh-Pasek (Eds.), *Play = learning: How play motivates and enhances children's cognitive and social-emotional growth* (pp. 74–100). New York: Oxford University Press.

Bewick, T. (1885). *The fables of Aesop: And others, with designs on wood*. London: B. Quaritch.

Blakemore, J. E. O., & Centers, R. E. (2005). Characteristics of boys' and girls' toys. *Sex Roles, 53*(9/10), 619–633. https://doi.org/10.1007/s11199-005-7729-0.

Bodrova, E., & Leong, D. J. (2015). Vygotskian and post-Vygotskian views on children's play. *American Journal of Play, 7*(3), 371–388. https://www.journalofplay.org/.

Browne, B. A. (1998). Gender stereotypes in advertising on children's television in the 1990s: A cross-national analysis. *Journal of Advertising, 27*(1), 83–96. https://doi.org/10.1080/00913367.1998.10673544.

Burghardt, G. M. (2005). *The genesis of animal play: Testing the limits*. Cambridge, MA: MIT Press.

Convention on the Rights of the Child. (1989, November). *United Nations Human Rights Office of the High Commissioner*. https://www.ohchr.org/en/professionalinterest/pages/crc.aspx. Accessed on March 29, 2019.

Crenshaw, K. (1989). Demarginalizing the intersection of race and sex: A black feminist critique of antidiscrimination doctrine, feminist theory, and antiracist politics. *University of Chicago Legal Forum, 1989*, 139–167. Retrieved from https://chicagounbound.uchicago.edu/uclf/vol1989/iss1/8/.

DeLoache, J. S., Cassidy, D. J., & Carpenter, C. (1987). The three bears are all boys: Mothers' gender labeling of neutral picture book characters. *Sex Roles, 17*(3/4), 163–178. https://doi.org/10.1007/BF00287623.

Ginsburg, K. R. (2007). The importance of play in promoting healthy child development and maintaining strong parent-child bonds. *Pediatrics, 119*(1), 182–191. https://doi.org/10.1542/peds.2006-2697.

Goldstein, J. H. (1994). Introduction. In J. H. Goldstein (Ed.), *Toys, play, and child development* (pp. 1–5). New York: Cambridge University Press.

Gutwald, R. (2017). Girl, LEGO Friends is not your Friend! Does LEGO construct gender stereotypes? In R. T. Cook & S. Bacharach (Eds.), *LEGO and philosophy: Constructing reality brick by brick* (pp. 103–112). New York: Wiley.

Hains, R. C. (2014). *The princess problem: Guiding our girls through the princess-obsessed years.* Naperville, IL: Sourcebooks.

Hall, S. (1990). Cultural identity and diaspora. In J. Utherford (Ed.), *Identity: Community, culture, difference* (pp. 222–237). London: Lawrence & Wishart.

Hall, S. (1997). *Representation: Cultural representations and signifying practices.* Newbury Park, CA: Sage.

Hirsh-Pasek, K., Golinkoff, R. M., Berk, L. E., & Singer, D. G. (2009). *A mandate for playful learning in preschool: Presenting the evidence.* New York: Oxford University Press.

Hovorka, J. (2012). Women/chickens vs. men/cattle: Insights on gender–species intersectionality. *Geoforum, 43,* 875–884. https://doi.org/10.1016/j.geoforum.2012.02.005.

Johnson, D. (2014). Figuring identity: Media licensing and the racialization of LEGO bodies. *International Journal of Cultural Studies, 17*(4), 307–325. https://doi.org/10.1177/1367877913496211.

Karniol, R., Reichman, S., & Fund, L. (2000). Children's gender orientation and perceptions of female, male, and gender-ambiguous animal characters. *Sex Roles, 43*(5/6), 377–393. https://doi.org/10.1023/a:1026651427146.

Katz, E. (2013). The history of birth control in the United States. In R. Green (Ed.), *History of medicine* (pp. 81–102). New York: Haworth Press.

Kaufman, S. B., Singer, J. L., & Singer, D. G. (2012, March 6). The need for pretend play in child development. *Psychology Today.* https://www.psychologytoday.com/us/blog/beautiful-minds/201203/the-need-pretend-play-in-child-development. Accessed March 29, 2019.

King, C. R., Lugo-Lugo, C. R., & Bloodsworth-Lugo, M. K. (2011). Colonial claims: Indigenous people, empire, and naturalization. In *Animating difference: Race, gender, and sexuality in contemporary films for children* (pp. 53–74). New York: Rowman & Littlefield.

Klass, P. (2018, February 5). Breaking gender stereotypes in the toy box. *New York Times.* https://www.nytimes.com/2018/02/05/well/family/gender-stereotypes-children-toys.html. Accessed on March 29, 2019.

Kollmayer, M., Schultes, M.-T., Schober, B., Hodosi, T., & Spiel, C. (2018). Parents' judgements about the desirability of toys for their children: Associations with gender role attitudes, gender-typing of toys, and demographics. *Sex Roles, 79*(5/6), 329–341. https://doi.org/10.1007/s11199-017-0882-4.

Konzack, L. (2014). The cultural history of LEGO. In M. J. P. Wolf (Ed.), *Lego studies: Examining the building blocks of a transmedial phenomenon.* New York: Routledge.

LaDow, S. (1976). *A content-analysis of selected picture books examining the portrayal of sex roles and representation of males and females* (ERIC Document Reproduction Service No. ED123165). East Lansing, MI: National Center for Research on Teacher Learning.

Leaper, C., Breed, L., Hoffman, L., & Perlman, C. A. (2002). Variations in the gender-stereotyped content of children's television cartoons across genres. *Journal of Applied Social Psychology, 32,* 1653–1662. https://doi.org/10.1111/j.1559-1816.2002.tb02767.x.

LEGO systems records eleventh consecutive year of growth in U.S. toy market. (2016, February 11). PR Newswire Association. https://www.prnewswire.com/news-releases/lego-systems-records-eleventh-consecutive-year-of-growth-in-us-toy-market-300218844.html. Accessed on March 29, 2019.

Lévi-Strauss, C. (1966). *The savage mind.* London: Weidenfeld and Nicholson.

Medrano, K. (2017, December 29). Ancient and creepy doll head discovered in prehistoric child grave joins world's oldest known toy collection. *Newsweek.* https://www.newsweek.com/ancient-creepy-doll-head-discovered-prehistoric-child-grave-worlds-oldest-toy-764072. Accessed on March 29, 2019.

Melsky, R. (2019, January 3). *Announcing-boy, wonder! Prince wonder.* Accessed on June 30, 2019. https://princess-awesome.com/blogs/news/announcing-boy-wonder.

Melson, G. (2001). *Why the wild things are: Animals in the lives of children.* Cambridge, MA: Harvard University Press.

Merskin, D. (2002). Boys will be boys: A content analysis of gender and race in children's advertisements on the Turner Cartoon Network. *Journal of Current Issues & Research in Advertising, 24*(1), 51–59. https://doi.org/10.1080/10641734.2002.10505127.

Merskin, D. (2018). *Seeing species: Re-presentations of animals in media and popular culture.* New York: Peter Lang.

Morrow, V. (1998). My animals and other family: Children's perspectives on their relationships with companion animals. *Anthrozoös, 11*(4), 218–226. https://doi.org/10.2752/089279398787000526.

Murnen, S. K., Greenfield, C., Younger, A., & Boyd, H. (2016). Boys act and girls appear: A content analysis of gender stereotypes associated with characters in children's popular culture. *Sex Roles, 74,* 78–91. https://doi.org/doi.org/10.1007/s11199-015-0558-x.

Patt, M. B., & McBride, B. A. (1992). *Gender equity in picture books in preschool classrooms: An exploratory study.* Paper presented at the Annual Meeting of the American Educational Research Association, Atlanta, GA.

Peterson, S. B., & Lach, M. A. (1990). Gender stereotypes in children's books: Their prevalence and influence on cognitive and affective development. *Gender and Education, 2,* 185–196. https://doi.org/10.1080/0954025900020204.

Postman, N. (1982/1994). *The disappearance of childhood.* New York: Vintage.

Potasz, C., De Varela, M. J. V., De Carvalho, L. C., Do Prado, L. F., & Do Prado, F. G. (2013). Effect of play activities on hospitalized children's stress: A randomized clinical trial. *Scandinavian Journal of Occupational Therapy, 20*(1), 71–79. https://doi.org/10.3109/11038128.2012.729087.

Premack, D., & Woodruff, G. (1978). Does the chimpanzee have a theory of mind? *Behavioural and Brain Science, 1*(4), 515–526. https://doi.org/10.1017/S0140525X00076512.

Raymond, M. (2016). No one mourns an unnamed animal: Why naming animals might help save them. *Zoomorphic, 6.* http://zoomorphic.net/2016/09/no-one-mourns-an-unnamed-animal-why-naming-animals-might-help-save-them/. Accessed on March 29, 2019.

Reich, S. M., Black, R. W., & Foliaki, T. (2017). Constructing difference: LEGO set narratives promote stereotypic gender roles and play. *Sex Roles,* 1–14. https://doi.org/10.1007/s11199-017-0868-2.

Ritvo, H. (1985). Learning from animals: Natural history for children in the eighteenth and nineteenth centuries. *Children's Literature, 13,* 72–93. https://doi.org/10.1353/chl.0.0198.

Russ, S. W., & Fiorelli, J. A. (2010). Developmental approaches to creativity. In J. C. Kaufman & R. J. Sternberg (Eds.), *The Cambridge handbook of creativity* (pp. 233–249). New York: Cambridge University Press.

Shaw, V. (1998). *Sexual harassment and gender bias.* New York: The Rosen Publishing Group.

Shmukler, D. (1981). Mother-child interaction and its relationship to the predisposition of imaginative play. *Genetic Psychology Monographs, 104*(2), 215–235. https://doi.org/10.1037/h0080492.

Singer, J. (1994). Imaginative play. In J. H. Goldstein (Ed.), *Toys, play, and child development* (pp. 6–13). New York: Cambridge.

Singer, J. L., & Singer, D. G. (2005). Preschooler's imaginative play as precursor of narrative consciousness. *Imagination, Cognition, and Personality, 25*(2), 97–117. https://doi.org/10.2190/0KQU-9A2V-YAM2-XD8J.

Spinner, L., Cameron, L., & Calogero, R. (2018). Peer toy play as a gateway to children's gender flexibility: The effect of (counter) stereotypic portrayals of peers in children's magazines. *Sex Roles, 79*(5/6), 314–328. https://doi. org/10.1007/s11199-017-0883-3.

Thompson, T. L., & Zerbinos, E. (1995). Gender roles in animated cartoons: Has the picture changed in 20 years? *Sex Roles, 32*(9/10), 651–673. https://doi.org/10.1007/BF01544217.

Tipper, B. (2011). "A dog who I know quite well": Everyday relationships between children and animals. *Children's Geographies, 9*(2), 145–165. https://doi.org/10.1080/14733285.2011.562378.

Tuan, Y.-F. (1984). *Dominance and affection: The making of pets.* New Haven: Yale.

Van Pelt, C. (2017). LEGO farm and agricultural idealism. In R. T. Cook & S. Bacharach (Eds.), *LEGO and philosophy: Constructing reality brick by brick* (pp. 145–151). New York: Wiley.

Vygotsky, L. S. (1933/1966). Igra i ee rol v umstvennom razvitii rebenka, Voprosy psihologii [*Problems of psychology*], *12*(6), 62–76. Trans. N. Veresov and M. Barrs (2016). Play and its role in the mental development of the child. *International Research in Early Childhood Education, 7*(2), 3–25. Web.

Wade, L. (2014, January 31). *SocImages news.* https://thesocietypages.org/ socimages/2014/01/31/this-month-in-socimages-january-2014/.   Accessed on March 29, 2019.

Wainman, R., & Grant, R. (2017). Representation in plastic and marketing: The significance of the LEGO women scientists. In R. T. Cook & S. Bacharach (Eds.), *LEGO and philosophy: Constructing reality brick by brick* (pp. 113–122). New York: Wiley.

Walker, A. (1988). Foreword. In *The dreaded comparison* (pp. 13–14). New York: Mirror.

Weisgram, E. S., & Bruun, S. T. (2018). Predictors of gender-typed toy purchases by prospective parents and mothers: The roles of childhood experiences and gender attitudes. *Sex Roles, 79*(5/6), 342–357. https://doi. org/10.1007/s11199-018-0928-2.

Zimmerman, L. K. (2017). Preschoolers' perceptions of gendered toy commercials in the US. *Journal of Children and Media, 11*(2), 119–131. https://doi. org/10.1080/17482798.2017.1297247.

13

The Man Behind the Mask: Camp and Queer Masculinity in *LEGO Batman*

Kyra Hunting

The LEGO Batman Movie's tagline declares "Always be yourself…unless you can be Batman." But who exactly is Batman? Is he…

Adam West's spandex-clad, wholesome-with-a-wink caped crusader?

Michael Keaton's slender, slightly unstable Bat-that-goes-bump-in-the-night?

George Clooney's rubber-muscled, campy, knowing Bat?

Christian Bale's conservative, somber, militaristic Dark Knight?

LEGO Batman as voiced by Will Arnett opts to be none of and all of these Batmans. The animated film engages with a core concern of Bat-fans and Batman creators alike: What are we to make of *Batman's* conflicted history, its ever-shifting models of *masculinity*, and the question of what is going on behind Batman's mask?

The LEGO Batman Movie (hereafter *LBM*) holds a unique place in the Batman and LEGO film franchises. The only LEGO theatrical

K. Hunting (✉)
University of Kentucky, Lexington, KY, USA
e-mail: kyra.hunting@uky.edu

© The Author(s) 2019
R. C. Hains and S. R. Mazzarella (eds.), *Cultural Studies of LEGO*,
https://doi.org/10.1007/978-3-030-32664-7_13

film to date featuring a licensed character, it walks a tightrope between continuing the tonal and thematic features that made *The LEGO Movie* (hereafter *TLM*) a success and engaging substantially with the iconic, nearly century-old Batman character and methods. Jessica Aldred (2014) has identified licensed characters' reduction to their simplest, most iconic features as a key element of LEGO-licensed video games (p. 106). But as LEGO moved into video content and, particularly, theatrical-length films, licensed LEGO characters needed to be fleshed out consistently with the original source texts while retaining LEGO games' and short-form videos' light-hearted, parodic tones.

LBM also occupies a unique space in the Batman franchise's cinematic iterations. Batman represents a "fractured franchise" in comparison to other examples like *Star Wars* and *Harry Potter*. From film to film, Batman changes both tone and core elements, like the actor playing Batman; features of Batman's origin story; and his romantic interests. The differences between the Batman films made by Tim Burton (1989, 1992), Joel Schumacher (1995, 1997) and Christopher Nolan (2005, 2008, 2012) are dramatic enough to call into question whether Batman even constitutes a single franchise—or if, instead, Batman is best understood as several contiguous or contemporaneous franchises centered on a single character?

Such questions are well-suited to studies of the relationships between Batman's media texts, which often engage with each creative team's need to distinctly break from or reject previous iterations (Winstead 2015). But they pose a real challenge for LEGO, whose style in co-branded transmedia iterations depends on flattening differences between texts. As Aldred (2014) noted, LEGO-licensed video games such as *Indiana Jones* and *Star Wars* frequently compressed several movies into a single game, leaving *LBM* in a complicated spot. It could hew closely to a specific Batman variant, reiterating that version's origin story, narrative and ideology—likely a temptation, given Nolan's trilogy's success in redefining Batman in the minds of many fans—or create an entirely new narrative and variant with little-to-no relationship or reference to specific pre-existing Batman texts. This tactic had previously been used mainly in *LEGO Batman: The Videogame* which, unusually for *LEGO* games, offered an original plot.

Ultimately, *LBM* chose neither approach. Instead, it presents a storyline that is both novel and deeply rooted in an encyclopedic Bat-history. The film aligns itself through intertextual referentiality to Nolan and Burton's Batmans while resoundingly rejecting their ideologies—in part by drawing on the history and aesthetics of the much-maligned 1960s camp TV series and Joel Schumacher's camped-and-queered 1990s antecedent.

This chapter explores how *LBM* destabilizes and undermines the "hypermasculinity" aligned with the Batman character. The film deploys distinctive elements of *LEGO* media (like parody) to undermine this masculinity, and simultaneously activates and embraces Batman's often-maligned, marginalized queer and camp textual history in strategic ways.

LEGO Batman: Expanding the Conversation

LBM's hybridity places its study in relation to several scholarly conversations, drawing together the burgeoning "LEGO Studies" field with the long history of Batman research, while also touching on feminist media studies, children's media studies and queer theory. Jason Mittell (2014) described LEGO Studies as a bricolage "comprised of pieces from a variety of disciplinary sources" (p. 270) and explained that a focus on re-combinance and flexibility would best serve the study of LEGO (p. 273). I echo this sentiment, arguing that *LBM* must be understood as a LEGO film, a *Batman* film, and an animated children's film simultaneously.

LEGO scholarship has identified ongoing tensions between a LEGO ethic of creativity and imagination and prescribed "proper" uses and messages of LEGO materials (Hills 2016; Johnson 2014)—tensions central to *TLM* (Gregg 2018). Objects' ability to be broken apart, built and rebuilt—expressed as metaphor by the recombination of media characters in the LEGO world—is significant across LEGO's theatrical films. This includes *LBM*, which "levels up" Batman's standard villains with an array from other media including Voldemort, King Kong and The Wicked Witch of the West. This recombinance is central to LEGO, which is a "medium, a mediating substance through which ideas can be expressed, and with which art can be created" (Wolf 2014, p. xxii). Others have noted that LEGO adaptations have distinctive characteristics that allow them to avoid expectations of canonicity (Wolf 2014, p. xxiii) while creating characters that are clearly identifiable in relationship to their source texts using a "compelling suite of characteristics" that are iconic (Aldred 2014, p. 110). I argue that this makes LEGO versions of franchise characters particularly flexible and ripe for parodic engagement.

Parody is a key feature of media characters' remediation into the LEGO form. Robert Buerkle (2014) found parody central in both the *Batman* and Marvel games, which "provide an overtly generic story that evokes the common tropes of those franchises" whose pleasure comes in part from a communal celebration of "Batmany stuff" (p. 147). However, exactly which "Batmany stuff" is activated at what time is crucial. Neal Baker (2014) observed in his study of *Lord of the Rings*-themed LEGO sets that the retention and rejection of parts of a film or franchise can be understood as narrative choices (p. 40). Pushing this a bit further, I argue that when creators of LEGO media texts decide which textual "building blocks" to retain, reject or remediate from a source text or franchise, they engage in a central part of meaning-making in LEGO narrative media texts. Buerkle (2014) saw the parody in *LEGO Star Wars* as often celebratory and nostalgic (p. 127), but I argue that in *LBM,* intertextual choices can function as deeply ideological and critical.

The idea that LEGO is ideological and sometimes regressive is not new. Derek Johnson (2014) found that LEGO's construction of its brand and its adaptation to licensing attempted to "disavow complicity in the racial order" (p. 323), and indeed, the world of *LBM* is quite White. (For more information on race representation in LEGO minifigures, see Chapter 14 by Derek Johnson in this volume.) Scholars have also identified the "masculinization" of LEGO, with female LEGO users erased or segregated into their own toy and media brands (Black et al. 2016). These segregated LEGO worlds have been identified as reinforcing problematic gender scripts (Johnson 2014; Reich et al. 2017). Sanctioned masculinity tends to be associated with aggression (Luther and Legg 2010), physical strength (England et al. 2011;

Smith et al. 2010), power (Tanner et al. 2003), technical skills (Thompson and Zerbinos 1995), muscularity (Coyne et al. 2014; Wooden and Gillam 2016) and competition (Wooden and Gillam 2016). Alternative traits like emotional vulnerability or literacy, cooperation, dependency and nurturing are rarely valued in male characters' representations, with some limited and rare shifts (Åström 2015; Hentges and Case 2013).

Intense "masculinization" has also been endemic across the Batman franchise. Dafna Lemish (2010) argued that *Batman's* animated and live-action variants play "a primary role in many boy's development of male identity," representing a masculinity based on strength, bravery, muscularity, and an undefeatable heroism "adored by females" (p. 16). Most Batman histories understood the characters' development as defined, at least in part, by a homophobic response to readings of Batman and Robin as gay, with efforts to "shore up" Batman's masculinity and dis-identify with texts or elements that might validate this reading. Most scholars have located this conflict's origins with Dr. Frederic Wertham, who in *The Seduction of the Innocent* postulated comic books as the source of many pathologies (Brooker 2001; Shyminsky 2011; Tipton 2008) and memorably described Batman and Robin as a "wish dream of two homosexuals living together" (Burke 2013, pp. 12–13). DC responded quickly, initially by domesticating Batman, killing off Alfred, and introducing Batwoman and Batgirl into Batman and Robin's lives (Torres 1999). The history of Batman that followed is a cyclical return of the repressed. The 1960s Adam West *Batman* poked fun at this wholesome Batman in what was meant as stylish, nostalgic camp. William Dozier, who produced the first *Batman* television show, noted: "there will be no doubt that Batman and Robin like girls, even though they may be too busy fighting crime to have much time for them" (Torres 1999, p. 334). Despite Dozier's protestations, camp's deep connections to gay male subculture indeed cast doubt. When discussing the series' humor, Andy Medhurst quoted George Melly saying, "what were we laughing at? The fact that they didn't know that Batman had it off with Robin" (Medhurst 1991, p. 156). The 1960s camp series was wildly popular but has since been rejected by the plurality of Batman fans, becoming a "bad object" in the franchise. As a result, "since the 1960s [there] has been the painstaking re-heterosexualization of Batman" (Medhurst 1991, p. 159).

Tim Burton's *Batman* and *Batman Returns* resonated far more with comics *The Killing Joke* (Alan Moore 1988) and *The Dark Knight Returns* (Frank Miller 1986), purging nearly every trace of Adam West's camp Batman. However, subsequent films directed by Joel Schumacher (*Batman Forever, Batman and Robin*) broke from this rule, so freely reveling in camp and allusions to the 1960s series that mainstream Batman fans, and many critics, recoiled. This background brought us to the "modern" Batman. Defined by Chris Nolan's Batman trilogy and continued in the DC Extended Universe in *Batman vs. Superman*, the reigning Batman when *LBM* was made was hypermasculine, tortured, vengeful, steeped in militaristic technology and authoritarianism. This Batman engaged in intense violence, justified by framing his opponents as terrorists rather than criminals (Brooker 2012; Kellner 2013). The darker Batman already had the greatest credibility with comic book fans, and online fans elevated Nolan's *The Dark Knight* as a similar "gold standard" for Batman on film (Posada 2013). Nick Winstead (2015) argued that Nolan "de-queered" Batman by emphasizing this hypermasculinity and a heterosexual binary (p. 573), but we have heard this tale before. While *LBM* could have aligned itself with the most recent and lauded variant of Batman, it instead tackled the full "hybrid canon" (Winstead 2015, p. 575), critiquing the very hetero-hypermasculinity Nolan's films championed and embracing the exiled camp queerness of Batman.

Building with Bat History

LBM is not coy. It quickly reveals its playful, subversive relationship to Batman's hybrid canon. The film begins with a black screen and ponderous voice-over, then transitions to a variant of the Warner Bros. and DC logos—all stylized to echo the beginning of Nolan's *Batman Begins*. The narrative starts with Joker hijacking a plane, further positioning it in relationship to Nolan's films' investment in terrorism. When the pilot refuses to be frightened, the tone shifts into the mode of LEGO media texts: light and knowing, a parody of the source text. The pilot confronting the Joker refers to both the "two boats" from Nolan's *The Dark Knight* and "the parade and the Prince music" from Burton's *Batman*, indicating that more than a general understanding of Batman's textual history would be at play. Lest the viewer become too comfortable that *LBM* would only engage with fan-sanctioned "serious" Batman films, Joker quickly lists the villains he is working with, including the lesser-known Crazy Quilt, Orca, Calendar Man, and King Tut, a creation of the 1960s series. By displaying a detailed and precise intertextuality, it differentiates itself from many other LEGO texts and immediately establishes that the film's playground encompasses *all* of Bat-history.

The first appearance of Batman further reveals the film's complicated relationship with the twin poles of the dark Burton/Nolan Batman and the camp 1960s/Schumacher Batman. We are introduced to the character in drag, disguised as Gotham's female mayor. After revealing himself as Batman, facilitated by the flexibility of LEGO to quickly swap faces, he somberly tells the Joker, "Let's get nuts"—a reference to Michael Keaton's *Batman*. Here, his language and voice align with the grittier Batman despite appearing in drag, indicating that *LBM* is less invested in "de-queering" Batman than were its predecessors.

The song that provides the soundtrack for Batman's first fight, while objects burst into flames in the background, further elucidates this dynamic. The song, ostensibly written by Batman, celebrates masculinity, asks a sequence of questions about who the manliest man is, including references to hypermasculine concepts such as a gadget arsenal, wrestling a bear, and pursuing muscularity through "leg day." The answer to the questions posed by the song invariably is that *Batman* is this paragon of masculinity. But the song goes beyond parodic excess to a satirical critique of this masculinity, as he instructs his computer to "overcompensate," immediately framing his machismo as inauthentic. While superficially Metal, the song's riffs also tie it to the 1960s series' theme music. His masculinity is not even superficially pro-social like Nolan's Batman, as the song assures us that Batman doesn't pay his taxes. Nor is it marked as heterosexual, for during the fight, Batman is not tempted by Ivy's poison kiss: He comically prevents it by placing several penguins between them. This first sequence crucially demonstrates that the film's intertextuality goes beyond the Easter Egg tracking that fan Web sites embraced. The specific intertextual references and how they are deployed are ideologically significant: *LEGO Batman* performs hypermasculinity as a farce.

The end of this scene further frames Batman's masculinity—and its rejection of emotional availability—as the film's source of conflict. When Batman is ready to capture the Joker, the Joker retorts that Batman "has to choose," that he cannot both defuse a bomb to save the city *and* catch his "greatest enemy." An incredulous Batman retorts, "You think you're my greatest enemy?", using romantically framed language to deny Joker this status, saying that he likes "to fight around."

When Joker responds by saying, "I'm fine with you fighting other people if you want to do that, but what we have is special," Batman rebuffs him, saying, "Batman doesn't do 'ships. [...] Batman and Joker are not a thing. I don't need you. I don't need anyone. You mean nothing to me."

Importantly, in this speech, Batman does not reject the Joker specifically, but rather the idea of an emotional connection to *anyone*. His exaggerated display of masculinized independence and emotional invulnerability hurts and infuriates Joker, whose remaining villainous actions throughout the film seek to gain Batman's acknowledgement of something "special" between them. The thematic idea that Batman and Joker are linked could be connected to the dark Batman comic *The Killing Joke* (Moore 1988), but the scene's language instead encourages the viewer to see this conflict in romantic comedy terms.

In these first scenes, then, the film's stage is set. It deploys a complex and extensive historical intertextuality, positioning *LBM* in a fractured, warring franchise. It aligns its main character with the reigning hypermasculine Batman, only to undermine and mock this ideology. The danger it presents is not villainous greed for money or power, but the fall-out of Batman's own callous insensitivity to others' emotional needs. Appearing in drag and immediately interpreting Joker's identification as an arch-nemesis in romantic terms, this macho Batman is immediately queered. As such, we can see the film's intertextuality as political. In many ways, the film is a journey from the hypermasculine Burton/Nolan Batman to the embrace of a camp Schumacher/1960s Batman, as well as a familial, emotionally-in-touch Batman not quite aligned with either.

Gotham's Toxin: Masculinity

The "masculinity problem" is a constant refrain in LEGO's theatrical films. *TLM* and *LEGO Ninjago* both featured authoritarian villains who privileged "successful" masculinity's trappings: power, status (through respect or fear), aggression, ambition and control. The latter takes three forms in these films: control over technology through the possession of an "ultimate weapon" (such as superglue in *TLM* and a giant cat in *LEGO Ninjago*); control over their community; and self-control. Indeed, in *LEGO Movie 2* the depiction of a female antagonist who appears to control minds is a feint, with a hyper-masculine violent heroic figure ultimately filling the role of the villain. (For further exploration of this depiction, see Chapter 6 in this volume: "The Accursed Second Part: Small-Scale Discourses of Gender and Race in *The LEGO Movie 2*" by Matthias Zick Varul.) These figures further exhibit attributes associated with what Phillip Serrato called "mature masculinity": "self-confidence and emotional invulnerability" (2011, p. 82) which, in this context, allows the villains to carry out plots undeterred by protestations or emotional appeals. These characteristics define *TLM's* villainous President Business and *LEGO Ninjago's* Lord Garmadon, setting them apart from Emmett and Lloyd, the films' uncertain, eager-for-acceptance, emotional heroes.

These villainous traits align with many *Batman* texts' forms of heroism. Batman controls Gotham by instilling fear in criminals and through Bruce Wayne's respected status as a community businessman and philanthropist. His gadgets (described as "wonderful toys" by Joker in *Batman* and *LBM*) give him technological mastery and are framed as re-purposed militaristic weapons in *Batman Begins*. He is seen as a proficient fighter with great physical control within the first 3 minutes of *Batman Begins,* the first 6 minutes of *Batman* and the first 8 minutes of *LBM*. In most Batman media texts, even campier iterations, he is relatively stoic, breaking his restraint only to display anger. He displays additional masculine ideals not central to LEGO film villains, such as "physical strength, resiliency, and heterosexual desirability" (Brown 2016, p. 134), and his strength and muscular body are highlighted.

Even as Bruce Wayne, he can pull a steel building part off a worker at the beginning of *Batman vs. Superman*. In most films, women who cross Bruce Wayne and/or Batman's paths become besotted. As Jeffrey A. Brown (2016) argued, "superheroes have always represented the pinnacle of American cultural ideas about masculinity" (p. 131), and even when the genre is parodied, it further reinforces this hegemonic ideal.

LBM presents a dramatic break from this norm. Because it is a hybrid text, *LBM* depends on both the superhero genre and LEGO's other films, functioning as a genre, for meaning. As a result, Batman's hypermasculinity marks him as both the iconic hero Batman and as a LEGO villain. Therefore, when Joker sends Batman to the Phantom Zone, its gatekeeper cannot decide whether Batman is a bad guy. Nor can the film itself, which embraces some masculine traits associated with Batman across the franchise as ultimately necessary. For example, all the main characters including Robin, Alfred and Batgirl show some technological mastery to vanquish the villains Joker has released upon the city. One pivotal moment accommodates this by yoking the learning of technical mastery, in this case over "sick vehicles" and "advanced weaponry," to an emotional and familial moment in which Batman teaches Robin how to drive mid-battle. The masculine attributes that continue to be celebrated (particularly the emphasis on vehicles and weapons) fit neatly into the LEGO brand's other priorities that centralize collectability in both consumer practices and video games (Buerkle 2014).

Vanquishing villains is not *LBM*'s central problem, however. Instead, the literal splitting of the city by Joker's bomb represents the film's final challenge. Here, stereotypically feminine characteristics—not masculine ones—save the day when Batman listens to others and devises a plan based on cooperation: linking people to one another to form a chain to bridge the divide, pulling the ground together with a satisfying LEGO snap. Batman's plan only works, however, through his appeals to others and expressions of emotions. The chain represents a collaboration between Batman, his new friends, his former foes and all Gotham citizens. In contrast to his typical approach of working in isolation, Batman can only save the day through open communication.

LBM's communicative, stereotypically feminine conclusion is a fitting bookend for the film because the hypermasculinity represented by

Batman's introductory song is the source of most of the film's problems. Batman's insistence on emotional invulnerability and unwillingness to share his feelings with the Joker is the instigating action for the narrative, and the Joker's plot escalates simply because he wants to know Batman hates (loves) him. But Joker's plan depends on Batman behaving predictably. His attempt to get Batman to send him to the Phantom Zone could have been thwarted many times. If Batman had listened to Barbara/Batgirl when she offered to work together, instead of insisting on being a vigilante, he would not have pursued the Phantom Zone Projector. Further, he is self-confident to a fault, refusing to listen to Alfred and taking advantage of Robin to pursue his plans. His solution, like LEGO villains', is to gain control of the "ultimate weapon" (the Phantom Zone Projector). Barbara nearly stops him again when trying to smuggle the Projector into Arkham Asylum, but he sneaks it in anyway using a smoke bomb. Then, given one more chance when confronting the Joker in only his underpants, he mistakes Joker's baiting of him as trying to "entrap me into a relationship." In a moment of queer panic, Batman gives Joker exactly what he wants: A trip to the Phantom Zone.

When Batman himself arrives in the Phantom Zone, he is not held to account for these actions, but rather, for his lack of empathy, openness and emotional vulnerability. Flashbacks of him putting Robin at risk to get the bad guy, taking advantage of Robin's desire for connection, refusing to fulfill Robin's desire for a father, cruelly insisting that Alfred has no family, and even telling the "villain" that he means "nothing" to him serve as evidence that he is not a "good guy." Barbara and the Joker both foreshadowed this, telling Batman that he cannot be a hero if he "only cares about himself" and that he was his own "worst enemy," respectively. Even a traditional superhero film trope—Batman sending away Robin, Alfred and Batgirl for their own protection—is evoked as one of Batman's crimes. Batman tries to frame this along masculine lines, saying he was "protecting them," but he is corrected and told he is "protecting himself," de-prioritizing the characters' physical danger in favor of their emotional lives.

Halberstam (1998) argued that "'heroic masculinities' depend absolutely on the subordination of alternative masculinities" (p. 1), but *LBM* systematically deconstructs heroic masculinity, elevating instead the voices of "alternative masculinities" and women. While Robin's tendency toward camp is sometimes played for laughs, mostly affectionately, Batman's machismo is the more common target. The film also frames Robin as correct: his insistence on being involved and his attempts to soften and connect to Batman prove crucial in saving the day. The narrative and Batman himself also validate Barbara/Batgirl's message of collaboration ("It takes a village, not a Batman"), while Alfred presents a "preferred model" of masculinity: communicative, thoughtful, familial. Seen reading a book on "setting limits for your out-of-control child," Alfred is pivotal to reframing Batman's heroic masculinity as childish and destructive. Alfred also provides the key line linking *LBM* to Batman's history. Worried about Batman's behavior, he explains, "I've seen you go through similar phases in 2016, 2012 and 2008, and 2006, and 1997 and 1995 and 1989 and that weird one in 1966" (each date being the year of a release of a Batman film). Here, the film trades on the LEGO brand and its ability to compress multiple movies to leverage both its parody and critique of the franchise as a whole.

"Faggy and Funsies"

LBM's allusions to Batman's history are not treated equally. They function to embrace the parts of Batman's history most associated with camp and queerness. We see this at play in Alfred's quote above: Nearly every date listed was accompanied by an animated LEGO-style recreation of a scene from the film. The recreations of the Snyder, Nolan and Burton films display variations of dominant masculinity, with an animated *LEGO Batman* locked in combat, brooding, and in a heterosexual clinch, respectively. However, this *LBM* scene presents both Schumacher's films and the 1966 Adam West variant in live-action formats. Schumacher's films are compressed into a long still of the infamous nippled Batman suit, while West is shown doing the Batutsi—both significantly less "masculine" modes. The exceptional treatment of these two films in Alfred's list is telling: The only other live-action sequences in the film are clips from the romantic comedy *Jerry McGuire*, of which Batman is a secret fan. How should we interpret these clips, then? It becomes complicated. Within the film's context, the live-action clips align Schumacher's and West's films with "relationship movies" and Batman's secret vulnerability, but also the fictional world. However, within the context of the LEGO Cinematic Universe in *TLM*, *The LEGO Movie 2* and *LEGO Ninjago*, the films' live-action scenes represent the "real world," while the LEGO sequences are framed as stories or imaginary play. Regardless of which interpretation holds sway, while *LBM* is positioned in relationship to all the Batman films in this sequence, the franchise's two most maligned variants are given special consideration.

One could argue that Alfred's definition of the 1966 film as the "weird one" would validate its treatment as "abject" in the fandom, but the preponderance of its use in the film is more celebratory than critical. Later, Alfred appears in Adam West's light blue-gray Batman costume, explaining he "misses the '60s." Throughout, the jokes about 1960s Batman are friendly, frequently made at the expense of those who reject this Batman, rather than camp-Batman himself. For example, when Robin discovers the Batcave and its gadgets and vehicles, Batman only allows him to touch the "Bat Shark Repellant" because it is "useless"—but by the film's end, it proves highly effective, as Robin uses it to save Batman from Jaws. The Shark Repellant is given the "last laugh," and as a result, the objects of the joke are those who derided 1960s *Batman* and its iconography, not the film and series itself. By contrast, Batman comments that he doesn't "feel anything emotionally except for rage 24/7, 365 at a million percent. And if you think there's something behind, that you're crazy." This much more cutting joke targets the hypermasculine Batman with precision.

The embrace of "camp Batman" is thorough and serves as one way *LBM* further undermines the heteronormative hyper-masculine Batman. The film activates its intertextual relationship with camp Batman media alongside its narrative conflict in ways that push against Batman's "de-queering" to consider Batman/Bruce Wayne as a "queer construct" (Winstead 2015). In this chapter, I do not, by and large, conduct a queer reading of Batman. The queer potential of Batman, in general, has been well established by scholars like Will Brooker (2001), Andy Medhurst (1991) and Sasha Torres (1999), receiving such widespread cultural awareness that *SNL* has parodied it. *LBM*'s queerness is easily legible by those that revile and celebrate it alike. A religious-right group slammed *LBM* for being "pro-gay" and advocating for "gay adoption" (Reynolds 2017), while *The Root* described it as the "Brokeback Batman we've always wanted" (Johnson 2017). Both interpretations go for the "low hanging fruit": The religious right's critique highlights Batman telling Robin he is co-parenting with Bruce Wayne, leading the young ward to celebrate having "two dads" by singing "it's raining dads." Notably, the critique focuses on the simple reference to two dads while missing the much more subversive camp reference to the gay anthem "It's Raining Men." *The Root* fares better, acknowledging that the film is at its core a "gay love story," which it says is so obvious that a child in the theater yelled out, "just *tell him*" to Batman during the film screening attended by the reviewer (Johnson 2017).

LBM is indeed structured as a romantic comedy. The Joker repeatedly demands (as that young child observes) that Batman reveal his feelings for him. Doing so literally saves the world and frees Batman from his emotional hang-ups, leading him to healthy relationships with his "friend family" (Alfred, Batgirl and Robin). It doesn't quite end in a kiss, but it nearly does: After asking Joker about his abs, Batman and Joker pull closer and closer together to mend the gap in Gotham's streets. Staring into one another's eyes against a sunset, Batman promises, "I hate you forever."

Joker's queerness is not, in and of itself, unusual. Scholars have argued that the franchise's queerness was displaced onto the Joker in Burton's films and again in Nolan's (Brooker 2001, 2012), pathologized as the inverse to Batman's hetero-masculinity. Those who refer to Nolan's Joker's queerness often point to Heath Ledger's Joker's profession to Batman, "you complete me," in *Dark Knight*—a line that *LBM* depicts in its original romantic-comedy context in an excerpt from *Jerry Maguire*. The line's use in Nolan's film serves as evidence of Joker's sexualized obsession with Batman and is part of his "deviance," but in *LBM*, Batman's language is what first sexualizes and romanticizes the Batman-Joker dynamic. Whereas Joker initially seeks reassurance that he is

Batman's "greatest enemy," Batman's reply, "I'm fighting a few different people," introduces the language of dating. Joker later takes up this language, saying, "I'm off the market…I'm off the menu." Then, running his hands down his body, Joker taunts Batman: "You won't get to fight any of this anymore." This effort to bait and upset Batman works spectacularly, as Batman's world fades to gray after the villains are put in jail. Joker takes up more "romantic comedy" language as the film goes on, telling Batman that he runs away "from every other person in your life, but I'm the one you're always chasing"; and Batman's final revelation of his feelings is distinctly romantic and queer. When trying to convince the Joker, who has dramatically applied red lipstick, to help him save the city, Batman finally says:

> You're the reason why I get up at 4:00 in the afternoon, and pump iron until my chest is positively sick. You're the reason I've given up a life spent with Russian ballerinas and lady activewear models. And if it wasn't for you, I never would have learned how connected I am with all these people.

These lines are exceptionally dense: Batman suggests he sculpts his body for Joker's benefit, that he has eschewed the (heterosexual) attention of Russian ballerinas and activewear models (a specific reference to Bruce Wayne's playthings in *Batman Begins, The Dark Knight* and *Batman vs. Superman*), and that Joker's villainy *is* responsible for his emotional maturation. Feigning hetero-normative hypermasculinity left him a man-child whom Alfred needed to parent, but admitting his "relationship" with the Joker matured him, making him able to nurture and care about others.

Similarly, *LBM* embraces the use of camp, often aligned with villains like *Riddler* or *The Joker* in post-1960s Batman films; and camp's history is entangled with gay subculture. When Dozier (creator of the 1960s Batman) was referred to as the "King of Camp," he resoundingly rejected the term, saying he hated it because it sounded so "faggy and funsies" (Torres 1999)—yet his series became instantly associated with camp and, as a result, queerness in a way that twenty-first-century Batman has been designed to obliterate and deny. However, *LBM* embraces both camp style and Batman's camp history.

LBM validates Batman's camp history through costuming. Robin's costume closely approximates the 1960s Batman costume, heightened with a glittery cape. When dressed as Dick, his red sweater and white shirt are similar to Burt Ward's outfits in the *Batman* TV show. Robin tries on several costumes over the course of the film. Some are played for campy laughs; one is literally "flaming," and another (titled "Batryshnikov") turns him into a ballet dancer. But when he takes the "wrong path" after Batman is sent to the phantom zone, he selects a costume resembling Nightwing, Dick Grayson's darker, mature, and heterosexualized post-Robin identity. After Batman returns to fix things, he encourages Robin to change into the "right" costume: the short-shorted, brightly colored Robin outfit that at first made Batman uncomfortable.

Similarly, when Batgirl finally gets her costume, it is the purple-and-yellow variant most associated with the 1960s television show (and its animated '70s counterpart), instead of the more recent versions combining black, yellow and blue. This departs from the costume used in the straight-to-video *LEGO DC Comics Super Heroes: Justice League—Gotham City Breakout* released one year earlier. References to the 1960s tv show and, to a lesser extent, Schumacher's films are peppered throughout *LBM*. Variations on the 1960s series theme are played several times; the Batmobile's computer says "Atomic batteries to power, turbines to speed"; and Batman's adoring crowds greet him with a sign saying "Batman Forever." The film even steers into Wertham's critique with Batman appearing early on in a "dressing gown."

While the film is replete with references to the Burton, Nolan and Snyder films, the references to camp Batman are particularly significant for two reasons. First, their inclusion is notable in a historical context that frequently has attempted to marginalize and erase these texts because of their associations with a queered camp masculinity. Secondly, the text deploys these references in crucial moments. Robin uses a weapon from the 1960s series to save Batman, and in the film's penultimate battle, the 1960s series signature "BAM" and "POW" exclamations appear on screen, accompanying their punches. The last line prior to the film's "epilogue" is Batman saying, "Holy family photo, Batman"—famous phrasing from the 1960s series that Schumacher brought back in *Batman and Robin*. Furthermore, the film is interlaced with new forms of camp, not explicitly referring to previous Bat-texts. A belligerent, unhappy Batman is cheered by his "favorite" thing: a "Tuxedo dress-up party," introduced with bright colors and disco music. When testing Robin on his ability to follow commands, Batman has him *plie* and *relevé* while his shorts briefly become a tutu. Joker does not hold the claim to camp excess in this film; his neon-carnivalesque makeover of Wayne Manor is almost humdrum compared to the excess already there.

Family Without Heteronormativity

LBM's narrative's queerness, its intertextuality, and its deployment of camp are complemented by a subtle-but-persistent rejection of heteronormativity across the film (quite unusual for a children's movie). While Harley is Joker's lover throughout most of the franchise, he calls her "girl buddy" in their first interaction in *LBM*. She never demonstrates jealousy over Joker's obsession with Batman, instead playing the catty girlfriend who tells him he is "too good for Batman." Batman is smitten with Batgirl on first sight, but the film rapidly, inexplicably drops his puppy-love attraction to her; it seems there only to explain his being distracted enough to "accidentally" adopt Robin. The film assures us that no future Batman/Batgirl romance is in the works, having Batman describe her as "my platonic coworker buddy, who's a girl and just a friend." The line is played for laughs; it's awkward, and the LEGO parody form is clearly at play. But what is being parodied? It isn't really Batman's friendship with a girl. The joke instead targets our discomfort with *LBM*'s lack of a romantic resolution, which is often central to superhero films. Furthermore, Batman's fleeting interest in Batgirl is inexplicable in a traditional film narrative, but it resonates with other Batman film texts that see him flit from Vicki Vale to Catwoman to Meridian Chase and back again.

Finally, the two scenes where Batman watches *Jerry Maguire* are the film's most inexplicable moments. In the first such scene, when Batman is revealed to be isolated and lonely, he watches the film alone. He laughs when Tom Cruise says "you complete me" to his love interest and then looks beside himself sadly. The scene is reprised at the film's end, but his three new friends join him both in viewing and in laughing at this line, demonstrating that the inclusion of others has enriched his life. But the question remains: What is funny about "you complete me?" It is telling that the film's only moments of clear heterosexual romance are punchlines to a joke the audience is not fully in on.

The film's ending privileges family, without the requirement of heteronormativity. This is historically and intertextually significant. Some have characterized Batgirl's original introduction as a response to Wertham and the Comics Code (Brooker 2001). Placing Batman at the head of a "Batman family" was intended to "avoid any further questions" about Batman and Robin's sexuality (Burke 2013, p. 13); but here, Batgirl is dismissed as a romantic interest for Batman, fulfilling a more motherly role to Robin, instead. The family is explicitly defined as a "friend family" by the Joker, who seems to acknowledge its value. The film gives no explicit credence to the idea of Batman and Robin as a couple, however. Indeed, *LBM* firmly places Robin in the position of "son"—what Medhurst calls the "approved fantasy" (1991, p. 160)—but does so while retaining the possibility that both Robin (identifying as his theme song the disco song "Fly Robin Fly") and Batman (who eschews Russian ballet dancers for a raucous fight with the Joker) are queer. Alfred, Robin, Batman and Batgirl are, indeed, a family, but one entirely divorced of the heteronormative expectations of romantic or biological ties. They fit nicely with what Kath Weston describes as "chosen families": a kinship structure pivotal to queer life (1991). In the repeated bonding rituals of "dress up" parties and the play with different variants of the language of father and son, there is even a hint of "drag families." Amazingly, the films closing song, "Friends are Family" by an artist with the deliciously campy name "Oh, Hush," includes the refrain "friends are the family you can choose." (Note that Weston's book is titled *Families We Choose*.)

Like many children's films, including *LEGO's* other theatrical offerings, *LBM* centers the importance of family relationships. It is exceptional, however, for centering an entirely "*chosen* family." The possibility of biological or romantic connections are cut off. Robin's age is slippery in the film: Although he is slightly smaller, Robin is not animated as dramatically less physically mature than other LEGO figures, and yet he is simultaneously worried about bedtime and ready to learn to drive. This makes his role as Batman's son one of mentorship and affective connection, rather than dependence. Finally, the film privileges family but also asserts that family is, on its own, insufficient. Batman's friend family is vital for his personal transformation, but the implicitly queer Joker instigates the change.

The new "Bat Family" cannot succeed without the villains. While *Batman* and *Batman Begins* evoke Joker's queerness as abject—the "other" that threatens to frighten or contaminate Gotham (Medhurst 1991, p. 161)—here, Joker's queerness is necessary (even redemptive). Winstead describes the "key lore" of *The Dark Knight* as "Batman containing the queer as an agent of chaos and disruption" (Winstead 2015, p. 581). But the Joker in *LBM* is not contained by Batman. Rather, he helps reveal Batman's queerness and, in so doing, facilitates Batman finding happiness with a family. Batman's attempt at containment—sending the threatening queer potential of Joker to the Phantom Zone—makes things worse. Only when Batman opens up to camp, to the help of others, and to sharing his feelings with the Joker can Batman save the day—and himself.

Conclusion

In his meditation on Batman and its "painstaking re-heterosexualization" since the 1960s (Medhurst 1991, p. 159), Medhurst (1991) complained that camp Batman had become "anathema to serious Bat-fans" and critiqued the tendency to treat camp Batman and dark Batman as mutually exclusive. He noted that if he could accept "the swooping eighties' vigilante…why are they so concerned to trash my camp crusader? Why do they insist so vehemently that Adam West was a faggy aberration, a blot on the otherwise impeccably butch Bat-landscape?" (p. 162). Historically, the Batman franchise has been a battle between those who enjoy its camp and queer pleasures and, more frequently, those who insist upon a grittier, darker, more heterosexual Batman. *LBM* takes advantage of LEGO's invitation to build something new with whatever blocks are on hand to demonstrate that we can, indeed, have both.

Taking parts of Bat-history that many fans have been denied or have rejected, *LBM* builds on its parodic play with the franchise by suggesting Batman's hypermasculinity is the farce—his real mask—and that Batman's campier history is an authentic, necessary part of who and what Batman is.

Freed from an allegiance to canon by the norms of the LEGO brand (Wolf 2014), *LBM* builds a brighter, more community-centered, queerer world for the not-so-Dark Knight.

References

Aldred, J. (2014). (Un)blocking the transmedial character: Digital abstraction as franchise strategy in Traveller's Tales' LEGO Games. In M. J. P. Wolf (Ed.), *LEGO studies: Examining the building blocks of transmedial phenomenon* (pp. 105–117). New York, NY: Routledge.

Åström, B. (2015). Postfeminist fatherhood in the animated feature films *Chicken Little* and *Cloudy with a Chance of Meatballs*. *Journal of Children and Media, 9*(3), 294–307. https://doi.org/10.1080/17482798.2015.104814.

Baker, N. (2014). Middle-earth and LEGO (re)creation. In M. J. P. Wolf (Ed.), *LEGO studies: Examining the building blocks of transmedial phenomenon* (pp. 40–54). New York, NY: Routledge.

Black, R. W., Tomlinson, B., & Korbkova, K. (2016). Play and identity in gendered LEGO Franchises. *International Journal of Play, 5*(1), 64–76. https://doi.org/10.1080/21594937.2016.1147284.

Brooker, W. (2001). *Batman unmasked: Analyzing a cultural icon.* New York, NY: Bloomsbury.

Brooker, W. (2012). *Hunting the Dark Knight: Twenty-first century Batman.* New York, NY: I.B. Tauris.

Brown, J. A. (2016). The superhero film parody and hegemonic masculinity. *Quarterly Review of Film and Video, 33*(2), 131–150. https://doi.org/10.1080/10509208.2015.1094361.

Buerkle, R. (2014). Playset nostalgia: *LEGO Star Wars: The Video Game* and the transgenerational appeal of the LEGO video game franchise. In M. J. P. Wolf (Ed.), *LEGO studies: Examining the building blocks of transmedial phenomenon* (pp. 118–152). New York, NY: Routledge.

Burke, L. (2013). A fan's history. In L. Burke (Ed.), *Fan phenomena: Batman* (pp. 10–21). Chicago, IL: Intellect Books.

Coyne, S. M., Linder, J. R., Rasmussen, E. E., Nelson, D. A., & Collier, K. M. (2014). It's a bird! It's a plane! It's a gender stereotype!: Longitudinal associations between superhero viewing and gender stereotyped play. *Sex Roles, 70*(9), 416–430. https://doi.org/10.1007/s11199-014-0374-8.

Dozier, W. (Producer). (1966–1968). *Batman* [Television series]. Hollywood, CA: 20th Century Fox Television.

Dozier, W. (Producer), & Martinson, L. H. (Director). (1966). *Batman: The Movie* [Motion Picture]. United States: Twentieth Century Fox.

England, D. E., Descartes, L., & Collier-Meek, M. A. (2011). Gender role portrayal and the Disney princesses. *Sex Roles, 64*(7), 555–567. https://doi.org/10.1007/s11199-011-9930-7.

Franco, L., Roven, C., Thomas, E. (Producer), & Nolan, C. (Director). (2005). *Batman Begins* [Motion Picture]. United States: Warner Bros. Pictures.

Garger, M., Lee, R., Lin, D. Lord, P., McKay, C., Miller, C. (Producer), Bean, C., Fisher, P., & Logan, B. (Director). (2017). *The Lego Ninjago Movie* [Motion Picture]. United States: Warner Bros. Pictures.

Gregg, P. B. (2018). Brick-olage and the LEGO/brand axis. *The Popular Culture Studies Journal, 6*(1), 29–44.

Gruber, P., Peters, J. (Producer), & Burton, T. (Director). (1989). *Batman* [Motion Picture]. United States: Warner Bros. Pictures.

Halberstam, J. (1998). *Female masculinity*. Durham: Duke University Press.

Hentges, B., & Case, K. (2013). Gender representations on Disney Channel, Cartoon Network and Nickelodeon broadcasts in the United States. *Journal of Children and Media, 7*(3), 319–333. https://doi.org/10.1080/17482798.2012.729150.

Hills, M. (2016). LEGO Dimensions meets Doctor Who: Transbranding and new dimensions of transmedia storytelling? *Icono14, 14*(1), 8–29. https://doi.org/10.7195/ri14.v14i1.942.

Johnson, D. (2014). Chicks with bricks: Building creativity across industrial design cultures and gendered construction play. In M. J. P. Wolf (Ed.), *LEGO studies: Examining the building blocks of transmedial phenomenon* (pp. 81–104). New York, NY: Routledge.

Johnson, J. (2017). *The Lego Batman Movie* is the Brokeback Batman we've always wanted. *The Root*. Retrieved from https://www.theroot.com/the-lego-batman-movie-is-the-brokeback-batman-we-ve-alw-1792203215. Accessed on November 3, 2018.

Kellner, D. (2013). Media spectacle and domestic terrorism: The case of the Batman/Joker cinema massacre, review of education, pedagogy, and cultural studies. *Review of Education Pedagogy, and Cultural Studies, 35*(4), 157–177. https://doi.org/10.1080/10714413.2013.799364.

Lee, R., Lin, D. (Producer), Lord, P., & Miller, C. (Director). (2014). *The LEGO Movie* [Motion Picture]. United States: Warner Bros. Pictures.

Lemish, D. (2010). *Screening gender on children's television: The views of producers around the world.* New York, NY: Routledge.

Lin, D., Lord, P., Miller, C. (Producer), & McKay, C. (Director). (2017). *The LEGO Batman Movie* [Motion Picture]. United States: Warner Bros. Pictures.

Lin, D., Lord, P., Miller, C. (Producer), & Mitchell, M. (Director). (2010). *The LEGO Movie 2: The Second Part* [Motion Picture]. United States: Warner Bros. Pictures.

Luther, C. A., & Legg, J. R., Jr. (2010). Gender differences in depictions of social and physical aggression in children's television cartoons in the US. *Journal of Children and Media, 4*(10), 191–205. https://doi.org/10.1080/17482791003629651.

Macgregor-Scott, P. (Producer), & Schumacher, J. (Director). (1997). *Batman & Robin* [Motion Picture]. United States: Warner Bros. Pictures.

Medhurst, A. (1991). Batman deviance and camp. In R. E. Pearson & W. Uricchio (Eds.), *The many lives of the Batman: Critical approaches to a superhero and his media* (pp. 149–163). New York, NY: Routledge.

Miller, F. (1986). *Batman: The dark knight returns.* New York, NY: DC Comics.

Mittell, J. (2014). Afterword: D.I.Y. disciplinarity—(Dis)Assembling LEGO studies for the academy. In M. J. P. Wolf (Ed.), *LEGO studies: Examining the building blocks of transmedial phenomenon* (pp. 268–274). New York, NY: Routledge.

Moore, A. (1988). *Batman: The killing joke.* New York, NY: DC Comics.

Nolan, C., Roven, C., Thomas E. (Producer), & Nolan, C. (Director). (2008). *The Dark Knight* [Motion Picture]. United States: Warner Bros. Pictures.

Posada, T. (2013). Canonizing *The Dark Knight*: A digital fandom response. In L. Burke (Ed.), *Fan phenomena: Batman* (pp. 78–89). Chicago, IL: Intellect Books.

Reich, S. M., Black, R. W., & Foliaki, T. (2017). Construction difference: Lego set narratives promote stereotypic gender roles and play. *Sex Roles, 79*(5–6), 285–298. https://doi.org/10.1007/s11199-017-0868-2.

Reynolds, D. (2017). Religious right blasts *Lego Batman* for 'Pro-gay propaganda.' *Advocate.* Retrieved from https://www.advocate.com/

film/2017/2/22/religious-right-blasts-lego-batman-pro-gay-propaganda. Accessed on November.

Roven, C., Snyder, D. (Producer), & Snyder, Z. (Director). (2016). *Batman v. Superman: Dawn of Justice* [Motion Picture]. United States: Warner Bros. Pictures.

Serrato, P. (2011). From "booger breath" to "the guy": Juni Cortez grows up in Robert Rodriguez's *Spy Kids* trilogy. In A. Wannamaker (Ed.), *Mediated boyhoods: Boys, teens, and young men in popular media and culture* (pp. 81–96). New York, NY: Peter Lang.

Shyminsky, N. (2011). "Gay" sidekicks: Queer anxiety and the narrative straightening of the superhero. *Men and Masculinities, 14*(3), 288–308. https://doi.org/10.1177/1097184X10368787.

Smith, S. L., Pieper, K. M., Granados, A., & Chouetti, M. (2010). Assessing gender-related portrayals in top-grossing G-Rated films. *Sex Roles, 62*(11), 774–786. https://doi.org/10.1007/s11199-009-9736-z.

Tanner, L. R., Haddock, S. A., Zimmerman, T. S., & Lund, L. K. (2003). Images of couples and families in Disney feature-length animated films. *The American Journal of Family Therapy, 31*(5), 355–373. https://doi.org/10.1080/01926180390223987.

Thompson, T. L., & Zerbinos, E. (1995). Gender roles in animated cartoons: Has the pictured changed in 20 years? *Sex Roles, 32*(9/10), 651–673. https://doi.org/10.1007/BF01544217.

Tipton, N. G. (2008). Gender trouble: Frank Miller's revision of Robin in the *Batman: Dark Knight* series. *The Journal of Popular Culture, 41*(2), 321–336. https://doi.org/10.1111/j.1540-5931.2008.00505.x.

Torres, S. (1999). The caped crusader of camp: Pop, camp, and the Batman television series. In F. Cleto (Ed.), *Camp: Queer aesthetics and the performing subject—A reader* (pp. 330–343). Ann Arbor: University of Michigan Press.

Weston, K. (1991). *Families we choose: Lesbians, gays, kinship.* New York, NY: Columbia University Press.

Winstead, N. (2015). "As a symbol I can be incorruptible": How Christopher Nolan de-queered the Batman of Joel Schumacher. *The Journal of Popular Culture, 48*(3), 572–585. https://doi.org/doi.org/10.1111/jpcu.12228.

Wolf, M. (2014). Prolegomena. In M. J. P. Wolf (Ed.), *LEGO studies: Examining the building blocks of transmedial phenomenon* (pp. xxi–xxv). New York, NY: Routledge.

Wooden, S., & Gillam, K. (2016). *Pixar's boy stories: Masculinity in a postmodern age.* Lanham, MD: Rowan and Littlefield.

14

A License to Diversify: Media Franchising and the Transformation of the "Universal" LEGO Minifigure

Derek Johnson

Prior to The LEGO Group's embrace of media licenses like *Star Wars* in 1999, the ubiquitous minifigure's faces and hands had always been cast in a yellow plastic meant to identify an unmarked, universal, implicitly White racial identity. The need to represent the explicitly racialized bodies of popular screen characters and stars prompted minifigure bodies' diversification, now produced in colors like "light nougat" and "reddish brown."[1] Even as LEGO's diversified its licensed products over the next fifteen years, its public disclosures, promotions and self-produced screen narratives (like *The LEGO Movie*) continued to present racially differentiated bodies as anomalies, favoring a corporate alignment with the standard yellow minifigure's unmarked racial universalism (Johnson 2014b).

Since 2015, however, LEGO's licensed products have revealed an intensification of this embrace of diversity at the levels of both race and gender, where non-White and non-male bodies have become a more pervasive part of the construction play on offer. On one hand, the

D. Johnson (✉)
University of Wisconsin-Madison, Madison, WI, USA
e-mail: drjohnson3@wisc.edu

© The Author(s) 2019
R. C. Hains and S. R. Mazzarella (eds.), *Cultural Studies of LEGO*,
https://doi.org/10.1007/978-3-030-32664-7_14

White-Black binary that initially prompted LEGO to distinguish the Black character Lando Calrissian from the rest of *Star Wars'* White cast has given way to multi-hued minifigures production based on characters played by Asian and Latinx actors, too (like Chirrut Imwe, Baze Malbus and Cassian Andor from *Rogue One*). On the other, LEGO encourages consumers to build generic "army building" minifigures (like anonymous Rebel and Imperial soldiers included alongside these hero *Star Wars* characters) from an increasingly diverse pool of pieces. These new pieces—building blocks of embodied difference—include not only minifigure heads in several different colors and printings, but also new hairpieces meant to broaden the scope of gender and race differentiated bodies that can be made with LEGO.

This chapter interrogates this intensification in LEGO's commitment to diversity through its contributions to major media franchises—as well as LEGO's potential to apply these principles to its new independent product brands. First, the chapter situates this diversification of representational choices in minifigure design against casting politics in the media franchises from which LEGO draws. As Hollywood's licensed partner, LEGO follows suit in contributing to pro-social, politically conscious brand identities, exploiting diversity's value as marketers increasingly imagine target consumers in terms of changing demographics and global growth potential (particularly in Asia). Secondly, however, the chapter considers how The LEGO Group's participation in media franchising's diversity politics reinforces its own brand positioning within the construction toy market. While LEGO follows suit, it also applies industrial diversity discourses to its corporate brand, design and representational practices beyond media-themed products. Lastly, then, even as claims about the "universal" qualities of the minifigure persist within LEGO's marketing, this chapter asks how LEGO innovates design practices and logics of differentiation in new product lines that imagine consumers—and their play objects—as raced and gendered subjects. With that in mind, the chapter argues that LEGO's licensed practice is more than a field of socially differentiated representation that parallels its more universalized modes of representation: It is also the site from which challenges to politics of universality can emerge.

In building this argument, this chapter extends previous research I have conducted examining LEGO's recent efforts to both build stronger appeals to inclusivity and redesign its minifigure product to accommodate greater differentiation between gendered and raced bodies (Johnson 2014a, b). The launch of the LEGO Friends theme in 2012, for example, represented an effort to design new products imagined as a separate space of girls' construction play, avoiding the disruption of other product themes' existing boy-appeal. This redesign included gendered alternative to minifigures called "mini-dolls." As LEGO design director Rosario Costa claimed, girls "needed a figure they could identify with, that looks like them" (Wieners 2011). This claim's dubious gender essentialism reveals fissures in the ideology of universality surrounding the minifigure, questioning its ability to serve all consumers' needs. Moreover, these mini-dolls followed a decade of experimentation in LEGO's media licensed product, borrowing its palette of colors to represent different skin tones—a key development in licensed minifigure production now carrying over to new product brands controlled exclusively by LEGO. This chapter will explore some of those linkages, asking how the intersections and representational logics of these design practices have accelerated amid changing industrial discourses and branded orientations toward diversity and inclusion.

As in that previous research, the construction of gender scripts, racial privileges and the politics of differentiating bodies continue to drive the inquiry; but here, those considerations increasingly intersect with interrogation of corporate social responsibility strategies (Banet-Weiser 2012; Ouellette 2018) through which the discourses and practices of culture industries extend from investment in pro-social values like diversity and global cosmopolitanism as means of extending brands and markets. The bodies that children can construct with LEGO minifigures and other construction play elements matter: They are material interfaces by which many children understand participation (and implicit limits thereof) in the creativity of construction play. The LEGO Group claims that "Through the power of play, we inspire children of all ages" ("Responsibility Report 2017" 2017, p. 3). By extension, the possibilities of what bodies children can and cannot build with LEGO speak to who the company imagines as part of its branded culture of play.

Thus, this chapter reveals how LEGO's media diversity discourses—in which the company invests in part as a result of its licensing strategies—have refigured those possibilities, while at the same time showing how LEGO has absorbed those diversity values across its wider catalog. In tracing these relationships, we can see both how the licensing practices of media franchising can be a catalyst for more diverse and inclusive cultural commodities and how that capacity for change gets incorporated within the culture industries' design, product differentiation and branding strategies.

Diverse Characters and Product Differentiation

LEGO's ongoing partnership with Disney as a *Star Wars* franchise licensee significantly pushed its product design practices into the industrial politics of diversity and inclusivity—somewhat ironically, given the firestorm of controversy surrounding the franchise's merchandising more generally. Anticipating the release of *Star Wars: Episode VII—The Force Awakens* during the holiday season, Disney and its merchandising and retail partners coordinated a September 2015 marketing event called "Force Friday" highlighting all the newly available consumer products in conjunction with the film's marketing. As paratexts (Gray 2010), these products would shape the as-yet-unreleased film's reception, with the marketing blitz creating expectations and signaling which characters might be of the greatest importance and value. However, as Suzanne Scott (2017) explores, this merchandising downplayed the role of Rey, the female character centered in the trailers and revealed in the final film as the new, light saber wielding Jedi protagonist empowered by the Force. In response, commodity activists used social media to ask "#WheresRey?", disappointed that the film's arguable advances in providing strong female characters did not extend to the merchandise. These products instead reflected conservative industry assumptions that the target audience of men and boys would prefer to see themselves reflected in the available merchandise (even as this did result in greater marketing attention being paid to the non-White character, Finn).

Hashtag activists took toy manufacturer Hasbro to task for failing to include Rey in its first wave of action figures to accompany the film.

LEGO's *Force Awakens* toys received less criticism by comparison, perhaps because they took a different approach in incorporating both gender diversity and non-White representations. Most obviously, Rey was conspicuously present in LEGO's merchandising of *The Force Awakens*—no one would need to ask where she was. Retailing at $19.99, the cheapest and thus most plentiful, accessible construction set related to the film was 75099 Rey's Speeder, a 193-piece representation of the hovering vehicle she pilots early in the film. This set included a Rey minifigure complete with both the helmet that covers her face in the sequence and a separate hairpiece that could be used with the feminine face printed on the head piece beneath the helmet. LEGO could have withheld the alternate hairpiece to limit this Rey figure's use to speeder piloting alone; indeed, LEGO regularly offers minor minifigure variants of different characters, rather than providing alternate heads and hairpieces in the same set, to motivate sales of multiple sets. But LEGO did not make this choice here. To be fair, the inclusion of that helmet could have helped to mitigate concerns about the marketability of a female character, masking her gender identity; the box art features an image of the feminine-faced Rey minifigure in the corner, but the larger action scene presents a faceless and thus more genderless warrior. However, regardless of any potential equivocation, LEGO was unafraid of making Rey this product's center of attention, including only one other character minifigure: the nameless, faceless "Unkar Henchman." Rey was not necessarily the center of the whole *Force Awakens* line: The key art shared across all product instead featured villain Kylo Ren. In terms of minifigure placement, however, LEGO most frequently relied upon the Rey character, including her in both the cheapest and the most expensive set (the 1329-piece 75104 Millennium Falcon at $149.99), suggesting her character had high value, too. The consumer who purchased all seven sets in the first *Force Awakens* product wave would thus ultimately collect two minifigures each of Rey and the droid BB-8, while characters like Finn and Kylo Ren would appear only in single sets. While Rey was therefore less rare, this relative accessibility and ubiquity presented a definite answer to the question, "#WheresRey?"

Perhaps more important, however, were the representational innovations introduced by LEGO's *The Force Awakens* product. The Finn minifigure was preceded by only a handful of non-White characters from media narratives that LEGO had produced in minifigure form. Like most of those figures, the face of Black British actor John Boyega was represented in "reddish brown" in contrast to the "light flesh" of Rey or the standard yellow of non-licensed minifigures. Much as toymaker Mattel had previously engaged in the practice of dye-dipping to create Black Barbie dolls (duCille 1996), prior Black minifigures like Lando had shared the same hair mold with White characters like Han Solo, just cast in a different color. However, Finn also featured for the first time a new hairpiece that more clearly differentiated him from White characters. Starting with its *Force Awakens* line, LEGO also began incorporating phenotypical representation in its "army building" minifigures beyond those that represented specific named characters played by actors of specific racial and gender identity. Instead, in sets like 75101 First Order Special Forces TIE Fighter, LEGO offered generic, nameless minifigure heads and bodies in colors other than yellow or "light flesh." The "First Order Officer" included in the TIE Fighter set was clearly non-White and moreover allowed for a greater range of phenotypical difference to be incorporated into the imagined worlds of LEGO play, as this minifigure was cast in "medium dark flesh" and not the same "reddish brown" used for Finn (or Lando before him). In this way, LEGO figured the possibility of racial difference as a deeper, more integrated part of the ways consumers might build their *Star Wars* universe. Similarly, the First Order Officer in the larger 75104 Kylo Ren's Command Shuttle set disrupted the ubiquity of White male embodiment in the Star Wars universe (and its industrial marketing). Rather than another nameless male henchman to accompany the named Kylo Ren and General Hux figures in the Command Shuttle, this First Order Officer featured a feminine face. The presentation of that face in "light flesh" plastic certainly extended the prevalence of Whiteness in the First Order command structure, but it helped pry open a space to imagine female power within that hierarchy. Lest we put too much emphasis on the dubious merits of female and non-White empowerment within the overtly fascistic power dynamics of the

First Order, it should also be noted that the 75140 Resistance Troop Transporter from the second wave of *Force Awakens* product in early 2016 engaged in the same diversification of the franchise's Resistance faction's ranks, providing a nameless female solider in addition to the hero General Leia minifigure.

Undoubtedly, LEGO's moves here follow shifts in on-screen representations and greater attention to the politics of diversity within industrial management of the *Star Wars* universe. The ability of LEGO to produce minifigures based on non-White or female characters like Rey, Finn and pilot Poe Dameron depended on a broader professional investment in diversity in casting that had rendered the population of *Force Awakens* far less homogenous compared to previous franchise entries. In the summer before the film's release, director J.J. Abrams and producer Kathleen Kennedy articulated this conscious effort as "a big commitment" (Statt 2015). The Hollywood trade press later portrayed this commitment as quantifiable, citing script analysis that proved significant increases in on-screen speaking time for women and non-White characters (Lopez 2017b), while other critics noted that four women enjoyed any spoken lines across the whole of the original 1977–1983 trilogy (Wade and Riseman 2017). Beyond speaking roles, the population of *Force Awakens* also looked different. In the original trilogy, female and non-White characters like Princess Leia and Lando Calrissian, respectively, were token exceptions in a universe where any gathered crowd—whether Rebel pilots in hidden bases or Imperial officers crewing their stations—would be uniformly White and male. In Abrams' film, however, women and people of color filled these everyday background roles, weaving diversity more profoundly into the texture of the universe (a change recognized by fans) (Hayes 2015). Even the First Order now seemed to embrace women and people of color, its fascism suggested to be a human supremacism communicated by the comparably greater presence of aliens in the Resistance. As produced by LEGO, then, minifigures like the First Order Officers were part of a concerted reorientation of the franchise toward greater diversity and inclusivity.

This shift only intensified a year later when products released in conjunction with *Rogue One* reflected the racial diversity of the film's cast.

Multiple characters played by Asian actors, including Chirrut Imwe and Baze Malbus, differentiated LEGO's new product from all the *Star Wars* building sets that had previously operated in a binary of Black and White. Their inclusion in LEGO form extended their centrality to the film's broader marketing. Industry reports noted that "two of China's biggest stars," Donnie Yen and Jiang Wen, had been cast in these roles explicitly out of "a bid to bring Chinese fans deeper into the 'Star Wars' universe." Although Chinese box-office returns for *Rogue One* were ultimately disappointing, these characters figured as global selling points who could be positioned "front and center" in marketing the film (Brzeski 2016). As a licensee, LEGO thus participated in Disney's conscious Asian outreach efforts through its production and marketing of Yen and Wen's characters in minifigure form.

However, the *Star Wars* franchise does not stand alone in Hollywood through this investment in diverse casting and service to global audiences. On the contrary, studios like Disney have developed broader strategic commitments to diversity and other values of corporate social responsibility ("Corporate" 2017). As one report in trade publication *Variety* (Lopez 2017a) maintained, box-office profitability could be positively correlated to on-screen diversity, particularly as the share of White filmgoers dropped amid changing US demographics and the growing importance of Asian markets in the global box office. Comscore market analyst Paul Dergarabedian provided the powerful quote that even "if you want to take the most absolute cynical view and say that everything in Hollywood is powered by the almighty dollar, then it still makes sense to have more diverse movies" (Lopez 2017a). As Aynne Kokas (2017) has argued in this context, Hollywood has also increasingly recognized the value of courting global audiences, particularly large emerging audiences in China—another factor leading casting directors, studio executives and marketers to embrace inclusivity. As such, *Vanity Fair* author Yohana Desta (2016) marked 2016 as "The Year Disney Started to Take Diversity Seriously" and presented "more inclusive visions of everything from classic musicals to a galaxy far, far away." At that time, the company had promised to feature ethnic minority leads in a quarter of its live-action films in the subsequent two years, while motion picture production president Sean Bailey attested,

"Inclusivity is not only a priority but an imperative for us, and it's top of mind on every single project" (Ford 2016). African-American director Ava DuVernay (who would direct Disney's 2018 *A Wrinkle in Time*) validated the company's efforts as "really killing it across the board in terms of the depth of the bench and the commitment to an inclusive slate" and credited Disney executives like Bailey for being "really, really forward-thinking" (Desta 2016).

In addition to this forward-thinking promise, Disney also sought to manage criticism of its representational practices—particularly in relation to concurrent accusations of whitewashing in superhero narratives like the *Doctor Strange* film and the *Iron Fist* television series. Both of these Marvel Studios projects foregrounded White heroes in stories with orientalist themes. According to trade reports in *Variety*, then, Hollywood's commitment to diversity "isn't entirely a rosy picture" (Holloway and Lang 2016) as companies like Disney repositioned and defended themselves. "That transition of diversity from the back burner to the hot stove," Daniel Holloway and Brent Lang (2016) wrote, "has changed the way that casting directors operate." Thus, as casting directors and studio development executives responded to these opportunities and criticisms, media franchises have gradually shifted their character (and characters). Disney's Marvel Studios franchise, for example, has gradually expanded and diversified the ranks of the Avengers superhero team over the course of more than twenty films since 2008. Until 2014, the series alternated between solo films for three White male heroes—Iron Man, Captain America and Thor— and team-up films like *The Avengers* with an expanded but still all-White group of six primary heroes (including the female spy, Black Widow). In this early period, "diversity" translated to the supporting of presence of Black mentor figures, best friends and sidekicks like Nick Fury, War Machine, The Falcon and Heimdall. The franchise's expansion from 2014 and beyond, however, followed Disney's strategic and public revaluation of diversity as a corporate value. In that context, *Black Panther* and *Captain Marvel* created a space for non-White and female-led films; *Spider-Man: Homecoming* (co-produced with Sony) resituated the White hero within a more diverse high school setting; and tokenism was arguably reduced as the huge ensemble casts of *Captain America: Civil*

War and *Avengers: Infinity War* accommodated more than one woman or person of color at a time.

The Force Awakens was therefore not isolated in its attempts to inject further diversity into franchise media production and marketing. Instead, it spoke to wider corporate efforts to rework the media franchise universes offered to consumers. As a licensee of these franchises, The LEGO Group surely found itself following suit. In the wake of *Force Awakens*, many other licensed LEGO themes also intensified their offerings of female and non-White minifigures. The LEGO Marvel Super Heroes line, for example, followed the course set by the increasingly diverse casting practices of the Marvel Cinematic Universe. 2016 brought Falcon and Agent 13 minifigures based on the *Captain America: Civil War* film, as well as the Ancient One from *Doctor Strange*, while 2017 introduced new female characters from *Thor: Ragnarok*, including Hela and Valkyrie, a dark-skinned Asgardian who further diversified the potential for building women of color in LEGO form. A Wasp minifigure followed the next year in conjunction with *Ant-Man and the Wasp*. At that same time, an exclusive minifigure set designed for a Toys "R" Us retail promotion also featured (alongside another War Machine) the Asian mystic Wong, who played a supporting role in both *Doctor Strange* and *Avengers: Infinity War*, inserting Asian bodies into the play of Marvel Superheroes for the first time.

Meanwhile, even as LEGO focused its efforts on supporting Marvel's film properties, it continued to offer more diverse representations in its sets based on comics characters. While sets released in this period included new characters such as She-Hulk, perhaps most notable is the inclusion of Ms. Marvel in the 2017 set 76076 Captain America Jet Pursuit. LEGO based this Ms. Marvel minifigure upon the Kamala Khan character whose solo comic book series launched in 2014 as part of a line-wide editorial interest in placing more diverse superheroes at the center of its publishing strategy. The 2012–2016 campaign, referred to as "Marvel Now!", sought to attract a new readership to Marvel's comic book product, an editorial mandate that encouraged creative teams to reinterpret existing characters and explore a broader range of hero identities. For example, writer Cullen Bunn was given the reins to the legacy superhero team *The Defenders* in order to shine "a spotlight on a few lesser-known Marvel characters" and reimagine it as an "all-female team" (Ching 2012). The next year, Brian Wood would similarly write an all-female *X-Men* title. By 2014, Marvel's interest in diversity led to high-profile announcements about the prioritization of female and non-White characters. Editor-in-chief Joe Quesada appeared on *The Colbert Report* to announce that an African-American character would take on the mantle of Captain America, as Sam Wilson would set aside his role as The Falcon to take over from the White hero Steve Rogers. Meanwhile, Thor's identity would be inherited by a mystery female character, with Marvel editor Wil Moss promising, "The new Thor continues Marvel's proud tradition of strong female characters like Captain Marvel, Storm, Black Widow and more. And this new Thor isn't a temporary female substitute—she's now the one and only Thor, and she is worthy" (Graser 2014). Kamala Khan extended this strategy: Adopting the legacy of Ms. Marvel (after its previous steward Carol Danvers embraced the Captain Marvel moniker), Khan is a young Muslim American from Jersey City grappling with her overlapping religious, teen, fan and superhero identities. She constructs her superhero persona with a costume that evokes influences from traditional *shalwar kameez* styles, rather than the sexualized look previously embodied by Danvers (Dev 2015). Editor Sana Amanat described the series as extending from the company's "desire to explore the Muslim-American diaspora from an authentic perspective" (Duke 2013).

LEGO's embrace of this interpretation of Ms. Marvel thus imports this representation of Muslim-American identity and authentic costuming into the materiality of the minifigure. Here, too, LEGO's representational diversity followed market logics set into motion at the broader level of the branded media franchise from which it draws. LEGO's decision to embrace Ms. Marvel in 2017 occurred at the same time that Disney and Marvel provided significant support for the character elsewhere in the media and retail sectors. In August 2017, for example, the Disney Store was "gearing up for the Halloween season" with the sale of a Kamala Khan dress-up costume (Cohen 2017). That same year, Marvel and Disney announced plans for an animation franchise called *Marvel Rising,* in which Ms. Marvel played a key role as part of a female-led and racially diverse team of heroes including America

Chavez, Quake and Squirrel Girl (Dinh 2017). Ms. Marvel's existence in LEGO form, in other words, spoke more to the character's placement in the management of a larger media franchise than any activist stance by The LEGO Group.

Meanwhile, through the DC Super Heroes theme (produced through a license with Warner Bros. Consumer Products, not Disney), LEGO expanded its roster of female minifigures beyond Wonder Woman, Batgirl and Harley Quinn to include Starfire, Supergirl and Lois Lane in 2015; Katana and Talia al Ghul in 2016; and Cheetah, Killer Frost, Mera and Batwoman in 2018. LEGO also contributed new product to the larger DC Super Hero Girls sub-brand (Tussey and Bak 2019), offering in 2017 new construction sets accompanied by the "mini-dolls" developed for the LEGO Friends theme. These mini-dolls emphasized female DC characters including Batgirl, Harley Quinn, Lena Luthor, Poison Ivy, Supergirl, Bumblebee, Mad Harriet and Eclipso. LEGO's increase in production of DC minifigures based on non-White characters was less stark. The Bumblebee mini-doll joined minifigures based on Cyborg and Firestorm in representing Black super hero characters, but the racial difference of Katana did not require visual acknowledgment due to the character's facemask, while the Arabic identity of Talia and her Ra's al Ghul were similarly undifferentiated by LEGO designers.

However, the production of *The LEGO Batman Movie*—and its attendant construction sets—did generate in 2017 more significant moves toward conscious representation of racial difference within the building elements offered to consumers. Although the characters of Barbara Gordon/Batgirl and her father, Commission Gordon, had previously been coded as White in most DC Comics, films and even previous LEGO sets, the film darkened the skin tones for both characters (in this case, using "medium dark flesh" plastic) and cast Rosario Dawson, an actor of Puerto Rican and Cuban descent, to voice Barbara. The choice to "race-bend" (Lopez 2012, p. 432) these key characters suggests LEGO recognized the value of diversifying superhero product in both film and merchandising markets. Batgirl serves doubly in that capacity, offering consumers not just a female point of identification with superhero construction play, but a non-White one, as well.

The LEGO Batman Movie also followed the casting of African-American actor Billy Dee Williams as Harvey Dent in the 1989 *Batman* film, employing the actor to reprise the character after his transformation into the villain Two-Face, now represented in the LEGO film in "medium dark flesh" colors. Chief O'Hara—a male police character from the 1966 *Batman* television series—is similarly gender-swapped in the new film. The dozens of villains and supporting characters featured also enabled LEGO to produce several more female and/or non-White characters across its branded product lines, including Mayor McCaskill, Magpie, Tarantula, Aaron Cash, Hawkgirl Mime, March Harriet, Apache Chief, Black Canary, Black Vulcan and an unnamed Police Officer. More recently in 2018, LEGO made Jessica Cruz and Hal Jordan minifigures available as promotional items in the *Aquaman: Rage of Atlantis* home video release and DK Publishing's *Build Your Own Adventure* book, replicating DC Comics' efforts to extend the Green Lantern mantle to female and non-White heroes. While it is difficult to determine whether the push to bend characters like Batgirl and O'Hara toward more diverse representation came from LEGO or its production partners at Warner Bros., LEGO has clearly shifted from cautiously including female and non-White characters in its construction sets to actively seeking out opportunities to provide them to consumers.

The *Harry Potter* theme's resurgence in 2018 similarly reflected this shift in representational strategy, while also pointing to some newer LEGO marketing practices behind it. As with the original 2001–2007 and 2010–2012 product themes, new products released in 2018 offered multiple opportunities to collect minifigures based on the three core White heroes Harry, Ron and Hermione: Each appears in at least three of the five 2018 offerings, not counting additional appearances in small point-of-sale and promotional items. However, the need to differentiate product on the basis of its exclusive minifigure offerings also prompts LEGO to include in those same sets secondary and even tertiary characters whose marginality can be a marketing asset. Thus, alongside multiple Harrys, Rons and Hermiones, these kits include lesser-known (and never before produced) characters like Hufflepuff student Susan Bones, or the Trolley Witch who sells Chocolate Frogs on the Hogwarts Express. Moreover, the expansion of LEGO's licensed product lines created opportunities for a greater number of products and scope of representation within them as the combination of collectability, production differentiation and representational difference collided. For example, the *Harry Potter* construction theme, like *The LEGO Batman Movie*, is supported by a line of Collectible Minifigures: blind-bag items which contain a mystery character. The sales of these items are motivated by searches for rare or in-demand characters, and at $3.99 each, these Collectible Minifigures support a wider range of characters beyond those than that LEGO uses to anchor product marketed in excess of $99.99 or more. Thus, the *Harry Potter* Collectible Minifigure series features characters with cult followings like Luna Lovegood, but also supporting characters of color, like Harry's brief love interest Cho Chang and his roommate Dean Thomas—neither produced in any way during earlier iterations of LEGO's *Harry Potter* theme. In just one year, LEGO represented a far more diverse and inclusive Wizarding World than it had in nine years of previous production.

Building Diversity Beyond Media Licenses

These examples do not include other licensed LEGO themes introduced since 2015, such as *Jurassic Park*, *Overwatch*, *Powerpuff Girls* and more. Whereas it was once easy to count single, tokenistic exceptions to White male ubiquity in these licensed media products, LEGO has invested in a somewhat more complex matrix of social differentiation within its product differentiation strategies. This acknowledgment of representational shifts is not intended to celebrate unproblematic corporate "progress," however; The LEGO Group has largely followed the lead of Disney and other Hollywood studios that pursue diversity and inclusivity from recognition of its market value. Construction toy design licensed to work with media brands borrows not only familiar characters explicitly marked by race and gender, but also market strategies for exploiting those differences.

Nevertheless, The LEGO Group's willingness to embrace the market strategies accompanying its media licenses also tracks with its own construction of corporate social responsibility through a commitment to the ideals of diversity as well as its own parallel attempts to reach new markets through product redesign. In the 2013 corporate "Responsibility Report" released by The LEGO Group a year after the introduction of LEGO Friends, for example, the company articulated an "aim…to ensure that we apply sufficient gender awareness in our product design and marketing development" and touted "new Gender Marketing Guidelines [that] underline how to strike a balance when creating communication and products that appeal to both boys and girls…ensuring that children are not being subjected to, or limited by, gender stereotypes" (Responsibility 2013, p. 55). Although LEGO is generally less vocal about racial politics, the Friends mini-doll served the pursuit of corporate branding at this level as well. Initially, abandonment of the standard minifigure's yellow skin tones and the adoption of those used in media licensed themes allowed one of the five main Friends characters, Andrea, to be coded as non-White. In 2017, however, LEGO announced that these main characters would have "a slightly different look" going forward—most notably with Olivia now having darker skin, too, although some consumers also perceived additional changes designed to code Emma as Asian (Tran 2017). With the change explained as a response to child consumers who "told us that they would like even more differentiated characters," the race of these characters was a conscious question of product design—and redesign—positioned in corporate disclosures as a response to consumers' social needs.

The LEGO Group also maintains its own interests in the value of diversity in a global marketplace where consumers and competitors in Asia increasingly figure as part of corporate strategy. Given the demand for its product and its premium price, LEGO has contended with unlicensed consumer product manufacturers in Asia who offer low-cost pirated alternatives in local markets. These competitors do not honor the intellectual property claims of media licensing partners any more than those of The LEGO Group. Thus, Chinese consumers can easily find alternatives to official LEGO product in which copycat companies like Lepin precisely reproduce the product and packaging offered in themes like LEGO *Star Wars* or Super Heroes. These products demonstrate untapped market potential in Asia, as well as The LEGO Group's frustrations in managing its brands there. In 2017 and 2018, however, LEGO emerged victorious in Chinese court cases that found companies like Lepin to be engaged in unfair practices, creating new possibilities for competition in this market ("Toymaker" 2018). A more aggressive Asian outlook was thus accompanied by a commitment to developing new kinds of LEGO product. When LEGO announced in 2018 a series of products exclusive to Asia, it newly deployed the yellow minifigure to participate in the valuable Chinese market's "iconic new year traditions." The Chinese New Year's Eve Dinner set centered on "a Chinese family reuniting to celebrate the lunar new year in a traditional home," while The Dragon Dance offered "a symbol of Chinese Culture" (Tran 2018). Yet unlike the 1998–1999 Ninja theme that marked racial difference by adding slanted eyes to the default yellow minifigure head, these Asia-exclusive sets utilized the same heads and face printing used in other LEGO themes, relying upon the clothing prints on minifigure torsos and legs to convey local difference as a cultural rather than phenotypical one. Thus, even as the "standard" yellow minifigure continued to be an important component in the construction of LEGO bodies, its meanings showed some signs of change—no longer a refusal of difference based in universality, but a more flexible component to be used in the production of local difference.

In such ways, LEGO is both following the lead of Hollywood and incorporating discourses of diversity shared with major media franchises within its own corporate branding strategies. Notably, recent "Responsibility Reports" (2016, 2017) issued by The LEGO Group do not speak as explicitly to the values of diversity in product design as those that had accompanied LEGO Friends, placing greater emphasis on environmental impact and focusing instead on the politics of gender in internal hiring practices. As an articulation of corporate cultural identity, the Responsibility Reports seem most interested in highlighting product design diversity when the feted introduction of new product supports those concerns. Nevertheless, across claims of corporate social responsibility and the management of difference within licensed media franchises, LEGO continues to grapple with the possibilities of rendering social difference buildable through its interlocking elements. While efforts in the realm of licensing depended on The LEGO Group's interest in borrowing the recognizable faces and bodies of franchised media characters, other efforts have relied upon a different kind of borrowing in which the company confronts consumers with the gendered and raced buildability of their own faces and bodies.

Licensing Consumer Identity

This move toward representing the body of the consumer unfolded across two different specialty LEGO products introduced in 2017 and 2018. The first was the Mosaic Maker, an in-store experience in which shoppers could step into a photo booth to have their faces scanned, leaving with a printed set of instructions for creating a mosaic of that image out of a kit of 1 × 1 LEGO tile elements. The London LEGO brand store introduced this product in 2017 (at a cost of 99 GBP), and it arrived the next year at other locations throughout Europe, Asia and the rest of the world (in the United States, this service costs $129.99) (Admin 2018). Despite the price, the final product generated from the Mosaic Maker would not be a full-color rendering. Mosaic Maker users received a standardized kit of 4500 tiles evenly distributed across only four grayscale colors plus yellow for the background. LEGO designers anticipated that not all faces would need the same number of each color; any one 48 × 48 portrait would only use 2304 of those tiles. The 2196 extra tiles exist only to accommodate variation in human difference. The number of excess pieces required to produce a full-color mosaic in tiles of the same color as LEGO minifigures—including "reddish brown," "nougat," "light flesh," and "medium dark flesh" and potentially many more—would almost surely require more variation in pieces that would make a standardized building kit untenable. Moreover, in producing a grayscale rendering, the Mosaic Maker dodges the question of which phenotypes might be privileged or rendered invisible by LEGO's current palette for representing racial difference. Instead, all faces are transformed into black and white.

In this way, the Mosaic Maker confronts designers and consumers alike with the representational practices and politics of LEGO building and the problems of universality. Even after LEGO introduced flesh-toned minifigures in its licensed sets, the company continued to assert that the ubiquitous yellow minifigure represented an unmarked, universal form of representation that anyone could identify with—but that universalism often produced Whiteness as an unmarked default category, as themes like Pirates and more sought to modify the yellow-faced minifigure to represent different racialized and ethnicized people (Johnson 2014b, pp. 314–315). While the Mosaic Maker provides a universal kit with which to self-represent oneself in LEGO form, it does not present any single configuration of tiles as the ideal from which other uses might deviate. Although The LEGO Group would no doubt avoid overtly discussing the racial politics of these design choices, it is worth imagining the calculations designers made to ensure every consumer would have enough pieces to render their own face, no matter how light or dark—as well as the decision-making process behind the choice to offer equal numbers of white, black, light gray and dark gray tiles—rather than assuming that the "average" consumer would need more of any one type. Such calculations matter as the Mosaic Maker kit presents the consumer with the possibility of self-representation in which one's identity extends from the potential to be visualized through LEGO. While the Mosaic Maker did not depend upon the minifigure by which licensed media products are increasingly differentiated, it nevertheless extended LEGO's negotiation of the politics of representing bodies that carry pre-existing identities and meanings tied to race and gender. In doing so, this engagement with social difference has further pushed LEGO from its previous investment in universalism.

A second LEGO product similarly presented consumers with the opportunity for self-representation, but this time in closer proximity to the company's engagement with the faces and bodies of recognizable media figures. In 2016, The LEGO Group announced a new product line called BrickHeadz, building on its existing investment in licenses from popular media franchises. Comparable in their cute aesthetic to Bobbleheads and the highly popular Funko Pop figures, the new BrickHeadz sought to compete in the licensed collectibles market by offering similarly scaled figures with more involved building instructions than LEGO's minifigures (Gerald 2016). Like the minifigure, however, BrickHeadz drew upon popular media franchises.

The first eight product offerings were characters based on Marvel and DC Super Heroes, followed by other BrickHeadz based on *Star Wars*, *Pirates of the Caribbean*, *Harry Potter*, Disney Princesses and more. In April 2018, however, LEGO released a product called 41597 Go Brick Me, a 708-piece kit retailing for $29.99 that allowed the user to design their own BrickHeadz figures. As suggested by the product's name and packaging, this kit encouraged consumers to make models of their own bodies that might sit alongside all the licensed BrickHeadz in the line. Unlike the Mosaic Maker, these suggested uses prompted builders to use differently colored tiles to try to match their skin tones and other distinguishing physical features. The Go Brick Me box featured three images of real people holding their BrickHeadz, each having built a figure whose hair color, skin tone, clothing and accessories matches their own. The choice of models—one dark-skinned male, one light-skinned female and one light-skinned male—further sells the Go Brick Me kit by virtue of its capacity for a range of embodied differentiation. Go Brick Me invites the consumer to cast oneself in LEGO form and, in that process, consider the best building strategies with which to represent the one's identity markers as defined by physical characteristics. The product page on LEGO's retail Web site promises enough "specially selected LEGO bricks for different hairstyles and skin color, plus there are two kinds of glasses, a sticker sheet to personalize your builds, and a brick separator" ("Go" n.d.).

The Go Brick Me kit thus imagines skin tone as a crucial point of identification in the construction of LEGO selves, extending licensed minifigure logics while also bringing new markers of difference into LEGO play by turning attention to the consumer's identity—something just as raced and gendered as the character and actor likenesses of media licensing. In fact, the online product page for Go Brick Me explicitly calls attention to the linkages between creative self-representation and licensed media franchises, instructing: "Mash up your own LEGO BrickHeadz persona with other famous BrickHeadz characters, to create a supercool hybrid version of yourself" ("Go" n.d.). Go Brick Me treats the consumer's own body as a likeness that requires—as does any licensed character—more careful attention to identity and markers of difference than the yellow minifigure's standard universality allowed.

In terms of race and gender, that yellow minifigure presented difference as deviation from a privileged norm: The addition of wigs, painted red lips and other markers of difference to create female minifigure faces established all the basic, unmarked smiley faces as male by default; the creation of different skin tones to make franchised characters' racial identities legible implied that preceding yellow minifigure faces could not accommodate Black, Asian or indigenous bodies in their unmarked Whiteness (Johnson 2014b). Yet in attempting to make buildable the bodies of media franchise characters and consumers alike, LEGO supplants universal logics with the increasing recognition of how race and gender might be constructed from its product kits. This is not to celebrate the complete erasure of LEGO universality: Go Brick Me packaging design does display a plain white BrickHeadz figure to invoke the idea of a blank slate, invoking White as a default. Yet even so, the packaging models holding their clearly racialized creations show that even this white default must be modified with "light flesh" tiles to signify a racialized Whiteness. In this sense, identity is not a default, but something actively built in and through LEGO play—where the marketing of the kit commodifies those social differences. Just as LEGO deploys the likeness and identities of franchise characters as means of differentiating dozens of building kits made up of very similar construction elements, it relies upon consumers' investment in their own embodied identity to support new products like Go Brick Me.

Conclusion

Even as LEGO expands its capacity to represent diversity across franchised minifigures, Friends mini-dolls, BrickHeadz and Mosaic Maker products, the yellow minifigure continues to have a privileged place in corporate branding and to anchor product themes like Ninjago and LEGO City, among others. However, the standard yellow minifigure increasingly sits in parallel to these competing practices and discourses of gender and race differentiation through which The LEGO Group manages its integral relationship with the media industries and its own branded claim to corporate social responsibility. LEGO's licensing strategies do not just borrow characters and strategies of inclusion from the media industries: They also ultimately seek ways to create brand power out of the potential for consumers to confront social difference in the worlds of construction play.

This chapter has argued that such shifts depend on the increasingly integral relationships between LEGO and its media licensing partners and have gradually offered a wider range of identification to users of its product. However, my intent has not been to celebrate the efforts of The LEGO Group and its partners in this arena; instead, these changes operate as part of the branded identities of products and corporations alike. Although I am interested in the close relationship between them, I stop short of claiming that LEGO's participation in media licensing programs caused shifts in its other product lines. Instead, I hope to have shown how the two operated in parallel—and often in intersection—in a corporate context defined by the shared concerns of social corporate responsibility, assumptions about changing consumer demographics and interest in global markets as represented by the promise of China. The consumers' ability to build different kinds of bodies out of LEGO emerges out of the ongoing strategic construction of media franchises, target audiences and global markets.

Note

1. These color names are drawn from the "LEGO Moulding Colour Palette" that the LEGO Ambassador Network released to enthusiast blogs including *The Brick Fan* in May 2016 (see Tran 2016).

References

Admin. (2018). *LEGO Mosaic Maker coming to New York!* The Brick Blogger. http://thebrickblogger.com/2018/06/lego-mosaic-maker-coming-to-new-york/. Accessed on June 4, 2018.

Banet-Weiser, S. (2012). *Authentic^{TM}: The politics of ambivalence in a brand culture*. New York: New York University Press.

Brzeski, P. (2016). "Rogue One" lands China release date. *Hollywood Reporter*. https://www.hollywoodreporter.com/heat-vision/rogue-one-lands-china-release-date-953678. Accessed on December 7, 2018.

Ching, A. (2012). *Marvel NOW! gets an all-female team of FEARLESS DEFENDERS*. https://www.newsarama.com/10480-marvel-now-gets-an-all-female-team-of-fearless-defenders.html. Accessed on April 1, 2019.

Cohen, J. (2017). *Disney Store is selling an official Ms. Marvel costume*. Comic Book Resources. https://www.cbr.com/disney-official-ms-marvel-costume/. Accessed on December 7, 2018.

Corporate social responsibility update 2017. (2017). The Walt Disney Company. https://www.thewaltdisneycompany.com/wp-content/uploads/2017 disneycsrupdate.pdf. Accessed on December 7, 2018.

Desta, Y. (2016). The year Disney started to take diversity seriously. *Vanity Fair*. https://www.vanityfair.com/hollywood/2016/11/disney-films-inclusive. Accessed on December 7, 2018.

Dev, A. (2015). American Muslims were proud of "Kamala Khan". *The Times of India*. https://timesofindia.indiatimes.com/city/bengaluru/American-Muslims-were-proud-of-Kamala-Khan/articleshow/42473218.cms. Accessed on December 7, 2018.

Dinh, C. (2017). *Marvel to launch new animation franchise "Marvel Rising"*. Marvel.com. https://www.marvel.com/articles/marvel-to-launch-new-animation-franchise-marvel-rising. Accessed on December 7, 2018.

duCille, A. (1996). *Skin trade*. Cambridge: Harvard University Press.

Duke, A. (2013). *Marvel's newest superhero is a Muslim-American teen*. CNN. https://www.cnn.com/2013/11/06/showbiz/ms-marvel-muslim-superhero/index.html. Accessed on April 1, 2019.

Ford, R. (2016). Black Santa and hip-hop "Oliver Twist": Disney's diversity push. *Hollywood Reporter*. https://www.hollywoodreporter.com/news/black-santa-hip-hop-oliver-twist-disneys-diversity-push-942983. Accessed on December 7, 2018.

Gerald. (2016). *LEGO announces their brand new BrickHeadz range!* Geek Culture. https://geekculture.co/lego-announces-their-brand-new-brickheadz-range/. Accessed on December 7, 2018.

Go Brick Me. (n.d.). *LEGO shop*. https://shop.lego.com/en-US/product/Go-Brick-Me-41597. Accessed on December 7, 2018.

Graser, M. (2014). Marvel introduces first female Thor in new comicbook series. *Variety*. https://variety.com/2014/biz/news/marvel-introduces-first-female-thor-in-new-comicbook-series-1201262561/. Accessed on December 7, 2018.

Gray, J. (2010). *Show sold separately: Promos, spoilers, and other media paratexts.* New York: New York University Press.

Hayes, B. (2015). *"Star Wars: The Force Awakens" and the little casting choice that makes a huge impact.* Screen Crush. http://screencrush.com/star-wars-diversity-casting/. Accessed on December 7, 2018.

Holloway, D., & Lang, B. (2016). Casting directors under pressure to represent today's America in film, TV. *Variety.* https://variety.com/2016/tv/features/diversity-movies-tv-casting-directors-1201905037/. Accessed on December 7, 2018.

Johnson, D. (2014a). Chicks with bricks: Building creative identities across industrial design cultures and gendered construction play. In M. J. P. Wolf (Ed.), *LEGO studies: Examining the building blocks of a transmedial phenomenon* (pp. 81–104). New York: Routledge.

Johnson, D. (2014b). Figuring identity: Media licensing and the racialization of LEGO bodies. *International Journal of Cultural Studies, 17*(4), 307–325. https://doi.org/10.1177/1367877913496211.

Kokas, A. (2017). *Hollywood made in China.* Berkeley: University of California Press.

Lopez, L. K. (2012). Fan activists and the politics of race in *The Last Airbender. International Journal of Cultural Studies, 15*(5), 431–445. https://doi.org/10.1177/1367877911422862.

Lopez, R. (2017a). Despite dollars in diversity, Hollywood still averse to making inclusive films. *Variety.* https://variety.com/2017/film/news/diversity-box-office-winners-hollywood-1202603438/. Accessed on December 7, 2018.

Lopez, R. (2017b). Women and non-White characters are speaking more in recent Star Wars movies. *Variety.* https://variety.com/2017/film/news/star-wars-diversity-dialogue-bechdel-test-rogue-one-1202633473/. Accessed on December 7, 2018.

Ouellette, L. (2018). MTV: #ProsocialTelevision. In D. Johnson (Ed.), *From networks to Netflix: A guide to changing channels* (pp. 147–156). New York: Routledge.

Responsibility report 2013. (2013). *The LEGO Group.* https://www.lego.com/r/www/r/aboutus/-/media/aboutus/media-assets-library/progress-report/lego_group_responsibility_report_2013.pdf?la=en-US&l.r=-1861804705. Accessed on December 7, 2018.

Responsibility report 2016. (2016). *The LEGO Group.* https://www.lego.com/en-us/aboutus/responsibility/our-policies-and-reporting/responsibility-report-2016-downloads. Accessed on December 7, 2018.

Responsibility report 2017. (2017). *The LEGO Group*. https://www.lego.com/r/www/r/catalogs/-/media/catalogs/aboutus/csr/reports/2017_responsibility%20report_final_online_2.pdf?l.r=-1411253497. Accessed on December 7, 2018.

Scott, S. (2017). #wheresrey? Toys, spoilers, and the gender politics of franchise paratexts. *Critical Studies in Media Communication, 34*(2), 138–147. https://doi.org/10.1080/15295036.2017.1286023.

Statt, N. (2015). Director J.J. Abrams weighs in on diversity in the Star Wars universe. *CNET*. https://www.cnet.com/news/director-j-j-abrams-weighs-in-on-diversity-in-the-star-wars-universe/. Accessed on December 7, 2018.

Toymaker Lego wins court case against Chinese copycats. (2018). *Reuters*. https://www.reuters.com/article/us-lego-china-copyright/toymaker-lego-wins-court-case-against-chinese-copycats-idUSKCN1NA2QF. Accessed on December 7, 2018.

Tran, A. (2016). LEGO 2016 color palette. *The Brick Fan*. https://www.thebrickfan.com/lego-2016-color-palette/. Accessed on December 7, 2018.

Tran, A. (2017). LEGO Friends 2018 design change explained. *The Brick Fan*. https://www.thebrickfan.com/lego-friends-2018-design-change-explained/. Accessed on December 7, 2018.

Tran, A. (2018). LEGO Asia region exclusive set images. *The Brick Fan*. https://www.thebrickfan.com/lego-asia-region-exclusive-set-images/. Accessed on December 7, 2018.

Tussey, E., & Bak, M. (2019). Get your cape on: Target's invitation to the DC Universe. In D. Herbert & D. Johnson (Eds.), *Point of sale: Analyzing media retail*. New Brunswick: Rutgers University Press.

Wade, C., & Riseman, A. (2017). See every line spoken by a woman in the original Star Wars trilogy. *Vulture*. https://www.vulture.com/2015/12/star-wars-all-female-lines-excluding-leia.html. Accessed on December 7, 2018.

Wieners, B. (2011). LEGO is for girls. *Businessweek*. https://www.bloomberg.com/news/articles/2011-12-14/lego-is-for-girls. Accessed on December 7, 2018.

Index

GPSR Compliance
The European Union's (EU) General Product Safety Regulation (GPSR) is a set
of rules that requires consumer products to be safe and our obligations to
ensure this.

If you have any concerns about our products, you can contact us on

ProductSafety@springernature.com

In case Publisher is established outside the EU, the EU authorized
representative is:

Springer Nature Customer Service Center GmbH
Europaplatz 3
69115 Heidelberg, Germany